# A SEMIOTIC THEORY
# OF LANGUAGE

**Advances in Semiotics**
*Thomas A. Sebeok, General Editor*

# A SEMIOTIC THEORY OF LANGUAGE

By

Sebastian Shaumyan

INDIANA UNIVERSITY PRESS
*Bloomington and Indianapolis*

Manufactured in the United States of America

Library of Congress Cataloging-in-Publication Data

Shaumyan, Sebastian.

    A semiotic theory of language.

    (Advances in semiotics series)
    Bibliography: p.
    Includes index.
    1. Applicative grammar.  2. Semiotics.  3. Linguistics
—Methodology.  I. Title.  II. Series.
P164.S5  1987    401'.41    85-46033
ISBN 0-253-30472-5

1 2 3 4 5 91 90 89 88 87

# Contents

## III. *Genotype Grammar*

## IV. *Phenotype Grammar*

## V. *Linguistic Methodology*

# *Preface*

This book is intended as an inquiry into the essence of language.

According to a widespread view effectively promulgated by Noam Chomsky during recent decades, natural languages are psychological objects, and therefore linguistics must be a part of psychology. The characterization of language that is proposed here is at odds with this view. True, linguistic processes in the minds of the speaker and the hearer are accompanied by psychological phenomena. But logical processes in the human mind are also accompanied by psychological phenomena; nobody, however, regards logic as a part of psychology. Although logical processes involve psychological processes, logic is independent of psychology, because logic has a specific subject matter for which psychological considerations are irrelevant: rules of deduction and the construction of deductive systems.

Language has a unique ontological status, because, on the one hand, it exists only in human consciousness, but, on the other, man is forced to treat it as an object that exists independently of him. Languages are not psychological objects, but they are not biological or physical objects, either—rather, they belong to a special world, which can be called the world of sign systems, or the semiotic world. The essential property of this world is that genetically it is the product of human consciousness, but ontologically it is independent of human consciousness.

Although psychological phenomena accompany linguistic processes in the human mind, linguistics is independent of psychology, because psychological considerations are irrelevant for understanding sign systems. Language is a tacit social convention shared by the members of the linguistic community; the infringement of this social convention makes the speaker run the risk of being incomprehensible or ridiculous. Language as a network of social conventions is what linguistics is all about. Social conventions are supraindividual; they are logically independent of psychological processes that may be connected with them in the minds of individuals.

Linguistics is completely independent of psychology. Psychology of speech is not even an auxiliary science of linguistics. Investigation of linguistic phenomena by methods of psychology is, of course, possible, and it is important. But a necessary prerequisite for such investigation is the previous establishment of linguistic facts: psychology of speech presupposes linguistics as its basis.

Languages are semiotic objects, and therefore linguistics must be considered a part of semiotics. This view of linguistics requires a linguistic theory based on an analysis of semiotic properties of language. I have developed such a theory. It has two components: *applicative grammar* and the *two-level phonology*.

The first version of applicative grammar was introduced in 1965 (Shaumyan, 1965). Further developments of the theory were presented in Shaumyan, 1974, 1977, and 1983. The history of the earlier stages of applicative grammar is presented in Guentchéva-Desclés, 1976. In this book I propose a new version of applicative grammar, which is the result of my latest theoretical research.

The new version of applicative grammar includes two important innovations: 1) a formal calculus of functional superposition, which assigns to words syntactic types, indicating their inherent syntactic functions and syntactic functions superposed onto the inherent syntactic functions; and 2) a system of semiotic laws constraining the formalism of applicative grammar; these laws make falsifiable claims about language. The formal calculus of functional superposition and the semiotic laws allow one to gain new insights and to make sense of cross-linguistic phenomena that there is no way of accounting for using the currently accepted linguistic theories.

Applicative grammar is significant in that, in contrast to existing linguistic theories, it provides means to detect genuine language universals in whose terms it is possible to establish correct cross-linguistic generalizations and construct insightful syntactic typologies. The past decade has seen a major revival of interest in linguistic typology. It is clear by now that typological studies utilizing a broad cross-linguistic data base are fundamental to the future progress of theoretical linguistics. Like any other contemporary linguistic theory, applicative grammar is dependent largely on typological data and argumentation.

There is a tendency in much current linguistic research to attempt to reduce essentially different phenomena to variations on a basic pattern modeled on the investigator's native language or languages related to it, and then to claim universality for this oversimplified model. Applicative grammar combats this type of reductionism by means of a theory of language universals that allows for the basic diversity of the world's languages.

The proposed semiotic laws are valid in both grammar and phonology. Therefore, it is appropriate to regard the new version of applicative grammar as a part of a more general linguistic theory including both grammar and phonology. This theory I call the semiotic theory of language.

The phonological part of the proposed semiotic theory of language develops the ideas of my two-level theory of phonology introduced in 1962 (Shaumyan, 1962, 1968). A reader familiar with my previous phonological works will notice that although the premises of the two-level theory of phonology have not changed, the novel version of this theory contains significant innovations in its conceptual system. These innovations are a fruit of my recent inquiry into the semiotic nature of phonological systems.

The crucial change concerns the treatment of the relation between phonological and phonetic notions. In my phonological theory as it was presented in my book on problems of theoretical phonology (Shaumyan, 1962, 1968), I regarded the phoneme and the distinctive features as purely functional units completely devoid of physical substance. That was done in order to oppose the confusion of functional and physical levels of sounds and acoustic features that was characteristic for all schools of classic phonology (Hjelmslev included: true, he also considered the phoneme to be a purely functional unit, but he confused the functional and physical levels with respect to the notions of distinctive features by relegating them to the status of merely elements of the physical substance of language). While now as before I do insist on a strict distinction between functional and physical levels of sounds and their acoustic properties, I have found a more adequate solution to the problem of the distinction of these levels.

Rather than oppose phonemes and sounds, distinctive features and acoustic features as purely functional and physical elements, I treat the phoneme and the distinctive feature each as a unity of opposites, and I introduce theoretical constructs: sound/diacritic and acoustic feature/diacritical feature. These theoretical constructs are dualistic entities with complementary conflicting aspects whose conceptual structure is similar to such theoretical constructs as wave/particle in physics and use-value/exchange-value in economics.

In view of these conceptual changes, we must redefine the goals of phonology. Rather than confine itself to the study of the functional level of sounds, phonology has to study the interplay between the functional and physical levels of language sounds.

I redefine the main goals of phonology as follows: 1) a strict separation of the functional and physical levels of language sounds; and 2) the study of the interplay between the functional and physical levels of sounds.

The proposed redefinition of the goals of phonology based on a more sophisticated treatment of phonological notions as dual entities is important for experimental phonetics. At present, there is a dangerous gap between phonology and experimental phonetics: on the one hand, phonologists often ignore experimental phonetics, and on the other, experimental phoneticians are sometimes hostile to phonology, because they do not see how phonology can explain some new results in experimental studies of speech sounds that seem to contradict the theoretical postulates of phonology.

The study of the interplay of the functional and physical levels as one of the main goals of phonology will restore communication between phonology and experimental phonetics.

The two-level theory of phonology is diametrically opposite to generative phonology—a part of the generative-transformational grammar currently in vogue. Generative phonology was introduced around 1959. By making out of an inferior type of phonological theory a straw man for their attacks, Halle and Chomsky argued that the phonemic level does not exist, that the only levels that do exist are the morphophonemic level (which was renamed systematic phonemics) and the phonetic level. That meant a revolution: phonology had to go into limbo, because it was replaced by a new discipline—generative phonology. The two-level theory demonstrates that the arguments against the existence of the phonemic level are groundless; it rehabilitates the phonemic level and phonology and demonstrates that generative phonology is false because it mixes the phonemic level with the morphophonemic level and confounds synchronic morphophonemic processes with diachronic ones.

The rehabilitation of the phonemic level and of phonology by the two-level theory means not a return to old phonology but an advance to a new idea of phonology based on the laws of semiotics. The insights and discoveries of the two-level theory give a new significance to old concepts of phonology.

Throughout this book, care has been taken to clearly present alternative views and theories. At this point a thorough exposition of linguistic methodology is given in the context of the general methodology of science. That has been done on account of the importance of linguistic methodology; linguistic methodology is important for anyone who intends to study or develop linguistics, since without knowledge of linguistic methodology it is impossible to comprehend and correctly evaluate linguistic theories.

Methodology has the following valuable points:

1) It sets standards for testing ideas critically—it is a tool of critical transaction. Notice that critical standards make sense when they are shared by the international community of linguists. Methodology calls for the critical evaluation of ideas using internationally shared standards. At this point methodology is an efficient medicine against any kind of provincialism in linguistics.

2) Being a tool of critical transaction, methodology is at the same time a heuristic tool—it helps to find ways of arriving at new ideas. Critique of the goals, concepts, laws, and principles of phonological and syntactic theories helps one to choose the right goals and methods, to discover and solve new problems—to organize phonological and syntactic research in the right direction.

3) Methodology sharpens one's capacity for speculative thinking. Some characteristic features of speculative thinking are: the ability to comprehend and perform imaginary experiments; the ability to understand reality in terms of ideal entities; the ability to transcend experimental data; and an aesthetic sense discriminating between beautiful and ugly abstract patterns—beauty is manifested by different types of universal structures that constitute the essence of reality, and a sense of beauty may have a heuristic value. Capacity for speculative thinking can be compared to an ear for music. If one does not have an ear for music, nothing can help. But if one does have an ear for music, the theory of music can sharpen this capacity. By the same token, methodology sharpens

one's capacity for speculative thinking, which is a necessary condition for imaginative, creative research.

By comparing alternative views and theories in the light of linguistic methodology, the reader will be able to form his own views on current issues in linguistics.

In writing this book, I was at pains to combine the greatest possible intelligibility with a precise analysis of the linguistic ideas. I have attempted to lay bare the intellectual depth and the beauty of the conceptual world of contemporary linguistics.

I proceed as follows. Chapter 1 provides an analysis of the fundamental concepts of the semiotic theory of language. In chapter 2 I present the novel version of the two-level theory of phonology. In chapter 3 I argue that two levels must be distinguished in grammar: the level of universal functional units, called the genotype level, and the level of syntagmatic units that realize the functional units, called the phenotype level; this chapter presents an outline of the concepts, principles, and laws of genotype grammar. In chapter 4 I present an outline of phenotype grammar. In chapter 5 the semiotic theory of language is discussed in the light of the general principles of the logic of science and linguistic methodology.

In preparing the final version of this book, I have benefited from innumerable discussions with and the insights of Jean-Pierre Desclés and Zlatka Guentchéva, to whom I express my appreciation. I gratefully acknowledge useful comments from Judith Aissen, Peter Cobin, Warren Cowgill, Laurence Horn, Adam Makkai, Edith Moravcsik, Alexander Schenker, Edward Stankiewicz, and Rulon Wells. To my children Olga and Alex, I am indebted for their performance of the somewhat arduous task of preparing the manuscript and for their helpful suggestions.

This book is a culmination of my research, which I started at the Academy of Sciences, U.S.S.R., and continued at Yale University. Some of my previous works on applicative grammar were written jointly with P. A. Soboleva, to whom I am indebted for her significant contributions at the earlier stages of the development of applicative grammar.

I gratefully acknowledge financial assistance from the A. Whitney Griswold Faculty Research Fund and the Department of Linguistics, Yale University, in connection with the preparation of the manuscript of this volume.

# I.

# The Aim and Structure of the Semiotic Theory of Language

## 1. A Semiotic Definition of Language

Linguistics is the scientific study of language. The first thing to notice about this definition is that the word *language* is in the singular without the indefinite article, not in the plural. Linguistics takes an interest primarily not in individual languages but in common features of all languages. The notion of language is an abstraction that characterizes the common properties of all languages.

This abstraction of linguistics can be compared with the abstraction of biology. Zoology and botany are concerned with individual organisms. Biology, however, takes interest not in individual living organisms but in life, that is, in those biological functions, such as growth, metabolism, reproduction, respiration, and circulation, that are common properties of all living organisms.

The word *language* is applied not only to such languages as English, Russian, French, or Chinese—which are called *natural* languages because they evolved spontaneously—but also to a variety of other systems of communication. For example, chemists, mathematicians, logicians, and computer scientists have constructed for particular purposes notational systems that are also called languages: languages of chemistry, mathematical languages, languages of logic, programming languages for computers. These are *artificial* languages. The word *language* applies also to systems of animal communication: one speaks of the language of bees, the language of ants, etc.

Linguistics is concerned with the notion of language primarily as it is applied to natural languages. Therefore, the word *language* is understood in linguistics usually in the sense of natural language, and so I will use this word.

Let us now define the notion of language. What is it?

Language is a complicated phenomenon that can be studied from many points of view. Consider the production of speech sounds. It involves different configurations and movements of the speech organs, constituting a physiological phenomenon. Speech sounds have various acoustic properties—an acoustic phenomenon. The produced speech sounds must be detected and decoded by the human auditory system, which to this end has evolved special perceptual mechanisms for detecting and decoding speech cues—a physiological phenomenon. As an instrument of thought, language is a part of the human mind—expression of thought involves psychological and cognitive processes. Language is connected with human culture—this connection constitutes an anthropological phenomenon. Finally, as a system of signs used as an instrument of communication and an instrument of the expression of thought, language is a social phenomenon of a special sort, which can be called a *semiotic* phenomenon. (The word *semiotic* is derived from Greek *sēmeion*, 'sign'). A system of signs as a semiotic phenomenon has a unique ontological status, because, on the one hand, it exists only in human consciousness, but on the other hand, man is forced to treat it as an object that exists independently of him. Sign systems belong to a special world, which can be called the world of sign systems, or the semiotic world. The essential property of this world is that genetically it is the product of human consciousness, but ontologically it is independent of human consciousness.

With respect to language, we are in the position of the six blind men and the elephant. The story goes that one of the blind men, who got hold of the elephant's leg, said that the elephant was like a pillar; a second, who was holding the elephant by its tail, claimed that it was like a rope; another, who came up against the elephant's side, asserted that it was like a wall; and the remaining three, who had the elephant by the ear, the trunk, and the tusk, insisted that it was like a sail, a hose, and a spear.

Like the elephant in that story, language can be approached from different sides. It can be studied from the point of view of biology, physics, psychology, logic, anthropology, philosophy, and, finally, semiotics (a general theory of sign systems).

While under these circumstances the study of language requires an interdisciplinary approach, there exists a hierarchy of different approaches to language. The decisive approach has to be the semiotic one, because the semiotic aspect of language constitutes the essence of language as an instrument of communication and an instrument of thought. While all other aspects are indispensable for the existence of language, they are subordinated to semiotics because they make sense only as manifestations of the semiotic nature of language.

A question arises: What properties characterize the semiotic aspect of language?

To answer this question is to give a *semiotic definition* of language.

I define *language as a sign system* characterized by the following properties: 1) two semiotic strata, 2) sequencing, 3) use of rules, 4) structure, 5) hierarchical stratification, and 6) semiotic relevance.

1) *Two semiotic strata.* Natural languages differ from other semiotic systems in that they have two semiotic strata. In natural languages the primitive semiotic system of signs is overlaid by a secondary semiotic system of diacritic linguistic elements. In distinction from natural languages, artificial languages of

mathematics, physics, chemistry, and other abstract sciences make do with only systems of signs.

The necessity of a secondary semiotic system in natural languages is explained by the limited capacity of the human memory. Natural languages are so richly endowed with a large number of various signs that without diacritic elements it would be impossible to remember all of the signs. Memorizing and the use of signs in natural languages are possible only because any sign can be represented as a sequence of diacritic elements, whose number is strictly limited and compassable. As for artificial languages, since they do not possess a large number of signs, they do not need a system of diacritic elements. Of course, artificial languages with two semiotic strata are possible in principle, but such artificial languages must be considered analogues of natural languages.

Let us now introduce basic concepts characterizing the sign stratum and the diacritic stratum.

I suggest two primitive concepts for the sign stratum:

1. Sign of: $X$ is a sign of $Y$.
2. Meaning of: $Y$ is a meaning of $X$.

These concepts refer to relations rather than to objects. Speaking of signs, we mean a binary relation 'sign of'; speaking of meanings, we mean a binary relation 'meaning of'.

*Sign of.* $X$ is a sign of $Y$ if $X$ means $Y$, that is, if $X$ carries the information $Y$. For instance, the sound sequence *bed* carries the information 'bed', it means 'bed'; therefore, *bed* is a sign of 'bed'.

A sign is not necessarily a sound sequence. It may be the change of a stress (compare *cónvict* and *convíct*), an alternation (compare *take* and *took*), a change of a grammatical context (compare *I love* and *my love*), or a change of word order (compare *John killed Mary* and *Mary killed John*). There may be a zero sign; for example, if we compare *quick, quicker,* and *quickest*, we see that *er* is a sign of the comparative degree and *est* is a sign of the superlative degree, but the positive degree is expressed by the absence of any sound sequence with *quick*, that is, by a zero sign.

The opposition *sign:meaning* is relative. There may be an interchange between these entities. For example, letter $p$ in the English alphabet normally denotes the sound $p$. But when we refer to the English letter $p$, we use the sound $p$ as a name, that is, as a sign of this letter. Further, the meaning of a sign may serve as a sign of another meaning. Thus, *lion* is a sign of a large, strong, carnivorous animal. This meaning of the sign *lion* can be used as a sign of a person whose company is very much desired at social gatherings, for example, a famous author or musician.

It follows from the foregoing that the proposed concept of the sign is considerably broader than the common concept of the sign.

*Meaning of.* The proposed concept of meaning is much broader than the traditional understanding of the term *meaning*. My concept of meaning covers all kinds of information, including various grammatical relations. As was shown above, the notion of meaning is relative: a meaning may be a sign of another meaning.

We must strictly distinguish between the notions 'sign' and 'sign of', and between the notions 'meaning' and 'meaning of'. The notion 'sign of' is a binary relation between a vocal product or other elements called a *sign* and a concept called the *meaning* of the sign. A sign and its meaning are members of a binary relation 'sign of'. For example, neither the sound sequence [teɪbl] nor the concept 'table' is a linguistic fact: the first one is a physical fact, and the second one is a fact of thought; only as the members of the relation 'sign of' are they linguistic facts: a sign and its meaning. If we denote the relation 'sign of' by the symbol $\Sigma$, the sign by the symbol $s$, and the meaning by the symbol $m$, we get the formula

(1)      $s\Sigma m$

This formula reads: the element $s$ is the sign of the concept $m$.

In accordance with the conventional terminology for members of binary relations, we will call $s$ the predecessor with respect to the relation $\Sigma$, and $m$ the successor with respect to the relation $\Sigma$.

The relation 'meaning of' is the converse of the relation 'sign of'. (The notion of the converse of a binary relation $R$ is defined in logic as follows: given a binary relation $R$, the relation $\breve{R}$, called the converse of $R$, holds between $x$ and $y$ if, and only if, $R$ holds between $y$ and $x$, and vice versa; for example, the relation *longer* is the converse of the relation *shorter*, and, vice versa, the relation *shorter* is the converse of the relation *longer*.) Introducing $\breve{\Sigma}$ as the name of the relation 'meaning of', we get the formula

(2)      $m\breve{\Sigma}s$

where $m$ is the predecessor and $s$ is the successor with respect to $\breve{\Sigma}$. This formula (2) reads: the concept $m$ is the meaning of the sign $s$.

Linguistic signs have various degrees of complexity. Language does not offer itself as a set of predelimited linguistic signs that can be observed directly. Rather, the delimitation of linguistic signs is a fundamental problem that presents great difficulties and can be accounted for only at a later stage of our study. In the meantime, I will work with words as specimens of linguistic signs. Although the theoretical definition of the notion of the word is maybe even more difficult than the definition of other linguistic signs, the word as a linguistic sign has an advantage of being familiar as an item of our everyday vocabulary. The term *word* does not need introduction; rather, it needs explication. For the present purpose, it is important that the basic semiotic properties that characterize words are valid for linguistic units in general.

Let us now turn to the second semiotic stratum of language, which can be called the diacritic stratum. In order to characterize this semiotic stratum, I will introduce the binary relation 'diacritic of'. Just as we distinguish between the notions of the sign and of the binary relation 'sign of', so we must distinguish between the notions of the diacritic and of the binary relation 'diacritic of'.

The first term of the relation 'diacritic of' is sounds, and the second term is a sign. If we denote 'diacritic of' by the symbol $D$, the sounds by $p^1$, $p^2$, . . . , $p^n$, and the sign by $s$, we get the formula

(3)     $p^1$, $p^2$, $p^n$ $D$ $s$

Sounds $p^1$, $p^2$, . . . , $p^n$, constituting the first term of the relation 'diacritic of', I call *phonemes*.

The function of phonemes is to differentiate between signs. A sound taken as a physical element is not a linguistic element; it turns into a linguistic element only as a phoneme, that is, as a first term of the relation 'diacritic of'. Signs are second terms of the relation 'diacritic of', because they are differentiated from one another by phonemes.

Here is a concrete example of the relation 'diacritic of': In the word *pin*, the sounds *p, ɪ, n* are the first terms of the relation 'diacritic of', and the sign *pɪn* is a second term of this relation. The sign *pɪn* has a meaning, but the sounds *p, ɪ, n* do not have meaning: they are used to differentiate the sign *pɪn* from other signs, such as *bɪn, pen, pɪt, hɪp*, etc.

It should be stressed that while a sign has a meaning, a phoneme does not have a meaning; it has only a *differentiating function*—and therein lies the essential difference between signs and phonemes.

We are now ready to formulate the *Principle of the Differentiation of Signs*:

> If two signs are different, they must be differentiated by different sequences of phonemes.

In order to understand why a diacritic, that is, phonemic, stratum is indispensable for any human language, consider a sign system that is simpler than any human language and has only two phonemes. Call them phonemes $A$ and $B$. Phonemes $A$ and $B$ are diacritics, that is, signals that do not have meaning but are used to produce signs. Call the class of signs produced by phonemes $A$ and $B$ the *lexicon* of the sign system. If the sign produced must have one-phoneme length, this sign system will be able to produce only two signs. Its lexicon can be increased, however, if it can produce signs by combining the phonemes in pairs: $AA$, $AB$, $BA$, $BB$ give four signs. If it can combine the two phonemes in triplets, eight signs will be produced: $AAA$, $AAB$, $ABA$, $ABB$, $BAA$, $BAB$, $BBA$, $BBB$. The longer the sequence, the larger the lexicon. The general rule is: $m$ different phonemes in sequences of length $n$ provide $m^n$ different signs.

Since the potential size of the lexicon increases exponentially as the length of the sequences increases linearly, sequencing is an efficient way to achieve a large lexicon with a limited number of different phonemes.

2) *Sequencing.* Auditory signs can be unfolded only in time. Auditory signs have only the dimension of time, in contrast to visual signs (nautical signal, etc.), which can have simultaneous groupings in several dimensions. The signs of human language, being auditory, are presented in succession; they form *sequences.* Sequencing is such an obvious property of language that it seems too simple; nevertheless, it is fundamental, and its consequences are innumerable.

An illustration of the power of sequencing was given above with respect to the diacritic stratum: a small set of phonemes can be arranged in different sequences to form thousands of different signs. No less powerful is sequencing with respect to sign stratum: thousands of signs in the lexicon of language are arranged in different sequences to form an enormous variety of sentences.

3) *Use of rules.* Language is a rule-governed sign system. In order to understand why such should be the case, let us focus on sequencing.

We cannot make unlimited use of the sequential strategy, because of the possibility of error. If we want to be able to recognize errors, not all possible sequences must be meaningful. Therefore, we must admit sequences longer than they would be if the sequential strategy were fully exploited. That is, we must admit *redundancy* in terms of communication theory.

Human languages are redundant because it is impossible for us to pronounce all conceivable sequences of phonemes. Let us illustrate this assertion in terms of written English. It has been estimated that if the sequential strategy were fully exploited, the English alphabet of 26 letters would give 26 possible one-letter words, 676 possible two-letter words, 17,576 possible three-letter words, and 456,976 possible four-letter words—a total of 475,254 words, or about the number in *Webster's New International Dictionary.* But this dictionary has a great many words with more than four letters.

Redundancy exists also on the sign-stratum level: not every sequence of words is admissible. We can say *John bought an interesting book,* but *Interesting an bought book John* does not make sense and is therefore inadmissible. It has been estimated that human languages are about 75 percent redundant; that is, if some language could use all possible sequences of letters to form words and all possible sequences of words to form sentences, its book would be about one-quarter the length of the books of the existing human languages.

Redundancy is useful because it decreases the possibility of errors. We hear words more accurately in sentences than in isolation because we know that some sequences of words are inadmissible.

Our problem now is: How do we know which sequences are admissible and which are not? Can it be a matter of memory?

Memorization is of no use, because there are too many possible phonemic sequences and too many possible sentences. It has been estimated that each successive word is, on the average, chosen from 10 alternatives possible in that context. That means there are about $10^{10}$ grammatical sentences 10 words long. Because there are fewer than $3.6 \times 10^9$ seconds per century, we would not have the time to memorize all of the admissible 10-word sequences, even if we could work at a rate of one second per sentence. And even if we could, we would know only the 10-word sentences, which are a small fraction of all the sentences we would need to know.[1]

If memorization is out of the question, we must assume that a system of rules is incorporated into any language that makes it possible to discriminate between admissible and inadmissible sequences. A *grammar* is a description of this system of rules.

It should be noted that the same expression can be constructed in different ways. For instance, the passive sentence *"Hamlet" was written by Shakespeare* can be constructed in two ways: either by directly combining the predicate *was written* with other parts of the sentence, or by deriving this sentence from the active sentence *Shakespeare wrote "Hamlet."* In accordance with these two possibilities, two different sets of rules are used.

The equivalence of different constructions of the same expression is an important phenomenon called the *polytectonic property.* The polytectonic property is characteristic of natural languages, while the artificial languages of mathematics and logic are generally *monotectonic;* that is, every expression in these artificial languages has a unique construction (Curry, 1961; 1963: 60).

4) *Structure.* The question arises: How does language have the potential to produce an infinite number of sentences? The answer is: Through sentences' having structure.

What, then, is the structure of a sentence?

To exhibit the structure of an object is to mention its parts and the ways in which they are interrelated. The structure of sentences can be illustrated by the following example. Suppose that for the words in a given sentence we substitute other words, but in a way that still leaves the sentence significant. Suppose we start with the sentence

(4)     *John married Mary.*

For *John* we substitute *Boris;* for *married, visited;* and for *Mary, Bill.* We thus arrive at the sentence

(5)     *Boris visited Bill.*

Sentence (5) has the same structure as (4). By substituting other nouns for *John* and *Mary* and other verbs for *married* in (4), we will get an enormous amount of various sentences having the same structure. The structure of all these sentences can be characterized by the following formula:

(6)     *Noun + Verb + Noun*

We find two types of relations here: 1) relations between the parts of the sentence, in our case the relations between the first noun and the verb, between the verb and the second noun, and between the first noun and the second one; and 2) relations between words that can be substituted for one another, in our case between *John, Boris,* and other nouns that can be substituted for one another, and between the verbs *married, visited,* and other verbs that can be substituted for one another. Relations of the first type are called *syntagmatic relations,* and of the second type, *paradigmatic relations.*

The structure of a sentence is a network of syntagmatic relations between its parts and paradigmatic relations between each part and all other expressions that can be substituted for it.

Not only sentences possess structure, but also words and sequences of phonemes. Suppose we start with the word *teacher;* let us substitute *read* for *teach* and *ing* for *er.* We thus arrive at the word *reading.* The possibility of replacing *teach* and *er* with other elements shows that the word *teacher* possesses structure: there is a syntagmatic relation between *teach* and *er,* and there are paradigmatic relations between *teach* and other elements that can be substituted for *teach,* on the one hand, and between *er* and other elements that can be substituted for *er,* on the other.

Suppose now that we start with the sequence of phonemes *man.* By interchanging *m* and *p, a* and *e, n* and *t* respectively, we obtain different words, namely, *pet, pen, pan, met, men, mat.* This possibility of interchanging the phonemes shows that sequences of phonemes possess structure. Thus, in *man* there are syntagmatic relations between *m, a,* and *n* and paradigmatic relations between each of these phonemes and other phonemes that can be interchanged with it.

To establish the structure of a sentence or of any other sequence is to mention its parts and the syntagmatic and paradigmatic relations that characterize it. It is structure that makes the number of possible sentences and other sentences of a language unlimited.

I will use the term *contrast* to designate syntagmatic relations and the term *opposition* to designate paradigmatic relations.

5) *Hierarchical stratification.* Let us take the Latin expression *i* 'go (imperative)'. It is the shortest possible expression, and at the same time it is a complete sentence that contains a variety of heterogeneous elements. What are these elements?

1. *i* is a sound, that is, a physical element;

2. *i* is a phoneme, that is, a diacritic, a functional element that differentiates linguistic units;

3. *i* is a root (a lexical morpheme), that is, an element that expresses a concept;

4. *i* is a part of speech (an imperative form of a verb);

5. *i* is a part of a sentence (a predicate);

6. *i* is a sentence, that is, a message, a unit of communication.

These elements belong to different levels of language; in other words, *i* is *stratified.* I have chosen a one-sound expression deliberately, in order to show that the difference between the levels of language is qualitative rather than quantitative: although linguistic units of a higher level are usually longer than units of lower levels—for example, a word is usually longer than a morpheme, and a sentence is longer than a word—what is crucial is not the length of expressions but their *function;* language is stratified with respect to different functions of its elements.[2]

What are the functions of these elements?

1. Sounds per se do not have any function, but they embody phonemes and linguistic units with various functions.

2. Phonemes have a diacritical, or distinctive, function.

3. Morphemes have a function of signifying concepts:

    a) root concepts, such as *child-, king-, govern-, kin-,* and

    b) nonroot concepts of two kinds:

        b1) subsidiary abstract concepts, such as *-hood, -dom, -ment, -ship* (*childhood, kingdom, government, kinship*), and

        b2) syntagmatic relations, such as *-s* in (*he*) *writes* or *-ed* in (*he*) *ended.*

4. Parts of speech—nouns, verbs, adjectives, adverbs—have a symbolic function; that is, they name the elements of reality.

5. Parts of sentences have a syntactic function as elements of a message.

6. Sentences have a communicative function; that is, they are messages—units of communication.

Besides the above functions, there is an important function called *deixis* (which comes from a Greek word meaning 'pointing' or 'indicating'). Deixis is a function of demonstrative and personal pronouns, of tense, of concrete cases, and of some other grammatical features that relate a sentence to the spatio-temporal coordinates of the communication act.

Finally, in terms of the three essential components of the communication act—the speaker, the hearer, and the external situation—to which reference may be made, a sentence has one of the following functions: a *representational* function, a *vocative* function, or an *expressive* function. A sentence has a representational function if it describes a situation referred to by the speaker; it has a vocative function if it serves as a directive imposing upon the addressee some obligation (a sentence in the imperative mood, interrogative sentence, etc.); it has an expressive function if it refers to the speaker's wishes or emotions.

The foregoing shows that the notion of linguistic level is a *functional* notion. This notion is central to linguistic theory. There are very complex hierarchical relationships between linguistic levels. For instance, the level of sounds (for generality, this level can be considered a zero-function level) is subordinated to the phonemic level, the level of words is subordinated to the level of sentences, etc.

To discover laws that characterize linguistic levels and hierarchical relationships between them is the main concern of linguistic theory.

The above examples are meant only to give the reader a glimpse into the stratification of language. A rigorous systematic description of linguistic levels and relationships between them will be given in the course of the book.

6) *Semiotic relevance.* Many people think of language as simply a catalogue of words, each of which corresponds to a thing. Thus, a particular plant, say an oak, is matched in the English language with a particular sound sequence that has an orthographic representation *oak*. From this point of view, differences between languages are reduced to differences of designation; for the same plant the English say *oak*, the Germans *Eiche*, the French *chêne*, the Russians *dub*. To learn a second language, all we have to do is to learn a second nomenclature that is parallel to the first.

This idea of language is based on the naive view that the universe is ordered into distinct things prior to its perception by man. It is false to assume that man's perception is passive. Far from it. Man's perception is guided by the language he uses; and different languages classify items of experience differently. True, to a certain point there may exist some natural division of the world into distinct natural objects, such as, for example, different species of plants, but on the whole, speakers of different languages dissect the universe differently. Different languages produce different dissections of the universe.

Here are some examples of different dissections of the universe by different languages.

The solar spectrum is a continuum that different languages dissect differently. So the English word *blue* is applied to a segment of the spectrum that roughly coincides with the Russian zones denoted by the Russian words *sinij* and *goluboj*. Two segments of the spectrum denoted by the English words *blue* and *green* correspond to one segment denoted by the Welsh word *glas*. The English word *wash* corresponds to two Russian words, *myt'* and *stirat'*. In English, *wash* occurs in both *wash one's hands* and *wash the linen,* but Russian uses the verb *myt'* with respect to washing one's hands and the verb *stirat'* with respect to washing the linen. The English verb *marry* corresponds to two Russian expressions: *marry* translates into Russian differently in *Peter married Mary* and *Mary married Peter.* English makes a difference between *to float* and *to swim* (*wood floats on water, fish swim in water*), while Russian uses the same word *plavat'* in both cases. English makes a difference between *to eat* and *to drink*, while Persian uses the same word *khordan* in both cases (*gušt khordan* 'to eat meat', *may khordan* 'to drink wine'). The Latin word *mus* corresponds to two English words, *mouse* and *rat*.

The same holds for grammar. For example, in Russian, the grammatical morpheme *-l* means, depending on the context, either a past event or a past event preceding another past event. It covers the area that is covered in English by two tenses—the past tense and the past perfect tense. The present tense in Russian corresponds to two tenses in English—the present indefinite tense and the present continuous tense. Modern Russian analyzes the notion of number into a singular and a plural, while Old Russian (like Ancient Greek and some other languages) added a dual. There are languages that add a trial (like most Melanesian languages) or a quadral (like the Micronesian language on the Gilbert Islands). Similar facts are well known.

Every language presents its own model of the universe. This property of languages is called *linguistic relativity*. The notion of linguistic relativity was advanced by Humboldt, but it was most clearly formulated by Sapir and Whorf.

Why does every language give a relative picture of the world?

Linguistic relativity can be explained as a consequence of the *Principle of Semiotic Relevance:*

> The only distinctions between meanings that are semiotically relevant are those that correlate with the distinctions between their signs, and, vice versa, the only distinctions between signs that are relevant are those that correlate with the distinctions between their meanings.

Let us examine linguistic relativity in the light of the Principle of Semiotic Relevance.[3] Consider the above examples. The English word *wash* has different meanings in the context of the expressions *wash one's hands* and *wash the linen*. But the distinction between these two meanings is irrelevant for the English language, because this distinction does not correlate with a distinction between two different sound sequences: in both cases we have the same sound sequence denoted by *wash*. Therefore, these two meanings must be regarded not as different meanings but as two *variants* of the same meaning. On the other hand, the meaning of the Russian word *myt'*, which corresponds to the meaning of the English *wash* in *wash one's hands*, and the meaning of the Russian word *stirat'*, which corresponds to the meaning of the English *wash* in *wash the linen*, must be regarded as different meanings rather than variants of the same meaning as in English, because the distinction between the meanings of Russian *myt'* and *stirat'* correlates with the distinction between different sequences of sounds, and therefore is relevant for the Russian language. A similar reasoning applies to the other examples. As to the relevant and irrelevant distinctions between signs, consider, for instance, the substitution of ə for ɪ in the penultimate syllables of terminations such as *-ity*, *-ily*, such as ə'bɪlətɪ for ə'bɪlɪtɪ (*ability*). Since the distinction between the two signs is not correlated with a distinction between their meanings, this distinction is irrelevant, and therefore they must be regarded as variants of one and the same sign. Another example: The distinction between the signs *nju* and *nu* is not correlated with a distinction between their meanings. Therefore, these signs are variants of the same sign denoted by a sequence of letters *new*.

One may wonder whether the Principle of Semiotic Relevance results in circularity: while the relevant distinctions between meanings are defined by their correlation with the distinctions between their signs, at the same time the relevant distinctions between signs are defined by the distinctions between their meanings. As a matter of fact, this principle does not result in circularity. The point is that the relation 'sign of' makes signs and meanings interdependent: distinctions between signs do not determine the distinctions between meanings, nor do distinctions between meanings determine the distinctions between signs; each kind of distinctions presupposes the other. Neither the distinctions between signs nor the distinctions between meanings should be taken as primitive. What is really primitive is the correlation of distinctions between sounds and distinctions between meanings. There is no circularity here, because both relevant distinctions between signs and relevant distinctions between meanings are determined by their correlation.

The Principle of Semiotic Relevance is an empirical principle reflecting the nature of human language, and therefore all consequences of this principle are also empirical and bear on the nature of human language.

The notion of relevance is relative: what is relevant from one point of view may be irrelevant from another. Semiotic relevance means relevance from a semiotic point of view. What is irrelevant from a semiotic point of view may be relevant from an extrasemiotic point of view. Thus, the distinction between *rat* and *mouse* is irrelevant in Latin, but it is relevant from a zoologist's point of view. The distinction between ingesting food and drink is irrelevant in Persian, but it is relevant from a physiologist's point of view. A distinction between some colors irrelevant for a language may be relevant from a painter's point of view.

The meaning of a sign is an entity that has dual aspects: semiotic and extrasemiotic. The extrasemiotic aspect of meaning is rooted in the culture of people who speak a given language. There is a permanent conflict between the semiotic and extrasemiotic aspects of the meaning: what is relevant from a semiotic point of view may be irrelevant from an extrasemiotic, cultural point of view; and, vice versa, what is relevant from an extrasemiotic, cultural point of view may be irrelevant from a semiotic point of view. This conflict is resolved in a speech act: a successful act of communication presupposes that the speech situation rooted in the common cultural background of the speaker and hearer transforms the semiotic aspect of the meaning into the extrasemiotic, so that the transmitted message can be properly understood by the hearer.

Every language as a specific model of the universe is a rigid cognitive network that imposes on the speakers and hearers its own mode of the classification of the elements of reality. But cognition is not divorced from communication. Human practice, human activity rectifies the rigid cognitive structures of a language in the process of communication.

Linguistic relativity as it was formulated by Humboldt, Sapir, and Whorf is valid with respect to the cognitive structures of language, but it must be supplemented by the notion of the duality of the meaning of the linguistic sign, which explains why in the process of communication people are able to transcend a rigid cognitive framework imposed on them by the language they use.

The Principle of Semiotic Relevance has empirically testable consequences. The validity of this principle depends on whether counterexamples could be found that would invalidate it. What evidence would serve to invalidate it?

Consider ambiguity. If the Principle of Semiotic Relevance were invalid, then we could distinguish different meanings no matter whether or not they were correlated with different sound sequences. Let us take the sentence *I called the man from New York*. This sentence is ambiguous; it has two very different meanings: 'I called the man who is from New York' or 'From New York, I called the man'. One cannot distinguish between the two meanings, because they are not correlated with different sequences of signs. Or take a case of phonological neutralization: German *rat* may mean either *Rad* or *Rat*, but speakers of German do not distinguish between these meanings, because they are not correlated with different sound sequences. This ambiguity can be resolved by different contexts only because there exist oppositions, such as *Rade : Rate*.

No explanation of puns or jokes would be possible without an understanding of the Principle of Semiotic Relevance. Consider: *Why did the little moron throw the clock out the window? To see time fly.* Or: *Why didn't the skeleton jump out of the grave? Because he didn't have the guts to.* The ambiguity of the expressions *time flies* and *to have the guts to do something* can be explained by the absence of a correlation between the differences in meaning and the differences between sound sequences.

In all the above examples, a suspension of a distinction between different meanings is the result of the suspension of a distinction between different signs.

## 2. The Principle of Semiotic Relevance and Homonymy

The Principle of Semiotic Relevance calls for reconsidering the traditional notion of homonyms.

A *homonym* is defined as a word or expression that has the same sound as another but is different in meaning. For example, the noun *bear* and the verb *bear* are said to be homonyms of each other, or simply homonymous. In terms of signs, homonyms are different signs that have the same form, that is, the same sound. The relation between two homonyms can be represented by the following diagram:

(1)

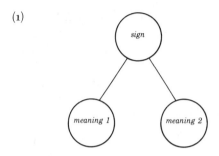

The notion of homonyms contradicts the Principle of Semiotic Relevance, which holds that different signs must be different in form, that is, in sound or in some other marker. A correct diagram for two different signs must be

(2)

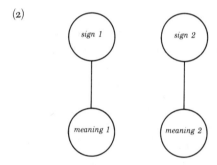

In the light of the Principle of Semiotic Relevance, what is called a homonym is one sign rather than two (or more) signs. This sign can be represented by the diagram

(3)

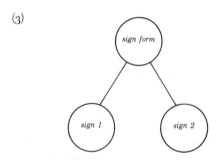

The sign in (3) can be called a *polyvalent sign*.

Under the Principle of Semiotic Relevance, meaning 1 and meaning 2 in (1) belong to the same class of meanings, no matter how different they are; hence the ambiguity of the sign in (1). To distinguish between meaning 1 and meaning 2, we must have two different signs corresponding to these meanings, as in the diagram

(4)

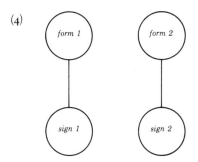

The sign in (3) can be viewed as a suspension of the distinction between the signs in (4). And the ambiguity of the sign in (3) can be viewed as a suspension of the distinction between the meanings in (4), which is a counterpart of the suspension of the distinction between signs.

We can formulate the *Principle of Suspension* as a corollary of the Principle of Semiotic Relevance:

> If a distinction between a sign $X$ and a sign $Y$ is suspended through replacing them with a single sign $Z$, then the meanings of $X$ and $Y$ combine to form a single class of meanings designated by $Z$.

Let me illustrate this principle. Consider the following sentences:

(5)  a. *John killed a* bear.
  b. *Her husband is such a* bear *that nobody likes him.*
  c. *These letters* bear *no dates.*
  d. *What is the Russian word for* bear?

The meanings of *bear* in (5a) and (5b) are different—in (5a) *bear* designates an animal, and in (5b) *bear* designates a man through a metaphor—but they constitute a single class of meanings since they are designated by the same sign *bear*. The meanings of *bear* in (5a) and (5c) are different and belong to different classes of meanings, because they are designated by different signs: *bear + the place of a term* in (5a) and *bear + the place of a predicate*. As was pointed out in section 1.1, a sign is not necessarily a sound sequence—it may be a context. Here we have a case of signs that are combinations of sound sequences and grammatical contexts. It is to be noted that not every change of a context means a change of a sign. Thus, the contexts of *bear* in (5a) and (5b) are different, but these contexts are lexical and therefore cannot constitute different signs.

In (5d), *bear* is taken out of the grammatical contexts of (5a, b, and c). Therefore, it must be viewed as the result of the suspension of the distinction between the two signs *bear* + *the place of a term* and *bear* + *the place of a predi-cate*. Hence, it is ambiguous.

In current linguistic literature, both 'homonymy' and 'ambiguity' are used as related notions. The present analysis of these notions is their theoretical expli-cation based on the Principle of Semiotic Relevance. While ambiguity as ex-plicated above is a consequence of the Principle of Semiotic Relevance, we have to reject homonymy as incompatible with this principle.

Since the terms *ambiguous sign* and *ambiguity* are not well defined in current linguistic literature, I propose the terms *polyvalent sign* and *poly-valence* as designating more precise concepts based on the Principle of Semi-otic Relevance.[4]

### 3. Saussure's Notion of the Sign

The notion of the sign proposed above differs from Saussure's notion (Saus-sure, 1966:65–70). Saussure considers a sign to be a bilateral entity consisting of a signifiant and a signifié.

Saussure seems to have introduced his notion of the sign in order to dispel the widespread misconception according to which a language is merely a no-menclature or a stock of labels to be fastened onto preexistent things. Thus, he wrote:

> I call the combination of a concept and a sound-image a *sign*, but in current usage the term generally designates only a sound-image, a word, for example (*arbor*, etc.). One tends to forget that *arbor* is called a sign only because it car-ries the concept "tree," with the result that the idea of the sensory part implies the idea of the whole. (Saussure, 1966:67)

Saussure's concern about dispelling the naive view of language as a stock of labels used as names for preexisting things is understandable. But it is difficult to accept his claim that *arbor* is called a sign because it carries the concept 'tree'. True, the expression *arbor* is a sign because of its being in a particu-lar relation to the meaning 'tree'. Similarly, a man is a husband because of his having a wife. But it does not follow that a husband is a combination of two people.

Saussure fails to see the difference between two sharply distinct notions: 1) the notion that a thing $X$ belongs to a class $K$ through its having a relationship to another thing $Y$, and 2) the notion that the thing $X$ and the thing $Y$ together form a whole, that is, a member of the class $K$.

One might argue that by saying that "*arbor* is called a sign only because it carries the concept 'tree'" in conjunction with his decision to use the term *sign* to designate the combination of a concept and a sound-image, Saussure did not mean that the concept is part of the sign but simply wanted to justify the intro-duction of a new notion into linguistics—a bilateral linguistic unit consisting of a signifiant and a signifié. One might argue that we should not cavil at Saussure's unfelicitous wording of his thought.

Let us then accept the term *sign* as an arbitrary label for designating the bilateral linguistic unit consisting of a signifiant and a signifié. And let us consider whether linguistics needs this bilateral unit.

The least one can say about the sign in the sense of a bilateral linguistic unit consisting of a signifiant and a signifié is that this notion is gratuitous. Actually, since the traditional notion of the unilateral sign, if correctly explicated, involves reference to meaning, linguistics does not need the notion of the sign as a bilateral linguistic unit. What linguistics needs is a correct explication of the traditional notion of the unilateral sign. As was shown in section 1.1, neither the sign nor the meaning must be taken as a primitive notion. The primitive notions are to be the relation 'sign of' and its converse 'meaning of'. The sign and the meaning are the terms of these binary relations.

The relations 'sign of' and 'meaning of' are asymmetric: the sign communicates the meaning, but the meaning does not communicate the sign. Semiotically, the meaning is subordinate to the sign. Therefore, taking the sign as a unilateral unit, we do not exclude the reference to meaning but view the sign and the meaning in the right perspective. One proof that the notion of the bilateral sign unnecessarily complicates linguistic theory is that both Saussure himself and the linguists who adhere to his terminology constantly fall back into the unilateral-sign terminology.

Under the present explication, the sign remains unilateral, and we do not need the notion of a bilateral linguistic unit.

The notion of the bilateral sign unnecessarily complicates linguistic terminology and precludes the use of the good term *sign* in its traditional sense, which is quite useful for linguistics, if correctly explicated.

There might be other objections against the notion of the bilateral sign. One is this: If we conceive of the word as a unilateral sign, then such a word as *bear* with different meanings will be characterized as a polyvalent unilateral sign. But if we conceive of the word as a bilateral sign, then we have to say that there are two homonymous signs *bear*$_1$ and *bear*$_2$, which have a common signifiant. And, as was shown in section 1.2, the notion of homonymy is untenable on semiotic grounds.

By introducing some new distinctions and definitions, we probably could resolve the above difficulty. But that would add new complications to the unnecessary complication involved in the notion of the bilateral sign.[5]

## 4. Linguistics as a Part of Semiotics

As was shown above, language can be studied from different points of view, but a semiotic approach is crucial for comprehending the essence of language. Since natural languages are only a subclass of possible sign systems, a study of natural languages in a context of a general theory of possible sign systems is indicated. This theory is called semiotics. The principles and laws of semiotics apply to the study of natural languages, as well as to other sign systems. Therefore, linguistics must be regarded as a part of semiotics. We can define linguistics as a part of semiotics that deals with natural sign systems, that is, with natural languages.

Given the definition of linguistics as a part of semiotics, we have to look for the specific features of linguistics as a semiotic discipline. To this end we must consider the question, What is the specific difference between natural languages and all other kinds of sign systems?

Any natural language must be an adequate means of expressing the conceptual network of the human mind; that is, any natural language must be a sign system, which can have as many distinct signs as there are distinct concepts in the conceptual network of the human mind and which can create as many signs as are necessary to express new concepts in the processes of human cognition and communication. This feature of any natural language can be called the property of *cognitive flexibility* of natural languages. Being cognitively flexible, any natural language is an extremely rich, variable, and productive sign system. This feature of natural language makes it possible always to translate a message expressed in some sign system into a message expressed in a natural language, whereas the reverse is not true: not every message expressed in a natural language can be translated into a message expressed in some other sign system.

As a direct consequence of its cognitive flexibility, any natural language has a system of diacritics. To be cognitively flexible, a natural language must have the capacity of producing a potentially infinite number of signs. The system of diacritics serves as a means for the production of signs. Owing to a system of diacritics, any sign can be produced by combining diacritics; so any sign is nothing but a combination of diacritics.

Cognitive flexibility is a fundamental property of any natural language. Owing to this property, any natural language is a remarkably rich, complex, and infinitely variable and productive system of signs. From the point of view of cybernetics, natural languages belong to a type of systems that are called in cybernetics *very large systems*.

What, then, is a very large system, as understood in cybernetics?

In cybernetics the concept 'large system' refers to a system with a large number of distinctions. The larger the system, the larger the number of its distinctions. A very large system will have a very large number of distinctions. The words *very large* are used in cybernetics to imply that, given some definite observer with definite resources and techniques, the system beats him by its richness and complexity: so that he cannot observe it completely, or control it completely, or carry out the calculations for predictions completely.

Natural languages belong to such 'very large systems' because each natural language has a very large number of distinctions.

How, then, can a child learn a natural language, which is a very large system? How can a child acquire a system that beats him by its richness and its complexity?

The acquisition of a natural language by a child will remain a mystery unless we assume a hypothesis whereby there is available a simple sign system that underlies natural languages and controls their functioning. I call this simple sign system the *linguistic genotype*. The linguistic genotype is a common semiotic basis underlying all natural languages. Natural languages, in this sense, are embodiments of the linguistic genotype, and the functioning of every natural language simulates the functioning of the linguistic genotype. We can assume that a child acquires a natural language through the linguistic genotype, which, of course, does not exist independently of natural languages but is, so to say, built into them. Thus, the process of acquiring a natural language through the linguistic genotype must be conceived of as an unconscious process. But it is essential to assume that the linguistic genotype has an objective existence as a common semiotic basis of natural languages.

To study the linguistic genotype is to study the common semiotic properties of natural languages, that is, to study the basic semiotic laws of the functioning of natural languages.

The treatment of linguistics as a part of semiotics contrasts with a fairly widespread view that linguistics is a part of psychology.

True, linguistic processes in the human mind involve psychological phenomena. But logical processes in the human mind also involve psychological phenomena; nobody, however, views logic as a part of psychology. Although logical processes involve psychological processes, logic is independent of psychology, because logic has a specific subject matter for which psychological considerations are irrelevant: rules of deduction and the construction of deductive systems.

Although psychological phenomena accompany linguistic processes in the human mind, linguistics is independent of psychology, because psychological considerations are irrelevant for understanding sign systems. Apart from some marginal cases of onomatopoeia and related phenomena, the signs of human language are arbitrary and conventional. Language is a tacit social convention shared by the members of the linguistic community; the infringement of this social convention makes the speaker run the risk of being incomprehensible or ridiculous. Language as a network of social conventions is what linguistics is all about. Social conventions are supraindividual; they are logically independent of the psychological processes that may be connected with them in the minds of individuals.

Linguistics is completely independent of psychology. The psychology of speech is not even an auxiliary science of linguistics. The investigation of linguistic phenomena by methods of psychology is, of course, possible, and it is important. But a necessary prerequisite for such investigation is the previous establishment of linguistic facts: psychology of speech presupposes linguistics as its basis.

### 5. The Goals of Linguistic Theory and the Semiotic Basis of Abstraction

Observing natural languages makes obvious the many differences among them; not only are genetically unrelated languages, such as English and Chinese, very dissimilar, but languages that have a common origin, such as English and German, also differ from one another in many important ways. And yet, one can also discover important similarities among languages. Thus, the grammar of every language includes a system of obligatory syntactic functions. For instance, not every language differentiates between nouns and verbs, but every language must differentiate between the two basic components of a sentence: predicates and their terms.

On the other hand, although languages may vary greatly one from another, the possibilities of variation among languages are not unlimited: there are regular patterns of variation among languages that are limited by intrinsic functional and structural properties of signs. For instance, languages may vary in word order patterns, but these patterns can be reduced to a limited number of types determined by the intrinsic linearity of sign sequences in human speech. Language typology is possible only because there are functional and structural constraints on possible differences among languages.

Linguistic similarities and differences seem to be determined by some unknown factors that constitute the essence of natural languages. Therefore, linguistic similarities and differences must be recognized as significant phenomena that provide clues to the understanding of what a natural language is. These phenomena must be explained in terms of principles that account for the essence of natural languages.

The basic question of linguistic theory must be: What factors contribute to the similarities and differences between natural languages?

To answer this question, linguistic theory must achieve the following goals:

First, it must define the essential properties of natural language as a special kind of sign system.

Second, it must state linguistic universals, that is, all necessary or possible consequences of the properties of natural language as a sign system.

Third, it must explain facts of individual languages; that is, it must subsume these facts under classes of phenomena characterized by the principles and laws it has stated.

Fourth, it must construct insightful typologies and grammars of individual languages.

In accordance with the distinction of two semiotic strata in a natural language—the system of signs and the system of diacritic elements—linguistic theory consists of two parts: *phonology* and *grammar*. Phonology is the study of the system of diacritic elements, and grammar is the study of the system of signs.

In pursuing its goals, linguistic theory faces the following problem: What basis could we provide for justifying our abstractions? How can we distinguish between correct and incorrect abstractions? What abstractions have cognitive value, and what abstractions, far from having cognitive value, distort linguistic reality and hamper progress in linguistics? For example, what basis could we provide for such abstractions as deep structure in transformational grammar, underlying phonological representations in generative phonology, the universal notion of subject in various linguistic theories, and so on? A linguistic theory that lacks a reliable basis for its abstractions is built on thin ice.

The problem of justifying abstractions is central to any linguistic theory. As a matter of fact, all important discussions and controversies in contemporary linguistics turn around this basic problem, which so far has not been resolved satisfactorily.

Having come to grips with the above problem, I propose to constrain abstractions by tracing out the consequences of the semiotic principles, such as the Principle of Semiotic Relevance explained above and related principles, which will be presented in the following chapters of the book. If the assumption that the semiotic aspect of language constitutes its essence is correct, then tracing out consequences of the semiotic principles will be a necessary basis for a principled choice between conflicting abstract hypotheses advanced for the explanation of linguistic phenomena.

## 6. Synchronic Linguistics and Diachronic Linguistics

Languages change constantly. The evolution of a language is a succession of its different states in time. Evolution implies at least two different states: an initial state and a final state. Evolution has structure: any two successive states of a language are interrelated with each other by some regular correspondences. These correspondences can be stated as a series of rules. Two types of facts are distinguished: 1) paradigmatic and syntagmatic oppositions between linguistic units coexisting at a given state of a language—*synchronic* facts, and 2) correspondences between the successive states of a language—*diachronic* facts.

We want to find out, of course, how synchronic and diachronic facts are connected to each other. The answer is paradoxical: Diachronic facts are responsible for and at the same time irrelevant to the synchronic structure of a language.

Here is an example of the interrelation of the synchronic and diachronic phenomena (Saussure, 1956:83–84). In Anglo-Saxon, the earlier forms were *fōt:fōti, tōþ:tōþi, gōs:gōsi*, etc. These forms passed through two phonetic changes: 1) vowel change (umlaut): *fōti* became *fēti; tōþi, tēþi; gōsi, gēsi*; and 2) the fall of final *-i: fēti* became *fēt; tēþi, tēþ; gēsi, gēs* (Modern English: *foot:feet; tooth:teeth; goose:geese*). A comparison of the two states of the evolution of English—the Anglo-Saxon state and the Old English state—shows that the synchronic rules of the formation of the plural were different in both instances: in Anglo-Saxon the plural was marked simply by the addition of an -*i*; in Old English the plural was marked by the opposition between vowels.

Although the plural formation in Old English evolved from the plural formation in Anglo-Saxon, the former was logically independent of the latter. The synchronic statement of the rule of plural formation in Old English has nothing to do either with the above phonetic changes or with the rule of plural formation in Anglo-Saxon.

This example shows that synchronic facts are logically independent of diachronic facts. Hence, linguistics bifurcates into two branches: *synchronic linguistics* and *diachronic linguistics*.

A language as an instrument of communication is a synchronic system. Therefore, synchrony is logically prior to diachrony. The synchronic study of languages is the fundamental task of linguistics and a necessary prerequisite for the diachronic study. Synchronic linguistics takes precedence over diachronic linguistics.

*Synchronic* should not be confused with *static*. Any synchronic system contains archaisms and innovations consisting of newly coined words, new metaphorical uses of words, etc.; deviations from the received phonetic, grammatical, and lexical standards occur that may represent both remnants of the past and germs of the future development. These phenomena have nothing to do with *static:* they characterize the dynamic aspects of the synchronic system. Therefore, the term *static linguistics*, which is sometimes used as a synonym of *synchronic linguistics*, is inappropriate.

In accordance with the distinction of the two semiotic strata in language, synchronic linguistics consists of two parts: 1) phonology—the study of the diacritic stratum of language; and 2) grammar—the study of the sign stratum of language. I take the term *grammar* in a broad sense. It covers not only the notion of grammar in the narrow sense, but also semantics and everything pertaining to the study of the linguistic units that constitute the sign stratum of language.

## 7. Language Variation

Language changes not only in time but also in space and with respect to the stratification of a linguistic community into social classes and ethnic groups.

In accordance with the variation of a language in different geographical territories, we distinguish different *dialects* of a language. The term *dialect* applies to every regional form of a given language without any implication that a more acceptable form of the language exists distinct from the dialects. This use of the term *dialect* does not imply a judgment of value. For example, every American speaks a dialect—New England dialect, Southern dialect, etc. Speakers of these dialects never feel that they speak anything but a form of American English that is perfectly acceptable in all situations.

The term *dialect* also has quite a different use. When applied to languages such as Russian, German, or Italian, the term in current use implies a judgment of value: dialects are contrasted with a national language—for example, German has different dialects, but there is a form of German that is not a dialect but a language. There are Germans who do not speak any German dialect but the German language. In this sense, dialects are contrasted with a language not as particular forms of a linguistic system with its general form but as particular forms with a particular form that is accepted nationwide.

Dialects arise as a result of a decrease in the frequency and intimacy of contact between various sections of the population separated from one another by different geographical localization. But the diminution of the frequency and intimacy of contact may be a result of a social and ethnic stratification of a linguistic community. Therefore, it is appropriate to use the term *dialect* to distinguish not only varieties of a language in space but also varieties conditioned by a social and ethnic stratification of a linguistic community. In current linguistic literature, the terms *social dialect* (*sociolect*) and *ethnic dialect* are used in this sense. Examples of social and ethnic dialects are the working-class dialect in England (cockney) and black English in the United States.

Dialects of a language can be viewed not only in synchronic but also in diachronic perspective. If we combine the space perspective with the time perspective, we can distinguish four types of linguistic systems reflecting different kinds of abstraction from time or space:

1) a linguistic system with time and space excluded (*monochronic monotopic* linguistic system);

2) a linguistic system with time excluded and space included (*monochronic polytopic* linguistic system);

3) a linguistic system with time included and space excluded (*polychronic monotopic* linguistic system); and

4) a linguistic system with both time and space included (*polychronic polytopic* linguistic system).

The first and second types of linguistic systems relate to synchronic linguistics, and the third and fourth types of linguistic systems relate to diachronic linguistics. In this book I will deal exclusively with the first type.

## 8. The Semiotic versus Generativist Notion of Language

Noam Chomsky, the founder of a linguistic theory called generative-transformational grammar, once defined language as follows:

> From now on I will consider a *language* to be a set (finite or infinite) of sentences, each finite in length and constructed out of a finite set of elements. (Chomsky, 1957:12)

Defining the goals of linguistic theory, he wrote:

> The fundamental aim in the linguistic analysis of a language $L$ is to separate the *grammatical* sequences which are the sentences of $L$ from the *ungrammatical* sequences which are not sentences of $L$ and to study the structure of grammatical sentences. (Chomsky, 1957: 12)

Furthermore, Chomsky defined the grammar of a language as follows:

> The grammar of $L$ will thus be a device that generates all of the grammatical sequences of $L$ and none of the ungrammatical ones. (Chomsky, 1957: 12)

What strikes one in these definitions of language and grammar is Chomsky's complete disregard of the fact that language is a sign system.

As a supposedly superior alternative to the semiotic notion of language as a sign system, Chomsky suggested a notion of language as a set of sentences.

As an alternative to the notion of grammar as a system of rules that constitutes an integral part of language, Chomsky suggested a notion of grammar that is not a part of language but is an external device for generating a language understood as a set of sentences.

Let us not argue about definitions. After all, every linguist, like every other scientist, has the right to define his terms in his own way. What matters is not definitions in themselves but the empirical consequences of such definitions. So, let us consider the empirical consequences of Chomsky's notions of language and grammar.

If we accept the notion of language as a sign system, we cannot investigate grammar independently of meaning, because linguistic units are signs, and a sign as a member of the binary relation 'sign of' cannot be separated from its meaning. A sign separated from its meaning is no longer a sign but merely a sequence of sounds—a purely physical phenomenon.

If, on the other hand, we do not include the notion of the sign in the definition of language and base this definition on some other set of notions, as Chomsky used to do, then we are free to consider grammar to be independent of meaning. According to Chomsky, "grammar is autonomous and independent of meaning" (Chomsky, 1957: 17). As a special case, he considered syntax to be an autonomous component of grammar distinct from semantics.

To support his claim that the notion 'grammatical' cannot be identified with 'meaningful', Chomsky devised an example of a sentence that was allegedly nonsensical but grammatically correct:

*Colorless green ideas sleep furiously.*

As a matter of fact, the nonsensical content of this sentence has no bearing on the question of whether or not its grammatical structure is meaningful. Chomsky confounded the notion of *grammatical meaning* with the notion of *lexical mean-*

*ing.* But we must distinguish between lexical meaning and grammatical meaning. No matter whether or not from the standpoint of lexical meaning a sentence is nonsensical, if the sentence is grammatically correct, it is grammatically meaningful. So, the above sentence contains the following grammatical meanings: the noun *ideas* signifies a set of objects, the verb *sleep* signifies a state *ideas* are in, the adverb *furiously* signifies the property of *sleep*, and the adjectives *colorless* and *green* signify two different properties of *ideas*. Grammatical meanings are *categorial* meanings, that is, the most general meanings characterizing classes of words and other linguistic units. If this sentence did not have grammatical meanings, we could not even decide whether it is nonsensical or not. We consider this sentence nonsensical because of the conflict between the grammatical and lexical meanings: the grammatical meanings of the adjectives *colorless* and *green* and the verb *sleep* assign contradictory properties and a highly unlikely state to the object denoted by the noun *ideas;* the adverb *furiously* assigns a strange property to a state denoted by the verb *sleep.*

Compare the following expressions:

(1)     *round table*
(2)     *round quadrangle*

The meaning of (2) is nonsensical, because the grammatical, that is, categorial, meanings of its words conflict with the lexical meanings: the grammatical meaning of *round* assigns a contradictory property to the object denoted by the noun *quadrangle.* Expression (1) makes sense, because its lexical and grammatical meanings are in keeping with each other.

Consider the following verses from *Alice in Wonderland* by Lewis Carroll:

> 'Twas brillig, and the slithy toves
> Did gyre and gimble in the wabe;
> All mimsy were the borogoves,
> And the mome raths outgrabe.

Do these verses make sense? Yes, of course, they do, for although they contain made-up nonsense words created by Lewis Carroll, we understand that *did gyre and gimble* signifies some actions in the past, *in the wabe* signifies a localization in some object, *slithy* signifies a property of the set of objects called *toves,* etc.

What, then, are grammatical meanings?

Grammatical meanings are morphological and syntactic categories. These categories are represented in the above verses by the plural suffix *-s,* the preposition *in,* the auxiliary verbs *did* and *were,* the conjunction *and,* the article *the,* and the word order.

Affixes, prepositions, conjunctions, etc. all have meaning because they are signs, and signs presuppose meaning. The notion of the meaningless sign is no better than the notion of the round quadrangle.

An analysis of a sentence into immediate constituents is impossible without an analysis of meaning. Consider the sentence

(3)    *The mother of the boy and the girl will come soon.*

This sentence admits of two analyses into immediate constituents:

(4)    *The mother (of the boy and the girl) will come soon.*
(5)    *(The mother of the boy) and the girl will come soon.*

We can analyze these two sentences differently because they have two different grammatical meanings.

Let us now have one possible complete analysis of sentence (3) into its immediate constituents:

(6)    (((The mother) (of ((the boy) (and (the girl)))))((will come) soon)).

If we disregard the meaning of (3), (6) is not the only possible way of analyzing (3) into immediate constituents. We could have constituents such as

(7)    (mother of)           ((boy and) the)       (and the)
       ((mother of) the)     (come soon)           ((and the) (girl will))
       (girl will)           (boy and)             (of the)

An analysis of a sentence into immediate constituents without an analysis of the meaning of the sentence admits of any arbitrary bracketing.

Why do we not analyze the sentence as shown in (7)? Because this analysis contradicts the semantic connections between words.

Any analysis of phrases into immediate constituents presupposes an analysis of semantic connections between words. A syntactic analysis presupposes a semantic analysis.

It is clear from the foregoing that an autonomous grammar independent of a semantic analysis is impossible unless we are resigned to doing a sort of hocus-pocus linguistics.

Here a further question arises: How did Chomsky manage to avoid unacceptable constituents, such as (*mother of*) or (*of the*) in the above example?

He did the trick by tacitly smuggling an analysis of meaning into an analysis of immediate constituents. But, smuggling semantic analysis into syntax cannot be an adequate substitute for a straightforward, consistent analysis of meaning as a part of syntax.

It should be noted that in the first version of generative-transformational grammar (1957), Chomsky was not concerned about semantics at all. However, he introduced a semantic component into the second version of his grammar (1965). That did not mean a change of his conception of an autonomous grammar independent of meaning: his grammar remained autonomous because the semantic component was conceived of as a component interpreting syntactic structures established independently of meaning. Clearly, the perverse idea that syntactic structures can be established without recourse to an analysis of meaning has persisted in all versions of generative-transformational grammar.

As a matter of fact, Chomsky inherited the idea of autonomous grammar from the distributionally oriented type of American structuralism, in particular from the works of his teacher Zellig S. Harris, who was concerned in grammatical description primarily with specifying patterns of occurrence and cooccurrence of elements. Harris worked without reference to meaning. His aim was to develop a method for representing grammatical structures of sentences without reference to semantic criteria; it was assumed that semantic statements would follow from purely formal syntax constructed independently of meaning.

Generative-transformational grammar is essentially a recasting of American distributional structuralism into a formal system. The new idea introduced by Chomsky was *generation*. He declared that structuralism was merely taxonomic, and he opposed his generative system to it as an explanatory model.

In order to evaluate the methodological significance of the notion of generation, let us consider some other important notions used in Chomsky's works.

One fundamental factor involved in a speaker-hearer's performance is his knowledge of grammar. This mostly unconscious knowledge is referred to as *competence*. Competence is distinct from *performance*. Performance is what the speaker-hearer actually does; it is based not only on his knowledge of language but also on many other factors—memory restrictions, distraction, inattention, nonlinguistic knowledge, beliefs, etc.

Chomsky uses the term *grammar* in two senses: 1) on the one hand, the term is used to refer to the system of rules in the mind of the speaker-hearer, a system that is normally acquired in early childhood; 2) on the other hand, it is used to refer to the theory that the linguist constructs as a hypothesis concerning the actual internalized grammar of the speaker-hearer.

Grammar in the sense of a linguistic theory is called a hypothesis, because the internalized grammar in the mind of the speaker-hearer is not available for immediate observation.

Chomsky assumes that the grammar in the speaker-hearer's mind is not an ordinary grammar but a generative grammar. He constructs his theoretical generative grammar as a hypothesis about the real grammar in the speaker-hearer's mind.

Chomsky assumes further that since the generative grammar in the speaker-hearer's mind is not available for immediate observation, the only way to draw conclusions about it is from the results of its activity, that is, from the properties of the set of sentences it has generated. Under this assumption, only those aspects of a generative grammar in the speaker-hearer's mind are relevant that cause generation of a particular set of sentences under consideration.

By analyzing all available sentences produced by this allegedly "generative" grammar in the speaker-hearer's mind, Chomsky constructs his theoretical generative grammar, which serves as a hypothesis about the generative grammar in the speaker-hearer's mind. Since only those aspects of generative grammar in the speaker-hearer's mind are considered relevant that cause it to generate a set of sentences, the only thing that is required from theoretical generative grammar is a capacity for generation of the same set of sentences that is available for immediate observation. To verify a theoretical generative grammar therefore means to establish that it is capable of producing this set of sentences.

The idea of a theoretical generative grammar as a hypothesis about the generative grammar in the speaker-hearer's mind looks very attractive, but it is actually a mistaken idea. If nothing is required of a theoretical generative grammar except that it generate correct sentences for a given language, then it must be considered unverifiable as a hypothesis about the real grammar in the speaker-hearer's mind.

But what is wrong with generative grammar as a theoretical hypothesis?

Generative grammar aims at constructing a mathematically consistent system of formal rules. But mathematical consistency does not guarantee a correct description of reality.

Using a mathematical formalism, we can posit a system of rules for deriving sentences from certain basic linguistic objects. Granted that these rules work, does it mean that they present a reasonable model of the real rules of a language we are describing? No, it does not. From the fact that a mathematical design works, one cannot conclude that language works in the same way. Real rules of real language are empirical dependencies between truly basic linguistic objects and sentences that are derived from them because of an empirical necessity. But empirical necessity should not be confused with logical necessity. In accordance with the laws of logic, true statements can be logically necessary consequences of both true and false statements. Let me illustrate that with two examples.

We can deduce the true statement *Butterflies fly* from two false statements by constructing the following syllogism:

(1)     *Cows fly.*
(2)     *Butterflies are cows.*
(3)     *Butterflies fly.*

In accordance with the rules of logic, the deduction of (3) from (1) and (2) is a logical necessity. But the logically necessary connection between (1) and (2), on the one hand, and (3), on the other hand, conflicts with empirical necessity.

Another example: Suppose we construct a calculus in which we posit some false initial statements such as $2=5$, $3=7$, and so on. Suppose, further, that this calculus has the following derivation rule: If $x=y$, then $x$ can be substituted for $y$ and $y$ can be substituted for $x$. By applying this rule, we can derive true statements from the initial false statements, for example: $2=2$, $3=3$, $5=5$, $7=7$, and so on. The logically necessary connection between these true statements and the initial false statements from which they are derived conflicts with empirical necessity.

If a linguist claims that his mathematical design is a model of the grammar of a real language, it is not enough for him to show that grammatically correct sentences can be derived by applying formal rules to certain initial objects. He also bears the burden of proving that the initial objects are not fictitious, that logically necessary derivations in his formal system correspond to empirically necessary derivations in the real system of a real language.

A linguist who claims that his formal system corresponds to the real system of a real language can validate his claim by basing his argumentation on an analysis of semiotic properties of language.

Generativism is unacceptable as a methodological postulate because it confounds logical necessity with empirical necessity. Granted that generative-transformational grammar is able to generate only true linguistic objects of the surface structure of a language (actually, it is far from being able to do so), this fact in itself does not guarantee that this grammar is not fictitious. Generative-transformational grammar based on the fictitious notion of deep structure and fictitious phonological entities conflicts with the functional properties of language as a sign system.

Fictionalism and generativism are two sides of the same coin. There is nothing wrong with the mathematical notions of algorithm and generation; rules of algorithmic type, when properly applied to particular domains, can be an important mathematical aid in empirical research. But generativism is a different story. Generativism as a methodological postulate is an attempt to justify fictitious entities in linguistics by devising mechanistic rules that convert fictitious linguistic entities into observable linguistic objects. Inventing and manipulating mechanistic rules are the only way to justify fictitious entities, but all of that has nothing to do with explanation—rather, it all is akin to reflections in curved mirrors.

The only right alternative to generativism is the semiotic method with its concept of semiotic reality. The semiotic method does not reject mathematical notions of algorithm and generation as useful tools of linguistic research. Rather, it rejects generativism as a methodological postulate. The choice of a mathematical tool is not crucial; what is crucial is to associate our mathematical tool with a correct hypothesis about language, and that can be done only by applying the semiotic method.

We can construct different systems that will generate the same set of sentences. If so—which system is the right system?

There is no way to answer this question if the only thing we require of a generative model is that it generate correct sentences for a given language. The only way to solve our problem is to study the properties of language as a sign system. Then and only then will we be able to make a right choice between different ways of constructing sentences of a given language. The correct system of rules must respect linguistic stratification; it must respect functional properties of linguistic units; it must respect the distinction between synchrony and diachrony, and so on. In other words, we must use the semiotic method, which provides the necessary criteria for an evaluation of linguistic models.

Generativism is unacceptable because it aims at constructing arbitrary mechanistic rules that either distort linguistic reality or at best have zero explanatory value.

Generativism distorts linguistic reality in the following ways:

1) It confounds the phonological level with the morphological level.

2) As a result of 1), it rejects the phonological level.

3) It uses fictitious entities called *deep structures* and fictitious phonological representations.

4) It confounds the constituency relations with linear word order, which involves an inferior formalism that is inadequate for a study of linguistic relations and formulating linguistic universals.[6]

Chomsky writes a lot on the philosophy of language. A discussion of his philosophical views is outside the scope of this book. Suffice it to make a few comments on his claim that his linguistic theory relates to the ideas of Humboldt. He claims that his notion of competence as a system of generative processes is related to Humboldt's concept of *free creativity.* Chomsky writes:

> We thus make a fundamental distinction between *competence* (the speaker-hearer's knowledge of his language) and *performance* (the actual use of language in concrete situations). . . . This distinction I am noting here is related to the *langue-parole* distinction of Saussure; but it is necessary to reject his concept of *langue* as merely a systematic inventory of items and to return rather to the Humboldtian conception of underlying competence as a system of generative processes. (Chomsky, 1965:4)

The works of Humboldt are not easy reading. But anyone who is familiar with these works and is able to understand them can see that Chomsky's notion of competence as a system of generative processes has no relation whatsoever to Humboldt's ideas.

The most often quoted passage from Humboldt's main linguistic work contains a succinct characterization of the essence of language as he understood it:

> In itself language is not work (*ergon*) but an activity (*energeia*). Its true definition may therefore be only genetic. It is after all the continual intellectual effort to make the articulated sound capable of expressing thought.* (Humboldt, 1971: 27)

---

*Original text: "Sie [die Sprache] ist kein Werk (*Ergon*), sondern eine Thätigkeit (*Energeia*). Ihre wahre Definition kann daher nur eine genetische sein. Sie ist nämlich die sich ewig wiederholende Arbeit des Geistes, den articulirten Laut zum Ausdruck des Gedanken fähig zu machen" (Humboldt, 1836: 41).

Obviously Chomsky confounds his notion 'generative' with Humboldt's notion 'genetic'. If one does not base one's speculations on the etymological affinity of the words *generative* and *genetic* but concentrates his intellectual powers on understanding what he reads, he will see that the above passage, in the context of the whole of Humboldt's work, has the following meaning.

By stating that language is not work (*ergon*) but an activity (*energeia*), Humboldt really meant that language is a constantly changing instrument of expressing thought and that expressive activity is a constant struggle by the individual to adapt the meaning of linguistic form for the thought he wants to express.

Humboldt conceives of the word as a bilateral unit—a combination of sign and meaning. Here is what he writes about the notion of the word:

> By the term 'words' we mean the signs of individual concepts. The syllable forms a sound unit, but it only becomes a word when there is some significance attached to it; this often requires a combination of several such units. Therefore, in the word two units, the sound and the idea, coalesce. Words thus become the true elements of speech; syllables lacking significance cannot be so designated.*
> (Humboldt, 1971: 49)

Humboldt's conception of the word as a bilateral unit consisting of sign and meaning is in keeping with the conception of the word in modern semiotics and has nothing in common with Chomsky's conception of autonomous grammar independent of meaning, with its unilateral linguistic units.

Humboldt's conception of language as an activity (*energeia*) has nothing in common with the mechanistic rules of generative grammar. Rather, it is in keeping with the conception of language in modern semiotics as a dynamic conventionalized conceptual system that is in a state of constant flux as a result of the constant struggle of individuals to adapt linguistic form to the thoughts they want to express.

Generativism must be abandoned. By saying that generativism must be abandoned, I do not mean to say that linguistics must return to one of the earlier varieties of structuralism—we have to attain a higher level of comprehension by reconstructing the old concepts in the framework of new formal systems based on semiotics. That will be genuine progress, not a return to worn old concepts.[7]

---

*Original text: "Unter Wörten versteht man die Zeichen der einzelnen Begriffe. Die Silbe bildet eine Einheit des Lautes; sie wird aber erst zum Worte, wenn sie für sich Bedeutsamkeit erhält, wozu oft eine Verbindung mehrer gehört. Es kommt daher in dem Worte allemal eine doppelte Einheit, des Lautes und des Begriffes, zusammen. Dadurch werden die der Bedeutsamkeit ermagelenden Sylben nicht eigentlich so genannt werden können" (Humboldt, 1836: 74).

# II.

# *Phonology*

### 1. The Phoneme and Distinctive Features

When I was giving a semiotic definition of language, I introduced the notion of the phoneme, which I defined as a diacritic used to distinguish different signs. According to this definition, a phoneme is the first term of the binary relation 'diacritic of', whose second term is a sign. The notion of the phoneme was motivated by the analysis of natural languages as a *very large sign system.* It was shown that no natural language can do without a limited number of diacritics necessary for the production of an unlimited number of signs.

The notion of the phoneme was introduced without an analysis of its relation to the notion of sound. At that stage of our discussion, it was enough to justify the notion of the phoneme by characterizing it merely as a diacritic without regard to the most difficult *problem of identity*, which is central to modern phonology.

It is now time to tackle the problem of identity in phonology. I will start with an analysis of speech sounds that does not presuppose the notion of the phoneme. I will try to show, step by step, how the solution to the problem of identity of speech sounds calls for the notion of the phoneme. In this way we will get new insights into the nature of objects denoted by the term *phoneme*. A new definition of the phoneme will be given, and it will reflect a deeper understanding of this intriguing notion. The new definition will supplement the definition of the phoneme as a diacritic.

Let us now turn to the analysis of speech.

Phoneticians recognize that speakers segment speech into series of discrete elements called phonetic segments, speech sounds, or *phones*. A phonetic study of languages provides an inventory and description of the occurring phonetic segments.

Any phonetic transcription is an abstraction from the physical reality of speech. Although speakers segment speech into discrete elements, it is actually a continuous flow. That is why the same speech sound is pronounced differently on different occasions. Compare the words *tea* and *too*. The initial consonants in these words are denoted by the same letter *t*, but they are very different. Try to pronounce only the initial consonants. In one case, the articulation of sound *t* takes place in a vocal tract that is already prepared to make the front vowel *i;* in the other, the vocal tract is already prepared for the back vowel *u*. Because of the different shapes of the vocal tract, the two articulations produce different acoustic results.

Take acoustic records of the pronunciation of the words *tea* and *too* on speech spectrograms. You will not be able to find a point of an abrupt change from the consonant *t* to the vowel *i* or from *t* to *u*. It will be impossible to draw a line between the two successive sounds and say that everything before is a pure consonant and everything after is a pure vowel.

Because the sound flow is a continuum, there is a great intrinsic variability among speech sounds. *Speech sounds are modified by their environments.* That is a basic universal assumption concerning the nature of speech sounds, which I call the *Principle of Speech Sound Variability.*

The question is, How do we know which sounds are the same in a given language? What does it mean to say that two speech sounds are the same? What does it mean, for example, to say that the word *tight* has the same initial and final consonant? These two consonants are not the same: the initial consonant is aspirated, while the final one is not aspirated. In order to represent this difference, two symbols are needed: $t^h$ for the aspirated consonant and $t^-$ for the unaspirated consonant.

Actually, speakers of a given language classify sounds as the same and different unconsciously. One might assume that this classification is based on a natural physical similarity between sounds: two sounds are the same if they belong to the same sound type, and they are different if they belong to different sound types. But this assumption would conflict with the phenomenon that speakers of different languages may classify similar sets of sounds in quite a different way. Consider the following set of sounds:

(1)   $p^h$    $p^-$
      $t^h$    $t^-$
      $k^h$    $k^-$

The superscripts $^h$ and $^-$ designate aspirated and nonaspirated character of sounds respectively.

Speakers of English classify these sounds as three sound types: *p*, *t*, and *k*, while speakers of Eastern Armenian classify all six sounds as different.[1] Similarly, speakers of Old Greek would distinguish six sounds here. These different ways of classification are reflected in the alphabets of these languages: while English has only three letters for this set of sounds, Eastern Armenian and Old Greek have six letters corresponding to the distinction of the aspirated and nonaspirated stops.

It should be noted that in spite of all their imperfections, the alphabets of various languages more or less faithfully reflect classifications of sounds as the same or different, made unconsciously by speakers of these languages.

The phenomenon that sounds belonging to similar sound sets may be classified differently by speakers of different languages, I call *phonic relativity*. This
phenomenon needs to be explained. To explain phonic relativity is to answer
the question, What determines identity of speech sounds in a given language?

The problem of the identity of speech sounds is one of the most profound
problems of theoretical linguistics. This problem is especially complicated; it
involves a series of difficulties that cannot be solved by conventional methods of
abstraction. That is why it cannot so far be considered fully resolved.

In what follows I will present my own solution of the problem of the identity
of speech sounds; I then will compare it with the solutions proposed by others
and explain why I consider them inadequate.

To explain phonic relativity, we must search for some fundamental property
or properties of language from which this phenomenon could be deduced.

In our search we must rely on the *Principle of Differentiation of Signs*. This
principle holds that two different linguistic signs must be differentiated by different sequences of diacritics. For example, *din* and *bin* differ by alternating
sounds *d* and *b*, *din* and *den* differ by alternating sounds *i* and *e*, *din* and *dim*
differ by alternating sounds *n* and *m*. In order to demonstrate that a given set of
sounds can be used to distinguish different signs, we have to fix a set of words
that are distinguished from one another by alternative choices of one sound
from this set. Consider the following two sets of words:

(2)     *pool*     *lip*
        *tool*     *lit*
        *cool*     *lick*

These sets of words show that sounds $p^h$, $t^h$, $k^h$ before the vowel *u* and
sounds $p^-$, $t^-$, $k^-$ after the vowel *i* are used to distinguish different words.

Let me now introduce the notion of the *position of sounds*. The position of a
sound is its place in a sound sequence determined by its environment. Thus, in
*pin* the position of *p* is its place before the vowel *i*, the position of *n* is its place
after the vowel *i*, the position of *i* is its place between *p* and *n*. So in (2) we have
two positions for the stops: before the vowel *u* in the first set of words and after
the vowel *i* in the second set of words:

(3)     I          II
        $p^h$        $p^-$
        $t^h$        $t^-$
        $k^h$        $k^-$

In (3) we have two ordered sets of sounds, $p^h:t^h:k^h$ and $p^-:t^-:k^-$. The relations that order the sets of sounds in each position I call *concrete distinctive
oppositions*, and the terms of these relations I call *concrete phonemes*. Using
this terminology, we can say that in (3) we have two ordered sets of concrete
phonemes: $p^h$, $t^h$, $k^h$ *and* $p^-$, $t^-$, $k^-$.

The essential difference between concrete speech sounds viewed as merely physical and speech sounds viewed as concrete phonemes is that concrete phonemes are terms of concrete relations. The label *concrete distinctive oppositions* characterizes a specific semiotic function of these relations as relevant differences between signs.

Various properties of concrete distinctive oppositions I will call *concrete distinctive features*, and I will describe them in articulatory terms. Thus, in (3) the distinctive oppositions can be characterized as follows:

(4)  I          II
     $L^I$       $L^{II}$
     $A^I$       $A^{II}$
     $V^I$       $V^{II}$

In this diagram the symbol $L$ means 'labial', $A$ means 'alveolar', $V$ means 'velar', and the superscripts mean that the concrete distinctive features in the two positions are different because of different environments.

Any set of concrete phonemes ordered by concrete distinctive oppositions I call a *paradigmatic class of concrete phonemes*.

Having introduced new notions, I must restate the problem of the identity of speech sounds in terms of these notions. Now the problem has to be restated as follows: What determines the identity of concrete phonemes that occur in different positions?

Since concrete phonemes are relational entities, an identity of concrete phonemes must be a counterpart of an identity of concrete distinctive oppositions by which paradigmatic classes of concrete phonemes are ordered. Therefore, the problem of the identity of concrete phonemes amounts to the problem, What determines the identity of the structure (isomorphism) of paradigmatic classes of concrete phonemes?

In coming to grips with this problem, we discover the *Law of Phonemic Identity:*

> Two paradigmatic classes of concrete phonemes $K_i$ and $K_j$ are identical if their relational structure can be put into a one-one correspondence, so that to each concrete phoneme $x$ of $K_i$ there corresponds a concrete phoneme $y$ of $K_j$, and to each concrete distinctive opposition $r$ of $K_i$ there corresponds a concrete distinctive opposition $s$ of $K_j$, and vice versa. There is a one-one correspondence between concrete phonemes $x$ and $y$, and between concrete distinctive oppositions $r$ and $s$, if the difference between $x$ and $y$ and between $r$ and $s$ is reducible solely to the effect of positional variation.

Let us now try to explain the phenomenon of phonic relativity by the Law of Phonemic Identity.

Let us turn back to (1). Why is the set of six sounds presented in (1) classified as three sounds in English and as six sounds in Eastern Armenian or Old Greek? Because in English $p^h$ and $p^-$, $t^h$ and $t^-$, $k^h$ and $k^-$ are concrete phonemes belonging to two paradigms, the differences between the terms of these pairs are reducible to the effect of positional variation: the stops are aspirated in the syllable-initial positions and nonaspirated in others. In other words, the difference between the aspirated and nonaspirated stops in English is irrelevant from the point of view of their distinctive functions. In Eastern Armenian and Old Greek, however, all the above six sounds are concrete phonemes that occur in the same positions, that is, belong to the same paradigm so that the distinction between the aspirated and nonaspirated stops is relevant in these languages. Here is an example demonstrating the relevance of the distinction between the aspirated and nonaspirated stops in Armenian:

(5)     $p^hajt$ 'stick' : $pajt$ 'horseshoe'
        $t^ho\gamma$ 'let' : $to\gamma$ 'line'
        $k^hujr$ 'sister' : $kujr$ 'blind'

The foregoing shows that the problem of identity of speech sounds is solved by splitting the concept of the speech sounds into two different concepts: the speech sound proper and the concrete phoneme. The identity of speech sounds is determined by their physical analysis, while the identity of concrete phonemes is based on the Law of Phonemic Identity.

Concrete phonemes are physical entities, but the identity of concrete phonemes is logically independent of their physical properties. In order to demonstrate that, we have to show that the Law of Phonemic Identity predicts situations where different concrete phonemes are identical with respect to their physical properties and, reversely, two identical concrete phonemes are completely different with respect to their physical properties. One of the possible situations predicted by this law is this: Assume concrete phonemes $A$, $B$, and $C$ in position $P_i$ and concrete phonemes $B$, $C$, and $D$ in position $P_j$ so that the difference between $A$ of $P_i$ and $B$ of $P_j$, between $B$ of $P_i$ and $C$ of $P_j$, and between $C$ of $P_i$ and $D$ of $P_j$ is conditioned solely by the differences between the positional environments. Under the Law of Phonemic Identity, there is a one-one correspondence between the concrete phonemes, as shown by the following diagram:

(6)     $P_i$                 $P_j$
        
        $A$     ↔     $B$
        $B$     ↔     $C$
        $C$     ↔     $D$

The sign ↔ in the diagram means 'one-one correspondence'. This hypothetical situation predicted by the law lays bare the essential semiotic properties of concrete phonemes and concrete distinctive oppositions, so that they can be seen in an ideal pure form. What we see is that two different phonemes $B$ in position $P_i$ and $B$ in position $P_j$ (or $C$ in position $P_i$ and $C$ in $P_j$) are identical with respect to their physical properties, and, reversely, two identical concrete phonemes $A$ in position $P_i$ and $B$ in position $P_j$ (or $B$ in $P_i$ and $C$ in $P_j$, or $C$ in $P_i$ and $D$ in $P_j$) are completely different with respect to their physical properties. By the same token, two different distinctive oppositions $B:C$ in $P_i$ and $B:C$ in $P_j$ are identical with respect to their physical properties, and, reversely, two identical distinctive oppositions $A:B$ in $P_i$ and $B:C$ in $P_j$ (or $B:C$ in $P_i$ and $C:D$ in $P_j$) are completely different with respect to their physical properties.

This abstract hypothetical situation may have counterparts in concrete languages. Consider the following example from Danish.

The Danish sounds $t$ and $d$ occur in syllable-initial positions, for example, in *tag* 'roof' and *dag* 'day'. In syllable-final positions, however, $d$ and $ð$ occur, rather than $t$ and $d$, for example, in *had* 'hat' and *hað* 'hate'. The distribution of the sounds can be presented by the following diagram:

(7)  Syllable-initial position                    Syllable-final position
            $t, d$                                          $d, ð$

How must we classify these sounds?

From a physical point of view, there are three different sounds here: $t$, $d$, and $ð$. From a functional point of view, however, we must suggest a different classification. Since from a functional point of view sounds are always concrete phonemes, that is, terms of some concrete distinctive opposition, the first question we must ask is this: What are the concrete distinctive oppositions whose terms are the above sounds as concrete phonemes?

In order to answer this question, we must bear in mind that concrete distinctive oppositions are characterized by some set of concrete distinctive features, in terms of some acoustic-articulatory properties.

Let us start with the syllable-initial position. The difference between $t$ and $d$ is that the first sound is tense and the second sound is lax. So, the opposition $t:d$ in syllable-initial position is characterized by the opposition of the phonetic features *tense:lax*. The sound $t$ possesses the phonetic feature *tense*, and the sound $d$ possesses the phonetic feature *lax*, and these features characterize the concrete distinctive opposition of both sounds as concrete phonemes.

Let us now consider the sounds in the syllable-final position. What concrete distinctive features characterize the opposition $d:ð$ in the syllable-final position?

The sound $d$ is lax, and the sound $ð$ is fricative. So, the opposition $d:ð$ is characterized by the opposition of the phonetic features *lax:fricative*.

Let us compare the opposition *tense:lax* in the syllable-initial position with the opposition *lax:fricative* in the syllable-final position. We discover an identity of structure between the two oppositions: namely, the relation of the sound *d* to the sound *ð* in the syllable-final position is the same as the relation of the sound *t* to the sound *d* in the syllable-initial position. The point is that in the syllable-final position, *ð* can be considered lax with respect to *d*. As a matter of fact, although *d* is lax with respect to tense *t*, *d* must be considered tense with respect to *ð*.

We see that from a functional point of view, the distinctive feature *lax* in the syllable-final position is the same as the distinctive feature *tense* in the syllable-initial position, and the distinctive feature *fricative* in the syllable-final position is the same as the distinctive feature *lax* in the syllable-initial position.

If this analysis of the functional identity of the distinctive features is correct, we arrive at the following conclusion: from a functional point of view, *d* in the syllable-final position is identical with *t* in the syllable-initial position, and *ð* in the syllable-final position is identical with *d* in the syllable-initial position. The functional identity of the concrete phonemes is a counterpart of the functional identity of their distinctive features (that is, a counterpart of the functional identity of the distinctive oppositions in the syllable-final and the syllable-initial positions).

The results of our analysis can be represented by the following diagram:

(8)      Syllable-initial position                              Syllable-final position
                    *t*                        ⟷                          *d*
                    *d*                        ⟷                          *ð*

The arrows in the diagram mean the functional identity of the respective concrete phonemes.

We can present a similar diagram for the concrete distinctive features of the concrete phonemes presented in (8):

(9)      Syllable-initial position                              Syllable-final position
                    *T*                        ⟷                          *L*
                    *L*                        ⟷                          *F*

The symbol *T* means 'tense', the symbol *L* means 'lax', and the symbol *F* means 'fricative'. The arrows in the diagram mean the functional identity of the respective concrete distinctive features.

We see that the difference between *t* and *d* and between *d* and *ð* in the syllable-initial and the syllable-final positions is reducible to the effect of the physical variations of these concrete phonemes in these two positions. By the same token, the difference between the distinctive feature *tense* and the distinctive feature *lax* and between the distinctive feature *lax* and the distinctive feature *fricative* in the syllable-initial and the syllable-final positions is reducible to positional variations.

Here is one more example, which lays bare the complete logical independence between the functional and physical identity of concrete phonemes.

Consider the shift in the degree of the openness of vowels in Danish, as seen in the following diagram:

(10)   *Before* n        *Before* r
         i      ⟷      e
         e      ⟷      ε
         ε      ⟷      a
         a      ⟷      ɑ

There are four contrastive degrees of vowel openness in Danish. The four front unrounded vowels are normally realized (indicated in the diagram as before n) as i,e,ε,a. However, before r there occurs a uniform shift by one degree of openness, yielding the paradigmatic class e,ε,a,ɑ. While this change modified the physical characteristic of each vowel, the relation between vowels remained constant. The vowel i in the position before n and the vowel e in the position before r are functionally identical, because they are the highest vowels in their respective positions. The vowel e before n and the vowel e before r are functionally not identical, because the first e has the second degree of openness, while the second e has the first degree of openness. We arrive at the conclusion that the differences between concrete phonemes that are in one-one correspondence are reducible solely to the effects of the physical variations of the concrete phonemes in the positions before n and r.

An analysis of all the relations between vowels in this diagram shows a complete logical independence between the functional and physical identity of concrete phonemes.

The discussion of the problem of the identity of sounds has shown that the notion of the identity of sounds must be split into two logically independent notions: the functional identity of sounds as concrete phonemes and the physical identity of sounds as sounds proper. By the same token, the notion of the identity of phonetic features must be split into two logically independent notions: the functional identity of phonetic features as concrete distinctive features and the physical identity of phonetic features as phonetic features proper.

In accordance with the distinction between the functional and physical identity of sounds, we distinguish two types of objects: classes of functionally identical concrete phonemes and classes of physically identical sounds. Both classes of sounds are logically independent.

Just as we must distinguish between the functional and the physical identity of sounds, so we must distinguish between the functional and the physical identity of phonetic features. In accordance with the distinction between the functional and physical identity of phonetic features, we must distinguish between two types of objects: classes of functionally identical phonetic features as concrete distinctive features, and classes of physically identical phonetic features as phonetic features proper. Both classes of phonetic features are logically independent.

Having introduced important distinctions between concrete phonological and phonetic objects, properties and relations, and classes of these objects, properties and relations, I have to introduce necessary terms corresponding to these distinctions.

A class of concrete phonemes I will call an *abstract phoneme.*

A class of concrete distinctive oppositions will be called an *abstract distinctive opposition.*

A class of concrete speech sounds will be called an *abstract speech sound,* or *sound type.*

A class of concrete phonetic features will be called an *abstract phonetic feature.*

As was said above, distinctive features are characteristics of distinctive oppositions in terms of articulatory or acoustic labels. Of course, these labels should be understood not in a physical but in a functional sense.

Our system of phonology has two levels: physical and functional. It can be represented by the following diagram:

| **Functional level** | Concrete phonemes | Abstract phoneme (a class of identical concrete phonemes): | Concrete distinctive features (or concrete distinctive oppositions): | Abstract distinctive features or distinctive oppositions (a class of identical concrete distinctive features or oppositions): |
|---|---|---|---|---|
| | $'a_1'$, $'a_2'$, $'a_3'$, . . . | $'A'$ | $'d_1'$, $'d_2'$, $'d_3'$, . . . | $'D'$ |
| **Physical level** | Concrete speech sounds: | Abstract speech sound or sound type (a class of physically identical concrete speech sounds): | Concrete articulatory or acoustic features: | Abstract articulatory or acoustic features (a class of physically identical articulatory or acoustic features): |
| | $a_1$, $a_2$, $a_3$, . . . | $A$ | $d_1$, $d_2$, $d_3$, . . . | $D$ |

It is convenient to treat a class of identical concrete phonemes as occurrences of one and the same phoneme in different positions. In order to do that, we must use a special type of abstraction, which can be called an *identifying idealization*. It is interesting to compare our approach with what the Russian mathematician Markov writes on the concept of the abstract letter:

> The possibility of establishing identity between letters allows us, by way of *abstraction by identification*, to set up the notion of an abstract letter. The application of that abstraction consists in a given case in that we actually speak of two identical letters as of *one and the same letter*. For example, instead of saying that in the word 'identical' two letters enter, which are identical with 'i', we say the letter 'i' enters in the word 'identical' twice. Here we have set up the concept of an abstract letter 'i' and we consider concrete letters, identical to 'i', as representatives of this *one* abstract letter. *Abstract letters* are letters considered with a precision up to identity. (Markov, 1954: 7–8)

Under identifying idealization, I will treat identical concrete phonemes as occurrences of one and the same abstract phoneme—or simply of one and the same phoneme. For example, the word *tɪtɪleɪt* 'titillate' will be treated as consisting of three occurrences of the phoneme *t*, two occurrences of the phoneme *ɪ*, one occurrence of the phoneme *l*, and one occurrence of the phoneme *eɪ*.

By the same token, I will treat identical concrete distinctive oppositions or distinctive features as occurrences of one and the same abstract distinctive opposition or abstract distinctive feature—or simply of one and the same distinctive opposition or distinctive feature.

A question arises: How must we denote classes of identical concrete phonemes? Consider, for instance, the example from Danish in (8). There we have two classes of identical concrete phonemes: *t,d* and *d,ð*. How must we designate these classes?

There are two methods of designating any class of elements: either we invent special symbols to designate classes of elements, or we choose any element in a given class and regard it as representing this class.

In our case, we can either invent new symbols to designate a given class of identical concrete phonemes, say '*t*' or '*d*', or regard one of the sounds as the representative of this class. The second method is more convenient. We choose a concrete phoneme, minimally dependent on its environment, as representing a given class of concrete phonemes. Since in our example the concrete phonemes in the syllable-initial position are less dependent on their environment than the concrete phonemes in the syllable-final position, we regard the concrete phonemes *t* and *d* in the syllable-initial position as representing classes of concrete phonemes.

An analogous reasoning applies to the concrete distinctive features *tense* (*T*), *lax* (*L*), and *fricative* (*F*) in the Danish example (9). There we have two classes of functionally identical phonetic features: [*T,L*] and [*L,F*]. To denote these classes, we can either invent new symbols or regard the concrete distinctive features $T$ and $L$ in position $P_1$ as representatives of the respective classes of concrete phonemes.

Let us compare the definition of the phoneme as a diacritic and the definition of the phoneme as a class of identical concrete phonemes, that is, concrete speech sounds that function as terms of distinctive oppositions. These definitions complement each other. The first definition abstracts from the speech flow as a physical continuum with variable sounds; it defines the phoneme without regard to its realization in the speech flow. The second definition is an operational definition, which establishes the relation of the phoneme as a diacritic to speech sounds.

Our discussion has shown that speech sounds possess a dual nature—physical and functional. Every speech sound splits into two objects: a physical object and a functional object. Both types of objects are logically independent. Functional and physical identity are complementary and at the same time mutually exclusive concepts. A sound as a member of a class of physically identical objects is a sound proper, but as a member of a class of functionally identical objects, it is a fundamentally new object—a phoneme. As a unity of contradictory objects—functional and physical—a speech sound is a combined object: a sound/diacritic. This combined object I call the phoneme.

What is the logical relation between the concept of the phoneme and the concept of the sound?

These are heterogeneous concepts that belong to different abstraction levels: functional and physical. Between the phoneme and the sound there can exist neither a relation of class membership nor a relation of class inclusion, since the phoneme and the sound belong to basically different abstraction levels. The relation between the phoneme and the sound is similar not to the relationship between the general notion of the table and individual tables, but to the relation between such notions as, let us say, the notion of commodity to the notion of product. Between the commodity and the product there is neither a relation of class membership nor a relation of class inclusion. The commodity and the product relate to each other as notions that characterize the dual nature of an object. There is an analogous relation between the wave and the particle in physics.

The notion of the sound/diacritic reminds one of such notions as the wave/particle in physics, the commodity as a unity of use-value and exchange-value, that is, as the use-value/exchange-value in economics, etc. I use the metaphorical term *centaur concepts* to denote this type of notion, because the structure of these notions is reminiscent of centaurs, the fabulous creatures of Greek mythology, half men and half horses.

The requirement of the strict distinction between the functional and physical identity as logically independent notions I call the *two-level principle*. The theory based on this principle I call the *two-level theory of phonology*.

## 2. Physical and Functional Segmentation of the Speech Flow

Besides the strict distinction between functional and physical identity, we should also distinguish between and not confuse the functional and physical segmentation of sounds. Research in the field of spectrographic analysis of speech sounds has demonstrated that there exists a natural segmentation of the speech flow into sounds independent of functional segmentation. Thus, G. Fant argues that linguistic criteria are irrelevant for determining the division of the speech flow into sounds. He writes:

> A basic problem in speech analysis is the degree of divisibility of the speech wave. The most common approach has been to start with the linguistic criteria in terms of a phonemic transcription and to impose this as a basis for division. By a systematic comparison of the sound patterns of different contexts it is possible to make general statements as to what sound features are typical for a particular phoneme. Such studies are necessary, but in order to avoid ambiguities in the labeling of the successive observable sound units, such an investigation should be preceded by an initial process of segmentation and description of the speech wave on the basis of its physical structure, and in terms of phonetic rather than phonemic units. There is no need for extensive investigation of this type in order to establish an objective basis for dealing with phonetic problems. . . . Detailed studies of this type lead to a description of the speech wave as a succession of sound units with fairly distinctly defined boundaries. (Fant, 1960: 21–22)

Some specialists in acoustic phonetics disagree with Fant and claim that the speech flow is continuous; they argue that there are no distinct boundaries between speech sounds: sounds blend into one another, creating transitions from one sound to another. From the standpoint of phonology, the important fact is that speakers segment the speech flow into discrete units, no matter what its acoustic properties are. The perception of speakers is what matters for phonology. If we accept the claim that the speech flow is continuous, then we have to explain the mechanism of perception that makes speakers segment speech flow into discrete units. Obviously, the problem needs further investigation. The starting point for phonology is the segmentation of the speech flow performed by the speakers, which in fact nobody questions. I apply the term *physical segmentation of the speech flow* to the segmentation performed by speakers. The functional segmentation of the speech flow contrasts with the physical segmentation of the speech flow. The aim of phonology is to discover the conditions of the functional segmentation of the speech flow.

A concrete phoneme is a minimal part of a linguistic sign that is a term of a distinctive opposition. A segmentation of a linguistic sign into a sequence of concrete phonemes may coincide with its segmentation into a sequence of sounds; in other words, a functional segmentation may coincide with a physical segmentation. But depending on the structure of a language, a minimal part of a linguistic sign may consist of two or more sounds. A sequence of two sounds may be interpreted as one or two concrete phonemes.

Two basic conditions can be stated that determine the functional interpretation of a sequence of two sounds:

CONDITION 1. Given an opposition of sequences of two sounds $\widehat{XY}$: XY, so that $\widehat{XY}$ is cohesive and XY noncohesive, $\widehat{XY}$ constitute one concrete phoneme and XY constitute two concrete phonemes.

Here are some examples of the opposition *cohesive:noncohesive:* A comparison of the Polish words *czy* [tši] 'if' and *trzy* [t|ši] 'three' shows that the only difference between these words is the homogeneous articulatory movement in *tš* in the former and its absence in the latter. We encounter the same opposition in the following pairs of Polish words:

(1)     *Czech* [t͡šex] 'Czech' : *trzech* [t|šex] 'of three'
        *czysta* [t͡šista] 'clean' : *trzysta* [t|šista] 'three hundred'
        *paczy* [pat͡ši] 'it warps' : *patrzy* [pat|ši] 'it looks'
        *oczyma* [ot͡šima] 'through the eyes' : *otrzyma* [ot|šima] 'will obtain'

In these examples physical cohesiveness and noncohesiveness are used as distinctive features. Only the opposition of cohesiveness and noncohesiveness is phonologically relevant. If this opposition did not exist, we could not use the physical cohesiveness of a sound sequence XY as a basis for concluding that these two sounds constitute an instance of a single phoneme; nor could we use the physical noncohesiveness of $X|Y$ as evidence that X and Y are instances of two different phonemes 'X' and 'Y'. By doing so we would substitute phonetic criteria for phonological ones, which is unacceptable.

The opposition between physical cohesiveness and noncohesiveness can also be called the opposition of strong and weak cohesion between sounds or the opposition of homogeneity and nonhomogeneity of sound sequences. This opposition is frequently created by the absence and presence of a morphemic or word boundary. Consider the following word pairs from Polish:

(2)     *podrzeć* [podžefiś] : *podżegacz* [pod-žegatš]
        'to tear up'            'instigator'
        *ocaleć* [otsal'efiś] : *odsadzać* [ot-sadzafiś]
        'to remain whole' 'to drive back'
        *dzwon* [dzvon] : *podzwrotnikowy* [pod-zvrotńikovi]
        'bell'                 'subtropical'

The sound sequences *dž, ts, dz* in the words *podrzeć, ocaleć, dzwon*, owing to the strong cohesion between the elements *d* and *ž*, *t* and *s*, *d* and *z*, constitute instances of the phonemes *ž, c,* and *ʒ*. The sound sequences *dž, ts, dz* in the words *podżegacz, odsadzać, podzwrotnikowy,* owing to the weak cohesion between the elements *d* and *ž, t* and *s, d* and *z,* constitute instances of the phonemic sequences *dž, ts,* and *dz.*

In English the sound sequence *tš* occurs inside of morphemes, but *t* and *š* can also be divided by a morpheme boundary or word boundary. Compare: *cheap, rich, butcher* and *court-ship, night-shift, nut-shell.* That creates an opposition *cohesiveness: noncohesiveness.* Hence, the sound sequence *tš* inside of morphemes must be interpreted as a single phoneme *č.*

> CONDITION 2. If in the sound sequence *XY* either *X* or *Y* is not interchangeable with other sounds or zero, then *XY* is an instance of a single phoneme 'Z'. If both *X* and *Y* are interchangeable with other sounds or zero, then *X* is an instance of the phoneme 'X' and *Y* is an instance of the phoneme 'Y'.

Let us clarify the two conditions using a concrete example, the sound sequence *tš.* According to these rules, this sequence can have the following interpretation depending on the various languages it occurs in.

If the sequence *tš* is semiotically indivisible, i.e., if in a given language neither *t* nor *š* can be substituted for, then the sequence *tš* is an instance of the phoneme 'č'. Such a case is a purely hypothetical one, since, to my knowledge, there exists no natural language in which both elements of the sequence would be noninterchangeable with other sounds or zero. However, there are languages in which *t* is not interchangeable with other sounds or zero, as, for instance, in the Spanish word *chino* [tšino] 'Chinese'. Eliminating *š,* we obtain *tino* [tino] 'tact'. The sound *t,* however, cannot be eliminated, since in Spanish words of the type *šino* are not admissible. That means that in Spanish *tš* is an instance of the single phoneme 'č'.

It should be emphasized that the degree of articulatory or acoustic unity of *tš* in English, German, or Spanish has absolutely no significance for determining whether *tš* constitutes an instance of one or two phonemes. What matters is only phonological interchangeability. That applies to any sound sequence. For instance, such sound sequences as *st, ps, bl, au, rs,* etc. could be interpreted as instances of single phonemes in one language but instances of two phonemes in another language.

There is also a condition for biphonematic interpretation of one sound. It can be formulated as follows:

> CONDITION 3. Given a sound sequence *XY* in a position $P_1$ and a sound *Z* in a position $P_2$, if *XY* is interpreted as two phonemes *XY* and if the difference between *XY* and *Z* is reducible solely to the effect of positional variation,

then $Z$ must be considered a realization of the phoneme sequence $XY$.

For example, in many Polish dialects nasalized vowels occur only before fricative consonants, and the sequences *vowel* + *nasal consonant* only before
stops, before vowels, and at the end of the word. Since the sequences *vowel* +
*nasal consonant* are interpreted as sequences of two phonemes, and since the
difference between the sequences *vowel* + *nasal consonant* and the *nasal
vowels* is reducible solely to the effect of positional variation, the nasal vowels
must be interpreted as realizations of the sequences *vowel* + *nasal consonant*.

### 3. Further Problems of Functional Identity

In certain positions in the speech flow, some sounds do not occur. For instance, in English words the voiced stops *b*, *d*, and *g* do not occur in the position after *s*. Consider the English words *spill* [spɪl], *still* [stɪl], and *scold*
[skould]. Since *b*, *d*, and *g* do not occur in the positions after *s*, words of the
type *sbɪl*, *sdɪl*, and *sgould* are impossible in English.

The nonoccurrence of some sounds in certain positions gives rise to a prob-
lem: can counterparts $x_1$, $x_2$, . . . , $x_n$ of sounds $y_1$, $y_2$, . . . , $y_n$, not occurring
in given positions, be considered functionally equivalent to sounds $x_1$, $x_2$,
. . . , $x_n$ in other positions where sounds $y_1$, $y_2$, . . . , $y_n$ do occur? In our case:
can counterparts $p$, $t$, $k$ of sounds $b$, $d$, $g$, not occurring in positions after *s*, be
considered functionally equivalent to $p$, $t$, $k$ in other positions where $b$, $d$, $g$ do
occur?

To answer these questions, we must base our analysis of the given situation
upon the concept of phonological opposition. In positions where the sounds $y_1$,
$y_2$, . . . , $y_n$ occur, the sounds $x_1$, $x_2$, . . . , $x_n$ are members of the phonological
oppositions $x_1:y_1$, $x_2:y_2$, . . . , $x_n:y_n$, and in positions where sounds $y_1$, $y_2$,
. . . , $y_n$ do not occur, sounds $x_1$, $x_2$, . . . , $x_n$ cannot be members of these oppositions. The phonetic feature distinguishing sounds $x_1$, $x_2$, . . . , $x_n$ from
sounds $y_1$, $y_2$, . . . , $y_n$ should be redundant if sounds $x_1$, $x_2$, . . . , $x_n$ do not
participate in phonological oppositions $x_1:y_1$, $x_2:y_2$, . . . , $x_n:y_n$. Therefore,
sounds $x_1$, $x_2$, . . . , $x_n$ in positions where sounds $y_1$, $y_2$, . . . , $y_n$ do not occur
cannot be functionally equivalent to sounds $x_1$, $x_2$, . . . , $x_n$ in positions where
sounds $y_1$, $y_2$, . . . , $y_n$ do occur.

In our English example, $p,t,k$ in *spill*, *still*, and *scold* do not participate in
the phonological oppositions $p:b,t:d,k:g$, because $b,d,g$ do not occur in the
position after *s*; therefore, the voiceless phonetic feature distinguishing $p,t,k$
from $b,d,g$ is redundant here.

$p,t,k$ in *spill*, *still*, and *scold* cannot be considered functionally equivalent to
$p,t,k$ in *pill* [pɪl], *till* [tɪl], and *cold* [kould] because $p,t,k$ in initial positions

before vowels participate in the phonological oppositions $p:b,t:d,k:g$ (compare *pill:bill, till:dill, cold:gold*), and so their voiceless phonetic feature serves as a distinctive feature contrasting with the voiced phonetic feature.

The voiceless phonetic feature of $p,t,k$ in initial positions before vowels is distinctive, while the same phonetic feature of $p,t,k$ in the position after $s$ is not distinctive. In the position after $s$ we have a *merger* of phonemes that are in opposition into one phonological unit. This merger is called *neutralization*, and the resulting new phonological unit is called an *archiphoneme*. The neutralization of $p:b,t:d,k:g$ results in the archiphonemes $P,T,K$, or $<p/b>,<t/d>$, $<k/g>$ in another notation.

In our English example, the nonvoiced stops $p,t,k$ will be denoted by $p,t,k$, the voiced stops will be denoted by $b,d,g$ and the archiphonemes will be denoted by $P,T,K$. The words *pill, till,* and *cold* will be transcribed *pɪl, tɪl,* and *kould,* and the words *spill, still,* and *scold* will be transcribed *sPɪl, sTɪl,* and *sKould.*

The concepts of neutralization and the archiphoneme presuppose each other and can in no way be disassociated from one another.

As another example of neutralization, I will take a neutralization of *voiced: voiceless* consonants in Russian. Consider the Russian words *kust* [kust] 'bush' and *gust* [gust] 'thick'; here we encounter the opposition $k:g$. The distinctive features that characterize this opposition are voicelessness and voicedness. But at the end of words this opposition is neutralized. Thus, in the words *luk* 'bow' and *lug* 'meadow' the otherwise contrasting phonemes $k$ and $g$ merge into a single archiphoneme $K$ (or $<k/g>$ in another notation), and as a result these words merge into a single homonymous sign *luK.*

In our Russian example, the archiphoneme $K$ in *luK* presupposes a phonetically conditioned alternation $g:k$ in such forms as *luga* 'of the meadow' and *luk* 'meadow'. Actually, the nondistinctiveness of certain phonetic features of sounds in positions where their counterparts do not occur is completely independent of the existence or nonexistence of phonetically conditioned alternations. Thus, the voiceless phonetic feature of $p,t,k$ in the English words *spill, still,* and *scold* is nondistinctive, although these sounds do not alternate with $b,d,g$ in other positions.

It goes without saying that the notion of phonetically conditioned alternations of phonemes cannot be dispensed with in phonology, because these alternations account for homonyms resulting from the merger of the phonemic shapes of words. But in the interest of a revealing account of this notion and that of distinctiveness, we should strictly distinguish between and not confuse these notions.

Let us now consider alternative solutions to our problem.

Linguists who include physical similarity of sounds in the definition of the phoneme consider any sort of restriction on the occurrence of sounds in particular positions to be a case of defective distribution, which does not affect the physical constitution of phonemes that occur in these positions. Therefore, these phonemes are considered identical with physically similar phonemes that occur in other positions. Thus, adherents of this approach would view *p,t,k* in English *spɪl*, *stɪl*, and *skould* as equivalent to *p,t,k* in *pɪl*, *tɪl*, and *kould*.

What should we think of this approach? It is true that the nonoccurrence of sounds in any position does not affect the physical constitution of sounds that occur in these positions. But since physical similarity is irrelevant for determining the functional equivalence of sounds, this approach is unacceptable.

It should be noted that we can speak of defective distribution of phonemes only in those cases where the sounds that do not occur in certain positions have no counterparts that do occur in these positions. For instance, in Russian *r* and *r'* do not occur in initial position before *n*: Russian words cannot begin with the phoneme combinations *rn* or *r'n*. Since *r* and *r'* have no counterparts in this position, the nonoccurrence of *r* and *r'* in this position should be considered a case of defective distribution of the phonemes *r* and *r'*.

### 4. Distinctive Features and Experimental Phonetics

As was shown above, every phoneme is characterized by a set of distinctive features. Since phonemes are functional segments ordered into linear sequences, the sets of distinctive features characterizing phonemes are also ordered into linear sequences.

The assumption that phonemes are characterized by linear sequences of sets (or bundles) of distinctive features lies at the basis of modern phonology, no matter how widely particular phonological theories differ from one another. This assumption has recently been challenged by some experimental phoneticians. Here are some of their arguments against the assumption that distinctive features are tied to linearly ordered functional segments of the special flow.

Consider duration. If duration functions as a distinctive feature, phonology includes it among other distinctive features of a functional segment. For example, in English duration serves as a functional cue distinguishing between long and short vowel phonemes, and the opposition of the distinctive features *short:long* must be considered a segmental property of phonemes. However, studies in experimental phonetics have shown that duration has many other linguistic functions that are not restricted to a single segment. It has been found, for example, that in English under certain conditions the phonological distinctive feature *voiced* does not correspond to the phonetic feature *voiced*. Perceptual tests with synthetic stimuli have shown that vowel duration is a sufficient cue for determining the perception of voicing in a final consonant: if you synthesize a sequence such as *jus*, with a voiceless *s*, and lengthen the duration of the vowel, listeners will begin to hear *juz*, even though there is no voicing present in the fricative (for a recent review of the experiments, see Wardrip-

Fruin, 1982). Similarly, it has been discovered that the *tense:lax* (*fortis:lenis*) distinction of stop sounds in German is not exclusively associated with the consonants themselves that presumably carry the distinctive feature of *fortis* and *lenis*, but that the distinction between words containing a fortis or lenis stop sound is characterized by a different distribution of the durations of the consonant and the preceding vowel. Thus, in the analysis of German word pairs such as *baten:baden* and *Laken:lagen*, the duration of the vowel and stop sequence remains approximately constant at the expense of its different distribution between the vowel and the consonant: in words such as *baten*, the vowel is shorter and the consonant is longer; while in words such as *baden*, the relationship is reversed—a shorter consonant follows a longer vowel (Kohler, 1981). Modern literature in experimental phonetics abounds in examples that seem to contradict the notion of the distinctive feature as a segmental property of the speech flow.

These findings of experimental phonetics have induced some linguists, in particular phoneticians, to question the validity of the phonological notion of the distinctive feature. Ilse Lehiste, in her recent paper on the experimental study of duration, writes:

> One of my longstanding complaints and criticisms of most current linguistic theories is the fact that they ignore the temporal aspects of spoken language almost completely. If duration enters into phonological theory at all, it gets segmentalized: [+long] may be included among the distinctive features of a segment. And this is where linguistic theory stops—implying that duration can have only a segmental function, i.e., that all duration can do is differentiate between short and long segments.
>
> Those phonologists who have some acquaintance with experimental phonetics have devoted considerable attention and effort to the study of temporal aspects of spoken language; unfortunately this seems to have had little or no impact on the theoreticians, who continue to manipulate segmental distinctive features to the exclusion of anything larger than a segment. I have said it before, and I will say it again: phonologists ignore phonetics at their own peril. The peril is that they may operate in a fictitious abstract sphere that has no connection with reality. In this abstract sphere, linguistic constructs are timeless. In the real world, spoken language unfolds itself in time. (Lehiste, 1984: 96)

Lehiste, like many other phoneticians, rejects the phonological notion of the distinctive feature, because she fails to see the fundamental difference between the functional and physical levels of the speech flow. Consider the above example concerning the sequence *jus*. True, if we synthesize the sequence *jus*, with a voiceless *s*, and lengthen the duration of the vowel, listeners will begin to hear *juz*, even though there is no voicing in the fricative. That is an interesting phenomenon. But does it undermine the notion of the distinctive feature as a segmental property? From a phonological point of view, the essential thing is the perception of the opposition *voiced:voiceless* rather than the acoustic properties that are involved in the perception. The essential thing is that although in the above experiment the sound *s* does not change, it is perceived as *z* when the preceding vowel is lengthened. What matters is that on the functional level we have the opposition *s:z*. This opposition is a phonological phenomenon that is no less real than the phonetic fact that acoustically the phoneme *z* is represented by the voiceless sound *s* plus the length of the preceding vowel.

Similarly, the discovery that in German the *tense:lax* distinction is associated with the length of the vowel that precedes the consonant does not undermine the phonological notion of the distinctive features *tense:lax*. What matters from a phonological point of view is not the distribution of vowel duration in words such as *baten:baden* but the perception of the consonants as the members of the distinctive oppositions *tense:lax*.

In accordance with the notion of the functional level of the speech flow, we can hypothesize that speech sounds as phonemes are perceived in a special processing area of the brain, different from that used for the perception of other types of sounds. This processing area of the brain can be called the area of functional perception. Functional perception transforms continuous suprasegmental acoustic phenomena into discrete segmental functional properties.

Phonological distinctive features are no less real than the phonetic phenomena that serve as cues to distinctive features.

The recent findings of experimental phonetics throw new light on the nature of speech sounds. If correctly interpreted, these findings lead to fresh insights into the duality of the speech flow. We understand better the relation between the functional and physical levels of the speech flow: what serves as a segmental property of speech sounds at the functional level is their suprasegmental property at the physical level.


## 5. Phonological Antinomies

In section 2.1 it was shown that phoneme and sound are heterogeneous concepts that characterize different levels of the speech flow: functional and physical. There is neither a relation of class membership nor a relation of class inclusion between the sound and the phoneme, because these concepts belong to basically different abstraction levels. The notion of the phoneme characterizes the dual nature of the segments of the speech flow, and therefore the phoneme constitutes a complex notion, the sound/diacritic. This complex notion is reminiscent of such notions as the wave/particle in physics and the use-value/exchange-value in economics. I suggested the metaphorical term *centaur concepts* to denote this type of notion because the structure of these notions is reminiscent of centaurs, the fabulous creatures of Greek mythology, half men and half horses.

In section 2.1, evidence for the dual nature of the segments of the speech flow was based on the discovery of the contradictory consequences from a pair of assumptions that both are taken as a characterization of essential properties of speech sounds. The two assumptions are:

1. Speech sounds are physical elements.

2. Speech sounds are elements whose function is to differentiate between linguistic signs in accordance with the Principle of Semiotic Relevance.

If the two assumptions are considered essential for the characterization of the basic properties of speech sounds, then we have to accept all consequences from these assumptions. Since the consequences are contradictory, we face what in my book on theoretical phonology I called *the antinomies of the paradigmatic and syntagmatic identification of phonemes* (Shaumyan, 1968: 37–44).

From assumption 1 it follows that different sounds cannot be identical, while assumption 2 predicts that different sounds can be identical.

By the same token, it follows from assumption 1 that a sequence of two sounds cannot constitute one segment, while assumption 2 predicts that a sequence of two sounds can constitute one segment.

In order to solve these antinomies, we have to regard speech sounds as complex objects having a dual nature: functional and physical.

In addition to the two antinomies, we discover a third, more general antinomy, which I have called *the antinomy of transposition* (Shaumyan, 1968: 31–37).

The antinomy of transposition is generated by the following two assumptions, which both characterize the essential properties of the phoneme:

Assumption 1: Phonemes are elements whose function is to differentiate between signs.

Assumption 2: Phonemes are acoustic elements.

Let us examine the consequences that can be drawn from these assumptions.

If assumption 1 is valid, then the acoustic substance of phonemes can be transposed into other forms of physical substance—graphic, chromatic, tactile. Any phoneme and any set of distinctive features can be presented not only as acoustic elements but as graphic, chromatic, or tactile symbols, as well. In order to see that, let us perform the following mental experiment. We will transpose phonemes into circles of identical dimension but different color, let us say in English the vowel *æ* into a blue circle, the vowel *e* into a brown circle, the consonant *k* into a green circle, the consonant *n* into a red circle, the consonant *t* into a yellow circle. The words *cat, ten, neck, net, can, tan* can then be represented as chains consisting of combinations of the differently colored circles, as shown in the following table:

(1)  Words  Circles
     *kæt*   green-blue-yellow
     *ten*   yellow-brown-red

| *nek* | red-brown-green |
| *net* | red-brown-yellow |
| *kæn* | green-blue-red |
| *tæn* | yellow-blue-red |

Hence, from assumption 1 it follows that phonemes can be transposed from acoustic substance into other forms of physical substance.

Let us turn now to assumption 2. If it is true that phonemes are acoustic elements, then it follows that they cannot be transposed into other forms of physical substance, since in that case they would cease to be themselves, i.e., acoustic elements.

Here we encounter an evident antinomy: both assumption 1 and assumption 2 are valid in respect to modern phonology; yet assumption 1 implies that phonemes can be transposed into other forms of physical substance, while assumption 2 implies a direct contradiction, i.e., that phonemes cannot be transposed into other forms of physical substance.

This contradiction constitutes an inherent theoretical difficulty, which can be termed the antinomy of transposition.

The antinomy of transposition may evoke the following objection. According to assumptions 1 and 2, a phoneme is, by definition, at the same time an element whose function is to differentiate between signifiants and an acoustic element. And since this definition is adequate for natural languages, the property of the differentiation between signifiants and the property of being an acoustic element are equally essential for the phoneme, and the bond between these two properties must be considered indispensable within the limits of natural languages. Therefore, we are not justified in deducing from assumption 1 that the phoneme can be transposed from acoustic substance into other forms of physical substance.

This objection can be answered as follows. If we regard definitions as convenient compressed descriptions of directly observed data, then, since in natural languages phonemes are always sound elements, we are not justified in separating the functional properties of the phoneme from its acoustic properties. But the subject matter of science comprises not only empirical data, not only what *is* but also what in principle *can be:* hence, if a mental experiment arrives at what can be, we disclose the essence of the studied subject. We regard the definition of the phoneme not as a convenient compressed description of an empirical fact but as a hypothesis about facts that are possible in principle. At the level of abstract possibility, the question arises whether the communicative function of a natural language would be violated if its acoustic substance were transposed into other forms of physical substance. Obviously, no such violation would occur. We are, therefore, justified in transposing phonemes, by means of mental experiment, from acoustic substances into other forms of physical substance. The results of the mental experiment contradict, however, the interpretation of the acoustic properties as the essential properties of the phoneme, since if the acoustic properties are essential properties of the phoneme, the phoneme cannot be transposed from acoustic substance into any other form of physical substance.

In order to resolve the antinomy of transposition, we must posit that although the phoneme and the sound are indissoluble, the phoneme is logically independent of acoustic substance. Saussure aptly compared linguistics with political economy, since both sciences are concerned with the notion of *value*. In his view, language is basically a system of pure values, and the phoneme is a particular instance of linguistic value. Let us continue Saussure's analogy of linguistics with political economy. A phoneme is the distinctive value of some acoustic substance. Speech sounds have distinctive values in the same way as commodities have exchange-values. Both the speech sound and the commodity have a dual character: the speech sound is a unity of the sound proper and the diacritic, while the commodity is a unity of an exchange-value and a use-value. The phoneme is logically independent of acoustic substance in the same way as the exchange-value of the commodity is independent of use-value, that is, of its physical properties. Here is how Marx characterizes the relation between the exchange-value of a commodity and its use-value, that is, its physical properties:

> The objectivity of commodities as values differs from Dame Quickly in a sense that 'a man knows not where to have it.' Not an atom of matter enters into the objectivity of commodities as values; in this it is the direct opposite of the coarsely sensuous objectivity of commodities as physical objects. We may twist and turn a single commodity as we wish; it remains impossible to grasp it as a thing possessing value. (Marx, 1977: 138)

Comparing speech sounds with commodities, we can say that just as not an atom of matter enters into the objectivity of commodities as values, so not an atom of acoustic substance enters into the objectivity of speech sounds as values. (In this quotation Marx uses the term *value* in the sense of 'exchange-value'.)

The key to understanding the dual character of speech sounds is the concept of the unity of opposites. This concept, known essentially since Nicolaus Cusanus as *coincidentia oppositorum*, a way of reasoning that has deeply influenced the musical thinking of Johann Sebastian Bach through his art of counterpoint in the fugue, lies at the very base of Hegel's dialectics. Hegel, in turn, has exerted a major influence on all modern philosophy, including that of Karl Marx. Hegel's notion of *dialectics* can be seen, essentially, as an ongoing conflict between opposites that constitute a unity.

A striking example of "the unity of opposites" in modern physics is the dual nature of light—or more generally of electromagnetic radiation. Radiation produces many paradoxical situations. For instance, when there are two sources of light, the intensity of the light at some place will not be necessarily the sum of the radiation from the two sources; it may be more or less. This situation is explained as the interference of the waves that emanate from the two sources: where two crests of the waves coincide, we have "more light" than the sum of the two; but we have "less light" where there is a coincidence of a crest and a trough. On the other hand, when ultraviolet light is shown on the surface of some metals, it can move the electrons from the surface of the metals. This situation, called the "photoelectric effect," is explained as a collision of light particles with electrons. The inescapable conclusion is that light must, therefore, consist of both particles and waves. Particles and waves constitute the *unity of opposites* in the phenomenon of electromagnetic radiation.

The discovery of the dual nature of electromagnetic radiation—reasonably well understood by the time of the 1927 International Conference on Physics held in Copenhagen, Denmark, and featuring such notable scientists as Niels Bohr, Max Planck, and Albert Einstein—created major conceptual difficulties unknown in classical Newtonian physics. In order to cope with these difficulties, Bohr introduced the famous "Complementarity Principle" into modern physics. The Complementarity Principle treats the particle picture and the wave picture as two complementary descriptions of the same phenomenon; each of them has a limited range of application, and both are needed to provide a complete description of the phenomenon under investigation.

The notion of *complementarity* dominates the thinking of modern physics. Bohr suggested that the Complementarity Principle is a methodological postulate that is valid outside of physics, as well. The notion of complementarity, therefore, is quite similar to the notion of the "unity of opposites" in Hegel's dialectics. It is quite certain that Bohr was well aware of the similarity.

Now, to take this discussion one step further, we must observe that the Complementarity Principle, as a methodological postulate, is very useful indeed, not only in physics, where it was first recognized, but in other sciences, as well. But in applying this postulate, one must beware of applying it trivially. The chief reason why the Complementarity Principle has become so famous is that the essential alternative pictures of reality seem to conflict with one another at first.

Now in my linguistic research I have discovered a nontrivial application of the Complementarity Principle most helpful in the understanding of linguistic phenomena.

In the final section of my book *Problems in Theoretical Phonology* (Shaumyan, 1968) I discuss the concepts of my phonological theory from the point of view of the Complementarity Principle.

Speech sounds have a *dual character*—physical and functional. Functional and physical identity are complementary in the sense of the unity of opposites; that is, they are complementary and at the same time mutually exclusive and contradictory concepts.

Consider, for instance, the Danish consonants *t* and *d* in syllable-initial and syllable-final positions. Physically these consonants are not identical; the *t* is "voiceless" and the *d* is "voiced." But their physical nonidentity "conflicts" with their functional properties: in Danish the syllable-initial *t* is functionally identical with the syllable-final *d* sound.

Consider the physical segmentation of the flow of speech. The sequence *–ts–* consists, both in English and in German, of two physical segments, a *t*-like sound followed by an *s*-like sound, as in the English word *cats* and the German word *zehn*, the number 'ten'. But from a functional point of view, *–ts–* constitutes one segment in German (frequently spelled with the letter *z*) but always two separate ones in English. Thus, just like the physical and functional identity, physical and functional segmentation are complementary and at the same time mutually exclusive and contradictory concepts.

A sound as a member of a class of physically identical objects is a sound proper, but as a member of a class of functionally identical objects, it is a fundamentally new object, a diacritic. A unity of contradictory objects—functional and physical—a "speech sound" is a combined object: the best way to characterize it would be to call it a *sound/diacritic*. A sound/diacritic is thus a unity of opposites similar to such unities of opposites as the wave/particle in physics and the exchange-value/use-value in economics.

In order to denote this type of notion I have introduced a new term. The new term, mentioned above, is *centaur concepts*. I regard the phoneme as a centaur concept, as a sound/diacritic, which constitutes a radical departure from various current concepts of this notion.

### 6. Some Misconceptions about the Phonological Antinomies

The three phonological antinomies were first stated in my book on theoretical phonology (Shaumyan, 1968). These antinomies were criticized by Kortlandt (1972: 29–33) and Fischer-Jørgensen (1975: 343–45). Both linguists advance similar arguments against the phonological antinomies. I will focus on Kortlandt's criticism, because it is more detailed.

Criticizing the antinomy of transposition, Kortlandt writes:

> From the model outlined here two statements evolve (Šaumjan, 1968: 35):
> (1) Phonemes are elements whose function is to differentiate between signifiants.
> (2) Phonemes are acoustic elements.
> The first statement leads Šaumjan to the following conclusion:
> If it is true that the function of phonemes is to differentiate between signifiants then it follows that there exists an inherent possibility of transposing the acoustic substance into other forms of physical substance—graphic, chromatic, tactile. Any system of distinctive features and phonemes can be presented not only as acoustic properties but as graphic, chromatic or tactile symbols as well.
> However, "if it is true that phonemes are acoustic elements it follows that they cannot be transposed into other forms of physical substance since in that case they would cease to be themselves, i.e. acoustic elements" (1968: 36). According

to Šaumjan, the resulting contradiction, which he calls the 'antinomy of trans-position,' constitutes an inherent theoretical difficulty in Trubetzkoy's model of the phoneme.

The reasoning is clearly incorrect. If we substitute 'green table' for 'pho-nemes,' 'thing' for 'elements,' and 'colour' for 'function,' we obtain something like this:

(1) A green table is a thing whose color is green.

(2) A green table is a table.

If it is true that the colour of a green table is green then it follows that there exists an inherent possibility of transposing its table-ness into other forms of thing-ness. However, if it is true that a green table is a table it follows that it cannot be transposed into other things since in that case it would cease to be a table.

Analogy is a bad argument and I am no supporter of the kind of debating ex-hibited in the preceding paragraph, but it certainly shows that a bit of superficial logic does not make up for the lack of explicitness with regard to the underlying assumptions. Šaumjan's reasoning would hold true if the first statement were reversible, but that is clearly not the case if the second statement holds. (Kort-landt, 1972: 29)

As we can see from this quotation, Kortlandt's refutation of the antinomy of transposition is based on his claim that the first statement (about the differ-entiating function of the phoneme) is irreversible (i.e., the reverse statement "Elements whose function is to differentiate between signifiants are phonemes" is not true).

Kortlandt's argument seems irresistible, and yet it is wrong. The point is that, contrary to Kortlandt's claim, the reverse statement is true, because the essence of a phoneme is in its distinctive function. Any phoneme represented by some acoustic element remains the same phoneme no matter into which other physi-cal substance it is transposed. The antinomy of transposition is a conflict be-tween the physical nonidentity of two physical substances and their functional identity. In order to solve the antinomy of transposition, we have to recognize the logical independence of the functional and physical identity of speech sounds and introduce the centaur concept *sound/diacritic*.

I do not mind the use of analogies in reasoning, but Kortlandt's analogy be-tween a phoneme and a green table is pure nonsense. A green table is a thing whose color is green. But from this statement it does not follow that a green table can be transposed into some other green thing, say, into a green apple, because green color is not an essential property either of a table or of an apple. The difference between the green color of a table and the distinctive function of a phoneme is that the distinctive function is an essential property of a pho-neme, and, therefore, a phoneme can be transposed from its acoustic sub-stratum as long as other physical substances have the same distinctive function, while green color is not an essential property of a table, and therefore a green table has nothing in common with a green apple or a green crocodile.

As regards the antinomies of the paradigmatic and syntagmatic identification of phonemes, Kortlandt agrees with them but makes certain reservations. Thus, with respect to the paradigmatic identification of phonemes, he writes:

> There is, however, one possible identification which Šaumjan does not take into consideration, though it violates neither the functional nor the physical properties of the phoneme. He writes:
>
> if, in accordance to statement 1, phonemes possess a function of differentiation between signifiants, then phonemes which occur in different positions can be altered in respect to their phonation is sharply as desired as long as they do not get confused with one another. (1968: 41)
>
> According to this view, one could, strictly speaking, regard any pair of sounds as variants of one and the same phoneme provided only that they are in complementary distribution: thus [q] in position $P_1$ can be identified with [ć] in position $P_2$, and subsequently [k] and [k'] can be identified in accordance with their acoustic properties. It follows that Šaumjan's antinomy cannot be logically derived from his statements 1 and 2 alone, but that it rests upon an additional assumption concerning the mutual relations between phonemes as well. This does not diminish the value of his argument because such an assumption is explicitly present in Trubetzkoy's work. (Kortlandt, 1972: 32)

Kortlandt's claim that the antinomy of the paradigmatic identification of phonemes rests upon an additional assumption concerning mutual relations between phonemes is wrong. That is not an additional assumption but a direct consequence of statement 1 characterizing phonemes as diacritic elements. The alleged additional assumption is not present in Trubetzkoy's work. As a matter of fact, Trubetzkoy was unaware of phonological antinomies, and therefore he failed to see the logical independence of the functional and physical identity of phonemes. Thus, in determining conditions under which two speech sounds can be considered realizations of two different phonemes or variants of a single phoneme, he lumped together functional and physical criteria. One of his basic rules is formulated as follows:

> Rule III. If two sounds of a given language, related acoustically or articulatorily, never occur in the same environment, they are to be considered combinatory variants of the same phoneme.

This rule, as well as some other crucial statements in Trubetzkoy's work, which will be discussed below, clearly show that he failed to discover phonological antinomies and was unaware of the logical independence of functional and physical identity of speech sounds, as well as of the logical independence of functional and physical segmentation of the speech flow.

In discussing the antinomy of the syntagmatic segmentation, Kortlandt claims that this antinomy rests upon an additional assumption that there exists a natural segmentation of the speech flow into sounds that does not coincide with the syntagmatic segmentation. Kortlandt fails to see that that is not an additional assumption but a characterization of the speech flow resulting from the conflict between the consequences that directly follows from the two initial statements defining the essential properties of phonemes.

### 7. Remarks on Bohr's Complementarity Principle and Dialectics

Now that I have set forth the two-level theory of the phoneme, it will be useful to consider it in a broad methodological context of the logic of science. I intend to relate the two-level theory of phonology to the Complementarity Principle, which is of considerable significance in the comprehension of certain fundamental epistemological situations that possess an analogous character although they arise in various and at first glance unconnected areas of knowledge.

The discovery of the Complementarity Principle is the achievement of the outstanding Danish physicist Niels Bohr. First, Bohr formulated the Complementarity Principle as a purely physical principle; later, however, he extended its validity also to other areas of knowledge, above all to biology and psychology. At the present time the Complementarity Principle is interpreted as a general methodological principle that characterizes a definite epistemological situation.

The essence of the Complementarity Principle is described by Bohr as follows:

> In order to characterize the relation between phenomena observed under different experimental conditions, one has introduced the term complementarity to emphasize that such phenomena together exhaust all definable information about the atomic objects. Far from containing any arbitrary renunciation of customary physical explanation, the notion of complementarity refers directly to our position as observers in a domain of experience where unambiguous application of the concept used in the description of phenomena depends essentially on the conditions of observation. (Bohr, 1958: 99)

In illustrating the Complementarity Principle, we can turn to the problem of the nature of light. Contemporary physics teaches that light has a dual nature and, consequently, that diffusion of light cannot be described by a single theory. To describe it, we must resort, writes the Polish physicist L. Infeld, to two theories, the corpuscular theory and the wave theory (Infeld, 1950: 108).

The corpuscular theory and the wave theory cannot be reduced to one another. They are at once mutually exclusive and mutually complementary. This paradoxical epistemological situation where the examined phenomenon can be exhaustively described only by means of mutually exclusive and at the same time mutually complementary theories necessitates the creation of syncretic

dual concepts; in the given case, such a dual concept is the concept of cor-
puscle/wave. Other examples of syncretic dual concepts are time/space and
mass/energy.

If we revert from physics to phonology, a linguist who observes the sounds of
language must inevitably admit that as an observer of the sound properties of
language, he is forced to utilize two kinds of experimental methods: on the one
hand, the sounds of language can be subjected to experimental investigation in
respect to their acoustic nature or to the physiological conditions of their formation, and on the other hand, it is possible to introduce different kinds of experiments with linguistic informants with the view of establishing objective
phonemic contrasts present in a given language.

These two kinds of experimental methods of investigation can be called the
physical and the semiotic experimental methods of investigation in phonology.
The specific epistemological character of these experimental methods consists
in the fact that their results cannot be united into a single picture. Their results
are mutually exclusive and, at the same time, mutually complementary. As
proof we can examine the problem of the identity of the sounds of language.
For instance, investigation of the consonants $t$ and $d$ using the physical experimental methods discloses an essential difference between these consonants: $t$ is
voiceless and tense, and $d$ is voiced and lax. But as was shown above, in Danish
the syllable-initial $t$ is functionally identical to the syllable-final $d$. We see that
the results of physical and semiotic methods of investigation of the Danish consonants $t$ and $d$ cannot be united into a single picture. If we attempted to do
that, we would encounter an irreconcilable contradiction: we would have to admit that the consonants $t$ and $d$ are both identical and nonidentical. In order
to avoid this contradiction, as well as other analogous contradictions present
in the observation of other sounds of natural languages, we have to admit that
the pictures of the identity of the language sounds obtained by semiotic experimental methods of investigation are mutually exclusive and, at the same
time, mutually complementary. Hence, we encounter an epistemological situation that is analogous to epistemological situations encountered in physics and
in other sciences. All such situations are embraced by the Complementarity
Principle.

The sounds of language possess a dual nature, as does light (on another plane,
of course).

As was said above, I suggest the term *centaur concepts* to cover a class of
syncretic concepts in various sciences, such as time/space, mass/energy, use-
value/exchange-value, sound/diacritic, etc.

The Complementarity Principle is generally recognized in contemporary
physics and logic of science. It is an independent discovery of Bohr's, but there
is a striking similarity between this principle and the principle of the unity of
opposites, which constitutes the heart of the dialectical method proposed by
Hegel and widely used by Marx in his works. Bohr was aware of the similarity

of the two principles, and he used the term *dialectics* to characterize the general methodological and epistemological significance of the Complementarity Principle. Thus, he wrote:

> The complementarity mode of description does indeed not involve any arbitrary renunciation on customary demands of explanation but, on the contrary, aims at an appropriate dialectic expression for the actual conditions of analysis and synthesis in atomic physics. . . . The epistemological lesson we have received from the new development in physical science, where the problems enable a comparatively concise formulation of principles, may also suggest lines of approach in other domains of knowledge where the situation is of essentially less accessible character. An example is offered in biology where mechanistic and vitalistic arguments are used in a typically complementary manner. In sociology, too, such dialectics may often be useful, particularly in problems confronting us in the study and comparison of human cultures, where we have to cope with the element of complacency inherent in every national culture and manifesting itself in prejudices which obviously cannot be appreciated from the standpoint of other nations.
>
> Recognition of the complementary relationship is not least required in psychology, where the conditions for analysis and synthesis of experience exhibit a striking analogy with the situation in atomic physics. (Bohr, 1948: 317–18)

## 8. An Illustration: How the Functional View of Speech Sounds Gave Birth to One of the Greatest Discoveries in the History of Linguistics

The functional view of sounds is significant to the extent to which it increases our understanding of natural languages. I will describe the revolutionary break in linguistics brought about by the functional view of sounds. I mean the birth of Saussure's theory of the vowel system in the Indo-European parent language.

Indo-European had a vowel alternation $e:o:\emptyset$, which appeared in diphthongs as $ei:oi:i$, $eu:ou:u$, and $er:or:r$.

Examples from Greek:

| (1) | Present Tense | Perfect | | Aorist (Past tense) |
|---|---|---|---|---|
| | *e* | *o* | | *ø* |
| | *pétomai* | *pepótemai* | | *eptómen* |
| | 'I fly' | 'I have flown' | | 'I flew' |
| | | | | |
| | *ei* | *oi* | | *i* |
| | *peítho* | *pépoitha* | | *épiton* |
| | 'I persuade' | 'I am persuaded' | | 'I persuaded' |
| | | | | |
| | *er* | *or* | | *r* |
| | *dérkomai* | *dédorka* | | *édrakon* |
| | 'I see' | 'I see' (Perf. in the sense of Pres.) | | 'I saw' |

In addition, one finds in Indo-European a different kind of alternation, namely, $\bar{a}:\bar{o}:a$. Examples from Greek (Doric dialect) and Latin:

(2)

| | $\bar{a}$ | $\bar{o}$ | $a$ |
|---|---|---|---|
| Greek | *phāmí* 'I speak' | *phōnā́* 'voice' | *phatós* 'said (past participle)' |
| Latin | | *dōnum* 'gift' | *datus* 'given' |
| | *stāre* 'to stand' | | *status* 'standing' |

Ferdinand de Saussure argued that the alternation $\bar{a}:\bar{o}:\breve{a}$ is not different from the alternation $e:o:\emptyset$, since from a functional point of view the long vowels $\bar{a}$ and $\bar{o}$ must be interpreted as combinations of the short vowels $e$ and $o$ with a hypothetical sound $A$.

Saussure realized that if the long vowels in these alternations were interpreted as a combination of the short vowel with $A$, the two kinds of alternations, which before had looked entirely different, would become quite the same:

(3)  $ei:oi:i$
$eu:ou:u$
$eA:oA:A$

Under this hypothesis, the examples in (2) can be interpreted:

(4)

| | | | |
|---|---|---|---|
| Greek | *phāmí* = *pheAmí* | *phōnā́* = *phoAnā́* | *phatós* = *phAtós* |
| Latin | | *dōnum* = *doAnum* | *datus* = *dAtus* |
| | *stāre* = *steAre* | | *status* = *stAtus* |

Saussure advanced his hypothesis in 1879, which was to mark a turning point in the history of linguistics, although the functional and structural point of view that it represented was too strange to his contemporaries for it to meet with any general understanding. Ferdinand de Saussure was twenty-one when he published his famous *Mémoire sur le système primitif des voyelles dans les langues indo-européennes* (1879). This work was at least fifty years ahead of the linguistics of its time. Only in 1927, after the Hittite language had been deciphered, were the facts predicted by Saussure's theory discovered. The Polish linguist Jerzy Kuryłowicz showed that the Hittite laryngeal $h$ corresponds to the phoneme $A$ hypothesized by Saussure (Kuryłowicz, 1977). Here are some facts that confirm Saussure's theory:

(5)

| | Latin | Tokharian | Hittite | |
|---|---|---|---|---|
| | *pāscunt* | *pāskem* | *pahsanzi* | 'they feed, support' |
| | *novāre* | | *newaḫḫ* | 'innovate' |

## 9. Alternative Theories of the Phoneme and the Distinctive Features

"Often it is only after immense intellectual effort, which may have continued over centuries, that humanity at last succeeds in achieving knowledge of a concept in its pure form, in stripping off the irrelevant accretions which veil it from the eyes of the mind" (Frege, 1884: vii). These words of the great German logician apply to phonology no less than to any other branch of knowledge. More than a half-century has passed since the concept of the phoneme was introduced into the science of language, but even at the present time the problem of the definition of the phoneme cannot be considered to have been fully resolved.

Wherein lies the essence of the problem that concerns the definition of the phoneme?

Every definition of a concept is arbitrary, since every scholar can define any concept in a way that is to his advantage. From this point of view, the definitions of concepts are not concerned with the essence of the matter, and arguments concerning such definitions can hold only terminological interest. Although the definitions of concepts are in themselves arbitrary, we can regard any definition of a concept as a statement that has an explanatory function. In this case the definition of the concept answers the question "What is the nature of $x$?": for example, "What is the nature of light?", "What is the nature of meaning?", "What is the nature of truth?", etc. Since the definitions of concepts that are based on the formula "What is the nature of $x$?" require on the part of the scholar a deep penetration into some sphere of reality, and are at the same time formulated not in the form of single, isolated statements but in the form of an entire system of statements, such definitions can be called theories, as well; for example, the "definition of light" can be called the "theory of light," the "definition of meaning" the "theory of meaning," the "definition of truth" the "theory of truth." The aforementioned words of Frege do not apply to all definitions of concepts; they apply only to definitions of concepts based on the formula "What is the nature of $x$?", because this type of concept definition in particular presents fundamental problems that are rooted in the process of human knowledge. The history of science shows that the struggle for progress in any field of knowledge often takes on a form of a conflict of pro and con definitions of concepts based on the formula "What is the nature of $x$?" Conflicts of this type have existed in connection with the concept of the phoneme over the past fifty years. The question is, then, which definition of the phoneme based on the formula "What is the nature of $x$?", i.e., which phoneme theory, reflects most closely the linguistic reality?

Let us now turn to a comparison of the two-level theory of the phoneme and the distinctive features presented in this book with alternative theories.

The notion of the phoneme as a class of functionally equivalent concrete phonemes is a novel concept that marks a decisive progress in understanding the essence of the phenomenon different phoneme theories have tried to explain.

The notion of the phoneme as a class of sounds is not new. Rather, it is very old; and the notion of the phoneme as a class of sounds is popular in current linguistic literature, too. What is missing is the understanding of the principle on which the classes of sounds are abstracted. As a matter of fact, all existing phonological theories that operate with the notion of the phoneme as a class of sounds have their abstraction on the principle of physical similarity of sounds, which makes these theories worthless.

N. S. Trubetzkoy severely criticized all phonological theories that abstracted classes of sounds on the basis of their physical similarity. His aversion to these theories was so strong that he tried to define the notion of the phoneme without regard to the class concept. He defined the phoneme as follows:

> Phonological units that, from the standpoint of a given language, cannot be analyzed into still smaller successive distinctive units are phonemes. (Trubetzkoy, 1969: 35)

This definition of the phoneme is based on the notion of the phonological unit, which is defined as follows:

> By (directly or indirectly) phonological or distinctive opposition we thus understand any phonic opposition capable of differentiating lexical meaning in a given language. Each member of such an opposition is a *phonological* (or *distinctive*) unit. (Trubetzkoy, 1969: 33–34)

Trubetzkoy's definition of the phoneme is significant in that it is based on the notion of the distinctive opposition. At the same time, this definition disregards the notion of class. The reasons for this disregard are psychologically understandable. Trubetzkoy ignores the class concept for fear that it will open the door to the treatment of the phoneme as a phonetic rather than a phonological concept, that is, for fear that the phoneme will be treated as if it belonged to the same level as the sound. Of course, this fear was justified; that is confirmed by the subsequent development of phonology. Thus, the concept of the phoneme as a class of physically related sounds dominated American descriptive linguistics and was very popular elsewhere, too. The following definition is typical:

> The phoneme is "a class of sounds which: (1) are phonetically similar and (2) show certain characteristic patterns of distribution in the language or dialect under consideration." (Gleason, 1955: 261)

As was shown above, linguists who include physical similarity of sounds in the definition of the phoneme as a class of sounds do not accept the notion of neutralization and consider any sort of restriction on the occurrence of sounds in particular positions to be a case of defective distribution. This view is, of course, consistent with the notion of the phoneme as a class of physically similar sounds, but then one may wonder whether the linguists who accept this notion of the phoneme understand why they need the term *phoneme*. The term *phoneme* makes sense only as a label for a specific functional concept radically different from the ordinary notion of the sound, or else this term is worthless as an aid to understanding linguistic reality: it functions solely as an honorific for what is called the sound in ordinary phonetics.

Trubetzkoy was unaware that the solution to the problem lies in the contrast of two kinds of classes of sounds: 1) physical classes of sounds and 2) functional classes of sounds as members of concrete distinctive oppositions, that is, as concrete phonemes. This contrast, rooted in the dual nature of speech sounds, was to be discovered.

In spite of his insistence on a consistent functional approach, Trubetzkoy was not consistent in many respects himself. Thus, his rules for the determination of phonemes are not free from confusion of the phonological point of view with the phonetic approach. Here are some examples of this confusion.

In defining conditions under which two speech sounds can be considered realizations of two different phonemes, and under what conditions they can be considered phonetic variants of a single phoneme, Trubetzkoy formulated four rules. Rule III reads:

> If two sounds of a given language, related acoustically or articulatorily, never occur in the same environment, they are to be considered combinatory variants of the same phoneme. (Trubetzkoy, 1969: 49)

Clearly, this rule is false: whether two sounds of a given language are related acoustically or articulatorily or not has no bearing on whether they are variants of the same phoneme or not. We know that two identical sounds can belong to different phonemes, and, vice versa, two acoustically unrelated sounds can be variants of the same phoneme.

In formulating rules for distinguishing between a single phoneme and a combination of phonemes, Trubetzkoy proposes the following rule:

> Rule II.—A combination of sounds can be interpreted as the realization of a single phoneme only if it is produced by a homogeneous articulatory movement or by the progressive dissolution of an articulatory complex. (Trubetzkoy, 1969: 56)

Under this rule, such combinations of sounds as *ks* or *st* can never be interpreted as a single phoneme, because these combinations of sounds are not produced by a homogeneous articulatory movement.

Clearly, this rule is false: whether a combination of sounds is produced by a homogeneous movement or not has no bearing on whether this combination must be interpreted as two phonemes or one phoneme. We know that *ks* or *st* can be interpreted as either two phonemes or one phoneme, depending on the system of phonological oppositions in a given language.

Let us now turn to the notion of the distinctive feature. It is generally assumed that there is a one-one correspondence between distinctive features and phonetic features (acoustic or articulatory) that correlate with them. In other words, an isomorphism is assumed between a set of distinctive features and a set of phonetic features that correspond to the distinctive features. In accordance with this assumption, the distinctive features are expressed in the same terms as the phonetic features that are supposed to correspond to the distinctive features.[2]

As was shown above, the view that there is a one-one correspondence between distinctive features and acoustic features conflicts with the semiotic nature of phonological opposition. The distinctive feature does not correspond to elementary units on the phonetic level. As a matter of fact, the distinctive feature is a class of functionally equivalent phonetic features. This insight, which is a logical consequence of a purely theoretical deductive analysis, finds confirmation in experimental phonetics, provided the experimental data are interpreted correctly.

For example, it has been known for decades that in English the vowel preceding a voiceless consonant is shorter than the same vowel preceding a voiced consonant. Perceptual tests with synthetic stimuli have shown that vowel duration is a sufficient one for determining the perception of voicing in a final consonant: if a sequence with a voiceless consonant is synthesized, such as *jus*, and the duration of the vowel is lengthened, listeners will begin to hear *juz*. Thus, the duration of the vowel contributes to the perception of a phonetic feature, namely, voicing in the adjacent consonant. This experiment shows that the distinctive feature 'voicing' may have two phonetic variants—'+voicing' and '−voicing'—depending on the environment. The situation when the phonetic feature '−voicing' is perceived as '−voicing' in one type of environment and as '+voicing' in another type of environment is analogous to the situation when a gray circle is perceived as a white circle inside of a black circle and as a black circle inside of a white circle.

Trubetzkoy also gives an alternative definition of the phoneme as "the sum of the phonologically relevant properties of a sound" (Trubetzkoy, 1969: 36), which is similar to the definition formulated earlier by R. Jakobson. In other words, the phoneme is defined as a bundle of distinctive features (Bloomfield, 1933).

Trubetzkoy's alternative definition of the phoneme is incorrect, because it confounds an analysis of an object into its components with an analysis of a class of objects into its characteristic properties. A phoneme is a minimal component of a sound-form. For example, a sound-form *bed* consists of three minimal components, that is, phonemes *b*, *e*, and *d*. But distinctive features are not components of a phoneme. Rather, they are characteristic properties of a class of functionally equivalent sounds. Thus, such distinctive features as 'labial', 'stop', and 'voiced' are not components of the phoneme *b*; rather, they are characteristic properties of the class of sounds denoted by the symbol *b*.

The identification of phonemes with bundles of distinctive features had unfortunate consequences: it induced some linguists to treat the phoneme as a fictitious entity. The following claim is typical:

It is not the phoneme, but rather the distinctive feature which is the basic unit of phonology: this is the only unit which has a real existence. (Martinet, 1965: 69)

As a matter of fact, the basic unit of phonology is the phoneme. Distinctive features are not units of phonology. They are only functional characteristics of classes of sounds that are phonemes.

## 10. Phonological Syntagmatics

### 10.1 Phonological Units

In the foregoing sections I discussed the notions of the phoneme and the distinctive feature. Every phoneme is characterized by a set of distinctive features. In a phonological system there are as many different sets of distinctive features as there are different phonemes.

I turn now to an examination of sequences of phonemes in a language.

All languages have rigid constraints on sequences of phonemes. Sequences that are admissible in one language may be inadmissible in another language. For instance, the sequences of phonemes *rt* and *nr* occur at the beginning of a word in Russian but do not occur in this position in English. Both English and Russian allow *pr* but not *rp* as initial consonantal clusters. In initial position, the cluster of three consonants *str* is allowed, but all other combinations of these three phonemes are inadmissible: *srt, rst, rts, tsr,* and *trs* are impossible. In every language the occurring sequences of phonemes represent only a very small percentage of the theoretically possible sequences.

Sequential units resulting from the fact that some phonemes contract relations with one another are called *syllables*. The structure of the syllable depends on the relations that can be contracted by the phonemes. These relations are governed by special rules.

The syllable is a minimal sequential phonological unit. There are larger phonological units. Every phonological feature is characterized by what Trubetzkoy called the culminative function. According to Trubetzkoy, the culminative function is represented by accents that signalize how many full words the speech flow is composed of. An accent sets off one and only one syllable of the word at the expense of and in contrast to the other syllables of the same word. Thus, the culminative function makes one syllable the center of the word, and all its other syllables are made the satellites of the central syllable.

Trubetzkoy attributed the culminative function only to word accents. But this function can also be attributed to vowel features as characterizing the segment of the speech flow constituting syllable nuclei. Just as the accents signalize how many full words the speech flow is composed of, the vowel features of the segments of a word signalize how many syllables a word is composed of. The vowel feature sets off one and only one segment of a syllable at the expense of and in contrast to the other segments constituting the syllable. Thus, the vowel feature makes one segment the center of a syllable, and the other segments of the syllable are made satellites of its central segment.

From the point of view of the culminative function, there is a complete analogy between the structure of the syllable and the phonological structure of the word.

The main consequence of the above characteristic of the culminative function is that the central and noncentral phonemes of a phonological unit can be in opposition only to phonemes of the same type; that is, vowels can be in opposition only to vowels, and consonants only to consonants. In other words, vowels and consonants can never occur in the same position. This conclusion is opposed to a fairly widespread view that vowels and consonants can occur in identical phonological positions.

Our theoretical conclusion can be confirmed by an experiment based on the following operational definition of the notion 'phonological opposition':

(1)     OPERATIONAL DEFINITION. A given phonological unit $X$, which is a part of a larger phonological unit $Y$, is in phonological opposition to a phonological unit $Z$ if the substitution of $Z$ for $X$ does not destroy the structure of $Y$.

Our theoretical conclusion can be confirmed by the following experiment. Consider, for example, the words *paw* [pɔ] and *eat* [it]. Let us assume the following opposition:

(2)     | $P_1$ | $P_2$ |
        |-------|-------|
        | $p$   | $ɔ$   |
        | $i$   | $t$   |

On this assumption, we must be able to freely substitute $p$ for $i$ and, vice versa, $i$ for $p$, or $ɔ$ for $t$ and, vice versa, $t$ for $ɔ$, since by definition any phonemes that oppose each other in identical positions can be substituted for each other. As a result of our assumption, we will get impossible syllabic structures: either $iɔ$, which at best can be counted as two syllables, not one syllable, or $pt$, which is no syllable at all. These substitutions violate operational definition (1) because they destroy the structure of the respective syllables.

Since the phonological positions must be defined with respect to the structure of the syllable, the analysis of (2) is clearly incorrect. The correct analysis must be

(3)     | $P_1$ | $P_2$ | $P_3$ |
        |-------|-------|-------|
        | $p$   | $ɔ$   | $\varnothing$ |
        | $\varnothing$ | $i$ | $t$ |

where symbol $\varnothing$ signifies an empty position.

It is clear from the foregoing that vowels and consonants can never occur in identical phonological positions. We should not confound the notion of the phonological position with the place in a phoneme string. For example, pɔ and it are phoneme strings with an underlying syllable structure. If we take these words merely as phoneme strings, then the consonant p in pɔ correlates with the vowel i in it as the phonemes that occupy the first place in both strings. But if we approach both strings from the point of view of their syllable structure, then, as was shown above, the vowels and consonants in these strings do not constitute oppositions, because they occur in different phonological positions.

There is parallelism between the relation of central and noncentral phonemes in a syllable and the relation of central (stressed) and noncentral (unstressed) syllables in a phonological word. The central and noncentral syllables of phonological words can be in opposition to syllables of the same type; that is, central syllables can be in opposition only to central syllables, and noncentral syllables can be in opposition only to noncentral syllables. Consider the word *rampage*, which can be stressed either on the first or on the second syllable: ˈræmpeɪdʒ or ræmˈpeɪdʒ.

The variants of the word *rampage* are opposed as follows:

(4)     zero–ræm–peɪdʒ
        ræm–peɪdʒ–zero

In addition to the culminative function, the stress may have the distinctive function, which must be considered its secondary function. The distinctive function of the stress presupposes the culminative function, but the reverse is not true: the stress may not, and usually does not, have the distinctive function. Here is an example of words that are in opposition with respect to the culminative and the distinctive functions: *tórment* and *tormént*. This opposition can be represented by the following diagram:

(5)     zero–tór–ment
        tor–mént–zero

One might wonder why we could not oppose the first syllable and the second syllable of ˈræmpeɪdʒ to the first and second syllable of ræmˈpeɪdʒ as follows:

(6)     ˈræm–peɪdʒ
        ræm–ˈpeɪdʒ

These substitutions would violate operational definition (1), because they would destroy the normal stress patterns of words. As a result of our substitutions, we would get impossible stress patterns: either ræm–peɪdʒ, a word without a stress at all, or ˈræm–ˈpeɪdʒ, with two equivalent stresses on the first and the second syllables of this word, which amounts to no stress at all—the two substitutions have the same result.

Similar considerations apply to the words *tórment* and *tormént*. The correct opposition of these words is presented in (5). If we assume the opposition

(7)     *tór–ment*
        *tor–mént*

then, by substituting the respective syllables, we will violate the operational definition, because we will obtain an incorrect stress pattern of words: either a word pattern without any stress on its two syllables, or a word pattern with two equivalent stresses on its syllables, which amounts to no stress at all.

The syllable and the phonological word differ in that the phonological word is a sign—that is, it has some meaning—while the syllable is not a sign; it does not have any meaning. Of course, there are languages, such as Vietnamese, that have only monosyllabic words. But also in this case syllables taken by themselves have no meaning: Vietnamese syllables have meaning only insofar as they are used as phonological words.

The syllable is a universal phonological unit: there are no languages lacking syllables. But the phonological word is not a universal phonological unit: there exist languages in which the stress does not fall on separate words.

For instance, French is quite interesting in this respect. L. V. Ščerba compares the function of stress in Russian:

> In Russian the speech flow is separated into words due to the fact that every word possesses verbal stress: *my čitáem knígu naúčnogo soderžánija* 'we are reading a scientific book'; this sentence possesses five stresses and five words. It is, of course, true that in Russian there exist some unstressed words, the so-called enclitics, and especially proclitics; yet this does not change the basic fact, since the number of such unstressed words is small; and since such words possess, as a rule, the character of movable prefixes and suffixes; moreover, the word which is affected by enclitics always preserves stress in its usual place. Therefore we talk in Russian about the 'verbal stress.' No analogy to this exists in French: there stress relates not to individual words but to a group of words, which represent a complete meaningful unit. The stress falls on the last syllable of the final word of the group unless the penult contains the so-called *e muet* (the only apparent exception to this is the pronoun *le* which can stand in the terminal position of such a group but remains under stress: *donne-le!*). The remaining words of the group remain unstressed, as can be seen from these examples: *un grand mouchoir de soie* 'a large silk handkerchief'; *je viendrai vous voir* 'I will come to see you'; *quelques minutes après* 'a few minutes later'; *en lisant le journal* 'while reading the newspaper'; *aussi vite qu'il pouvait* 'as fast as he could.' (Ščerba, 1948: 82)

These examples show that a number of stresses does not necessarily signalize the number of independent words in a given speech flow; in languages such as French, stresses signalize only the number of separate word groups in a given speech flow.

While in some languages stresses can correspond to units larger than separate words, namely, to word groups, in other languages they correspond to units that are smaller than words, as well. Let us take, for instance, the German word *Wachsfigurenkabinett* 'cabinet for wax figures'. In this word there occur three stresses: a primary one on the first syllable, and two secondary ones on the syllables *-nett* and *-gur-*. This example shows that in German, stress signalizes not only the number of separate words in a given speech flow but also the number of parts in a composite word. Comparing the function of stress in German with the function of stress in Russian, A. Martinet writes:

> In languages such as German the situation is clear: every element of the composite word preserves the stress which characterizes it as an individual word; the second syllable of the word *Figur* 'figure' always preserves its stress, independently of whether the word *Figur* constitutes an autonomous member of a sentence or a component of a composite word. Quite different is the situation in such languages as Russian where all components of the composite word, with the exception of one, lose their proper stress: the word *nos* 'nose' loses its stress and the timbre of its vowel when it becomes a component of the composite word *nosorog* 'rhinoceros'; in the German equivalent of this word, *Nashorn*, on the contrary, every one of the components preserves its proper stress; there occurs only the subordination of the stress of the component *-horn* to the stress of the component *Nas-*. Thus the *accentual unit* in Russian is the word, and in German the lexeme. (Martinet, 1949: 89)[3]

The largest phonological unit is the phonological sentence characterized by intonation. Intonation also characterizes word groups as parts of a sentence. The sentence and its parts characterized by intonation can be called intonational units. It should be noted that intonation has not only the culminative function, signaling how many sentences the speech flow consists of, but also the distinctive function. For example, the opposition between rising and falling intonation is used to differentiate between subordinate and main classes.[4]

### 10.2  Are Monovocalic Phonological Systems Possible?

The analysis of phonological units in 2.10.1 allows us to posit the following four universals:

(8)     LAW OF PHONOLOGICAL OPPOSITION:
          No language can have the opposition of vowels and consonants: vowels can be
          in opposition only to vowels, and consonants can be in opposition only to
          consonants.

(9)     LAW OF PHONOLOGICAL CONTRAST:
          Every language has the contrast of vowels and consonants.

(10)   LAW OF PHONOLOGICAL FUNCTIONS:
      In every language the distinctive function is obligatory for consonants and op-
      tional for vowels, since the culminative function is the only essential pho-
      nological function of vowels.

(11)   LAW OF MINIMAL VOCALISM:
      For every language, a possible minimal vocalism consists either of two vowels
      having the distinctive function or of one vowel having no distinctive function.

Recall that, by the definition in 1.1, the term *opposition* designates the paradigmatic relation, and the term *contrast* designates the syntagmatic relation.
   The above phonological laws are not inductive laws. Rather, they are consequences of the analysis of the semiotic properties of phonological systems. It
follows from the Law of Minimal Vocalism that there can be languages having a
monovocalic phonological system.
   The Law of Minimal Vocalism is based on the following assumptions. Since,
under the Law of Phonological Opposition, vowels can be in opposition only to
vowels, never to consonants, and any opposition presupposes at least two phonemes, then any vocalism having the distinctive function must consist of at least
two vowels. As to the culminative function, it is based on contrast, and since,
under the Law of Phonological Contrast, every language has the contrast of
vowels and consonants, the minimal vocalism, restricted only to the culminative
function, must be confined to a single vowel.
   Minimal phonological vocalism confined to a single vowel is a theoretical possibility supported by an analysis of the semiotic properties of the phonological
system. But it is an empirical question whether at present there exist languages
having a vocalism confined to a single vowel. Some linguists have claimed that
Kabardian and Abaza, North Caucasian languages, are phonologically unique
in that they have no vocalic opposition and are confined to a single vocalic
phoneme. This claim has been the subject of controversy (see Genko, 1955;
Kuipers, 1960; Allen, 1965; Szemerényi, 1964 and 1977; Lomtatidze, 1967;
Halle, 1970; Kumaxov, 1973; Colarusso, 1975).
   By the same token, Gamkrelidze and Mačavariani have considered the Proto-
Kartvelian phonological system to be monovocalic. Thus, Gamkrelidze, in an
article that summarizes the results of the massive phonological research on the
vocalism in Kartvelian languages, done by him and Mačavariani (1965), writes
as follows:

> We may envision an earlier stage of Common Kartvelian with no phonemic con-
> trasts between vowels, assigning the two vowels *e and *a as allophones to one
> original vowel, which later split into different phonemic units according to the
> character of its allophones. (Gamkrelidze, 1966: 80)

I intend to examine closely the hypotheses of monovocalism in Kartvelian
and North Caucasian languages in a separate work.

## 10.3 Phonological Structure of the Syllable

There are already a great number of publications on the phonological structure of the syllable. Among the earlier studies, the most important is the work
of Kuryłowicz (1948). Important recent contributions include the works of
Kahn (1976), Vennemann (1978), Halle and Vergnaud (1979), and Clements and
Keyser (1983), among others. A critical survey of these works is, however, outside the scope of this investigation. I shall examine the phonological structure
of the syllable only from the standpoint of the semiotic approach. As a point of
departure, I will take some notions about the syllable on which there has been
a convergence of opinion in the more recent literature. Then I will apply a semiotic analysis to these notions and will trace out its important consequences,
which throw new light on the phonological nature of vowels.

The syllable consists of three parts: 1) the *onset*, 2) the *nucleus*, and 3) the
*coda*. For example, in a syllable *bed*, *b* is the onset, *e* is the nucleus, and *d* is
the coda. The nucleus and coda combined are called the *core*. This analysis of
the syllable can be represented by the following constituency tree:

(12)

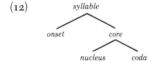

The phonemes that function as nuclei are called *vowels*. The phonemes that
do not function as nuclei are called *consonants*. A syllable can be reduced to its
nucleus, but never to its onset or coda. In other words, a syllable may consist
solely of a vowel but never solely of a consonant or a consonant cluster.

A syllable without a coda is called an *open* syllable, and a syllable with a coda
is called a *closed* syllable.

The above constituency tree specifies a hierarchy of the components of the
syllable. The onset and the core belong to the first level of the hierarchy, and
the nucleus and the coda to the second level.

In positing this hierarchy, we are able to explain some important properties
of the syllable.

In many languages the closed syllables either do not occur at all (as in Old
Russian) or occur very rarely (as in Georgian or Italian), while there are no languages in which all syllables begin only with vowels, that is, do not have onsets.
In languages where closed syllables occur, the occurrence of closed syllables
presupposes the occurrence of open syllables. That can be explained by the fact
that the opposition of the components *onset:core* is basic, because these components belong to the first level of the above hierarchy. This basic opposition
must occur in every language. On the other hand, the opposition of the components *nucleus:coda* is not basic, because these components belong to the second level of the hierarchy. Therefore, in some languages this opposition can be
reduced to the nucleus.

Other important phenomena explained by the above hierarchy are the *quantity* and the *intonation* of the syllable. There is an intimate relationship between the quantity or the intonation of the syllable and its core to the exclusion of its onset. The quantity of a syllable is determined by the core, that is, by the nucleus plus the coda, so that the equivalence holds:

(13)    *long nucleus = short nucleus + coda*

In many languages that have syllables whose core consists only of a short vowel, this vowel cannot be stressed: stress must pass onto a neighboring vowel. Such syllables are called *light*. A syllable whose core consists of a long vowel, two short vowels, a short vowel plus a consonant, or combinations of these is called *heavy*. The stress placement may depend on the distinction of light and heavy syllables. For instance, in Latin, stress is placed on the penultimate syllable of a word if it is heavy, and on the antepenultimate syllable if the penultimate syllable is light. Compare: 1) *rédigo* 'I drive back', 2) *redégi* 'I have driven back', and 3) *redáctum* 'driven back'. Stress is placed on the penultimate syllables in 2) and 3) and on the antepenultimate syllable in 1) in accordance with the rule of stress placement.

The intonation of a syllable extends onto the nucleus and a certain part of the coda. For example, in Lithuanian *ver̃kti* 'to cry', consisting of two syllables *ver̃k-ti*, the rising intonation extends onto the *e+r̃* of the syllable *ver̃k*.

The basic problem in defining the syllable is the definition of the syllable boundary. The definition of the syllable must be based on the syllable boundary as a primitive notion. Taking the notion of the syllable boundary as primitive, we can define the syllable as follows:

(14)    The *syllable* is a maximal string of phonemes between two syllable boundaries.

If we accept this definition of the syllable, we have to turn to the definition of the syllable boundary. To define the syllable boundary, I will introduce the notion of the *interlude*. I use the term *interlude* to denote a string of one or more consonants between two vowels—an intervocalic string of consonants.

An interlude may have either a binary or a unary structure. A binary interlude has two components: the left part, which constitutes the coda of the preceding syllable, and the right component, which constitutes the onset of the succeeding syllable. A unary interlude must be conceived of as a binary interlude reduced to its right component, which constitutes the onset of the succeeding syllable. It follows that the onset component is the constitutive component of the interlude: the coda component of the interlude presupposes the onset component, but the onset component does not presuppose the coda component.

The basic assumption in defining the syllable boundary is that there is an intimate relationship between word structure and syllable structure. Ideally, the same sequential constraints that operate at the beginning of a word should be operative at the beginning of a syllable; and the same sequential constraints that operate at the end of a word should be operative at the end of a syllable.

The syllable boundary is defined by the following principles:

1) The interlude constitutes the onset of the next syllable, unless the preceding syllable cannot be kept open because its vowel does not occur in word-final position. If that is the case, then as many consonants as necessary to provide the syllable with an admissible coda must be detached from the onset of the next syllable and transferred to the preceding syllable.

To illustrate the first principle, let us take words such as *eastern* and *tester*. The word *eastern* can be syllabified as *i$stərn*, where $ denotes the syllable boundary. But the word *tester* cannot be syllabified as *te$stər*, because this syllabification violates a sequential constraint in English by which the short vowels *e, u ,o,æ* are disallowed in word-final position. Since *te$ster* contains the vowel *e*, which does not occur word-finally, it must be resyllabified to yield *tes$tər*.

2) If the interlude does not occur in word-initial position, then as many consonants as necessary to reduce it to the admissible word-initial shape must be detached from it and transferred to the preceding syllable as coda.

These are the two main principles that define the syllable boundary. In addition, there are a few special principles of the syllable boundary which there is no need to discuss in this very general outline of phonology.

## 10.4 The Primary and Secondary Functions of
### Vowels and Consonants in the Syllable

In 10.1 it was shown that vowels differ from consonants in that vowels have the culminative function and consonants do not. A vowel constitutes the center, the nucleus, of a syllable, while consonants are in marginal positions; consonants are satellites of vowels. This phonological definition of vowels and consonants contrasts with the phonetic definition of vowels as sounds characterized by voice modified by various shapes of the oral cavity, and of consonants as sounds produced by the closure of air passages.

The proposed phonological definition of vowels and consonants is not generally accepted in the current phonological literature. While some linguists recognize that in many cases the roles played by phonemes in the syllable may be a useful basis for a functional distinction between vowels and consonants, they deny that this approach can be used for a universal phonological definition of vowels and consonants. For example, Martinet admits that it is mostly expedient to distinguish between phonological systems of vowels and consonants. He writes:

> What is expected of consonants and vowels is not that they should appear in the
> same contexts, that is they should be in opposition, but that they should follow

one another in the chain of speech; in other words, we expect them to be in contrast. (Martinet, 1960: 72)

But at the same time he makes the following reservation:

> This does not mean that certain sounds cannot, according to this context, function as the syllabic peak, which is normal for a vowel, or as the flanking unit of this peak, which is normal for a consonant. [i] in many languages is a syllabic peak before a consonant and the adjunct of such a peak before a vowel: e.g. French *vite* and *viens*. [1] is a syllabic peak, i.e. a vowel, in the English *battle* or Czech *vlk* 'wolf,' but a consonant in English *lake* or Czech *léto* 'year.' *In these circumstances there is no point in distinguishing two phonemes, one vocalic and the other consonantal.* (Martinet, 1960: 72–73; emphasis added)

The fact that sometimes consonants can be used as syllabic nuclei and vowels as satellites of the syllabic nuclei seems to be the evidence that a phonological definition of vowels and consonants based upon their function in the syllable cannot be universally valid. And yet, if correctly interpreted and understood, it does not undermine the universal validity of this definition. It is true that one and the same phoneme may function sometimes as a syllable nucleus and sometimes as a nonsyllabic phoneme in the same language. But we must distinguish between the primary and secondary functions of a phoneme. Thus, the primary function of vowels is to serve as syllable nuclei, while their secondary function is to serve as consonants. Conversely, the primary function of consonants is to serve as satellites of syllable nuclei, while their secondary function is to serve as syllable nuclei.

The distinction between the primary and secondary functions of vowels and consonants is based on their range. By the range of vowels and consonants I mean their distribution within a syllable. If the range of a phoneme is greater when it serves as a syllable nucleus than when it serves as a satellite, then the primary function of the phoneme is to be a syllable nucleus, and its secondary function is to be a satellite. Conversely, if the range of a phoneme is greater when it serves as a satellite than when it serves as a syllable nucleus, then the primary function of the phoneme is to be a satellite, and its secondary function is to be a syllable nucleus.

It is to be noted that the notion of the range of the phoneme has nothing in common with the statistical notion of frequency. The range of a phoneme is defined solely by its distributional possibilities. For example, Czech *r* and *l* as satellites occur in syllable-initial and syllable-final positions, while as syllable nuclei they occur only between consonants. Therefore, their primary function is to be satellites, while their secondary function is to be syllable nuclei. The French *i* as a syllable nucleus occurs between syllable-initial and syllable-final consonants, between zero onset and syllable-final consonants, between syllable-initial consonants and zero coda, while as a satellite it occurs only before vowels. Therefore, the primary function of the French *i* is to be a syllable nucleus, and its secondary function is to be a satellite.

### 10.5 Comments on the Notion 'Extrasyllabic Consonant'

The distinction between the primary and secondary functions of vowels and consonants in the syllable throws new light on the problem recently raised by Clements and Keyser (1983). They claim that in some cases long clusters of consonants may contain consonants that are not members of any syllable. Such consonants they call *extrasyllabic*. They characterize extrasyllabic consonants as follows:

> An extrasyllabic consonant is one which is not a member of any syllable. Typically, such consonants are separated from neighboring consonants by short neutral or voiceless vowels and are historically susceptible to processes which either eliminate them or incorporate them into well-formed syllables by means of processes such as vowel epenthesis, sonorant vocalization and metathesis. English has several such examples. The usual pronunciation of *knish* in Cambridge, Massachusetts, for example, inserts a short, voiceless schwa after the *k*. However, this is not a full schwa as is evidenced by its near minimal contrast with the word *canoe*. Other examples of extrasyllabic consonants in English include the initial consonants of the names *Pnin, Knievel, Zbiegniew, Khmer Rouge, Dvořák, Phnom Penh, Dmitri* and *Gdansk*, in usual pronunciations, not to speak of the *b* in common renderings of the name of the former Iranian minister *Ghotbzadeh*. (Clements and Keyser, 1983: 39–40)

Here is an example of extrasyllabic sonorants from Klamath (an American Indian language of Oregon), which Clements and Keyser represent in the following diagrams (Clements and Keyser, 1983: 121):

(15)

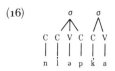

'lies down on the stomach'

(16)

σ        σ

C  C  V  C  C  V
|  |  |  |  |  |
n  l  ə  p  k̓  a

'mashes up with a round object'

Clements and Keyser have introduced the notion 'extrasyllabic consonant' in order to handle complex consonant clusters that are not parsable by the rules of their theory of the syllable. The difficulty lies not in the complexity as such but in that such consonant clusters are irregular in a given language and can be parsed as a part of a syllable neither by the rules of the theory of Clements and Keyser nor by the rules of any other viable theory of the syllable.

We can understand the motivation for the notion 'extrasyllabic consonant', but this notion does not seem to resolve the difficulty. Although this solution does away with irregular consonant clusters, a new difficulty arises: extrasyllabic consonants as such are heterogeneous elements, and by being heterogeneous elements they interfere with the sequential structure of the phonological word and make it irregular. This irregularity seems to be as odd as the irregularity of consonant clusters.

The answer to our problem is in the distinction between the primary and secondary functions of phonemes. Relying on this distinction, we can treat what Clements and Keyser call extrasyllabic consonants as syllable nuclei with or without satellites, depending on their number. Thus, the function of the second sonorant *l* in the Klamath word *willGa* and the sonorant *n* in the Klamath word *nlᵊpka* are counterparts of the function of the Czech sonorant *l* in the Czech word *vlk* 'wolf'. In this case, consonants have taken on the function of vowels, that is, the function of the syllable nucleus, as their secondary function. Similarly, in the above examples from English, such as *Gdansk* or *Zbigniew*, the consonants *g* and *z* have taken on the function of the syllable nucleus. Since this function is more unusual for *g* and *z* than for the sonorants *r*, *l*, *m*, and *n*, an ultra-short schwa is inserted to support the pronunciation of *g* and *z* in the usual position.

If we compare the solution to the problem of irregular consonant clusters using the notion 'extrasyllabic consonant' and using the distinction between the primary and secondary functions of the phoneme, we can see that the odds are in favor of the latter solution. The extrasyllabic consonant is an ad hoc notion introduced especially to solve the problem of irregular consonant clusters, while the primary and secondary functions of the phonemes are notions introduced on independent grounds to explain the structure of the syllable. The latter notions are an instance of even broader notions of primary and secondary functions of semiotic units, which are a cornerstone of semiotics and must be a cornerstone of any adequate linguistic theory. In addition, while the introduction of the notion 'extrasyllabic consonant' pretends to solve the problem of irregular consonant clusters, it generates a new difficulty, since, as was pointed out above, extrasyllabic elements are heterogeneous elements that make the structure of a phonological word seem irregular. Relying on the distinction between the primary and secondary functions of phonemes, we solve the problem of irregular consonant clusters not by introducing new notions but by treating some consonants as syllables with consonantic, rather than vocalic, syllable nuclei.

## 10.6 Prosodic Features

We are now ready to consider the notion 'prosodic feature'. Prosodic features can be defined as elements that characterize units of speech flow whose duration differs from the duration of phonemes. These units usually are larger than phonemes: a syllable or a phonological word, which consists of one or more syllables; they can, however, be smaller than the phoneme, as, for example, in the case when the syllabic nucleus splits into two consecutive units called *morae*.

In essence, prosodic features are subdivided into two groups: *accentual* and *nonaccentual*.

*Accent*, or *stress*, should be defined as the setting off of one syllable within a bisyllabic or a polysyllabic word. The basic function of stress is the so-called *culminative* (crest-forming) function, which consists in the fact that the accents signalize the number of independent words within the given speech flow. Since every self-contained word usually possesses only one stress, it follows that the number of stresses in any given speech flow determines the number of self-contained words, as well.

With respect to the place it occupies in the word, stress can be either *bound* or *free*. A stress is called a bound stress if in the given language it always falls in one and the same place (in Czech, for instance, the stress falls always on the first syllable, in Turkish always on the last syllable), or if its place is determined strictly by the phonemic structure of the word (in Latin, for instance, where the stress can fall on either the penult or the antepenult, its place is determined by the phonemic structure of the penult). A stress is called a free stress if it can occupy various places independently of the phonemic structure of the word; consequently, it possesses, aside from the culminative function, also the function of word differentiation (for instance, in Russian, where the stress is free, the words *píli* 'they drank' and *pilí* 'saw (imperative)' differ phonologically only with respect to their place of stress).

According to the manner of the setting off of the stressed syllable, we differentiate the following types of stress:

(a) *strong*, or *dynamic*, stress (the stressed syllable is set off by greater tenseness of its articulation);

(b) *quantitative* stress (the stressed syllable is set off by increased lengthening of the articulation of the vowel); and

(c) *tonal*, or *musical*, stress (the stressed syllable is set off by a change in the tone pitch).

Dynamic stress, which is innate in Russian, is rather widespread among the various languages of the world.

Quantitative stress is seldom encountered; it is found, for instance, in modern Greek.

Tonal stress, which is used by various languages of the world, can have several variations. In Lithuanian there exists an opposition of a rising and a falling intonation. In Swedish and Norwegian there exists an opposition of a simple and a complex stress; a simple stress consists of a falling and rising pitch (the direction of the tone movement is immaterial, since it changes with respect to dialect changes), while a complex stress consists of a falling-rising pitch.

Prosodic features that in one and the same word are relevant to more than one syllable are called *nonaccentual*. For example, in the African language Lonkundo there exists a contrast between the words *lòcòlò* 'palm fruit' and *lò-cóló* 'invocation' (the symbol ` represents a low-register tone, the symbol ´ a high-register tone). Nonaccentual prosodic features do not have the culminative function; their only purpose is word differentiation.

In order to simplify the description of prosodic features, it is useful to introduce the concept of the *mora*. The mora is the minimal segment of the speech flow that can be a carrier of a prosodic feature. In respect to the concept of the mora, a long vowel phoneme that, let us say, has a rising pitch can be regarded as a succession of two morae, the first of which is a carrier of a sharp tone of low register and the second, a carrier of a sharp tone of high register. On the other hand, if the long vowel has a falling pitch, it can be regarded as a succession of two morae, the first of which is a carrier of a sharp tone of high register and the second, a carrier of a sharp tone of low register. For instance, if we take the Lithuanian word *nósis* 'noise' (with a falling intonation) and the word *tākas* 'footprint, track' (with a rising intonation), we can regard each of these words as possessing three morae. In the word *nósis* the first mora is set off; in the word *tākas*, the second. A simplification of the description can be attained by reducing the twofold characteristic of intonation (quality of intonation and place of intonation) to a single characteristic (place of intonation), because the application of the concept of the mora makes the quality of intonation phonologically redundant.

The above discussion presents, in short, the classification of prosodic elements in modern phonology. It is unnecessary to go into further detail here.

Prosodic features have a purely relational nature; they are independent of definite phonic substance. The essential thing is that we distinguish between prosodic and nonprosodic elements, not because the substance of prosodic and nonprosodic elements is objectively different but because we get to them through two different analyses of the speech flow. Imagine a language that would allow only syllables of the type *mā* or *ba*, that is, fully nasalized or fully nonnasalized syllables. If we assume at the same time that in this language every word could have only one nasalized syllable, it becomes apparent that the function of nasality would be basically identical to the function of stress in such languages as, let us say, Russian, English, or German. This mental experiment is a logical consequence of the following statement, which I formulate as the *Principle of the Transposition of Phonological Structure:*

> Any phonological structure can be transposed from one phonic substance into another as long as the phonological relations characterizing this structure remain intact.

The Principle of the Transposition of Phonological Structure predicts that one and the same phonic substance can be used in one language as a prosodic feature and in another language as a nonprosodic feature. Consider the glottal stop. In Arabic the glottal stop is a phoneme of this language; in a few American Indian languages it is a distinctive feature characterizing glottalized phonemes. But in Lettish or Danish it is no longer a phoneme or a distinctive feature but, as it were, a kind of accent, that is, a prosodic feature.

In conclusion, a few words about nonaccentual prosodic features. One may wonder whether nonaccentual prosodic features could be treated simply as distinctive features. Thus, if we treated low-register and high-register tones as distinctive features, then we could treat *ò* and *ó* as two different phonemes, like *i* and *u* or *k* and *g*. This approach is certainly possible. However, it is consistent to regard different tones as prosodic features, because tones affect segments of the speech flow that do not necessarily coincide with phonemes: a given vowel phoneme may be pronounced with a sequence of tones, and a given tone may affect a number of vowels or fractions of vowels.

## 11. On Generative Phonology

Let us turn to the phonological theory called *generative phonology*. The bases of generative phonology were elaborated by Morris Halle and Noam Chomsky between 1955 and 1968, when their book *The Sound Pattern of English* was published.

Generative phonology constitutes the phonological component of generative-transformational grammar. The phonological component consists of two levels: the level of systematic phonemics and the level of phonetics. The level of systematic phonemics roughly corresponds to the morphophonemic level of non-transformational grammar, and the level of systematic phonetics roughly corresponds to the level of phonetics. The level of systematic phonemics consists of systematic phonemic representations of underlying forms, which are converted by phonological rules into systematic phonetic representations, which constitute the level of systematic phonetics.

The basic claim of generative-transformational grammar is that the phonemic level does not exist, and therefore—and this is a revolution—the old phonology must be rejected and replaced by a radically new discipline: generative phonology. Let us see whether this revolution is justified. In order to do so, we have to examine the arguments against the existence of the phonemic level.

In his book on Russian phonology, Morris Halle advanced an argument disposing of the phonemic level. He writes:

> In the Russian example discussed the morphophonemic representation and the rule concerning the distribution of voicing suffice to account for all observed facts. Phonemic representation, therefore, constitutes an additional level of rep-

resentation made necessary only by the attempt to satisfy Condition (3a). If Condition (3a) can be dispensed with, then there is also no need for the 'phonemic' representation. (Halle, 1959: 21)

Here is how Halle presents Condition (3a):

> A phonological description must include instructions for inferring (deriving) the proper phonological representation of any speech event, without recourse to information not contained in the physical signal.

He adds in a footnote:

> This requirement has played a particularly important role in the development of American linguistics. 'For a notation to be phonemic we require a bi-unique, one-one relation rather than a many-one relation (between representation and utterance—M.H.).' C. F. Hockett, Review of A. Martinet's Phonology as Functional Phonetics, *Language*, 27, 340 (1951).

Halle makes the following comments about Condition (3a):

> Condition (3a) is concerned with procedures that are essentially analytical. Analytical procedures of this kind are well known in all sciences. Qualitative and quantitative chemistry, electrical circuit analysis, botanical and zoological taxonomy, medical diagnosis are examples of disciplines concerned with discovering the appropriate theoretical representations (i.e., chemical formula, configuration of circuit elements, classification within the taxonomical framework, names of disease, respectively) of different complexes of observable data. Theoretical constructs are never introduced because of considerations that have to do with analytic procedures. Thus, for instance, it is inconceivable that chemistry would establish substances that can be identified by visual inspection as a category distinct from substances that require more elaborate techniques for their identification. Yet this is precisely the import of Condition (3a), for it sets up a distinction between phonemes and morphophonemes for the sole reason that the former can be identified on the basis of acoustic information alone, whereas the latter require other information as well.

> So important a deviation from a standard scientific practice can only be justified if it were shown that phonology differs from other sciences in such a way as to warrant the departure. This, however, has never been demonstrated. Quite to the contrary, it has been common to stress the essential similarity between the problems of phonology and those of other sciences. The conclusion, therefore, imposes itself that Condition (3a) is an unwarranted complication which has no place in a scientific description of language.

I agree with Halle's criticism of Condition (3a). One may, however, wonder whether the phonemic representation would satisfy Condition (3a). As a matter of fact, the phonemic representation, if it is to be linguistically significant,

should run counter to Condition (3a) rather than satisfy it. The two-level theory
of phonology is not based on analytical procedures. It is based on the Principle
of Semiotic Relevance.

An important consequence of the Principle of Semiotic Relevance is that
phonological representation should stand in a many-many relation to phonetic
representation; that is, one phonemic symbol might correspond to several phonetic symbols. Another important consequence of the Principle of Semiotic
Relevance is the necessity to strictly distinguish between distinctive and acoustic features: the former belong in phonemic representation, the latter in phonetic representation. Just as phonemes and sounds should be in many-many
relations, so distinctive features and acoustic features should be in many-many
relations, as well.

Let us now turn to the Russian example considered by Halle. He presents
the Russian words *mok li* 'was (he) getting wet?' and *mok by* 'were (he) getting
wet?', *žeč li* 'should one burn' and *žeč by* 'were one to burn' in three types of
transcription, as shown below:

(1)          *I*              *II*             *III*
        *mok l'i*       *mok l'i*       *mok l'i*
        *mok bi*        *mog bi*        *mog bi*
        *žeč l'i*       *žeč l'i*       *žeč l'i*
        *žeč bi*        *žeč bi*        *žeǯ bi*

Column I represents a morphophonemic representation, column II a phonemic representation, and column III a phonetic representation.

In Russian, voicing is distinctive for all obstruents except *c*, *č*, and *x*, which
do not possess distinctive voiced counterparts. These three obstruents are
voiceless unless followed by a voiced obstruent, in which case they are voiced.
At the end of the word, however, that is true of all Russian obstruents: they are
voiceless, unless the following word begins with a voiced obstruent, in which
case they are voiced.

The forms in column III can be deduced from the forms in column I by
the rule

(2)       *obstruent* → *voiced* in the context: _____*voiced obstruent.*

But if grammar is to generate the forms in column II, it cannot have one general rule (2), but instead of this rule it will have two rules, (3a) and (3b), the first
one linking the morphophonemic representation with the phonemic representation and the second one linking the phonemic representation with the phonetic representation:

(3)       a. *obstruent* → *voiced* in the context: _____*voiced obstruent*,
                                  except *c*, *č*, *x*;
          (b) *c*, *č*, *x* → *voiced* in the context: _____*voiced obstruent.*

Thus, assuming that there is a phonemic level, we cannot state the significant generalization that voicing assimilation applies uniformly to all obstruents. It is for difficulties of this type that Halle rejects a phonemic level.

What should we think about this example? To evaluate it properly, we have to make necessary corrections in the phonemic representation of the words. If we acknowledge the distinctive property of phonemes, we can see that the phonemic transcriptions *mok l'i* and *mok bi* are incorrect, since they do not take into account that at the end of the word all Russian obstruents can be only voiceless unless followed by a voiced obstruent, in which case they can be only voiced. The correct transcriptions are *moK l'i* and *moK bi*, because in these words the voicelessness of *k* is redundant and the voicing of *g* is redundant (symbol *K* denotes an archiphoneme restricted with respect to *voicelessness: voicing*, whose instances are sounds *k* and *g*).

Let us now compare the distinctive and redundant features of the phonemes presented in columns I and II.

1) In column I voicelessness is a distinctive feature of *k*, since *k* contrasts with *g*, and a redundant feature of *č*, since *č* has no voiced counterpart.

2) In column II voicelessness is redundant in *K* and *č*, and voicing is redundant in *g*. Therefore, they belong in the same class of obstruents with respect to the redundant features *voiceless: voiced*.

Accordingly, the correct phonological representation must be

(4)    *moK l'i*    *moK bi*    *žeč l'i*    *žeč bi*

Rule (2) applied to the correct phonological representation will give the output in column III. In this view rule (2) is phonemic rather than morphophonemic.

We conclude that rule (2) can be considered morphophonemic or phonemic, depending on whether the morphophonemic or the phonemic level is chosen as the starting point of phonological theory.

The question arises, Which level must we choose as the starting point of phonological theory?

The goal of phonology is the study of the system of distinctive oppositions. Therefore, the starting point of this theory is the phonemic level as an ideal system of distinctive oppositions whose properties are determined by the Principle of Semiotic Relevance. The ideal system of distinctive oppositions is not based on analytic procedures but is postulated as a theoretical construct from which possible systems of distinctive oppositions are deduced.

The goal of generative phonology is the study of the system of alternations. Therefore, the starting point of this theory is the morphophonemic level postulated as a theoretical construct.

A system of distinctive oppositions is an essential part of any human language. A system of alternations is a significant but not essential part of a human language. We cannot imagine a human language without a system of distinctive oppositions, but we can imagine one without a system of alternations.

Since both a system of distinctive oppositions and a system of alternations constitute the expression plane of a language, we must seek to integrate studies of these systems into a single phonological theory.

Is it possible to realize this integration in the framework of generative phonology?

Generative phonology deals with processes of mapping the morphophonemic level onto the phonetic level. To describe these processes, we do not need an intermediary level; the phonemic level is redundant with generative phonology. In view of that, it is difficult to see how the study of alternations can be integrated on the basis of generative phonology.

It is not clear how distinctive oppositions can be defined on the basis of alternations, but it is natural to define alternations on the basis of distinctive oppositions. Alternations are nothing other than a subset of distinctive oppositions that hold between allomorphs of morphemes.

In this view, the morphophonemic level, that is, the level of alternations, is a sublevel of the phonemic level, which is the level of distinctive oppositions. Hence, it is indicated to solve our problem within a phonological theory whose starting point is the phonemic level.

Since the morphophonemic level is a sublevel of the phonemic level, it is partially subordinated to the phonemic level. Therefore, the essential step towards the creation of an integrated phonological theory is to determine the nature of this subordination.

Our first observation is that we must distinguish phonetically conditioned and nonphonetically conditioned alternations. Nonphonetically conditioned alternations are a projection of diachronic processes onto the synchronic structure of a language. Consider the alternations *wiodę: wiedziesz* 'I lead: you lead', *biorę: bierzesz* 'I take: you take', *niosę: niesiesz* 'I carry: you carry' in Polish. The vocalic alternation *o: e* in these words is not phonetically conditioned as it was in Old Polish. In Old Polish this alternation was conditioned by nonpalatalized anterior lingual consonants. But in Modern Polish this conditioning has been lost, because in a later stage of development of Polish a new *e* appeared before nonpalatalized anterior lingual consonants as a result of the change of the reduced vowel ь into *e*. Thus, the phonetically conditioned alternation *o: e* of Old Polish has been projected into Modern Polish as a morphologically conditioned alternation *e: o*. In Modern Polish the change of *e* into *o* is not conditioned by nonpalatalized anterior lingual consonants, since *e* occurs before these consonants (for instance, in *sen* 'sleep'); it is conditioned by the verbal suffixes *−e* (first person singular present) and *−ą* (third person plural present). Here the suffixes *−e* and *−ą* can be viewed as operators that, when applied to stems ending in nonpalatalized anterior lingual consonants, imply the change of *e* into *o*.

We can posit the relation of implication between phonemic alternations and morphemes that condition phonemic alternations.

Abstracting from morphologically conditioned phonemic changes, we can posit ideal forms of morphemes underlying allomorphs. In our case the ideal forms of morphemes will be: *wied–*, *bier–*, *nies–*. They are ideal because they do not coincide with any of their allomorphs.

Besides morphologically conditioned alternations, there are phonetically conditioned alternations. For instance, we have the alternation d : T in the Russian words *sadu : saT* 'to the garden : garden'. This alternation is phonetically conditioned, since voiced obstruents automatically lose their voicing at the absolute end of words.

It should be noted that whereas morphologically conditioned alternations hold between the allomorphs of a morpheme, phonetically conditioned alternations hold between variants of the same allomorph. Thus, in our example the alternating parts of the Russian words, that is, *sad–* and *saT–*, should be considered variants of the same allomorph *sad–* rather than two different allomorphs.

We conclude that alternations are grounded in the synchronic structure of the phonemic level. Therefore, we must posit the following constraint on possible rules in the integrated phonological theory:

> No rules should be formulated in phonetic terms if they do not correspond to synchronic processes in the structure of the phonemic level.

I call this constraint the *Condition of Synchronic Motivation*. In accordance with this condition, we cannot formulate the alternation *e : o* in the above Polish example as a phonetic rule of the change of *e* into *o* before anterior lingual nonpalatalized consonants, since in Modern Polish vowel *e* occurs in this position.

The Condition of Synchronic Motivation is an effective bar to substituting diachrony for synchrony in phonological studies.

In constructing a phonological theory, we can choose between two approaches: either the morphophonemic level or the phonemic level hypothesized as theoretical constructs can be taken as a starting point of the theory. The morphophonemic level is the starting point of generative phonology; the phonemic level is the starting point of the two-level theory of phonology.

Since the morphophonemic level and the phonemic level are interrelated, we must seek to integrate the study of the two levels in a single phonological theory.

Since the phonemic level is redundant with generative phonology, it would be difficult to realize this integration on the basis of generative phonology.

The study of the phonemic and the morphophonemic levels can be naturally integrated within a theory that takes the phonemic level as its starting point.

Integrated phonological theory must have two basic goals: 1) the exploration of systems of distinctive oppositions as autonomous objects; and 2) the exploration of systems of alternations as objects partially subordinated to systems of distinctive oppositions.

Why should systems of distinctive oppositions be considered autonomous objects? Because they are completely independent of systems of alternations. Although systems of alternations play an important part in natural languages, they are not absolutely essential: we can imagine a language without a system of alternations, but no natural language can exist without a system of distinctive oppositions.

The basic methodological constraint on possible rules in integrated phonological theory is the Condition of Synchronic Motivation. This condition involves a consistent differentiation between phonetically conditioned and nonphonetically conditioned rules. Phonetically conditioned rules cover variations of sounds occurring in the speech flow as instances of phonemes and phonetically conditioned alternations of nonrestricted (or free) and restricted phonemes. Nonphonetically conditioned rules cover nonphonetically conditioned alternations (morphophonemic rules) and syllable structure (syllable structure rules).

The strict separation of functional and physical equivalence of sounds and acoustic features, functional and physical segmentation of the speech flow, and phonetically and nonphonetically conditioned alternations should be considered several of the universal constraints on the construction of phonological models. The study of universal constraints on the construction of phonological models is a basic methodological goal of an integrated theory of phonology.

In constructing phonological models, we may face the possibility of alternative choices; for instance, we may have to make a choice between a binary feature system (Jakobson, 1968; Chomsky and Halle, 1968) and a multivalued feature system (Ladefoged, 1971). The evaluation of different possibilities in constructing phonological models should be based partly on the abstract study of the properties of semiotic systems and partly on empirical evidence from linguistic typology, linguistic change, and comparative language acquisition studies by psycholinguists.

I have examined Halle's arguments against the existence of the phonemic level and have demonstrated that they are false. I have shown that the system of phonemic oppositions is an essential aspect of any phonological system, while morphophonological alternations are optional, in principle. Therefore, the phonemic level is a basic and autonomous level of any phonological system, while the morphophonemic level, which is dispensable in principle, is subordinated to the phonemic level.

Phonology is an indispensable part of linguistics as a discipline that studies the phonemic level of language.

Granted that the claim about the nonexistence of the phonemic level is false, and granted that phonology is an indispensable part of linguistics, one may wonder, however, whether generative phonology could be considered valuable not as a replacement for phonology but as a modern version of morphophonology. Let us now consider whether this more modest claim of generative phonology might be acceptable.

The fundamental error of generative phonology is disregard of the properties of language as a sign system that, as was shown above, are characterized by the

Principle of Semiotic Relevance and the Principle of Synchronic Stratification. The complete lack of understanding of the sign nature of language has led to disastrous consequences—to a confusion of synchrony and diachrony and a confusion of the phonemic level with the morphophonemic and phonetic levels.

Every state of a given language contains a series of layers that reflect different stages of its history. With respect to these layers, we can speak about the diachronic stratification of the state of a language. In the same way, the geological layers of the surface of the Earth reflect different stages of its history. But from a functional viewpoint, any language is synchronically stratified, and the synchronic stratification of a language sharply differs from its diachronic stratification. Moreover, these two stratifications, as is well known, conflict with each other. The diachronic stratification of a language is the object of internal reconstruction, which is part of the history of language. But it is one thing to study the diachronic stratification of a language as part of its history, and it is another thing to confound the diachronic stratification of a language with its synchronic stratification. And that is what generative phonology does.

In order to justify a confusion of synchrony with diachrony, Chomsky and Halle advanced a proposition that phonological rules are extrinsically ordered. This proposition is known as the *Ordering Hypothesis*. Chomsky and Halle say:

> The Hypothesis that rules are ordered . . . seems to us to be one of the best-supported assumptions of linguistic theory. (Chomsky and Halle, 1968: 342)

Chomsky and Halle's claim that the Ordering Hypothesis is one of the best-supported assumptions of linguistic theory is false. Any extrinsic ordering of rules is arbitrary and therefore unacceptable. True, language is a hierarchical system, but there must be an inner dependence between the rules of any natural hierarchy, rather than an extrinsic ordering. The order of rules may reflect the order of phenomena in time, but time order belongs to diachrony rather than synchrony.

Rule ordering is a formal device that creates a vicious circle in synchrony: the generation of phonological objects is justified by the Ordering Hypothesis, which in its turn is justified by the fact that ordered rules may generate phonological objects. That is a case of an arbitrary application of formal machinery to empirical facts, as discussed above in the section on the generativist notion of language (chap. 1, sec. 7). True, the generative model can generate phonological objects; but, as was shown above, from the fact that a mathematical design works, one cannot conclude that language works in the same way. The generative model is based on logical necessity, but logical necessity does not necessarily conform to empirical necessity. It may be in conflict with empirical necessity. And such is the case with respect to the formal machinery of generative phonology based on arbitrary rule ordering.

Generative phonology confounds functional description with internal reconstruction. Functional description belongs to synchrony, and internal reconstruction belongs to diachrony, but generative phonology lumps these two things together under the heading 'linguistic competence'. The rules of generative phonology pretend to characterize the linguistic competence of the speaker-hearer. It is clear, however, that the abstract underlying structures that are proposed as an input of these rules cannot characterize a language either as a tool of communication or as a tool of cognition. The rules of generative phonology have nothing to do with the competence of the speaker-hearer, for whom the only thing that matters is functional rather than genetic dependencies between the elements of his language.

The confusion of synchrony and diachrony involves other grave conceptual difficulties, of which I will speak later. Let me first discuss some examples of the confusion of synchrony and diachrony in generative phonology:

Consider the following alternations of the front vowels in English:

(5)  *iy:*   serene      *e:*   serenity
            obscene             obscenity

     *ey:*   profane     *æ:*   profanity
            inane               inanity

     *ay:*   divine      *ɪ:*   divinity
            sublime             sublimity

Chomsky and Halle propose the following underlying phonemic representations of morphemes:

(6)  *serēn*    *profǣn*    *divīn*
     *obsēn*    *inǣn*      *sublīm*

These abstract forms coincide with historical reconstructions that are retained by the orthography.

Chomsky and Halle propose three rules to produce the current phonetic forms: 1) a laxing rule, which applies before the *-ity* suffix; 2) a vowel shift rule, which changes *ɪ* to *ǣ*, *ē* to *ī*, and *ǣ* to *ē*; and 3) a diphthongization rule, by which *ǣ* becomes *æy*, *ī* becomes *iy*, and *ē* becomes *ey*. The derivations for *səriyn* and *sərɛnɪtɪ* are given below:

(7)  *serēn*    *serēn+iti*
                *seren+iti*    Laxing before *-ity*
     *serīn*                   Vowel shift
     *seriyn*                  Diphthongization

It is clear that Chomsky and Halle are doing an internal reconstruction, but they present it as if it were a synchronic phenomenon. The above three rules describe diachronic phonetic changes but are presented as if they describe synchronic processes characterizing the speaker-hearer's competence.

Chomsky and Halle confound synchrony with diachrony. This confusion is possible because the rules are ordered. But ordering the rules makes sense if it corresponds to a succession of changes in time; otherwise it is arbitrary. In our case, the ordered rules can be reasonably interpreted as describing a succession of phonetic changes in time; from a synchronic point of view, however, this ordering is arbitrary.

Two different notions are confused here: a diachronic notion of the phonetic change and a synchronic notion of the phonemic alternation. Phonemic alternations, rather than phonetic changes, belong to synchrony.

From a synchronic point of view, only one rule can be proposed here—a rule of phonemic alternations of *iy* with *e*, *ey* with *æ*, *ay* with *i* before the -*ity* suffix.

The confusion of phonetic changes with phonemic alternations is a consequence of the Ordering Hypothesis. Eliminate the rule ordering, and this confusion will be impossible.

Let us now turn to another example. According to Chomsky (1964:88–90), the following phonological rules are valid in English:

(8) $\begin{Bmatrix} k \\ t \end{Bmatrix} \to s$ in the context: _____ $+ [i,y]$      Rule (1)

(9) $[s,z] + [i,y] \to [š,ž]$ in the context: _____*Vowel*      Rule (2)

Thus, according to rule (1) we have

(10)    *opaque* → *opacity*
       *logic* → *logicism*
       *democrat* → *democracy*
       *pirate* → *piracy*

According to rule (2) we have

(11)    *race* → *racial*
       *express* → *expression*

(12)    *erase* → *erasure*
       *enclose* → *enclosure*
       *revise* → *revision*

If those phonological rules are regarded as unordered rules, having the form 'morpheme *X* realizes phoneme *Y* in the context of *Z*_____*W*', then they should be supplemented by the rule

(13) $\begin{Bmatrix} k \\ t \end{Bmatrix} + [i,y] \to š$ in the context: _____*Vowel*      *Rule* (3)

to explain such facts as *logician*, *delicious* (cf. *delicacy*), *relate* → *relation*, *ignite* → *ignition*, etc. However, rule (3) can be dispensed with if the first two rules are ordered in such a way that rule (2) is applied to the result of the application of rule (1).

A grammar containing rules (1) and (2), applied in the order named, will give the following derivations:

(14)    *lajik+yɨn*        *prezident+i*        *prezident+i+æl*
        *lajis+yɨn*        *prezidens+i*        *prezidens+i+æl*        (according to (1))
        *lajišɨn*                               *prezidenš+æl*         (according to (2))

A grammar containing rule (2) obviously lacks the generalization found in a grammar containing only rules (1) and (2) with ordered application. Moreover, it can be proved that a grammar containing rule (3) lacks other generalizations, as well. Thus, alongside rules (1) and (2) there is also the following rule:

(15)    $z \rightarrow s$ in the context: _____ $+iv$                              Rule (4)

e.g., *abuse* → *abusive*.

Now consider such forms as *persuade* → *persuasive* → *persuasion, corrode* → *corrosive* → *corrosion*, etc.

In a grammar that does not envisage ordered application of rules, these correspondences must be accounted for by means of the following two new rules, independent of rules (1), (2), (3), and (4):

(16)    $d \rightarrow s$ in the context: _____ $+iv$                              Rule (5)

(17)    $d + [i,y] \rightarrow \check{z}$ in the context: _____ *Vowel*                Rule (6)

However, if the rules are applied in a definite order, then rules (5) and (6) are superfluous. Generalizing rule (1) to apply to $d,t$ instead of $t$, we get the following derivation for *persuasive:*

(18)    *perswēd+iv*
        *perswēz+iv*        (according to (1))
        *perswēsiv*         (according to (4))

and for *persuasion:*

(19)    *perswēd+yin*
        *perswēz+yin*        (according to (1))
        *perswēžin*         (according to (4))

Such is the reasoning of Chomsky. This example is a vivid illustration of the importance of ordering phonological rules. However, in considering the above example, we come across the following difficulty.

In formulating rule (1), Chomsky obviously simplified it, because it is easy to find exceptions, such as *shake* → *shaky, might* → *mighty.* If it were only a matter of didactic exposition, these exceptions might be disregarded, because, even though rule (1) is simplified, the example given is very illustrative. However, careful consideration of the ordered rules used by Chomsky suggests that there must be a cardinal difference between them, which is not given in generative phonology.

Comparing rules (1) and (2), we find that they refer to cardinally different processes. Such cases as *shake* → *shaky, might* → *mighty* do not come under rule (1), because it is formulated as if it had to do with the phonological conditions of the transition:

(20) $\begin{Bmatrix} k \\ t \end{Bmatrix} \rightarrow s$ in the context: _____$[i,y]$

Actually, this transition occurs under morphophonological rather than phonological conditions. It does not occur in the context of definite phonemes; it occurs in the context of definite suffixes—suffixes of abstract nouns in this case: *-ity/-y, -ism.*

(21) $\begin{Bmatrix} k \\ t \end{Bmatrix} \rightarrow s$ in the context: _____$+ \begin{Bmatrix} \text{-ity/-y} \\ \text{-ism} \end{Bmatrix}$

This formulation is also a simplification, because to formulate rule (1) exactly, it would be necessary to consider the entire class of affixes, in the context of which the above phonological process takes place. However, the fundamental issue of the matter is as follows. Chomsky formulates this rule as if the phonological process occurred under definite phonological conditions, whereas we maintain that it occurs not under phonological but under definite morphological conditions, i.e., in the context of a definite class of affixes.

It is different with rule (2). The transition

(22) $[s,z] + [i,y] \rightarrow [š,ž]$ in the context: _____Vowel

takes place not under morphological but under phonological conditions, i.e., in the context of the adjacent vowel.

Thus, when formulating phonological rules in generative phonology, two kinds of phonological processes should be distinguished: 1) phonological processes occurring under definite morphological conditions, i.e., in the context of a definite class of affixes; and 2) phonological processes occurring under definite phonological conditions, i.e., in the context of definite distinctive features or phonemes.

Generative phonology does not differentiate between these two kinds of phonological processes. However, such differentiation is of fundamental importance.

Rules pertaining to the first kind of phonological processes will be called *morphophonological rules* (*M-rules*), and those pertaining to the second kind of processes will be called *phonological rules* (*P-rules*).

Let us now consider how to reformulate the above rules in the light of differentiating between the morphophonological and phonological levels of phonological processes.

To account for the facts given by Chomsky, it is sufficient to have two morphophonological rules and one phonological rule.

The morphophonological rules are

(23) $\left\{\begin{array}{c} k \\ t \end{array}\right\} \rightarrow s$ in the context: _____ $+ \left\{\begin{array}{c} \text{-ity/-y} \\ \text{-ism} \end{array}\right\}$        M-rule (1)

(24) $[z,d] \rightarrow s$ in the context: _____ $+iv$        M-rule (2)

The phonological rule is

(25) $[s,z] + [i,y] \rightarrow [š,ž]$ in the context: _____*Vowel*        P-rule (3)

Consistent differentiation between morphophonological and phonological rules is one of the essential aspects of treating phonological processes in synchronic linguistics.[5]

The above example illustrates a confusion of phonemic and morphophonemic levels in generative phonology, which is a second consequence of the Ordering Hypothesis. Eliminate rule ordering, and this confusion is impossible.

Finally, as a result of the confusion of synchrony and diachrony, generative phonology does not distinguish between distinctive functions of sounds and their physical properties. In other words, generative phonology confounds not only the phonemic level with the morphophonemic level, but also the phonemic level with the phonetic level.

From a formal point of view, the rules of generative phonology are of an algorithmic type; that is, these rules are instructions for converting a set of initial sequences of symbols into new sequences of symbols in a finite number of steps. These rules Chomsky calls *rewriting rules*. Rewriting rules, like any other mathematical formalism, can have cognitive value if they are combined with correct empirical hypotheses about the nature of reality. Otherwise, they are no more than a game with symbols.

Generative phonology seriously distorts linguistic reality. What is the cause of the errors and fallacies of generative phonology? The cause is the fetishistic approach to the notion of the formal rule. Generative phonology aims at constructing a mathematically consistent system of formal rules. But mathematical consistency does not guarantee a correct description of reality. A consistent system of formal rules must be combined with a correct hypothesis about reality. Otherwise, this system may be inappropriate. Generative phonology presents a good example of the tragic consequences of mathematical fetishism.

A question arises: Why did generative phonology have success in some quarters?

The answer is this: Generative phonology started with a severe critique of phonology, and this critique was justified in many respects. At the same time, a novel approach was emphasized which required a construction of formal systems analogous to formal systems in other sciences. Chomsky is a master of polemic, and his successful polemic against an inferior type of phonology accompanied with a promise of new linguistic vistas played a decisive role in the promotion of generative phonology.

There is also another side of the story.

Generative phonology is a theory that is dressed in mathematical garb. For a certain sort of mind, the glamour of mathematical garb has a powerful appeal regardless of the ideas underneath it. But not every mathematical formalism is easy to master. The formalism of generative phonology has the advantage of simplicity. Rewriting rules is a type of formalism that does not presuppose any knowledge of mathematics and can be readily mastered by anybody who is able to enjoy manipulating symbols.

The price of this simplicity is high: strip the mathematical dress off the body of ideas, and you will see that the naked body lacks substance. Nevertheless, generative phonology is a seductive game with symbols. This game with symbols, like any other game, is an exciting pastime. It can be emotionally very satisfying.

A question arises: Can generative phonology turn from a game with symbols into an activity having significant cognitive value?

Yes, it can if it gives up the Ordering Hypothesis, if it does not confound synchrony with diachrony and the phonemic level with the morphophonemic level and the phonetic levels. But then it will lose all of its attractions and will become ordinary phonology.

# III.

# *Genotype Grammar*

### 1. Two Levels of Grammar: Genotype Grammar and Phenotype Grammar

In accordance with the distinction of two semiotic strata in a natural language—the system of signs and the system of diacritic elements—linguistics consists of two parts: *phonology* and *grammar*. Phonology is the study of the system of diacritic elements, and grammar is the study of the system of signs.

A minimal sign is called a *morpheme*. For example, the word *speaker* consists of two morphemes: *speak-er, speak-* and *-er*. The word *above* consists of one morpheme.

Every combination of morphemes is called a *syntagm*. It follows from this definition that a word consisting of two or more morphemes is a syntagm; a combination of words is also a syntagm.

Morphemes, words, and groups of words can be called *syntagmatic units*. Besides syntagmatic units, a language has units of a different kind. If we approach language as an instrument of communication, we discover a new type of units, which can be called *functional units*.

The basic functional unit is the *sentence*. The communicative function of language is to transmit messages from the speaker to the hearer—in more general terms, from the sender to the receiver—and messages are transmitted by means of sentences. A word or a group of words does not transmit a message unless it functions as a unit of communication—a sentence.

The next basic functional unit is the *predicate*.

In terms of the notions *sentence* and *representation*, the predicate can be defined as the functional unit that represents a sentence. Here are some examples illustrating this definition. Consider the Russian sentence

(1)    *Ivan kupil knigu.*
       'John bought the book'.

We can delete the noun *knigu* 'the book' and get the correct sentence

(2)    *Ivan kupil.*
       'John bought'.

Or we can delete the noun *Ivan* 'John' and get the correct sentence

(3)      *Kupil knigu.*
         'Bought the book'.

Finally, we can delete both nouns, and again we will get a correct sentence:

(4)      *Kupil.*
         'Bought'.

In all these sentences, the constant element is the verb *kupil*, and this element is what is left after all the deletions because it represents the complete sentence; the verb *kupil* is the predicate of these sentences. True, if we take the English equivalent of the Russian sentence—*John bought the book*—we can delete only *the book*, but we cannot delete *John*; neither *bought the book* nor *bought* is a sentence in English. But that is because the rules of English grammar restrict the deletions of subjects. Still, in those cases when the deletion of the subject is possible, it is the verb that serves to represent the whole sentence. Compare the imperative sentences

(5)      *You come here, Jack, and you go over there, Mary.*

and its equivalent with the deleted subjects

(6)      *Come here, Jack, and go over there, Mary!*

We can delete all the other words and get finally

(7)      *Come and go!*

which syntactically represents the whole sentence. Since the predicate represents the sentence, it can be identical with the sentence in those cases when the sentence is complete without any other functional units. For instance, the Russian sentence

(8)      *Teplo.*
         'It is warm'.

has only a predicate *teplo*, which is identical with the whole sentence. Similarly, the English sentence

(9)      *Fire!*

has only a predicate *fire*, which is identical with the whole sentence.
    The next functional units are *terms*. The terms are the complements of the

predicate: they denote the participants of a situation denoted by the predicate. For example, in the sentence

(10)    *John slept.*

the predicate *slept* denotes the situation of sleeping, and the term *John* denotes a participant of this situation—the subject of the sentence. In

(11)    *John gave money to Bill.*

the predicate *gave* denotes the situation of giving, and the terms *John, money,* and *Bill* denote the participants of the situation—the subject *John,* the direct object *money,* and the indirect object *Bill.* As sentence (8) shows, a sentence can have no terms. But although a sentence can be without terms, every sentence must have a predicate.

Besides predicates and terms, a sentence may contain *predicate modifiers* and *term modifiers.* In languages that have adjectives and adverbs, adjectives serve as modifiers of terms, and adverbs usually serve as modifiers of predicates. For example, in the English sentence

(12)    *The red car was moving slowly.*

the adjective *red* is the modifier of the term *car,* and the adverb *slowly* is the modifier of the predicate *was moving.*

There are other functional units, but I will not discuss them here.

Functional units and syntagmatic units clearly belong to different levels of language. There is no one-one correspondence between them. Functional units can be realized not only by single words but by other syntagmatic units, as well:

1) A functional unit can be realized by a group of words:

(13)    *The weight of the snow on the roof caused the shed to collapse.*

In this sentence the first term is realized by the group *the weight of the snow on the roof,* and the predicate by the group *caused to collapse.*

2) A functional unit can be realized by a morpheme that constitutes a component of an incorporating complex. So, in Chukchee a lexical morpheme may be incorporated into a verb stem. This morpheme must be viewed as an optional affix that has a function of a term denoting an object. For example, such is the Chukchee lexical morpheme *kora* 'deer', incorporated in the verb *kora-janratgat* 'separated deer' in the sentence

(14)    *Jetynvyt korajanratgat.*
        'The hosts separated the deer'.

3) A functional unit is realized by a morpheme that is a component of a verbal form. There is no incorporation here, because morphemes of this type are

mandatory components of verbal forms. For example, in Georgian the conjugation of transitive verbs involves the realization of a term denoting a subject and a term denoting an object:

(15)    *mo-kl-a* 'he killed him'
        *mo-kal-i* 'you killed him'
        *mo-v-kal-i* 'I killed him'

The realization of functional units by morphemes of incorporating complexes and morphemes constituting mandatory components of verbal forms is common in Paleoasiatic, Caucasian, Semitic, and Bantu languages.

Functional units and the morphological units that realize them constitute different levels of linguistic structure, which should strictly be distinguished from each other. In accordance with this distinction, we must distinguish two types of syntactic connections: 1) syntactic connections between functional units and 2) syntactic connections between units that realize functional units, that is, syntactic connections between syntagmatic units. In current linguistic literature, these two different types of connections are very often confounded with each other. Consider, for instance, such very common statements as: 1) the predicate agrees with the subject; 2) the predicate governs the object. In the light of the foregoing, these statements are clearly incorrect. Predicate, subject, and object are functional units, while agreement and government are formal connections between syntagmatic units. Therefore, the correct statements will be, on the one hand: 1) the predicate has a subject relation with the term, 2) the predicate has an object relation with the term; and, on the other hand: 1) the verb agrees with the noun, 2) the verb governs the noun.[1]

We can think of the syntactic structure of a sentence as something independent of the way it is represented in terms of syntagmatic units. In this way we come up with two levels of grammar, which I call *genotype grammar* and *phenotype grammar*. Genotype grammar comprises functional units—predicates, terms, modifiers—and abstract operator-operand relations between these units. Phenotype grammar comprises syntagmatic units—morphemes and words—and connections between them in terms of linear order and their morphological properties. Such notions as agreement and government clearly belong in phenotype grammar.

The rules of genotype grammar are invariant with respect to various possibilities of their realization by phenotype grammar. The terms *genotype* and *phenotype* arc borrowed from biology, where genotype means a definite set of genes that is invariant with respect to its different manifestations called phenotype.

The distinction between the genotype and phenotype levels is of paramount importance for linguistic theory, because this distinction puts us on the road to the solution of the basic question of linguistic theory formulated above: What factors contribute to the similarities and differences between natural languages?

In order to see the significance of genotype grammar for formulating univer-

sal rules that are invariant with respect to their different manifestations, consider passivization rules.

Take an active-passive pair in English:

(16)    a. *Columbus discovered America.*
        b. *America was discovered by Columbus.*

In generative-transformational grammar, the relation between active sentences and passive sentences is treated by means of passive transformations.
There are quite a few proposals as to how passive transformations should be
stated. These proposals differ greatly in detail. But despite great differences in
detail, advocates of generative-transformational grammar agree that: 1) passive
in English applies to strings in which a noun phrase, a verb, and a noun phrase
occur in this order:

(17)        1                        2

        *Noun Phrase — Verb — Noun Phrase*

and 2) passivization involves postposing of the preverbal noun phrase and pre-
posing of the postverbal noun phrase:

(18)        2                        1

        *Noun Phrase — Verb $_{pass}$ — Noun Phrase*

Passive transformations clearly are rules stated in terms of linear order of
words. One may wonder whether universal rules of passivization can be stated
in terms of passive transformations. As a matter of fact, that cannot be done, for
the following reasons.

For one thing, since different languages have different word order, a statement of passivization in terms of the transformational approach will require a
distinct rule for each language where the order of the relevant words is different. Take, for example, the following active-passive pairs in Malagasy:

(19)    a. *Nahita ny  vehivavy ny  mpianatra.*
           saw     the woman    the student
           'The student saw the woman'.
        b. *Nohitan'ny        mpianatra ny  vehivavy.*
           seen (passive) the student    the woman
           'The woman was seen by the student'.

In Malagasy the verb is in the initial position, and the subject is normally in
the final position:

(20)

$$\overset{2}{\overparen{\qquad}}\qquad\overset{1}{\overparen{\qquad}}$$

*Verb — Noun Phrase — Noun Phrase*

In this formula of the active sentence, the noun phrase *1* is the subject and the noun phrase *2* is the object. Passivization involves the reversal of the order of the noun phrases:

(21)

$$\overset{1}{\overparen{\qquad}}\qquad\overset{2}{\overparen{\qquad}}$$

*Verb*$_{pass}$ *— Noun Phrase — Noun Phrase*

In terms of linear order of words, the rule of passivization in Malagasy is quite distinct from the rule of passivization in English.

There are languages where word order is irrelevant for the statement of the rule of passivization. Consider the following active-passive pair in Russian:

(22)    *a. Kolumb         otkryl     Ameriku.*
        Columbus (subject) discovered America (object)
        'Columbus discovered America'.
  *b. Kolumb-om      byla otkryta   Amerika.*
        Columbus-by (instr.) was  discovered America (subject)
        'America was discovered by Columbus'.

In Russian, active and passive sentences can have the same word order, because word order is irrelevant for passivization. Here passivization involves, besides passive marks on the verb, the change of case markings: the noun that is in the accusative case in the active sentence is in the nominative case in the passive sentence; the noun that is in the nominative case in the active sentence is in the instrumental case in the passive sentence.

It is clear that the universal rules cannot be stated in terms of operations on strings of words, that is, in terms of syntagmatic units. Word order, case markings, and verbal morphology are language-specific, and therefore they are irrelevant for the characterization of a language-independent universal rule of passivization.

In order to state a universal rule of passivization, we have to use the notions of the genotype level. On this level we face functional units rather than words and combinations of words. For our immediate purpose, we must treat the basic functional unit—the predicate—as a binary relation whose terms denote an agent and a patient. The rule of passivization must be stated as the operation of *conversion* on the binary relation. Conversion is an operation with the help of which, from a relation $R$, we form a new relation called the *converse* of $R$ and denoted by $\breve{R}$. The relation $\breve{R}$ holds between $X$ and $Y$ if, and only if, $R$ holds between $Y$ and $X$. The converse of the relation $>$, for example, is the relation $<$, since for any $X$ and $Y$ the formulae

(23)    $X < Y$    and    $Y > X$

are equivalent.

Passive predicate is the converse of active predicate. The conversion involves the exchange of positions between the term denoting an agent and the term denoting a patient. In the active construction, the primary term denotes an agent, and the secondary term denotes a patient. In the passive construction, the secondary term becomes the primary term, and the primary term becomes the secondary term. It should be noted that position, as a relational notion, is independent of the linear order of words. So, in the above example from Russian (22), although the primary term and the secondary term have exchanged their positions in the passive construction, their linear order has remained intact.

The statement of the rule of passivization as the conversion of active predicates is language-independent and therefore is universal. This rule of genotype grammar predicts the phenomena on the phenotype level of different languages. If the secondary term of an active sentence is the primary term of the corresponding passive, then it should stand in the same position in the passive sentence as do the primary terms of active sentences in languages where word order is not free. And if the primary term of an active sentence is the secondary term of the corresponding passive, then it should stand in the same position in the passive sentence as do the secondary terms of active sentences in languages where word order is not free. This prediction is confirmed by the facts of various languages of the world where word order is not free. In the above examples from English and Malagasy (16, 19), the secondary terms of the active sentences stand in the same positions in the passive sentences as do the primary terms of the active sentences, and the primary terms of the active sentences stand in the same positions in the passive sentences as do the secondary terms of the active sentences.

Another prediction concerns the morphological marker of the converse relation. Since conversion is an operation on the predicate, the passive predicate must be characterized by some morphological marker, while the morphological markers on the terms of the predicate are optional. This prediction is confirmed by the languages of the world. No matter how different are the morphological markers of the verbs that serve as manifestations of passive predicates, one thing remains constant: the mandatory use of some morphological marker of the passive predicate.

The foregoing shows the crucial significance of the distinction between the genotype and phenotype levels. Generative-transformational grammar ignores the genotype level and states the rules of grammar in terms of the phenotype level. As a result, generative-transformational grammar fails to provide cross-linguistically viable functional notions for the study of language universals.

## 2. The Basic Notions of Genotype Grammar

In the foregoing section I gave tentative definitions of some functional units of language. Now we are ready to study these notions in a more systematic way.

Any speech act involves a communication and three basic items connected with it—the sender, the receiver, and the external situation. According to whether the communication is oriented towards one of these three items, it can have respectively an expressive, vocative, or representational function.

I leave the expressive and vocative functions for the present and focus on the representational function of the communication. With respect to this function, the following postulate can be advanced:

If we abstract from everything in the language used that is irrelevant to the representational function of the communication, we have to recognize as essential only three classes of linguistic expressions:
a) the names of objects;
b) the names of situations;
c) the means for constructing the names of objects and the names of situations.

I call this postulate the *Principle of Representational Relevance*.

Names of objects are called *terms*. For example, the following expressions are used as terms in English: *a car, a gray car, a small gray car, a small gray car he bought yesterday*. Terms should not be confused with nouns. A noun is a morphological concept, whereas a term is a functional concept. Languages without word classes lack nouns but still have terms.

*Sentences* serve as the names of situations.

The means for constructing the names of objects and the names of situations are expressions called *operators*.

An operator is any kind of linguistic device that acts on one or more expressions called its *operands* to form an expression called its *resultant*. For example, in the English expression

(1)     *The hunter killed the bear.*

the word *killed* is an operator that acts on its operands *the hunter* and *the bear*; in *gray car* the expression *gray* is an operator that acts on its operand *car*. If an operator has one operand, it is called a *one-place* operator; if an operator has *n* operands, it is called an *n-place* operator.

It is important to notice that in accordance with the definition of the operator as a linguistic device, instances of an operator do not have to be only concrete expressions, such as words or morphemes. For instance, a predicate may be represented by intonation. So, in the following verse from a poem by the Russian poet A. Blok:

(2)     *Noč'. Ulica. Fonar'. Apteka.*
        'Night. Street. Lantern. Pharmacy'.

we have four sentences. In each of these sentences the intonation serves as an operator that acts on a term to form a sentence.

Another example of an operator that is not a concrete expression is truncation. For instance, *bel* 'is white' in the Russian sentence

(3)     *Sneg bel.*
        'The snow is white'.

is the resultant of truncation of the suffix *-yj* in the world *bel-yj* 'white'. Here truncation serves as an operator that acts on the adjective *bel-yj* 'white' to form the predicate *bel* 'is white'.

Let us focus on the operation of the combination of the operator with its operands. According to the definition of this operation in ordinary logic, an *n*-place operator combines with its operands in one step. This definition treats all operands as if they had an equally close connection with their operator. But usually an operator is more closely connected with one operand than another. For example, a transitive verb is more closely connected with the secondary term than with the primary term. Thus, in the above example (1), the transitive predicate *killed* is more closely connected with *the bear* than with *the hunter.*

Why are *killed* and *the bear* more closely connected than *killed* and *the hunter?* Because a combination of a transitive predicate with a direct object is equivalent to an intransitive predicate. That is why in some languages this combination can be replaced by an intransitive predicate. For example, in Russian *lovit' rybu* 'to catch fish' can be replaced by the intransitive verb *rybačit'* with the same meaning. And, vice versa, an intransitive verb can be replaced by a transitive verb with a direct object. For example, *to dine* may be replaced by *to eat dinner.* There is also other evidence of a close connection between a transitive verb and its direct object. Thus, nouns derived from intransitive verbs are oriented towards the subjects of the action (*genetivus subjectivus*), while nouns derived from transitive verbs tend to be oriented towards the objects of the action (*genetivus objectivus*). Compare *the dog barks:the barking of the dog* versus *they abducted the woman:the abduction of the woman.* The ambiguity of expressions such as *the shooting of the hunters* must be explained by the fact that although the verb *to shoot* is transitive, it can also be used as an intransitive verb; we can say *the hunters shoot* without specifying the object. Compare: *the boy reads the book:the boy reads.* The orientation of nouns derived from transitive verbs towards the object of the action is a universal tendency observed in typologically very different language groups.

To do justice to this phenomenon, we must redefine the combination of an $n$-place operator with its operands as a series of binary operations: an $n$-place operator is applicated to its first operand, then the resultant to the second operand, and so on. According to the new definition, an $n$-place operator combines with its operands in $n$ steps, rather than in one step as in ordinary logic. For example, any transitive predicate, which is a two-place operator, must be applied to the secondary term, then the resultant to the primary term. Thus, in the expression (1), the transitive predicate *killed* must be applied first to *the bear*, then to *the hunter:*

(4)     ((*killed the bear*) *the hunter*)

The new binary operation is called *application.*

The above informal explanation of the notion of application must now be presented as a formal statement called the *Applicative Principle:*

> An $n$-place operator can always be represented as a one-place operator that yields an $(n\text{-}1)$-place operator as its resultant.[2]

Examples of representing an $n$-place operator as a one-place operator: The two-place operator *killed* is represented as a one-place operator that is applied to its operand *the bear* and yields the resultant (*killed the bear*). The resultant is a $(2\text{-}1)$-place operator, that is, a one-place operator, which is applied to another term, *the hunter*, and yields the resultant ((*killed the bear*) *the hunter*). The new resultant is a $(1\text{-}1)$-place operator, that is, a zero-place operator, which is a sentence. This sentence is an abstract representation of the sentence

*The hunter killed the bear.*

The three-place operator *gave* is represented as a one-place operator that is applied to its operand *Mary* and yields the resultant (*gave Mary*). The resultant is a $(3\text{-}1)$-place operator, that is, a two-place operator. This two-place operator is represented, in its turn, as a one-place operator that is applied to another term, *money*, and yields the resultant ((*gave Mary*) *money*), which is a $(2\text{-}1)$-place operator, that is, a one-place operator. The latter is applied to the term *John* and yields a $(1\text{-}1)$-place operator (((*gave Mary*) *money*) *John*), which is an abstract representation of the sentence *John gave Mary money.*

On the basis of the Applicative Principle, I define the formal concepts *one-place predicate, two-place predicate,* and *three-place predicate* and the formal concepts *primary term, secondary term,* and *tertiary term.*

> DEFINITION 1. If $X$ is an operator that acts on a term $Y$ to form a sentence $Z$, then $X$ is a *one-place predicate* and $Y$ is a *primary term.*

DEFINITION 2. If X is an operator that acts on a term Y to form a one-place predicate Z, then X is a *two-place predicate* and Y is a *secondary term*.

DEFINITION 3. If X is an operator that acts on a term Y to form a two-place predicate Z, then X is a *three-place predicate* and Y is a *tertiary term*.

The opposition of a primary and a secondary term constitutes the *nucleus* of a sentence. These terms I call *nuclear*.

An *applicative tree* (henceforth AT) is a network of operators and operands combined by application. The sentence *He knocked down his enemy* can be presented by the following applicative tree:

(5)

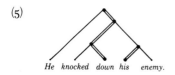

In an AT, operators are represented by double lines, and operands are represented by single lines. An AT presents the relation *operator:operand* independently of the linear word order, as can be seen from the following example:

(6)

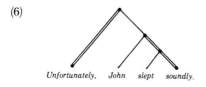

(7)

ATs (7) and (6) are equivalent from the relational point of view.

Any AT can be replaced by an equivalent linear formula with brackets. In the linear notation, by a convention, an operator must precede its operand, and both are put inside brackets.

(8)     (((DOWN KNOCKED) (HIS ENEMY)) HE)

(9)     (UNFORTUNATELY ((SOUNDLY SLEPT) JOHN))

Formula (8) replaces AT (5). Formula (9) replaces ATs (6) and (7), since it is invariant under the changes of word order.

In a linear formula, the brackets can be left out in accordance with the principle of leftward grouping. Applying this convention to the above linear formulae, we get

(10)   ((DOWN KNOCKED) (HIS ENEMY)) HE

(11)   UNFORTUNATELY ((SOUNDLY SLEPT) JOHN)

### 3. Constituency

Applicative structure represented by an applicative tree has two facets: part-whole relations called *constituency relations* and *dependency relations*. Operators and operands are interconnected by constituency and dependency relations.

An operator and its operand are in part-whole relation to the resultant of the operator. Therefore, a network of operators and operands presented by an applicative tree is at the same time a network of part-whole relations.

On the other hand, a network of operators and operands is also a network of *heads* and their *dependents*, because either the operator is the head and its operand is dependent, or, vice versa, the operator is dependent and its operand is the head.

I will first consider constituency.

*Constituency* is a part-whole relation that is defined in two steps. We first define *immediate constituents* and then give a definition of *constituents* based on the definition of immediate constituents:

> DEFINITION OF IMMEDIATE CONSTITUENTS:
> If expression *A* is an operator, expression *B* is its operand, and expression *C* is the resultant of the application of *A* to *B*, then expressions *A* and *B* are *immediate constituents* of expression *C*.

Examples: In AT (5) in the preceding section the operator *down* and its operand *knocked* are immediate constituents of the resultant *(down knocked)*; the operator *his* and its operand *enemy* are immediate constituents of the resultant (his enemy); the resultant *(down knocked)* is in its turn the operator of the resultant *(his enemy)*, and both of these expressions are immediate constituents of the resultant *((down knocked) (his enemy))*, which in its turn is the operator of *he*; *((down knocked) (his enemy))* and *he* are immediate constituents of the sentence *(((down knocked) (his enemy)) he)*.

In AT (6) and AT (7) in the preceding section, *soundly* and *slept* are immediate constituents of *(soundly slept)*; *(soundly slept)* and *John* are immediate constituents of *((soundly slept) John)*; *unfortunately* and *((soundly slept) John)* are immediate constituents of *(unfortunately ((soundly slept) John))*. (In representing immediate constituents, we place, by a convention, an operator before its operand.)

DEFINITION OF CONSTITUENTS:
If there exists a sequence of expressions $x_1, x_2, \ldots, x_n$ such that $x_i$ is an immediate constituent of $x_{i+1}$ (for $i = 1, 2, \ldots, n\text{-}1$), then $x_i$ is a *constituent* of $x_n$.

Examples: Every word $W$ in any sentence $S$ is its constituent, because, for any sentence $S$, there exists a sequence of expressions $x_1, x_2, \ldots, x_n$ such that $x_i$ is a word $W$ and $x_i$ is an immediate constituent of $x_{i+1}$ (for $i = 1, \ldots, n\text{-}1$). Thus, in the sentence presented in AT (5) in the preceding section, the word *knocked* is a constituent of the sentence *He knocked down his enemy*, because there exists a sequence of expressions *knocked, (down knocked), ((down knocked) (his enemy)), (((down knocked) (his enemy)) he)*, and every member of this sequence is an immediate constituent of the member that follows it. And every member of this sequence is also a constituent of the sentence *He knocked down his enemy*, because it is at the same time a member of the subsequence that satisfies the above definition of the constituent. For instance, *(down knocked)* is a constituent of the sentence in question because *(down knocked)* is a member of a subsequence *(down knocked), ((down knocked) (his enemy)), (((down knocked) (his enemy)) he)*, and every member of this subsequence is an immediate constituent of the member that follows it.

Note that I have defined immediate constituents and constituents independently of linear word order. In current linguistic literature, and in particular in generative-transformational grammar, the definition of immediate constituents includes the requirement that immediate constituents must be adjacent elements in a linear string. While in genotype grammar constituency is viewed as independent of linear word order, generative-transformational grammar confounds constituency with linear word order. That leads to serious difficulties, which will be discussed below.[3]

## 4. Dependency

It is possible to give a precise definition of the dependency relation on the basis of the part-whole relation between an operator, its operand, and the resultant of the operator.

DEFINITION OF DEPENDENCY:
Let expression $C$ be a resultant of operator $A$ applied to operand $B$. Either $A$ is the head and $B$ is its dependent, or $B$ is the head and $A$ is its dependent: if expression $C$ belongs in the same category as operand $B$,

then *B* is the *head* and *A* is its *dependent;* if expression *C* belongs in a different category from that of *B*, then *A* is the *head* and *B* is its *dependent.*

If operand *B* is the head and operator *A* is its dependent, then *A* is called the *modifier of the head.*

If operator *A* is the head and operand *B* is its dependent, then *B* is called the *complement of the head.*

Example: In

(1)     *Bill bought new books.*

the operator *new* is the modifier, and the operand *books* is its head, because the resultant (*new books*) belongs in the same category as *books* (both are terms); the operator *bought* is the head, and the operand (*new books*) is its complement, because the resultant (*bought* (*new books*)) belongs in a different category from that of (*new books*): (*bought* (*new books*)) is a predicate, but (*new books*) is a term; finally, the operator (*bought* (*new books*)) is the head, and operand *Bill* is its complement, because the resultant ((*bought* (*new books*)) *Bill*) belongs in a different category from that of *Bill:* the former is a sentence, and the later is a term.

The concepts 'head' and 'dependent' given in the above definitions are more general than those given in current linguistic literature. In so-called dependency grammar, dependency relations are defined only for the smallest constituents of a sentence, that is, for words. For example, the sentence

(2)     *A little boy looked intently at the picture.*

will be represented in dependency grammar by the following tree:

(3)

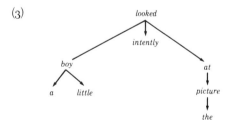

Dependency grammar is unable to represent dependency relations between functional units, while genotype grammar does represent these relations. So the above sentence will be represented in genotype grammar by the following dependency tree:

(4)

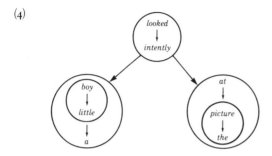

Starting from the notion of applicative structure, we are able to give a rigorous definition of the dependency relation presented above. Dependency is not a primitive concept: it must be defined. But dependency grammar is not able to give a satisfactory definition of this concept.

Richard A. Hudson in his recent paper gives a tentative solution to the problem of defining dependency (Hudson, 1980: 188–91). Using the term *modifier* as a synonym of the term *dependent*, he defines heads and modifiers in terms of the concepts 'frame' and 'slot'. According to Hudson, any filler of a slot in a frame is a modifier. But the concepts 'frame' and 'slot' cannot be taken as primitive, either; they also have to be defined. Rather than give a definition of these concepts, Hudson gives a list of heads and modifiers.

(5)

| *modifier* | *head* | *example* |
|---|---|---|
| object | verb | *likes(H) biscuits(M)* |
| subject | verb | *John(M) drowned(H)* |
| prep. obj. | preposition | *in(H) London(M)* |
| adjective | noun | *big(M) hands(H)* |
| genitive | noun | *my(M) hands(H)* |
| determiner | noun | *the(M) end(H)* |
| adverb | adjective | *very(M) big(H)* |
| rel. clause | noun | *people(H) who think that(M)* |
| comp. clause | comp. adj. | *bigger(H) than Mary was(M)* |

Any list of heads and modifiers cannot replace a definition of these concepts.

Taking the notion of applicative structure as a starting point, we are able to solve the problem of defining dependency. We give a rigorous definition of heads and dependents and draw an important distinction between two kinds of dependents: modifiers and complements.

## 5. Constituency and Dependency as Complementary Notions

Contemporary linguistic theory recognizes that there are two models of representation of the syntactic structure of a sentence: constituency representation and dependency representation. Generative-transformational grammar uses constituency representation, while some other grammatical theories favor dependency representation.

In current linguistic literature, controversy about the superiority of one type of syntactic representation over another approaches the intensity of a civil war. But as a matter of fact, there is no likelihood of forming a consistent description of grammatical structure using a choice of only one of the two possible models of representation. It seems as though one must use sometimes constituency representation and sometimes dependency representation, while at times it is possible to use either. The situation is rather like that in physics, where the phenomena of light are explained by two theories that complement each other—the wave theory of light and the quantum theory of light. Separately neither of them fully explains the phenomena of light, but together they do.

We are faced with a fundamental problem: Is it possible to combine constituency representation and dependency representation to form an integrated representation of syntactic structure? And if it is possible, will the integrated representation of syntactic structure lead to new significant insights into linguistic reality?

My answer to this question is affirmative. It is possible to form an integrated representation of syntactic structure that will lead to new significant insights into linguistic reality. In the foregoing sections it was shown how that can be done. Starting from the notion of applicative structure, I defined constituency and dependency as complementary notions that are reduced to the relations between an operator, its operand, and the resultant of an operator.

With the integration of the constituency and dependency models into the applicative model, the controversy over the superiority of one type of model over the other must come to an end. As a matter of fact, we cannot dispense with either model; both of them are necessary as complementary pictures of linguistic reality.

## 6. The Structure of the Sentence

### 6.1 The Notion of Syntaxeme

As was shown above, the level of functional units is universal, while the level of morphological units that realize the functional units is language-specific. The level of functional units I call the genotype level, and the level of syntagmatic units that realize functional units I call the phenotype level. Functional units are irreducible to any other type of units, they are ultimate units of the genotype level.

Neither words nor combinations of words belong to syntax proper. As a matter of fact, these are morphological units that realize functional units—the true units of syntax.

In order to set out the crucial significance of functional units as true units of syntax, I introduce the term *syntaxeme*. I suggest calling the functional unit the syntaxeme.

## 6.2 Predicate Frames

The construction of a sentence starts with a *predicate frame*. By a predicate frame I mean a combination of a predicate with an appropriate number of terms functioning as operands of the predicate.

The minimal sentence consists of two syntaxemes, one of which is the predicate, which normally designates a state of affairs or an event, while the other is the primary term, which refers to a participant whose role, whether active or passive, is emphasized by its choice as the primary term. The primary term contrasts with other terms as a pivot, that is, as a term having a privileged position in a sentence. In current linguistic literature, the primary term is called the subject. I will show below that the term *subject* is inappropriate, because it refers also to other notions that are incompatible with the notion of the pivot.

The primary term may be represented by a pronominal morpheme such as *I* in *I love* or by a morpheme that is a component of a verbal form, as in Latin *amo* 'I love'. The primary term may be represented by a word or a group of words, as in *John left* or *Poor John, whom I met yesterday, is very sick*. The primary term may be represented by a combination of a word and a pronominal morpheme or by a combination of a word and a morpheme that is a component of a verbal form, as in French *l'homme il marche* 'The man is marching' or in Latin *Caesar venit* 'Caesar came'. Semantically, the primary term may denote an agent, as in *John walks slowly*; a patient, as in *John was arrested*; or a beneficiary, as in *John was given the books*. It can also have some other meanings, which I will not discuss here.

According to the language concerned, the primary term may either have a case marker, such as nominative in Latin or Russian, or be marked by a position with respect to the predicate. For example, in English and French the primary term precedes the predicate, as in

(1)      a. *Tom beats Dick.*
         b. *Dick beats Tom.*

In (1a) *Tom* is the primary term and *Dick* is the secondary term; but in (1b), vice versa, *Dick* is the primary term and *Tom* is the secondary term.

The corresponding Russian sentences will be

(2)      a. *Tom b'et Dik-a.*
         b. *Tom-a b'et Dik.*

As these sentences show, the position of the primary term with respect to the predicate is irrelevant in Russian: in (2a) the predicate *b'et* is preceded by the primary term *Tom;* in (2b), however, the predicate *b'et* is preceded by the secondary term *Tom-a*. What matters is not the position but case markers: in both (2a) and (2b) the primary term is in the nominative case, which has a zero case marker, and the secondary term is in the accusative case, which has the case marker *-a*.

An important property of the primary term with respect to the secondary term and other terms is its indispensability. The secondary term or the tertiary term can be eliminated from a sentence, which will still remain a complete sentence. But that is normally not true of the primary term. For instance,

(3)     a. *Peter sells fruit (for a living).*
        b. *Peter sells (for a living).*
        c. *\* Sells fruit (for a living).*

After we eliminated the secondary term *fruit* from (3a), we got sentence (3b), which is normal. But the elimination of the primary term *Peter* has led to an inadmissible sentence (3c).

The predicate frame *predicate:primary term* can be reduced to a structure consisting only of one unit—the predicate. In this case the predicate becomes syntactically equivalent with the whole sentence that it represents. In many languages, such as Russian or Latin, sentences with a predicate and a zero term are quite normal. Compare Latin *pluit* 'it rains' or *ningit* 'it snows', Russian *žarko* 'it is hot'.

According to a fairly widespread view, sentences with terms are the result of the expansion of basic sentences consisting solely of a predicate; so, sentences without terms are regarded as basic, and sentences with terms are regarded as derived from the sentences containing predicates only. But, as a matter of fact, the contrary is true: the structure of the sentences containing predicates is a reduced structure based on the full structure *predicate:primary term*. This claim is based on the Principle of Maximum Differentiation discussed below: a complete sentence is a structure that permits the maximal differentiation of the members of the predicate frame. The opposition of the predicate and the primary term is eliminated in the sentence consisting of the predicate only. Still, according to its syntactic role, the predicate represents the complete sentence. A predicate can represent a complete sentence, but the reverse is not true: a complete sentence cannot be regarded as the representation of a predicate.

According to the above definition of the two-place and three-place predicates and the secondary and tertiary terms, a combination of the two-place predicate with a term is syntactically equivalent to the one-place predicate, and a combination of the three-place predicate with a term is syntactically equivalent to the two-place predicate. An obvious consequence of these definitions is that predicates are more closely connected with tertiary and secondary terms than with the primary term. The construction of a sentence containing more than one term goes on by incorporation of terms into predicates.

The closer connection between predicates and secondary and tertiary terms is manifested by the contraction of these predicates and their terms into simple predicates. Compare

(4)     *form a circle round* → *encircle*
        *give courage* → *encourage*
        *he watches weight* → *he is a weightwatcher*
        *he held her in a warm embrace* → *he warmly embraced her*

Predicates and terms can be expanded by various modifiers; we must distinguish *modifiers of terms* and *modifiers of predicates*.

An elementary term is normally represented by a noun. A modifier of a term is normally represented by an adjective but can also be represented by words that belong to other lexical classes. As was said above, the primary function of a verb is to be a predicate, but one of its secondary functions is to replace an adjective whose primary function is to be a modifier of a term. The primary function of a noun is to be a term, but one of its secondary functions is to serve as a modifier of a term. The primary function of a sentence is to be an independent unit of communication, but one of its secondary functions is to serve as a modifier of a term. Compare the following expansions of the elementary term represented by the noun:

(5)     *father*
        *the father*
        *the old father*
        *the old father of John*
        *the old father of John, who returned yesterday*

The modifier of a predicate is normally represented by an adverb, whose primary function is to be a modifier of a predicate. It can, however, be represented by other words, one of whose secondary functions is to serve as a modifier of a predicate. Compare

(6)     *He walked slowly.*
        *He walked in a hurry.*

An important syntaxeme is the *modifier of a sentence*. A modifier of a sentence is represented by an adverb or an adverbial phrase. Examples of modifiers of sentences:

(7)     *Probably, John will come back tomorrow.*
        *Unfortunately, it is too late.*
        *Last summer I visited Mexico.*

If we transpose a sentence into a term, we can embed one sentence into another sentence. We have already discussed one case of embedded sentences;

that is when a transposed sentence serves as a modifier of a term. But a sentence can also serve as a term of another sentence. For example, in

(8)     *I know that John has left.*

we find a sentence *John has left* that was transposed by means of the conjunction *that* into the secondary term of sentence (8).

In current linguistic literature, the term *clause* is sometimes used to denote a sentence that either is a part of another sentence or is combined with another sentence using a coordinating conjunction, such as *and, but,* etc.:

(9)     *John went to Boston, and Peter went to New York.*
        *Boris likes smoking, but I don't like it.*

Sentences can be *coordinated* and *subordinated*. The difference between the coordination and the subordination of sentences is this: coordinated sentences can interchange their positions in the structure of the sentence whose components they are, while this interchange is impossible between the main sentence and the subordinated sentence without a complete change of the meaning (which may make no sense at all) of the sentence whose components they are. So, if we take the above coordinated sentences (9), we can interchange their positions as follows:

(10)    *Peter went to New York, and John went to Boston.*
        *I don't like smoking, but Boris likes it.*

As an example of subordinated sentences, consider

(11)    *I did it, because they asked me to do it.*

If we interchange the positions of the components of this sentence, we will get a sentence with a completely different meaning:

(12)    *They asked me to do it, because I did it.*

As a matter of fact, the clause *because they asked me to do it* is a modifier of the clause *I did it*. If we take the above sentence (8) and try to interchange the position of its components, we will get complete nonsense:

(13)    **John has left that I know.*

## 6.3 Functional Transposition and Superposition

According to our definition of dependency, given an operator $A$ and an operand $B$, $A$ is the head and $B$ is its dependent, if $A$ transposes $B$ from one category into another. If an operator transposes its operand from one category into another, I call the operator a *transposer* and the operand, a *transponend;* and the process I call *transposition.*

Examples of transposition in English: The operator *of* applied to the term *table* transposes *table* from the category of terms into the category of modifiers of terms. The operator *is* applied to *table* transposes *table* from the category of terms into the category of predicates. The operator *that* applied to the sentence *John left Paris yesterday* transposes this sentence from the category of sentences into the category of terms (compare *I know John* and *I know that John left Paris yesterday*).

Neither constituency grammar nor dependency grammar has the means to handle transposition. But understanding the phenomenon of transposition is of paramount importance to linguistic theory. This phenomenon has far-reaching implications in both synchrony and diachrony.

Now I consider transposition more closely. The concept 'transposition' is different from the concept 'transformation' as used in generative-transformational grammar. In generative-transformational grammar, the term *transformation* refers to operations that effect changes in preestablished structures through deletion, substitution, or permutation of constituents. Transpositions require no deletion, substitution, or permutation; they are purely relational operations transferring expressions from one category into another. It should be pointed out that applicative grammar does not require transformations in the sense of generative-transformational grammar.

The concept 'transposition' makes it possible to reveal important relations between syntactic functions and words that have these functions. Word categories have a dual nature: on the one hand, they have some very general lexical meaning, and on the other hand, they have some definite syntactic function. So, nouns denote objects and at the same time function as terms in a sentence; adjectives denote fixed properties and at the same time function as modifiers of terms in a sentence; verbs denote changing properties and at the same time function as predicates of sentences; adverbs denote properties of properties and at the same time function as modifiers of predicates in sentences. These are inherent syntactic functions of the word categories, because these functions correlate with the lexical meanings of the word categories.

Since words are transposed from one category into another, they are at the same time transposed from one syntactic function into another. Thus, we come up with a classification of the syntactic functions in terms of 'primary' and 'secondary'. Primary syntactic functions are inherent syntactic functions of the word categories. Secondary syntactic functions are those that are acquired by words when they are transposed from their basic category into some other category.

Examples: The noun *milk* may function as a term in a sentence, and that is its primary function; by applying the operator *of*, we transpose this word into *of milk*, and now it functions as a modifier of a term, which is its secondary function; by applying the operator *is* to *milk*, we get *is milk*, which functions as a predicate of a sentence, and that is another secondary function of *milk*.

A sentence can also have primary and secondary syntactic functions. The primary function of a sentence is the function of being an independent unit of communication. Its secondary functions are functions of a term or a modifier. When a sentence is transposed into a clause, it receives a secondary function. Compare, for instance, *I know John* and *I know that John has left*.

There are languages that do not distinguish between lexical classes, such as Chinese. We must abandon the terms *verb* and *noun* when describing these languages. Still, we can discover predicative and nonpredicative functions in these languages, just as we can in languages that have lexical classes. They can be based on different modes of combinations of the expressions that constitute one and the same lexical class.

The interplay of primary and secondary syntactic functions of words is of fundamental importance for diachrony: when a word *A* receives a secondary function in a certain syntactic environment, there is a universal tendency to replace the word *A* with a word (or group of words) *B*, for which this function is a primary function. Owing to this tendency, nouns that have a secondary function of adverbs are replaced by adverbs (for instance, Romance adverbs in *-mente* are ancient instrumentals); adjectives that have a secondary function of terms are replaced by nouns, etc.

The phenomenon of transposition is crucial for the typological classification of languages of the world. For instance, the so-called inflexional languages (such as Latin or Russian) and analytic languages (such as English or French) have different types of transposers (flexions, on one hand, and prepositions, on the other hand). A classification of the languages of the world from the point of view of transposition must answer the fundamental question of universal grammar and language typology: In what way do languages differ with respect to the transposers they use?

The distinction of primary and secondary syntactic functions implies a view of syntactic processes that is different from the view of syntactic processes advocated by generative-transformational grammar.

Generative-transformational grammar regards syntactic nominal groups as a result of nominalization of sentences. In many instances this view is justified. There are, however, instances when it runs into difficulties. Consider, for example, the nominal structure 'adjective + noun'. *the blue sky* is not the result of the transformation of *the sky is blue*. In languages where the formal category of the adjective occurs, the primary syntactic function of the adjective is attributive, and the secondary is predicative.

As a matter of fact, from the standpoint of derivation, the nominal group is no less fundamental than the sentence. The nominal group is fundamental for the syntactic contrast *adjective : noun*, and the sentence is fundamental for the syntactic contrast *noun: verb*. The syntactic contrast between the adjective and the noun, on the one hand, and between the noun and the verb, on the other hand, is based on the semiotic *Principle of Maximum Differentiation*. The nominal group is characteristic of the maximum differentiation between the noun and the adjective, and the sentence is characteristic of the maximum differentiation between the noun and the verb. The syntactic contrast between the noun and the adjective is neutralized in the predicative position, and the syntactic contrast between the noun and the verb is neutralized in the attributive position. That is why *the sky is blue* must be regarded as derived from *the blue sky* rather than vice versa: *is blue* is a secondary function of *blue*. By contrast, *the moon shines* must be regarded as primary with respect to *the shining moon:* the participle *shining* is a secondary function of the verb.

In accordance with the Principle of Maximum Differentiation, both nominal groups and sentences are fundamental from the standpoint of the direction of derivation. Therefore, under some conditions nominal groups are derived from sentences, and under other conditions sentences are derived from nominal groups.

A process related to functional transposition is what I call *functional superposition*. Given a syntactic unit, superposition puts a secondary syntactic function over its primary one so as to combine them into a new bistratal syncretic function. For example, if by using the suffix *-tion*, we change the verb *to instruct* into a verbal noun *instruction*, we have a case of transposition: the noun *instruction* has no syntactic function whatsoever of a verb. If, on the other hand, by using the suffix *-ing*, we change the verb *to instruct* into a different kind of noun—the so-called gerund *instructing*—we will have a case of functional superposition: the verbal noun retains the syntactic functions of the verb *to instruct*. Thus, it can take an object in the accusative (*on instructing him*) and an adverb (*He suggested our immediately instructing them*). The suffix *-ing* I call a *superposer*, and the verb *to instruct*, with respect to the suffix *-ing*, I call a *superponend* of *-ing*. The suffix *-ing* superposes noun functions onto the verb functions of *to instruct* so as to combine them into a new syncretic verbal-nominal function.

Other examples of superposition: In Russian, the characteristic syntactic function of the instrumental case is to be an adverbial, but in addition, it can take on the function of the direct object, as in *Ivan upravljaet zavodom* 'John manages a factory'. This sentence can be passivized—*Zavod upravljaetsja Ivanom* 'The factory is managed by John'—because the instrumental in the active functions as an accusative case.

The characteristic function of the accusative case is to be the direct object, but in addition, it can take on the function of an adverbial, as in the Russian sentence *On rabotal celyj den'* 'He worked all day long'. In this sentence the accusative *celyj den'* can be replaced by an adverbial of time, such as *utrom* 'in the morning', *večerom* 'in the evening', etc. Compare: *On rabotal večerom* 'He worked in the evening'. This syntactic behavior of the accusative shows that it functions as an adverbial.

The characteristic function of the Russian dative is the role of an indirect object, but there is a large class of predicates that superpose the function of the subject onto it. For example, in:

(14)   *Vidja, čto   proisxodit, emu      stydno   za svoego   brata.*
        seeing what happens   him-Dat. ashamed for his-Refl. brother
        'Seeing what is happening, he feels ashamed for his brother'.

In (14) the dative *emu* has its characteristic function of the indirect object, but in addition, the predicate *stydno* superposes onto it the function of the subject, so that *emu* has three properties of a subject: 1) it controls Equi into a participle construction *vidja, čto proisxodit;* 2) it serves as an antecedent of the reflexive *svoego;* and 3) it precedes the predicate *stydno* (although Russian has a free word order, subjects normally precede predicates, while direct and indirect objects follow them).

As will be shown below, the notion of superposition is of paramount importance for understanding the structure of ergative languages.[4]

## 7. Valence and Voice

Now we can introduce the generalized concept of valence called the *valence of an operator.*

The valence of an operator is defined as the number of operands that the operator can be combined with. Accordingly, operators can be *univalent, bivalent, trivalent,* etc.

I call the valence of an operator the *generalized concept of valence,* since the ordinary concept of valence usually relates to predicates alone, and predicates are only a special class of operators.

By applying valence-changing rules, we can increase, decrease, or reorient the valence of a predicate. Here are some examples of the application of these rules:

*To fall* and *to rise* are one-place predicates. By changing the root vowels of these predicates, we derive two-place predicates from them: *to fell* and *to raise.* Compare

(1)     *a. The tree has fallen.*
       *b. Someone has felled the tree.*

(2)     *a. An arm rose.*
       *b. Someone has raised an arm.*

The Russian predicate *rugat'* is a two-place predicate like its English counterpart *to scold.* By applying the suffix *-sja* to *rugat',* we get the one-place predicate *rugat'-sja*. Compare the following Russian sentences and their English counterparts:

(3)     a. *On rugaet rebenka.*
        b. *He scolds a child.*

(4)     a. *On rugaet-sja.*
        b. *He scolds.*

Notice that although in (4b) *scolds* is used only with one term, that does not mean a decrease of its valence. A true decrease of the valence of a predicate takes place when some formal device is used, such as the suffix *-sja* in Russian. English does not have formal devices for decreasing the valence of predicates. When *to scold* is used as a one-place predicate, as in the above example, this use must be characterized as an incompletely realized two-place valence.

Compare now the following sentences:

(5)     a. *John killed Mary.*
        b. *Mary was killed by John.*

These two sentences have an equivalent meaning and an equal number of terms. Both *killed* and *was killed* are two-place predicates. But what is the difference between these predicates? The predicate *was killed* is the converse of *killed*, and it involves a permutation of terms: in the sentence (5a) the primary term denotes an agent (*John*), and the secondary term denotes a patient (*Mary*); and, as a result of the permutation of these terms, in (5b) the primary term denotes a patient (*Mary*), and the secondary term denotes an agent (*John*).

*Conversion* neither increases nor decreases the valence of a predicate; it is a *relational change of valence.*

The notion of conversion was defined above for two-place operators. But conversion can be applied to many-place operators. Consider the three-place predicate *to load* in the following sentence:

(6)     *They loaded goods on trucks.*

where *they* is a primary term, *goods* is a secondary term, and *trucks* is a tertiary term.

We can apply conversion to *loaded* and permutate the secondary and tertiary terms. We get

(7)     *They loaded trucks with goods.*

As a result of conversion, *goods* became a tertiary term and *trucks* became a secondary term.

Now we can generalize the notion of conversion as an operator applied to many-place relations.

DEFINITION OF CONVERSION:
The many-place relation $\breve{R}_n$ called the *converse* of the many-place relation $R_n$ holds between $x_1, \ldots, x_l, \ldots, x_i, \ldots, x_n$ if, and only if, the relation $R_n$ holds between $x_1, \ldots, x_i, \ldots, x_l, \ldots, x_n$.

In accordance with this definition, the conversion of any $n$-place relation $R_n$ involves a permutation of any two terms:

$$(8) \qquad \breve{R}_n \, x_1 \ldots x_l \ldots x_i \ldots x_n \equiv R_n \, x_1 \ldots x_i \ldots x_l \ldots x_n$$

The valence of an operator was defined above as the number of operators with which the operator can be combined. Now we can generalize the notion of valence by including in it the relational structure of the operator defined by the rules of conversion of operators. I will distinguish two types of valence: 1) *quantitative valence*—the number of operators with which an operator can be combined; and 2) *relational valence*—an orientation of an operator with respect to its operands determined by the rules of conversion.

Classes of operators generated by the valence-changing rule I call *valence classes of operators*. In the above examples we find the following valence classes: 1) *to fall, to fell;* 2) *to rise, to raise;* 3) *rugaet, rugaet-sja;* 4) *killed, was killed.*

Now we are ready to consider the notion of voice. It is helpful to define this notion with respect to the notion of valence.

I define *voice* as follows:

*Voice* is a grammatical category that characterizes predicates with respect to their quantitative and relational valence.

I regard this definition of voice as a generalization that covers various current notions of voice.

Starting from this definition of voice, we can develop a calculus of possible voices. The calculus will not tell us about the actual number of voices in every language; it will tell us how many voices a language can have. Clearly, no language has all possible voices. Languages differ from one another, in particular, by different sets of voices. That makes it possible to write a new chapter of language typology—a typology of voices.

The above definition of the voice has important consequences, which will be considered in the sections that follow.

## 8. The Typology of Sentence Constructions

We must distinguish two types of languages:

1) languages that have transitive constructions that are in opposition to intransitive constructions, and

2) languages that distinguish not between transitive and intransitive but rather between active and inactive (stative) constructions.

The first type is subdivided into two subtypes: a) accusative languages, such as Russian, Latin, or English, and b) ergative languages, such as Dyirbal. The second type is represented by many Amerindian languages, such as Dakota or Tlingit (these are called languages with the active system) (Klimov, 1973: 214–26).

The terms *accusative languages* and *ergative languages* are widely accepted conventional labels characterizing languages that do not necessarily have morphological cases; rather, they have syntactic counterparts of relations denoted by morphological cases. Thus, although Russian has morphological cases and English does not (short of a distinction between the nominative and accusative in personal pronouns: *I-me, he-him,* etc.), both Russian and English are called accusative languages, because word order and prepositions in English can express the same relations as morphological cases in Russian. For similar reasons, both Basque and Tongan are called ergative languages, although Basque has morphological cases and Tongan does not.

DEFINITION

The *transitive construction* is a sentence with a two-place predicate in which either the primary term denotes an agent and the secondary term a patient (in accusative languages), or the primary term denotes a patient and the secondary term an agent (in ergative languages).

The *intransitive construction* is a sentence with a one-place predicate and a primary term only, which does not differentiate between the agent and the patient: it may denote either an agent or a patient.

An example of synonymous transitive constructions in Dyirbal (an ergative language) and English (an accusative language) (Dixon, 1972):

(1)     a) *Ŋuma yabu+ŋgu buṛa+l.*
        b) *Mother saw father.*

The Dyirbal transitive *buṛa+l* corresponds to English *saw.* Dyirbal *ŋuma* corresponds to English *father.* Both denote an agent, but it is a primary term in Dyirbal, while it is a secondary term in English. Dyirbal *yabu+ŋgu* corresponds to English *mother.* Both denote an agent, but it is a secondary term in Dyirbal, while it is a primary term in English.

Examples of nondifferentiation between the agent and the patient in English intransitive constructions:

(2)     a) *Peter sells well.*
          (the primary term denotes an agent)
       b) *These books sell well.*
          (the primary term denotes a patient)

       c) *Automobiles are sold.*
          (the primary term denotes a patient)

       d) *Charles and Peter are fighting over Mary.*
          (*Charles* and *Peter* are both agents and patients)

The notions 'agent' and 'patient' are taken as primitive grammatical concepts.

To define the transitive and intransitive constructions, some linguists use the notions 'subject' and 'direct object' (for example, Perlmutter and Postal, 1984: 94–95). In terms of these notions, a sentence is transitive if it has both a subject and a direct object, and the sentence is intransitive if it has only a subject.

This characterization runs into difficulties.

First, since subject denotes both the topic and the agent, while direct object denotes a patient, which is a part of the comment, these notions can be used to characterize only the transitive construction in accusative languages: subject corresponds to the primary term denoting an agent, and direct object corresponds to the secondary term denoting a patient. These notions cannot be used to characterize the transitive constructions in ergative languages. Thus, in Dyirbal the primary term and the secondary term in a transitive construction each coincide partly with subject and partly with direct object: the primary term shares the property of topic with subject and the property of patient with direct object, and the secondary term shares the property of nontopic with direct object and the property of agent with subject.

The notion of subject also meets with difficulties in some accusative languages. Thus, Schachter (1976, 1977) has shown that in Philippine languages the notion of subject splits into two notions—the topic and the agent (*actor* in Schachter's terminology)—which are independent of each other: there are separate markers for the agent and for the topic. From the point of view of Philippine languages, other accusative languages merge the syntactic properties of the topic and the agent within a single sentence part—the subject, while from the point of view of other accusative languages, Philippine languages divide the syntactic properties of the subject between the topic and the agent.

Subject and direct object are not universal notions, but they are valid concepts in most accusative languages and must be defined in terms of two classes of notions: 1) primary term, secondary term; 2) agent, patient.

Second, the use of the notion 'subject' to characterize the primary term in the intransitive construction conceals its fundamental property of nondifferentiating between agents and patients.

The foregoing shows that subject and direct object are complex notions that cannot be used as valid universal constructs. They must be replaced by more fundamental, truly universal notions: primary and secondary terms, on the one hand, and agent and patient, on the other.

The transitive and intransitive constructions in accusative languages can be represented as follows:

(3)

|              | Unmarked terms | Marked terms |
|--------------|----------------|--------------|
| Transitive   | A              | P            |
| Intransitive | A/P            |              |

The transitive and intransitive constructions in ergative languages can be represented as follows:

(4)

|              | Unmarked terms | Marked terms |
|--------------|----------------|--------------|
| Transitive   | P              | A            |
| Intransitive | P/A            |              |

These tables show that transitive constructions in the ergative and accusative languages are mirror images of each other.

The opposition *primary term : secondary term* is central to the syntactic organization of any natural language. The range of primary terms is greater than the range of secondary terms: primary terms occur with both intransitive and transitive verbs, while secondary terms occur only with transitive verbs. Primary terms occurring with intransitive verbs must be construed as units resulting from a neutralization of the opposition *primary term : secondary term* that is associated with transitive verbs.

The syntactic opposition *primary term : secondary term* belongs in a class of relations characterized by the *Markedness Law:*

> Given two semiotic units A and B which are members of a binary opposition A : B, if the range of A is wider than the range of B, then the set of the relevant features of A is narrower than the set of relevant features of B, which has a plus relevant feature. (The range of a semiotic unit is

the sum of its syntactic positions. The term *relevant feature* means here an essential feature that is part of the definition of a semiotic unit.)

The opposition $A:B$ is the *markedness relation* between $A$ and $B$, where $A$ is the *unmarked term* and $B$ is the *marked term* of this opposition.

The Markedness Law characterizes an important property of natural languages and other semiotic systems. It makes a significant empirical claim that *mutatis mutandis* is analogous to the law concerning the relation between mass and energy in physics.

In languages with case morphology, primary terms are denoted by the nominative case in accusative languages and by the absolutive case in ergative languages. Secondary terms are denoted by the accusative case in accusative languages and by the ergative case (or its equivalents) in ergative languages.

The relation between primary and secondary terms is characterized by the *Dominance Law:*

The marked term in a sentence cannot occur without the unmarked term, while the unmarked term can occur without the marked term.

A corollary of the Dominance Law is that the unmarked term of a sentence is its central, its independent term. By contrast, the marked term of a sentence is its marginal, its dependent term. The unmarked term is the only obligatory term of a sentence.

The Dominance Law explains why the marked term is omissible and the unmarked term is nonomissible in a clause representing the opposition *unmarked term:marked term*. The marked term is omissible because the unmarked term does not entail the occurrence of the marked term. And the marked term is nonomissible because the marked term entails the occurrence of the unmarked term; that is, it cannot occur without the unmarked term. As a consequence of this law, languages manifest the following general tendency: ergatives can, but absolutives cannot, be eliminated in transitive constructions in ergative languages; accusatives can, but nominatives cannot, be eliminated in transitive constructions in accusative languages.

As a consequence of the Markedness Law, we can establish a hierarchy of syntactic terms which I will call the *Applicative Hierarchy:*

(5)     [*Primary term > Secondary term > (Tertiary term)*] *> Oblique term*

The brackets and parentheses have a special meaning in (5). The brackets embrace terms as members of the predicate frame: they are the operands of the predicate. The parentheses indicate that the tertiary term is marginal with respect to the primary and secondary terms, which are central to the predicate frame. The tertiary term is marked with respect to the secondary term, because the range of the secondary term is greater than the range of the tertiary term: the secondary term occurs in both transitive and ditransitive constructions, while the tertiary term occurs only in ditransitive ones. And oblique terms are marked with respect to the predicate frames, because the range of the predicate frames is greater than the range of oblique terms: the predicate frame occurs in every clause, while oblique terms occur only in some clauses. The oblique term is a term transposed into an adverbial that serves as an operator modifying the predicate frame.

Some languages have syntactic constructions that seem to be counterexamples to the claim that secondary terms occur only in transitive constructions and tertiary terms occur only in ditransitive constructions. Consider these Russian impersonal sentences:

(6)      a. *Menja tošnit.*
            me      nauseates
            'I feel nauseated'.
         b. *Mne  xolodno.*
            to-me is-cold
            'I am cold'.

In (6a) *menja* is the accusative of the pronoun *ja* 'I.' Accusative in Russian, as in other languages, indicates a secondary term, and therefore one may wonder whether *menja* is a secondary term that occurs here without a primary term. True, the inherent syntactic function of accusative is to be the secondary term of a sentence. But in impersonal sentences it can take on the function of the primary term, which is superposed onto its primary function. Thus, it may be equivalent to the primary term of a subordinate clause, which can be changed into a participial construction by eliminating the primary term:

(7)      *Kogda* ja *smotrju na eto,* menja *tošnit.*
         'When I look at this, I feel nauseated'.
         → *Smotrja na eto, menja tošnit.*
         'Looking at this, I feel nauseated'.

Similarly, in (7b) the dative *mne*, whose inherent syntactic function is to be a tertiary term, has taken on the function of a primary term, which is reflected in its syntactic behavior (like that of *menja* in (6a)): it can induce the change of a corresponding subordinate clause into a participial construction by eliminating an equivalent primary term.

The terms of a clause are mapped onto grammatical meanings characterizing the participants of the situation denoted by the clause. The primary and secondary terms are mapped onto *agent* and *patient*, which are central grammatical meanings in a clause. The oblique terms can be mapped onto grammatical meanings characterizing the spatial opposition *where : whence : whither : which way* (location, source, goal, instrument) and other grammatical meanings that are rooted in spatial meanings, such as time, beneficiary, recipient, etc. The important thing to notice is that agent and patient are universal grammatical meanings associated with the primary and the secondary terms, while other grammatical meanings vary from language to language: every language has its own set of concrete grammatical meanings associated with oblique terms.

The tertiary term has an intermediary place between central terms and oblique terms. On the one hand, it has something in common with central terms: it may alternate with the primary and the secondary terms, in contrast with oblique terms, which never alternate with the central terms. On the other hand, like oblique terms, it is mapped onto concrete meanings—mostly onto *beneficiary* or *recipient*, but also onto *instrument*, *goal*, and others.

The grammatical meanings of terms (such as *grammatical agent, grammatical patient*, etc.) in the sense of applicative grammar are not to be equated with Filmorean case roles (Filmore, 1968, 1977), the thematic relations of Gruber (1965), or the theta roles of Chomsky (1981, 1982) and Marantz (1984). For example, Marantz (1984: 129) assigns different rules to the object of the preposition *by* in passive constructions. Consider

(8)     a. *Hortense was passed by Elmer.* (agent)
        b. *Elmer was seen by everyone who entered.* (experiencer)
        c. *The intersection was approached by five cars at once.* (theme)
        d. *The porcupine crate was received by Elmer's firm.* (recipient)

Applicative grammar treats all objects of *by* in (8a–d) as grammatical agents. Marantz assigns roles to these terms, because he lumps together grammatical and lexical meanings. One must strictly distinguish between and not confuse lexical and grammatical meanings. Grammatical meanings are obligatory meanings that are imposed by the structure of language, while lexical meanings are variables depending on the context. The grammatical meaning 'agent' assigned to a term is a formal meaning that treats an object denoted by the term as an agent no matter whether or not it is a real agent. Thus, the objects denoted by the terms in (5b–d) are not real agents, but linguistically they are treated *as if* they were real agents. Since lexical meanings are closer to reality, a conflict often arises between the lexical and grammatical meanings of a term. We can observe these conflicts in (5b–d), while in (5a) the lexical meaning of the term agrees with its grammatical meaning.

Every word has a number of meanings: some of them are lexical meanings, and others are grammatical meanings. Although from a structural standpoint the grammatical meanings are the most important, they are the least conspicuous. To dispel any illusions, we must understand that the grammatical meanings of a word are not directly accessible; they are blended with the lexical meanings. The blend of grammatical meaning and lexical meaning constitutes a heterogeneous object.

The Russian linguist Aleksandr Peškovskij, who was far ahead of his time, wrote about the heterogeneity of the meaning of the word as follows:

> We warn the reader against the antigrammatical hypnotism that comes from the material parts of words. For us, material and grammatical meanings are like forces applied to one and the same point (a word) but acting sometimes in the same direction, sometimes in intersecting directions, and sometimes *in exactly opposite directions*. And here we must be prepared to see that the force of the material meaning, just like the stream of a river carrying away an object, will be *obvious*, while the force of the formal meaning, just like the wind blowing against the stream and holding back the same object, will require special methods of analysis. (Peškovskij, 1934:71)

From a formal, grammatical standpoint, *The boy is seen by him* behaves exactly in the same way as *The boy was killed by him*. Grammatically, *by him* is agent and *the boy* is patient in both sentences. The predicate *was seen* implies an agent and a patient in the same way as the predicate *was killed*. The difference between the two predicates lies in their lexical meaning. Both *was seen* and *was killed* imply a grammatical agent as the meaning of the oblique term *by him*. But the lexical meaning of *was killed* is in keeping with the grammatical notion of agent, while the meaning of *was seen* conflicts with this notion. Likewise, in the sentence *Her younger sibling hates her, sibling* is an agent from a grammatical point of view and an experiencer from a lexical point of view. The lexical notion of the experiencer and the grammatical notion of the agent conflict in a construction with the verb *hate*.

True, there is an interaction between lexical and grammatical meanings. So, the lexical meaning of the verb *visit* restricts the use of passive constructions with this verb: we can say *John visited Rome*, but *Rome was visited by John* cannot be used unless we mean to achieve a comic effect. But that in no way compromises the fundamental distinction between grammatical and lexical meanings.

The grammatical meaning 'agent' can be separated from lexical meanings by means of a thought experiment. If we replace the lexical morphemes of a word with dummy morphemes, we obtain the grammatical structure of a sentence in its pure form.

Here is an example of such an experiment (Fries, 1952: 71):

(9)     a) *Woggles ugged diggles.*
        b) *Uggs woggled diggs.*
        c) *Woggs diggled uggles.*
        d) *A woggle ugged a diggle.*
        e) *An ugg woggles diggs.*
        f) *A diggled woggle ugged a woggled diggle.*

All of these sentences clearly are transitive active constructions, owing to the specific word order and nominal and verbal morphemes. It is clear that the primary terms in these sentences mean 'agent', while the secondary terms mean 'patient'. Now we can relate passive constructions to all of these sentences:

(10)   a) *Diggles were ugged by woggles.*
       b) *Diggs were woggled by uggs.*
          etc.

It is clear that the preposition *by* introduces a term meaning 'agent' in these sentences.

Now let us substitute a lexical morpheme for a dummy root in a verb. If we substitute the morpheme *hate* for a dummy verbal root, we will get sentences such as

(11)   *Woggles hated diggles.*

We can relate a passive construction to (11):

(12)   *Diggles were hated by woggles.*

From the viewpoint of the lexical meaning of *hate*, the primary term *woggles* in (11) and the oblique term in *by woggles* in (12) mean 'experiencer'. But this meaning has nothing to do with the grammatical meaning of these terms ('agent'), which remains invariant under various substitutions of lexical verbal roots whose meaning may often conflict with the grammatical meaning of the terms.

Lexical meanings are the meanings of morphemes that constitute word stems, while grammatical meanings are the meanings of inflexional morphemes, prepositions, conjunctions, and other devices, such as word order. Most current American works on grammar disregard the fundamental opposition *grammatical meaning : lexical meaning* and confound these notions. Recently, Foley and Van Valin have proposed the notions of *actor* and *undergoer*, which they define as "generalized semantic relations between a predicate and its arguments" (Foley and Van Valin, 1984: 29). 'Actor' and 'undergoer' are abstract notions that roughly correspond to the notions of 'grammatical agent' and 'grammatical patient' in the sense of applicative grammar. Still, Foley and Van Valin present these abstract notions as purely empirical generalizations, without defining the basis of their generalization. The work lacks a distinction between grammatical and lexical meanings, which is a necessary basis for the above and all other abstractions in grammar. We arrive at grammatical notions by separating, by abstracting, grammatical meanings from lexical meanings.

Rejecting the use of the notions 'agent' and 'patient' in formulating syntactic rules in view of the alleged vagueness of these notions, some linguists, among them Chomsky, Perlmutter, and Marantz, insist on positing a distinct grammatical level opposed to the level of semantic roles and dependencies. They adduce the dichotomy *syntax versus semantics* and advocate an autonomous syntax independent of semantics.

The dichotomy *syntax versus semantics* is false, because signs cannot be separated from meaning. The correct dichotomy is *grammar versus lexicon* rather than *syntax versus semantics*. Although grammar and lexicon interact, the grammatical structure of a sentence is relatively independent of lexical morphemes, and linguistic theory must do justice to this fundamental empirical fact. That means that linguistic theory must reject any kind of confusion of grammar with lexicon and must advocate the notion of autonomous grammar, in the sense of autonomy from lexicon rather than semantics.

A clear distinction between grammatical and lexical phenomena is a necessary condition for precision, for avoiding vagueness in semantic analysis. Semantic notions such as 'agent' seem to be imprecise and vague because of the confusion of grammar and lexicon. As a grammatical notion, the notion of agent is clear and precise insofar as it correlates with structural grammatical markers.

Let us turn to the second type of sentence construction—to the *active* system characterized by the opposition *active constructions: stative constructions*.

Here is how Boas and Deloria (1941) characterize this opposition in their *Dakota Grammar*:

> There is a fundamental distinction between verbs expressing states and those expressing actions. The two groups may be designated as neutral and active. The language has a marked tendency to give a strong preponderance to the concept of state. All our adjectives are included in this group, which embraces also almost all verbs that result in a state. Thus a stem like to "sever" is not active but expresses the concept of "to be in severed condition," the active verb being derived from this stem. The same is true of the concept "to scrape," the stem of which means "to be in a scraped condition." Other verbs which we class as active but which take no object, like "to tremble," are conceived in the same way, the stem meaning "to be a-tremble." Active verbs include terms that relate exclusively to animate beings, either as actors or as objects acted upon, such as words of going and coming, sounds uttered by animals and man, mental activities and those expressing actions that can affect only living beings (like "to kill," "to wound," etc.). There seem to be not more than 12 active words that would not be covered by this definition. (Boas and Deloria, 1941: 1)

Active languages have special morphological markers for a distinction between active and stative predicates and between terms denoting agents and nonagents. There are three morphological types of active and inactive constructions: 1) constructions with morphological markers only for predicates; 2) constructions with morphological markers for both predicates and terms; and 3) constructions with morphological markers only for terms. These morphological types of active and inactive constructions can be presented in the following diagram (Klimov, 1977: 58):

(13)    *Active construction*     *Inactive construction*
  1. $T \text{——} P_{act}$          1. $T \text{——} P_{stat}$
  2. $T_{agent} \text{——} P_{act}$   2. $T_{nonagent} \text{——} P_{stat}$
  3. $T_{agent} \text{——} P$         3. $T_{nonagent} \text{——} P$

The important thing to notice is that the opposition of one-place and two-place predicates is not essential for active and inactive constructions. These constructions typically consist of predicates with a single term, which by definition is a primary term. If a secondary term occurs, it is always optional.

## 9. The Paradox of Ergativity and Functional Superposition

In terms of morphological case markers and the notions of subject and direct object, the ergative system in languages such as Basque or Avar has traditionally been viewed as the system of case markers whereby the intransitive subject is identified with the transitive direct object morphologically, while the transitive subject receives a unique case marker. The ergative system contrasts with the accusative system in languages such as Russian, Latin, or German, in which the intransitive and transitive subjects are treated morphologically alike, while the transitive direct object receives the unique case marker. That can be illustrated by the following examples from Basque and Latin:

(1)    Basque (Lafitte, 1962):
    a) *Martin ethorri da.*
       Martin-Abs. came Aux.-3-Sg.
       'Martin came'.
    b) *Martin-ek hourra igorri du.*
       Martin-Erg. child-Abs. sent Aux.-3-Sg.
       'Martin sent the child'.

(In Basque the ergative case marker is -(e)k; the absolutive case has a zero case marker. The auxiliary *da* is used when there is a third person singular intransitive subject, and the auxiliary *du* is used when there is a third person singular transitive subject and a third person singular transitive direct object.)

(2)    Latin:
    a) *Venator necavit lupum.*
       hunter-Nom. kill-Perf. wolf-Acc.
       'The hunter has killed the wolf'.
    b) *Venator venit.*
       hunter-Nom. come-Perf.
       'The hunter has come'.

Such facts are well known, but in the recent decade it has been discovered that in many ergative languages some syntactic rules apply to the absolutives in intransitives, and the ergatives in the transitive constructions, in the same way as they do to the intransitive and transitive subjects in accusative languages. That can be illustrated as follows:

In the syntax of accusative languages, there is a rule called *Equi-NP Deletion*, which deletes the subject of the embedded clause if it is the same as the subject of the matrix clause. Examples:

(3)     English:
        a) *John wants to dance.* (from *\*John wants [ John dance]*)
        b) *John wants to see Mary.* (from *\*John wants [ John see Mary]*)
        c) *John can walk.* (from *\*John can [ John walk]*)

There is a syntactic rule called *Subject Raising*, which promotes the subject of the embedded clause into the matrix clause (the term *raising* has a metaphorical meaning: in a syntactic tree diagram, the embedded clause is located lower than the matrix clause). Examples:

(4)     English:
        a) *Peter happens to love Nancy.* (from *It happens that Peter loves Nancy*)
        b) *Jerry seems to be working.* (from *It seems that Jerry is working*)

There is a syntactic rule called *Conjunction Reduction*, which operates by reducing two sentences to one or some other process. Examples:

(5)     English:
        a) *Harry and Bill are working.* (from *Harry is working and Bill is working*)
        b) *Ralph sold his old car and bought a new one.* (from *Ralph sold his old car, and he bought a new one*)

It has been observed that in many ergative languages, Equi-NP Deletion, Subject Raising, Conjunction Reduction, and some other syntactic rules apply to a particular class of noun phrases—to a particular class of terms—namely, absolutives in the intransitive constructions and ergatives in the transitive constructions. Here is an example of the application of Equi-NP Deletion in Basque (Anderson, 1976: 12):

(6)     a. *dantzatzerat joan da*
           dance-infin-*to* go he is
           'He has gone to dance'.
        b. *txakurraren hiltzera joan nintzen.*
           dog-def-gen kill-infin-*to* go I-was
           'I went to kill the dog'.
        c. *ikhusterat joan da.*
           see-infin-*to* go he-is
           'He$_i$ has gone to see him$_j$'.
           *'He$_i$ has gone for him$_j$ to see him$_i$'.

The operation of Equi-NP Deletion does not depend on the transitivity of the verb in the matrix clause; the rule is controlled by both transitive verbs such as *want* and intransitive verbs such as *go*. It should be noted, however, that it is always ergatives and never absolutives that are deleted in the embedded clause.

Here is an example of Subject Raising in Tongan (Anderson, 1976: 13):

(7)　　a. *'Oku lava ke hū 'a Mele ki hono fale.*
　　　　　　pres possible tns enter abs Mary to his house
　　　　　　'It is possible for Mary to enter his house'.
　　　　b. *'Oku lava 'a Mele 'o hū ki hono fale.*
　　　　　　pres possible abs Mary tns enter to his house
　　　　　　'Mary can enter his house'.

In (7a) the subject *'a Mele* has been raised from the embedded clause. The rule also applies to transitive embedded clauses:

(8)　　a. *'Oku lava ke taa'i 'e Siale 'a e fefine.*
　　　　　　pres possible tns hit erg Charlie abs def woman
　　　　　　'It is possible for Charlie to hit the woman'.
　　　　b. *'Oku lava 'e Siale 'o taa'i 'a e fefine.*
　　　　　　pres possible erg Charlie tns hit abs def woman
　　　　　　'Charlie can hit the woman'.

The syntactic behavior of the ergative *'e Siale* is similar to the syntactic behavior of subjects in English that are raised out of embedded clauses. Ergatives thus can be raised out of the complements of *lava* 'be possible' regardless of transitivity. The syntactic behavior of absolutives is similar to the syntactic behavior of direct objects in corresponding English sentences: like direct objects, absolutives cannot be raised out of embedded sentences:

(9)　　*'Oku lava 'a e fefine 'o taa'i 'e Siale.*
　　　　pres possible abs def woman tns hit erg Charlie
　　　　'The woman can be hit (by Charlie)'.

If the ergatives in (7), (8), and (9) are interpreted as subjects and absolutives as direct objects, then Subject Raising applies in Tongan in the same sense as in English.

On the basis of this observation, a number of linguists (among them, Anderson, 1976; Comrie, 1978, 1979; Dixon, 1979) claim that absolutives in intransitive constructions and ergatives in transitive ones constitute exactly the same syntactic class denoted by the term *subject* in accusative languages, and to fail to recognize that as such is to miss a generalization. Because of this generalization, languages such as Basque or Tongan are considered to be morphologically ergative but syntactically accusative.

The linguists who make this claim must be given credit for unearthing the facts of syntax that call for explanation. No matter whether or not we agree with their argument, we must recognize it and contend with its full force and subtlety. Let us consider this argument in detail.

In one of the most important contributions to the study of ergativity, Stephen R. Anderson adduces that on the basis of rules such as Equi-NP Deletion and Subject Raising, embedded intransitive and transitive subjects are no more distinguished in Basque, an ergative language, than in English, an accusative language, and that subjects and direct objects are discriminated in both languages alike. Anderson concludes: "Rules such as those we have been considering, when investigated in virtually any ergative language, point unambiguously in the direction we have indicated. They show, that is, that from a syntactic point of view these languages are organized in the same way as are accusative languages, and that the basically syntactic notion of 'subject' has essentially the same reference in both language types" (Anderson, 1976: 16). Anderson admits that Dyirbal is different from accusative languages with respect to its syntax, but he regards that as an insignificant anomaly. He writes: "Dyirbal, which as noted differs fundamentally from the usual type, is in fact the exception which proves the rule" (Anderson, 1976: 23).

The fact that the same rules, such as Equi-NP Deletion and Subject Raising, apply both to subjects in accusative languages and to ergatives in ergative languages calls for explanation. Anderson and other linguists who share the same views must be given credit for showing that this fact engenders a problem. The formulation of a new problem is often more essential than its solution. Given the failure of a solution to a new significant problem, one can never return to old ideas in order to find a new solution; one has to search for new concepts, which marks the real advance in science. The claim that the syntactic organization of most ergative languages follows the pattern of accusative languages may be questioned, but the arguments that have been advanced for this claim must be surmounted within a fresh conceptual framework. That will be not a return to an old idea but an advance to a new idea giving a new significance to the old concept of ergativity.

It cannot be denied that in most ergative languages, with respect to the application of Equi and Subject Raising, ergatives are similar to transitive subjects in accusative languages. But does this similarity justify the generalization that in ergative languages the NPs to which Equi and Subject Raising apply belong to the class of subjects?

To answer this question, we must bear in mind that the subject is a cluster concept, that is, a concept that is characterized by a set of properties rather than by a single property. The application of Equi and Subject Raising is not a sufficient criterion for determining the class of subjects. Among other criteria, there is at least one that is crucial for characterizing the class of subjects. I mean the fundamental *Criterion of the Nonomissibility of the Subject*. A nonsubject can be eliminated from a sentence, which will still remain a complete sentence. But that is not normally true of the subject. For instance:

(10)    a. *John paints a landscape.*
        b. *John paints.*
        c. **Paints a landscape.*

The Criterion of the Nonomissibility of the subject is so important that some linguists consider it a single essential feature for the formal characterization of the subject (Martinet, 1975: 219–24). This criterion is high on Keenan's Subject Properties List (Keenan, 1976: 313; Keenan uses the term *indispensability* instead of *nonomissibility*).

Omissibility should not be confused with ellipsis. Ellipsis is a rule of eliminating syntactic units in specific contexts, and the opposition *omission:ellipsis* is one of the important aspects of the syntactic structure of any natural language.

When we apply a rule of ellipsis, we can always recover the term that was dropped by ellipsis; but an omitted term cannot be recovered: if in *John ate clams* we omit *clams*, we get *John ate*, and *clams* cannot be recovered because, starting from *John ate*, we do not know which noun was omitted.

Every language has specific rules of ellipsis. Thus, in Latin the rule of ellipsis requires the use of predicates without personal pronouns. In Latin we normally say *Amo* 'I love'. That is a complete sentence with a predicate and a subject that is implied by the context. In Latin we may say *Ego amo* only in case we want to place a stylistic stress on the personal pronoun. In Russian, the rules of ellipsis are directly opposite to the rules of ellipsis in Latin: the normal Russian sentence corresponding to Latin *Amo* is *Ja ljublju*, without the ellipsis of the personal pronoun; but if we want to place a stylistic stress, we use ellipsis and say *Ljublju*. The Russian *Ljublju* is as complete a sentence as Latin *Amo*. Both sentences have a subject and a predicate.

Mel'čuk characterizes the Criterion of Nonomissibility as follows:

> Deletability (called also dispensability; see Van Valin 1977: 690) is a powerful and reliable test for the privileged status of any NP: if there is in the language only one type of NP which cannot be omitted from the surface-syntactic structure of the sentence without affecting the grammaticality of the latter or its independence from the linguistic content, then this NP is syntactically privileged. Note that in English it is GS [grammatical subject] (and only GS) that possesses the property of non-deletability among all types of NP. To put it differently, if a grammatical sentence in English includes only one NP it must be GS. (Imperative sentences like *Read this book!*, etc. do not contradict the last statement.) Based on such cases as *Wash yourself/yourselves!*, *Everybody stand up!* and the like, a GS—*you*—is postulated in their surface-syntactic structures, where this GS cannot be omitted. It does not appear in the actual sentence following some rules of ellipsis. As for pseudo-imperative sentences of the type *Fuck you, bas-*

*tard!*, these are explained away in the penetrating essay by Quang (1971). (Mel'čuk, 1983: 235–36)

The Criterion of the Nonomissibility of the Subject excludes the possibility of languages where subjects could be eliminated from sentences. Yet precisely such is the case with ergative languages, if we identify ergatives with transitive subjects and absolutives with intransitive subjects in intransitive constructions and with transitive objects in transitive constructions. In many ergative languages, we can normally eliminate ergatives, but we cannot eliminate absolutives from transitive constructions. Here is an example from Tongan (Churchward, 1953: 69):

(11)     a. *'Oku taki au 'e Siale.*
             'Charlie leads me'.
         b. *'Oku taki au.*
             'Leads me (I am led)'.

*'e Siale* in (11a) is an ergative. It is omitted in (11b), which is a normal way of expressing in Tongan what we express in English by means of a passive verb (Tongan does not have passive).

Notice that in accusative languages the opposition *subject : direct object* is normally correlated with the opposition *active voice : passive voice*, while ergative languages normally do not have the opposition *active voice : passive voice*. This fact has significant consequences. In order to compensate for the lack of the passive, ergative languages use the omission of ergatives as a normal syntactic procedure that corresponds to passivization in accusative languages (an absolutive in a construction with an omitted ergative corresponds to a subject in a passive construction in an accusative language), or use focus rules that make it possible to impart prominence to any member of a sentence (in this case either an absolutive or an ergative may correspond to a subject in an accusative language). Here is an example of the application of focus rules in Tongan (Churchward, 1953: 67):

(12)     a. *Na'e tamate'i 'e Tēvita 'a Kōlaiate.*
             'David killed Goliath'.
         b. *Na'e tamate'i 'a Kōlaiate 'e Tēvita.*
             'Goliath was killed by David'.

Sentence (12a) corresponds to *David killed Goliath* in English, while (12b) corresponds to *Goliath was killed by David*. In the first case, the ergative *'e Tēvita* corresponds to the subject *David* in the active construction, while in the second case, the absolutive *'a Kōlaiate* corresponds to the subject *Goliath* in the passive. The focus rule gives prominence to the noun that immediately follows the verb, that is, to *'e Tēvita* in (12a) and to *'a Kōlaiate* in (12b).

In Tongan, as in many other ergative languages, we are faced with a serious difficulty resulting from the following contradiction: if the class of subjects is characterized by the application of Equi and Subject Raising, then ergatives are subjects in transitive constructions and absolutives are subjects in intransitive constructions; but if the class of subjects is characterized by the Criterion of the Nonomissibility of the Subject, then only absolutives can be subjects in transitive constructions. Since we cannot dispense with either of these criteria, that creates contradiction in defining the essential properties of the subject.

One might question whether we cannot dispense with either criterion. What if we choose to define subject in terms of one and disregard the other? The answer is that no essential criterion can be dispensed with in a theoretically adequate definition, because any theoretically adequate definition must include all essential features of the defined concept. We could dispense with one of these criteria only if we considered one of them inessential, that is, relating to an accidental feature of subject. But, as is well known, nonomissibility is a nonaccidental, permanent, essential feature of subject: subject is nonomissible because it is a syntactically distinguished, central, highly privileged term of a sentence in a given language. On the other hand, the behavior of subject with respect to Equi-NP Deletion and Subject Raising is also essential; therefore, we cannot dispense with this criterion, either. The two criteria are essential in defining the notion of subject, but at the same time they contradict one another when the notion of ergative is equated with the notion of subject. This contradiction I call the *paradox of ergativity*.

To solve this paradox, we must recognize that *ergative* and *absolutive* cannot be defined in terms of *subject* and *object*, but, rather, these are distinct primitive syntactic functions.

Since the terms *ergative* and *absolutive* are already used for the designation of morphological cases, I introduce special symbols with superscripts which will be used when ambiguity might arise as to whether syntactic functions or morphological cases are meant: $ERG^F$ means the syntactic function 'ergative', while $ERG^C$ means the morphological case 'ergative'. Similarly, $ABS^F$ and $ABS^C$.

The syntactic functions 'absolutive' and 'ergative' should be strictly distinguished from the morphological cases 'absolutive' and 'ergative'. First, some languages, such as Abkhaz or Mayan languages, are case-less, but they have the syntactic functions 'absolutive' and 'ergative'. Second, the syntactic function 'ergative' can be denoted not only by the ergative case but also by other oblique cases and coding devices (including word order). Of course, we must establish operational definitions of the syntactic functions 'absolutive' and 'ergative'. An instance of such an operational definition is presented in section 10.1.

The syntactic functions 'ergative' and 'absolutive' must be regarded as primitives independent of the syntactic functions 'subject' and 'object'.

We can now formulate the Correspondence Hypothesis:

The morphological opposition of case markings $ERG^C:ABS^C$ corresponds to the syntactic opposition $ERG^F:ABS^F$, which is independent of the syntactic opposition *subject:object* in accusative languages.

The symbols $ERG^C$ and $ABS^C$ are generalized designations of case markings. So, $ERG^C$ may designate not only an ergative case morpheme but any oblique case morpheme, say a dative or instrumental, or a class of morphemes that are in a complementary distribution, such as case markings of ergative.

Let us now compare the two particular classes of terms to which the syntactic rules in question apply: 1) the intransitive and transitive subjects in accusative languages, and 2) the absolutives in intransitive clauses and ergatives in transitive clauses in ergative languages. The first class is homogeneous with respect to nonomissibility (both intransitive and transitive subjects are nonomissible terms), but the second class is heterogeneous with respect to this property of terms: the absolutives are nonomissible, while ergatives are omissible terms. The heterogeneity of the class of terms to which the syntactic rules in question apply in ergative languages is an anomaly that calls for an explanation. We face the problem: How to resolve the contradiction that the ergative, which is the omissible term of a clause, is treated under the rules in question as if it were the nonomissible term?

In order to solve our problem, let us now consider more closely the syntactic oppositions *ergative:absolutive* and *subject:object*. Both of these oppositions can be neutralized. Thus, ergatives and absolutives contrast only as arguments of two-place predicates. The point of neutralization is the NP position in a one-place predicate where only an absolutive occurs.

The question arises, What is the meaning of the syntactic functions *ergative* and *absolutive*?

Ergative means 'agent', which we will symbolize by $A$. Absolutive, contrasting with ergative, means 'patient'—henceforth symbolized by $P$. Since, in the point of neutralization, an absolutive replaces the opposition *ergative:absolutive*, it can function either as an ergative or as an absolutive, contrasting with ergative; that is, semantically it may mean either 'agent' (the meaning of an ergative) or 'patient' (the meaning of an absolutive contrasting with an ergative).

The absolutive is a neutral-negative (unmarked) member of the syntactic opposition *ergative:absolutive*, and the ergative is a positive (marked) member of this opposition. That can be represented by the following diagram:

(13)

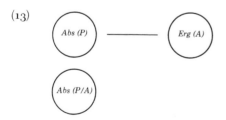

The meaning of subject and object is defined in terms of *A* and *P* as follows:

Object means *P*; subject contrasting with object means *A*. In the point of neutralization, subject replaces the opposition *subject : object*. Therefore, it can function either as subject contrasting with object or as object; that is, semantically, it may mean either 'agent' (the meaning of subject contrasting with object) or 'patient' (the meaning of object).

The subject is a neutral-negative (unmarked) member of the syntactic opposition *subject : object*, and the object is a positive (marked) member of this opposition. That can be represented by the following diagram:

(14)

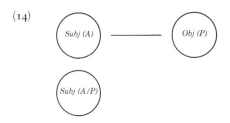

We come up with the opposition *unmarked term : marked term*. On the basis of this opposition, we establish the following correspondence between cases in ergative and accusative constructions:

(15)

| Opposition of markedness | Ergative construction | Accusative construction |
|---|---|---|
| Unmarked term | Absolutive | Subject |
| Marked term | Ergative | Object |

Examples of the neutralization of syntactic oppositions in English (an accusative language):

(16)   a. *John opened the door.*
       b. *John slept.*
       c. *The doors open.*
       d. *The doors are opened.*

In (16a), which is a transitive construction, the transitive subject *John* is an agent, and the transitive object *the door* is a patient. In the intransitive constructions, a subject denotes either an agent, as in (16b), or a patient, as in (16c) and (16d).

Examples of neutralization of syntactic oppositions in Tongan (an ergative language):

(17)   a. *Na'e inu   'a   e   kava 'e   Sione.*
       Past drink Abs. the kava Erg. John
       'John drank the kava'.

    *b. Na'e inu    'a    Sione.*
      Past drink Abs. John
      'John drank'.
    *c. Na'e lea    'a    Tolu.*
      Past speak Abs. Tolu
      'Tolu spoke'.
    *d. Na'e 'uheina 'a e ngoué.*
      'The garden was rained upon'.

In (17a) the ergative *'e Sione* denotes an agent, and the absolutive *'a e kava* denotes a patient. In (17b) the transitive *inu* is used as an intransitive verb; therefore, here we have the absolutive *'a Sione* instead of the ergative *'e Sione*. In (17c) the absolutive *'a Tolu* denotes an agent. In (17d) the absolutive *'a e ngoué* denotes a patient.

Speaking of the neutralization of syntactic oppositions in ergative languages, we should not confuse ergative languages with *active* (or *agentive*) *languages*. Some linguists consider active languages to be a variety of ergative languages. This view is incorrect: as was shown in section 8 of this chapter, active languages are polarly opposed to both ergative and accusative languages. Sapir distinguished the active construction (typified by Dakota) from both the ergative construction (typified by Chinook) and the accusative construction (typified by Paiute) (Sapir, 1917: 86). The ergative and accusative constructions are both based upon a verbal opposition *transitive:intransitive*, while for the active construction the basis of verbal classification is not the opposition *transitive: intransitive* (which is absent here) but rather a classification of verbs as *active* and *inactive* (*stative*). In a series of publications, G. A. Klimov has demonstrated the radical distinctness of the active construction from the ergative and accusative constructions and has provided a typology of the active constructions (Klimov, 1972, 1973, 1974, 1977). The notion of the active construction as radically distinct from the ergative construction is shared by a number of contemporary linguists (see, for example, Aronson, 1977; Dik, 1978; Kibrik, 1979). In active languages, the verbal classification as active and inactive correlates with the formal opposition of terms *active* (*agent*)*:inactive* (*patient*). Since this opposition is valid for both two-place and one-place predicates (a one-place predicate can be combined with a noun in an active or in an inactive case), the NP position in a one-place predicate cannot be considered a point of the neutralization of the opposition *active:inactive*. So, the notion of syntactic neutralization is inapplicable to active constructions. Therefore, the discussion below of the consequences of syntactic neutralization in ergative languages does not apply to active languages, where syntactic neutralization is absent.

The markedness relation between absolutive and ergative subject and object is defined by the Markedness Law (given on page 122):

> Given two semiotic units *A* and *B* which are members of a binary opposition *A:B*, if the range of *A* is wider than the range of *B*, then the set

of the relevant features of *A* is narrower than the set of the relevant features of *B*, which has a plus relevant feature.

The binary opposition *A : B* characterized by the Markedness Law is called the *markedness relation* between *A* and *B*; *A* is called the *unmarked term* and *B*, the *marked term* of this opposition.

Under the Markedness Law, absolutives and subjects are unmarked terms, and ergatives and objects are marked ones, because absolutives and subjects occur with both one-place and two-place predicates, while ergatives and objects occur only with two-place predicates.

The relation of markedness in a sentence is characterized by the Dominance Law (given on page 123):

> *The marked term in a sentence cannot occur without the unmarked term, while the unmarked term can occur without the marked term.*

A corollary of the Dominance Law is that the unmarked term of a sentence is its central, its independent term. By contrast, the marked term of a sentence is its marginal, its dependent term. I will call the unmarked term the *primary term* and the marked term the *secondary term.*

The Dominance Law explains why the marked term is omissible and the unmarked term is nonomissible in a clause representing the opposition *unmarked term : marked term.* The marked term is omissible because the unmarked term does not presuppose the occurrence of the marked term. And the unmarked term is nonomissible because the marked term presupposes the occurrence of the unmarked term; that is, it cannot occur without the unmarked term.

It is to be noted that the Dominance Law makes an empirical claim that must be validated by empirical research. But this law, like any other linguistic law, is an idealization of linguistic reality in the same sense as physical laws are idealizations of physical reality. Just as in physics empirical research discovers empirically explicable deviations from physical laws, so in linguistics empirical research has to discover empirically explicable deviations from linguistic laws. Empirically explicable deviations from a law should not be confused with real counterexamples that undermine the law. Thus, in (10) and (11) I gave some examples of the omissibility and nonomissibility of terms that can be explained by the Dominance Law. But it is easy to find apparent counterexamples to this law. For example, one could produce a sentence such as *John weighs 150 pounds* as such a counterexample. But here we have a semantically explicable deviation from the law rather than a counterexample. If we analyze such sentences, we discover a semantic constraint on the omissibility of the direct object: *If the meaning of the transitive predicate is incomplete without the meaning of the direct object, then the direct object cannot be omitted.* This constraint has nothing to do with the syntactic structure of a sentence; it belongs in the realm of semantics. There may be found other apparent counterexamples to the law that actually are deviations explicable by rules of ellipsis or some other clearly defined constraints.

We can now formulate a law that I call the Law of Duality:

> The marked term of an ergative construction corresponds to the unmarked term of an accusative construction, and the unmarked term of an ergative construction corresponds to the marked term of an accusative construction; and, vice versa, the marked term of an accusative construction corresponds to the unmarked term of an ergative construction, and the unmarked term of an accusative construction corresponds to the marked term of an ergative construction.

An accusative construction and an ergative construction will be called *duals* of each other.

The Law of Duality means that accusative and ergative constructions relate to each other as mirror images. The marked and unmarked terms in accusative and ergative constructions are polar categories, like, for example, positive and negative electric charges; a correspondence of unmarked terms to marked terms and of marked terms to unmarked terms can be compared to what physicists call 'charge conjugation', a change of all plus charges to minus and all minus charges to plus.

The proposed Law of Duality also reminds one of laws of duality in projective geometry and mathematical logic. For example, in logic duals are formed by changing alternation to conjunction in a formula and vice versa.

The Law of Duality is valid in phonology, as well. Consider, for instance, the opposition $d:t$ in Russian and the opposition $d:t$ in Danish. On the surface these two oppositions are the same. But, as a matter of fact, the Russian $d:t$ is a case of the opposition *voiced:voiceless*, and the Danish $d:t$ is a case of the opposition *lax:tense*.

In Danish the neutralization of the opposition $d:t$ results in $d$, which can represent either $d$ or $t$. So, $d$ is a neutral-negative (unmarked) member of the opposition $d:t$, and $t$ is a positive (marked) member of this opposition. That can be represented by the following diagram:

In Russian the neutralization of the opposition $d:t$ results in $t$, which can represent either $d$ or $t$. So, $t$ is a neutral-negative (unmarked) member of the opposition $d:t$, and $d$ is a positive (marked) member of this opposition. That can be represented by the following diagram:

We come up with the opposition *unmarked term : marked term* in phonology. On the basis of this opposition, we establish the following correspondence between members of the oppositions *lax : tense* and *voiced : voiceless*.

(18) 

| Opposition of markedness | lax : tense | voiced : voiceless |
|---|---|---|
| Unmarked phoneme | d | t |
| Marked phoneme | t | d |

Now we can apply the Law of Duality in phonology:

> The marked term of the opposition *lax : tense* corresponds to the unmarked term of the opposition *voiced : voiceless*, and the unmarked term of the opposition *lax : tense* corresponds to the marked term of the opposition *voiced : voiceless*; and, vice versa, the marked term of the opposition *voiced : voiceless* corresponds to the unmarked term of the opposition *lax : tense*, and the unmarked term of the opposition *voiced : voiceless* corresponds to the marked term of the opposition *lax : tense*.

Let us now turn to our main problem, which, in the light of the Markedness Law, can be restated as follows: How can we resolve the contradiction that ergative, which is the secondary (marked) term of a clause, is treated under the above rules as if it were the primary (unmarked) term of a clause?

In order to resolve this contradiction, we must rely on the notion of functional superposition introduced in section 6.3 of this chapter. Functional superposition means that any syntactic unit has its own characteristic syntactic function, but in addition, it can take on the function of any other syntactic unit, so that this function is superposed onto the characteristic function. The notion of functional superposition throws light on our problem. The important thing to notice is that only primary terms can appear in the intransitive clauses. An identification of a term of the transitive clause with the primary term of the intransitive clause involves a superposition of the function of the primary term in the intransitive clause onto the function of the given term of the transitive clause. Three possibilities are open: 1) only the primary term of a transitive clause can be identified with the primary term of an intransitive clause (no superposition); 2) only the secondary term of a transitive clause can be identified with the primary term of an intransitive clause (a superposition of the function of the primary term); or 3) both the primary and the secondary terms of a transitive sentence can be identified with the primary term of an intransitive sentence (no superposition or the superposition of the function of the primary term of an intransitive clause onto the secondary term of the transitive clause).

Accusative languages realize only the first possibility: both intransitive subject and transitive subject are primary terms. But all three possibilities are realized in ergative languages: 1) the syntactic rules in question are stated with reference to only absolutes in intransitive and transitive clauses (Dyirbal); 2) the syntactic rules in question are stated with reference to absolutes in intransitive clauses and ergatives in transitive clauses (Basque); and 3) the syntactic rules in question are stated with reference to absolutes in intransitive clauses and to absolutes and ergatives in transitive clauses (Archi, a Daghestan language; Kibrik, 1979: 71–72).

The notion of functional superposition in the ergative construction should not be confused with the notion of the pivot introduced by Dixon (1979). These notions have nothing in common. Rather, they are opposed to each other. While the notion of functional superposition, characterizing a syncretic property of syntactic units, reveals the radical distinctness of the syntactic structure of the ergative construction from the syntactic structure of the accusative construction, *pivot* is nothing but a descriptive term that glosses over this distinctness. Dixon uses symbol $S$ to denote an intransitive subject, symbol $A$ to denote a transitive subject, and symbol $O$ to denote a transitive object. Syntactic rules may treat $S$ and $A$ in the same way, or they may treat $S$ and $O$ in the same way: "we refer to $S/A$ and $S/O$ pivots respectively" (Dixon, 1979: 132). Dixon writes: "Many languages which have an ergative morphology do not have ergative syntax; instead syntactic rules seem to operate on an 'accusative' principle treating $S$ and $A$ in the same way" (Dixon, 1979: 63). Referring to Anderson (1976), Dixon relegates Basque and most other ergative languages (except Dyirbal and a few others) to a class of languages that have ergative morphology but accusative syntax. Thus, in spite of a different terminology, Dixon shares the same view as Anderson and other linguists who claim that the syntactic structure of ergative constructions in most ergative languages is identical with the syntactic structure of accusative constructions.

Why does functional superposition occur in ergative constructions and not in accusative constructions? This fact can be explained by a semantic hypothesis advanced on independent grounds. According to this hypothesis based on the semiotic principle of iconicity, the sequence *agent-patient* is more natural than the sequence *patient-agent,* because the first sequence is an image of a natural hierarchy according to which the agent is the starting point and the patient is the end point of an action. The semantic hierarchy *agent-patient* coincides with the syntactic hierarchy *transitive subject-direct object* in accusative languages, because transitive subject denotes agent and direct object denotes patient. But this semantic hierarchy contradicts the syntactic hierarchy *absolutive-ergative,* because absolutive, being syntactically a primary term, denotes 'patient', which is semantically a secondary term, and ergative, being syntactically a secondary term, denotes 'agent', which is semantically a primary term. Hence, under the pressure of the semantic hierarchy *agent-patient,* functional superposition assigns to the ergative the role of a syntactically primary term.

I propose the following definition of the notions 'accusative construction' and 'ergative construction':

1. The *accusative construction* and *ergative construction* are two representations of the abstract transitive/intransitive clause pattern: *primary term + transitive predicate + secondary term/primary term + intransitive predicate.*
2. Primary term is represented by *subject* in the accusative construction and by *absolutive* in the ergative construction. Secondary term is represented by *direct object* in the accusative construction and by *ergative* in the ergative construction.
3. The abstract clause pattern and its representations are characterized by the Markedness Law and the Dominance Law.
4. There is a correlation between the accusative and ergative constructions characterized by the Law of Duality.
5. The primary and secondary terms may exchange their functions, so that the function of the primary term is superposed onto the secondary term, and the function of the secondary term is superposed onto the primary term.

In order to make the rules Equi and Subject Raising valid for both accusative and ergative languages, we have to replace them with more abstract rules: *Equi-Primary Term Deletion* and *Primary Term Raising.* The generalizations expressed by these abstract rules solve the problem raised by Anderson. Contrary to his claim, there are neither subjects nor direct objects in ergative languages: ergative and absolutive are distinct primitive syntactic functions. What ergative and accusative constructions have in common is that they are different realizations of the abstract construction *primary term:secondary term.* The new abstract rules represent a correct generalization that cannot be captured in terms of the subject and direct object.

The rules Equi-Primary Term Deletion and Primary Term Raising lay bare the parallelism between the syntactic structure of the ergative construction in Dyirbal and the syntactic structure of the accusative construction, but a sharp difference between the syntactic structures of the ergative construction in Basque and similar ergative languages and the accusative construction. Since in Dyirbal the rules in question apply only to absolutives both in intransitive and in transitive constructions, the only difference between the ergative construction in Dyirbal and an accusative construction, say, in English, boils down to a mirror-image semantic interpretation: while primary terms in Dyirbal ergative constructions denote patients and secondary terms, agents, in any accusative construction, quite the reverse, primary terms denote agents and secondary terms, patients. Let us consider an example of the ergative construction from Dyirbal (Dixon, 1972):

(19)  *Yabu*        *ŋuma+ŋgu*       *buṛa+n.*
       mother       father+Agent     see+Past

```
primary,    secondary         ergative
patient     agent             predicate
'Mother was seen by father'.
```

Compare (19) with the English sentence

(20)    *Father      saw mother.*
        primary,    secondary
        agent       patient

We see that the syntactic function of *yabu* denoting a patient in (19) is a counterpart of the syntactic function of *father* denoting an agent in (20), while the syntactic function of *ɲuma+ŋgu* denoting an agent in (19) is a counterpart of the syntactic function of *mother* denoting a patient in (20).

Now, if we turn to a comparison of Basque and English, we discover a sharp difference between the syntactic structures of accusative and ergative constructions. Consider some examples from Basque discussed by Anderson (1976: 12; see (6) above):

(21)    *Dantzatzerat    jo-an     da.*
        dance-infin-*to*    go        he-is
        'He has gone to dance'.

(22)    *Txakurraren    hiltzera       joan      nintzen.*
        dog-def-gen     kill-infin-*to*    go        I was
        'I went to kill the dog'.

The deleted term from the embedded clause in the underlying structure has to be absolutive in (21) and ergative in (22).

In (22) the syntactic structure of the embedded ergative clause is very different from the syntactic structure of the embedded accusative clause in English, because the deleted ergative in the former has a syntactic behavior that is sharply distinct from the syntactic behavior of the deleted subject in the latter. While subject is an intrinsically primary term, ergative is an intrinsically secondary term. In (22) ergative functions as a primary term, but the function of the primary term is superposed onto ergative, whose characteristic intrinsic syntactic function is to serve as a secondary term. Since in (22) ergative functions as a primary term, the function of the secondary term is superposed onto absolutive, whose characteristic function is to serve as a primary term. The important thing to notice is that in transitive clauses similar to (22), neither ergative nor absolutive loses its characteristic function, and, consequently, absolutive can never be deleted in these clauses, while ergative can, in accordance with the Dominance Law, which holds that secondary terms presuppose primary terms, while primary terms do not presuppose secondary terms.

In summary, there is parallelism and at the same time a sharp difference between the syntactic structures of the ergative and accusative constructions. In order to do justice to both the parallelism and the difference, we have to state our generalizations and rules in terms of the abstract notions 'primary term' and 'secondary term'. The rules Equi-Primary Term Deletion and Primary Term Raising capture what ergative and accusative constructions have in common and at the same time reflect the laws and principles characterizing a profound difference between the two types of syntactic constructions.

Thus, we have come to a conclusion that is diametrically opposite to Anderson's view on ergativity. He claims that the majority of ergative languages, with the exception of Dyirbal and a few similar languages, have the same syntactic structure as accusative languages. We claim, on the contrary, that the syntactic structure of the majority of ergative languages differs sharply from the syntactic structure of accusative languages, with the exception of Dyirbal, whose syntactic structure exhibits parallelism with the syntactic structure of accusative languages, while not being identical with it.

The theory of ergativity advanced above I call the *Integrated Theory of Ergativity*, because, rather than opposing morphological ergativity and syntactic ergativity, this theory integrates the two notions of ergativity into a single notion of ergativity.

## 10. Some Implications of the Integrated Theory of Ergativity for Linguistic Typology

Now, after I have shown that the Integrated Theory of Ergativity resolves the fundamental problems posed by ergative constructions, I will put it to a further test by tracing out its consequences that bear upon linguistic typology. I will show that this theory is able to explain some further linguistic phenomena.

So long as everything proceeds according to his prior expectations, a linguist has no opportunity to improve on his linguistic theory. Improvements on a linguistic theory result from the search for explanations of anomalous facts.

The statement about the importance of anomalous facts for improving on linguistic theories needs to be qualified. Not all anomalies are equally important for a linguistic theory. For instance, irregular plurals in English, such as *mice* from *mouse*, are anomalous, but they are not crucial for a theory of English grammar: these facts belong in the lexicon. Only if *significant* anomalies can be demonstrated will there be a genuine theoretical issue to face.

A fact that is a significant anomaly for a given linguistic theory I call a *linguistic phenomenon*.

It follows from the definition of the linguistic phenomenon that this concept is relative to a given theory. A fact that is anomalous from the standpoint of one theory may be regular from the standpoint of another theory.

To explain a linguistic phenomenon is to subsume it under a conceptual framework from whose point of view it ceases to be anomalous and is considered regular.

In testing a linguistic theory, it is important to find out whether this theory can make sense of linguistic phenomena for which there is no way of accounting using the currently accepted theories and, in addition, of all those phenomena that contravene these theories.

Let us now consider further consequences of the Integrated Theory of Ergativity. These consequences will be presented under the following headings:

1. Ergativity as a grammatical category
2. Accessibility to relative clause formation
3. Voices in ergative languages
4. Split ergativity
5. The class of ergative languages
6. The practical results anticipated

## 10.1 Ergativity as a Grammatical Category

One fundamental consequence of this theory is that only those ergative processes can be considered formal ergative processes that correlate with ergative morphology.

I propose a broad definition of morphology that includes any coding device of a language. Under this definition, word order is part of morphology. The Abkhaz and Mayan languages are case-less, but since they have coding devices for marking case relations, these coding devices are covered by my definition of morphology.

Ergative expressions can be found in languages that do not have ergative morphology; that is, they are not distinguished by coding devices (Moravcsik, 1978). For example, as far as nominalizations are concerned, Russian, an accusative language, has ergative expressions: genitive functions as absolutive, and instrumental functions as ergative (Comrie, 1978: 375–76). In French and Turkish, both accusative languages, there are causative constructions that are formed on ergative principles (Comrie, 1976: 262–63); in French there are antipassive constructions (Postal, 1977).

Do ergative expressions not distinguished by coding devices belong to a distinct grammatical category, that is, to a distinct grammatical class?

A language is a sign system. And in accordance with the Principle of Semiotic Relevance, two different grammatical meanings are distinct if they correlate with different signs, that is, with different coding devices. Consequently, two classes of expressions belong to different grammatical categories if the difference between their grammatical meanings correlates with different coding devices. For lack of this correlation, the two classes belong to the same grammatical category.

In studying natural languages, one may discover various linguistic relations.

But if given linguistic relations are not distinguished from one another by at least one distinct coding rule, then they are variants of the same linguistic relation.

Ergative expressions can constitute a distinct grammatical category in a given language only if they are distinguished from other classes of expressions by at least one distinct coding rule.

In order to make my case concrete, I will consider ergative expressions in Russian. It is claimed that "as far as nominalizations are concerned, Russian has in effect an ergative system" (Comrie, 1978: 376). This claim is based on the following data.

In Russian, passive constructions can be nominalized. For example, we may have

(1)    a.  *Gorod razrušen       vragom.*
           city    has-been-destroyed enemy-by
           'The city has been destroyed by the enemy'.
    b.  *razrušenie  goroda vragom*
         destruction city-of  enemy-by
         'the city's destruction by the enemy'

(1b) is the nominalization of (1a). In (1b) the genitive *goroda* denotes a patient, the instrumental *vragom* denotes an agent, and the verbal noun *razrušenie* corresponds to a transitive predicate. This nominal construction correlates with a nominal construction in which a verbal noun corresponds to an intransitive predicate and genitive denotes an agent, for example:

(2)    *priezd vraga*
    arrival enemy-of
    'the enemy's arrival'

If we compare (1b) with (2), we can see that the patient in (1b) and the agent in (2) stand in the genitive (functioning as an absolutive), while the agent in (1b) stands in the instrumental (functioning as an ergative). Therefore, we can conclude that in Russian nominalizations involve ergativity.

Does ergativity constitute a distinct formal category in Russian nominal constructions?

Consider the following example of nominalization in Russian:

(3)    a.  *Ivan prenebregaet zanjatijami.*
          John neglects      studies
          'John neglects his studies'.
    b.  *prenebreženie Ivana    zanjatijami*
         Neglect       John(Gen) studies(Instr)
         'John's neglect of his studies'

The surface structure of (3b) is the same as the surface structure of (1b), but the instrumental *zanjatijami* denotes a patient rather than an agent, and the genitive *Ivana* denotes an agent rather than a patient. In this instance of nominalization, the instrumental *zanjatijami* functions as an object, and the genitive *Ivana* functions as a subject.

It is not difficult to find more examples of nominalization in which instrumentals denote patients rather than agents and genitives denote agents rather than patients. This type of nominalization occurs in a large class of verbs that take an object in the instrumental, such as *rukovodit'* 'to guide', *upravljat'* 'to manage', *torgovat'* 'to sell', etc.

All these examples show that Russian does not use any coding devices to make ergativity a distinct formal category in nominal constructions. True, ergativity differs from other relations denoted by the instrumental in Russian nominal constructions. But since ergativity is not distinguished from other relations in the opposition *instrumental : genitive* by at least one coding rule, ergativity does not constitute a distinct formal category and is simply a member of the class of relations denoted by the instrumental in Russian nominal constructions.

One may object to the above analysis of the ergative pattern and the meaning of the instrumental in Russian nominal constructions by pointing out that in Dyirbal and other Australian languages, the instrumental is used as an equivalent of both the ergative and the instrumental in other ergative languages. Why, one might ask, do I consider Dyirbal to have the grammatical category 'ergative' and deny that Russian has this grammatical category?

My answer is that any syntactic pattern must be considered in its relationship to the overall system of the language to which it belongs. The syntactic patterns with the instrumental are very different in Dyirbal and in Russian. True, the instrumental merges with the ergative in Dyirbal. But two instrumentals, one with the meaning 'agent' and another with the meaning 'instrument', can contrast within the same sentence in Dyirbal, which is impossible in Russian. Consider the Dyirbal sentence

| (4) | *Balan ḍugumbil* | *baŋgul yaraŋgu* | *baŋgu yaṛangu* | *balgan.* |
|-----|------------------|------------------|------------------|-----------|
|     | The woman        | [by] the man     | with the stick   | is-being-beaten |
|     | Absolutive       | Instrumental     | Instrumental     |           |
|     |                  | (=agent)         | (=instrument)    |           |

A similar sentence with agent-instrumental and instrument-instrumental is ungrammatical in Russian. These two instrumentals are in complementary distribution in Russian, while they contrast in Dyirbal. Besides, sentences with agent-instrumentals are basic, that is, unmarked, in Dyirbal, while in Russian, sentences with agent-instrumentals are passive constructions, that is, non-basic, marked constructions. Actually, Russian nominal constructions with agent-instrumentals are analogues of Russian passive constructions.

The above consequence is of paramount importance for typological research: with respect to ergativity, only those syntactic processes are typologically significant that are reflected by morphological processes.

Here are some phenomena that are typologically significant for the study of ergative processes: relativization, split ergativity, extraction rules (so called because they extract a constituent from its position and move it to some other position; the term *extraction rules* covers WH-Question, relativization, and focus), antipassives, and possessives.

The important thing to note is that the ergative processes connected with these phenomena have no counterparts in accusative languages; they characterize only different types of ergative languages.

In treating ergativity as a grammatical category, we come across the following question: Is ergativity identical with agentivity?

Under the definition of the grammatical category proposed above, ergativity is identical with agentivity if we define the meaning 'agent' as a class of meanings characterized by the same coding devices as the syntactic function 'ergative'.

The claim that agent is a grammatical category in ergative languages is opposed to the currently prevailing view that the notion 'agent' is a nonformal, purely semantic concept. Thus, Comrie writes:

> I explicitly reject the identification of ergativity and agentivity, [. . .] despite some similarities between ergativity and agentivity, evidence from a wide range of ergative languages points against this identification. (Comrie, 1978: 356)

To support his view, Comrie quotes examples, such as the following sentences from Basque (Comrie, 1978: 357):

(5)  *Herra -k     z  -erabiltza.*
     hatred -Erg. you-move
     'Hatred inspires you'.

(6)  *Ur-handia-k     d-erabilka eihara.*
     river     -Erg. it-move     mill-Abs.
     'The river works the mill'.

Such examples show that agentivity is denied a formal status in ergative languages because of the confusion of the lexical and grammatical meanings of nouns in the ergative case.

Lexical meanings are meanings of morphemes that constitute word stems, while grammatical meanings are meanings of inflexional morphemes, prepositions, conjunctions, and other formal devices, such as word order. Lexical meanings are not necessarily congruous with grammatical meanings they are combined with. There may be a conflict between the lexical and grammatical meanings of a word. For example, the grammatical meaning of any noun is 'thing', but the lexical meaning of a noun may conflict with its grammatical meaning. Thus, the lexical meanings of the words *table* or *dog* are congruous with their grammatical meanings, but the lexical meanings of *rotation* (process) or *redness* (property) conflict with their grammatical meaning 'thing'. The grammatical meaning of verbs is 'process'. In verbs such as *to give* or *to walk*, the lexical meanings refer to different actions, and therefore they are congruous with the grammatical meaning of the verbs. But consider the verbs *to father* or *to house*. Here the lexical meanings conflict with the grammatical meaning of the verbs. Lexical meanings are closer to reality than are grammatical meanings. The differences between word classes are based not upon the nature of elements of reality words refer to, but upon the way of their presentation. Thus, a noun is a name of anything presented as a thing; a verb is a name of anything presented as a process. If we confuse lexical and grammatical meanings, we will be unable to distinguish not only between main classes of words but also between any grammatical categories. A case in point is the grammatical category of agentivity.

From a grammatical point of view, any noun in the ergative case means 'agent', no matter what its lexical meaning is (that is, the meaning of the stem of the given noun). In Comrie's examples, the lexical meanings of *her-ra-k* in (33) and of *ur-handia-k* in (34) conflict with the meaning of the ergative case, which is a grammatical meaning. The ergative case has nothing to do with the objects of reality that the lexical meanings of nouns refer to. It has nothing to do with real agents; rather, the ergative case is a formal mode of presentation of anything as an agent, no matter whether it is a real agent or not. Contrary to the current view, the agent is a formal notion in ergative languages. This claim is based on a strict distinction between lexical and grammatical meanings.

While in ergative languages the agent is a grammatical category, it does not have a formal status in accusative languages. In these languages the agent is a variant of the meaning of the nominative, instrumental, or some other cases, or prepositional phrases. For example, we can use the term *agent* when speaking of passive constructions, but only in the sense of a variant of some more general grammatical category, because there are no distinct coding devices that separate the meaning 'agent' from other related meanings, such as the meaning 'instrument'. Thus, in English, *by* introduces an agent in the passive but can have other meanings, as well. Compare: *written by Hemingway* and *taken by force, earned by writing*, etc.

## 10.2 Accessibility to Relative Clause Formation

Constraints on the extractability of ergatives pose serious problems with respect to the Keenan-Comrie Accessibility Hierarchy (Keenan and Comrie, 1977). Recent investigations have revealed that processes such as relative clause formation are sensitive to the following hierarchy of grammatical relations:

(7)    *Subject > Direct object > Indirect object > Oblique NP >*
          *> Possessor > Object of comparison*

where > means 'more accessible than'.

The positions on the Accessibility Hierarchy are to be understood as specifying a set of possible relativizations that a language can make: relativizations that apply at some point of the hierarchy must apply at any higher point. The Accessibility Hierarchy predicts, for instance, that there is no language that can relativize direct objects and not subjects, or that can relativize possessors and subjects but not direct objects and oblique NPs.

The Accessibility Hierarchy excludes the possibility of languages where subjects were less accessible to relativization than were objects. Yet precisely such is the case with Mayan languages if the notion 'ergative construction' is defined on the basis of subject, as is done by the authors of the Accessibility Hierarchy, whose stance is representative of the views on ergativity. To see that, let us turn to Comrie's definition of the notions 'accusative construction' and 'ergative construction' (Comrie, 1978: 343–50; 1979: 221–23).

In speaking about the arguments of one-place and two-place predicates, Comrie uses the symbol $S$ to refer to the argument of a one-place predicate, and the symbols $A$ (typically agent) and $P$ (typically patient) to refer to the arguments of a two-place predicate. Where a predicate has the argument $P$, it is called a transitive predicate. All other predicates, whether one-place, two-place, or more than two-place, are called intransitive. An intransitive predicate can and usually does have an $S$, but it cannot have an $A$.

Using the three primitives $S$, $A$, and $P$, Comrie characterizes syntactic ergativity and syntactic accusativity (nominativity) as follows:

> In treating ergativity from a syntactic viewpoint, we are looking for syntactic phenomena in languages which treat $S$ and $P$ alike, and differently from $A$. Syntactic nominativity likewise means syntactic phenomena where $S$ and $A$ are treated alike, and differently from $P$. This distinction is connected with the general problem of subject identification: if in a language $S$ and $A$ are regularly identified, that is, if the language is consistently or overwhelmingly nominative-accusative, then we are justified in using the term *subject* to group together $S$ and $A$; if in a language $S$ and $A$ are regularly identified (consistent or overwhelming ergative-absolutive system), then we would be justified in using the term *subject* rather to refer to $S$ and $P$, that is, in particular, to refer to $P$, rather than $A$, of the transitive construction. (Comrie, 1978: 343)

In accordance with this characterization, Comrie arrives at the same conclusion as Anderson: he considers morphologically ergative languages, such as Basque or Tongan, to be syntactically accusative, because these languages treat $S$ and $A$ alike and differently from $P$; he considers Dyirbal syntactically to be ergative, because this language treats $S$ and $P$ alike and differently from $A$.

The weakness of such characterization is that the key notion 'to treat syntactically alike' is not analyzed adequately. What does it mean to say that Basque treats S and A alike? If it means only the application of the rules Equi-NP Deletion and Subject Raising, then, yes, Basque treats S and A alike and therefore must be regarded, according to this criterion, as a syntactically accusative language. But there is more to the syntax of the ergative construction than these rules. If we consider the markedness opposition and syntactic laws and phenomena associated with this key relation, then we conclude that Basque does not treat S and A alike. As a matter of fact, Comrie's characterization of ergativity runs into the same difficulties as Anderson's claim that we discussed in the previous section. But let us put aside these difficulties for now and turn to the Accessibility Hierarchy. Our question is, Can the Accessibility Hierarchy be regarded as a universal law? In order to answer this question, let us consider the facts of Mayan languages.

In Mayan languages, Equi-NP Deletion and other syntactic rules apply to ergatives in much the same way as they do in such languages as Basque or Tongan. Here is an example of Equi-NP Deletion in Quiche (Larsen and Norman, 1979: 349):

(8)    *Lee ak'aal*       *x-ø-u-chap*          *b'iin-eem.*
       THE CHILD    compl.-3sB-3sA-BEGIN    WALK-nominalizer
       'The child began to walk'.

Since Mayan ergatives meet Comrie's criteria of subjecthood, they must be considered subjects, and Mayan languages must be regarded as morphologically ergative but syntactically accusative languages.

Granted that Mayan ergatives must be defined as subjects, the Accessibility Hierarchy predicts that if Mayan languages allow relativization on absolutives, they must allow it also on ergatives. But, contrary to this prediction, in the Mayan languages of the Kanjobalan, Mamean, and Quichean subgroups, ergative NPs cannot as a rule be relativized (or questioned or focused), while absolutive NPs can. In order for an ergative NP to undergo relativization, it must be converted into a derived absolutive and the verb intransitivized through the addition of a special intransitivizing suffix. Here is an example of this process in Aguacatec (Larsen and Norman, 1979: 358):

(9)    *Ja ø-ø-b'iy yaaj xna7n.*
       asp. 3sB-3sA-HIT MAN WOMAN
       'The man hit the woman'.

(10)    a. *Na7 m-ø-b'iy-oon xna7n.*
           WHO dep.asp.-3sB-HIT-suffix WOMAN
           'Who hit the woman'?

b. *Ja ø-w-il yaaj ye m-ø-b'iy-oon xna7n.*
   asp. 3sB-1s-A-SEE MAN THE dep. asp.-3sB-HIT-suffix WOMAN
   'I saw the man who hit the woman'.
c. *Yaaj m-ø-b'iy-oon xna7n.*
   MAN dep.asp.-3sB-HIT-suffix WOMAN
   'It was the man who hit the woman'.

Here *-oon* is the intransitivizing suffix used to circumvent the constraints on extraction of ergatives (the term *extraction rules* is a cover term for relativization rules, focus rules, WH-Question).

The features of Mayan languages under discussion closely conform to those of the Dyirbal language, but while the Dyirbal absolutive meets Comrie's criteria of subjecthood, the Mayan absolutive does not.

Dyirbal does not allow relativization on ergatives; instead, the verb of the relative clause is intransitivized by adding the suffix *-ŋa-y*, and the ergative is replaced by the absolutive case (Dixon, 1972: 100). For instance, consider the Dyirbal sentence

(11)  *Yabu*          *ŋuma+ŋgu*     *buṛa+n.*
      MOTHER(ABS)    FATHER+ERG    SEE+PAST
      'Father saw mother'.

In sentence (11) the ergative is marked by *-ŋgu*. In order to be embedded into another sentence as a relative clause, sentence (11) must be antipassivized and ergative *ŋuma+ŋgu* replaced by absolutive *ŋuma+ø*. We may get, for example, the sentence

(12)  *ŋuma+ø*     *[buṛal+ŋa+ŋu+ø*           *yabu+gu]*      *duŋgara+nʸu.*
      father+ABS   see+ANTIPASS+REL+ABS    mother+DAT     cry+PAST
      'Father, who saw mother, was crying'.

We see that the facts of Mayan languages present strong evidence against the Accessibility Hierarchy. Does that mean that the Accessibility Hierarchy must be abandoned as a universal law? I do not think so. The trouble with the Accessibility Hierarchy is that it is formulated as a universal law in nonuniversal terms, such as subject, direct object, etc. To solve the difficulty, it is necessary to abandon nonuniversal concepts, such as subject and direct object, and to replace them with really universal concepts. The key to the solution of this difficulty is provided by applicative grammar.

From the point of view of applicative grammar, the Accessibility Hierarchy is a particular instance of the Applicative Hierarchy established on independent grounds as a consequence of the Markedness Law (sec. 8 of this chapter):

[*Primary term* > *Secondary term* > (*Tertiary term*)] > *Oblique term*

The Applicative Hierarchy is interpreted in accusative languages as

[*Subject* > *Direct object* > (*Indirect object*)] > *Oblique term*

and in ergative languages as

[*Absolutive* > *Ergative* > (*Indirect object*)] > *Oblique term*

We see that the confusion of ergatives with subjects is inconsistent with the Accessibility Hierarchy, which creates an irresoluble difficulty. The treatment of ergatives and subjects as different syntactic functions, on the other hand, leads to deeper understanding of the Accessibility Hierarchy, which results in its restatement on an abstract level in keeping with true basic syntactic universals: primary, secondary, and tertiary terms.

The revised Accessibility Hierarchy accounts both for the facts that motivated the original Accessibility Hierarchy and for the facts that have been shown to contravene it. The revised Accessibility Hierarchy excludes the possibility of languages where primary terms are less accessible to relativization than secondary terms. And this requirement applies both to accusative languages, where primary terms are interpreted as subjects and secondary terms as direct objects, and to ergative languages, where primary terms are interpreted as absolutives and secondary terms as ergatives. All the facts that support the original Accessibility Hierarchy support also the revised Accessibility Hierarchy. But, besides, the revised Accessibility Hierarchy is supported by the facts, like the above examples from Aguacatec, which contravene the original Accessibility Hierarchy. That is a significant result, which shows the importance of the abstract concepts of applicative grammar.

In conclusion, I want to dispel a possible misunderstanding of the concepts I have introduced. It was said above that in order to save the Accessibility Hierarchy, it is necessary to abandon the nonuniversal concepts 'subject' and 'direct object' and replace them with the universal concepts 'primary term' and 'secondary term'. The important thing to notice is that I suggest replacing one set of concepts with another set of concepts rather than one set of terms with another set of terms. The new terms *primary term* and *secondary term* designate a very different set of concepts from the concepts designated by the terms *subject* and *direct object*. One might argue that we could save the Accessibility Hierarchy by equating subject with absolutive and object with ergative. But this suggestion would obscure the essential difference between the three sets of concepts:

1) *primary term : secondary term,*
2) *subject : direct object,* and
3) *absolutive : ergative.*

No matter which terminology we use, we must distinguish between these three very different sets of concepts. The second and third sets of concepts are different interpretations (in accusative and ergative languages) of the first truly universal set of syntactic concepts.

### 10.3 Voices in Ergative Languages

One important consequence of the Law of Duality is that the opposition of voices in ergative languages is a mirror image of the opposition of voices in accusative languages: the *basic voice* in ergative languages corresponds to the *derived voice* in accusative languages, and the derived voice in ergative languages corresponds to the basic voice in accusative languages.

Since in accusative languages the basic voice is active and the derived voice is passive, that means that pure ergative languages cannot have a passive voice in the sense of accusative languages. Rather, pure ergative languages can have a voice that is converse in its effect to the passive of accusative languages—the so-called antipassive.

A split ergative language can have the passive voice only as a part of its accusative subsystem.

What is called the passive voice in ergative languages by Comrie and some other linguists cannot be regarded as the true passive from a syntactic point of view. Rather, it is a construction resulting from demotion of ergative. Thus, Comrie quotes the following sentence as an example of passive in Basque (Comrie, 1978: 370):

(13)    *Haurra    igorria          da.*
        child-Abs. send-Participle Aux.-3sg.

True, (13) could be translated into a passive clause in English: *The child was sent.* But the possibility of this translation has nothing to do with the syntactic structure of (13). Since in any transitive ergative clause absolutive means patient and ergative means agent, the demotion of ergative automatically involves the topicalization of absolutive. The crucial difference between the demotion of ergative and passivization is that passivization topicalizes the patient by means of the conversion of the predicate (*John sent the child: The child was sent by John*), while the demotion of ergative topicalizes the patient without any change of the predicate (cf. a detailed discussion of clauses with demoted ergatives in Basque in Tchekhoff, 1978: 88–93). I suggest calling the constructions with demoted ergatives *quasi-passive constructions.*

One might argue that the word *passive* should be used with reference to any construction involving the demotion of 'agent'. This use of the word *passive* would, of course, cover the constructions both with converted predicates and with predicates that remain unchanged. However, the question of how the word *passive* should be used is a pure terminological issue and involves nothing of substance. Granted that we accept the broader use of the word *passive*, the important thing is to distinguish between and not to lump together two very different types of passive constructions: 1) passive constructions with converted predicates involving the demotion of primary terms and the promotion of secondary terms to the position of primary terms; and 2) passive constructions with only the demotion of secondary terms denoting 'agents'. The real issue is: Can the two types of passive constructions occur in both accusative and ergative languages? The answer is no. The first type can occur only in accusative languages, the second type only in ergative languages.

Why is the first type possible only in accusative languages? Because, in accordance with the Law of Duality, a counterpart of the first type in ergative languages is its mirror-image, that is, antipassive, construction.

Why is the second type possible only in ergative languages? Because the second type involves the demotion of the secondary term denoting 'agent'. But in accordance with the Law of Duality, the secondary term of a clause denotes 'agent' in ergative languages and 'patient' in accusative languages. Therefore, while the demotion of the secondary term in an ergative construction makes it 'passive', the demotion of the secondary term in an accusative construction does not make it 'passive': the accusative construction remains active.

The above claims are deductive consequences of the Law of Duality. This law is subject to disconfirmation if counterexamples are found that cannot be explained as deviations motivated by special empirical conditions. The empirical study of voices in ergative languages in order to confirm or disconfirm the Law of Duality is one of the fascinating outcomes of the proposed theory of ergativity.

## 10.4 Split Ergativity

Ergative languages tend to exhibit various splits in case markings. These splits can be explained as conditioned by the properties of ergative constructions.

It is well known that in many ergative languages the ergative construction is confined to the past tense or the perfect aspect. How can we explain the correlation between ergative constructions and the tense/aspect?

Since in the ergative construction the primary term denotes patient, that means that the ergative construction presents the action from the point of view of the patient; therefore, the ergative construction focuses on the effect of the action. In the accusative construction the primary term denotes agent, which means that the accusative construction presents the action from the point of view of the agent; therefore, the accusative construction focuses on an action that has not yet been accomplished. Focusing on the effect of an action tends to correlate it with the past tense and the perfect aspect, while focusing on an action that has not yet been accomplished correlates it with the present, the future, the imperfect, and the durative aspects.

Similar explanations of the split in case marking conditioned by tense/aspect have already been proposed by other linguists (Regamay, 1954: 373; Dixon, 1979: 38). What, however, has passed unnoticed is that accusative languages present a counterpart of this split. Accusative languages tend to restrict the use of the passive constructions to the past tense and the perfect. For example, in Old Russian the use of passive constructions was unrestricted. In Modern Russian, however, the passive voice is confined to the past principles in the perfective aspect. Other types of passive construction have been replaced by constructions with reflexive verbs, which are used as a substitute for passive constructions. The explanation of this phenomenon suggests itself immediately if we accept the view that the passive construction is conceptually related to the ergative construction. Like the ergative construction, the passive construction presents the action from the point of view of the patient, and therefore it tends to correlate with the past tense and the perfective aspect.

Another major split in case marking is that involving personal pronouns. In most ergative languages, nouns and personal pronouns tend to have different patterns of case markings. For example, in Australian languages, pronouns usually have accusative case markings, while nouns have ergative case markings (Dixon, 1976). In Caucasian languages, nouns have ergative case markings, while pronouns mostly have an identical form for transitive agents and for patients. The noun/pronoun split in ergative languages can be explained on the same basis as the tense/aspect split. Since the ergative construction presents the action from the point of view of the patient, it cannot be used in situations where the action should be presented from the point of view of the agent, as in the case where we use personal pronouns (Blake, 1977).

A different type of split is analyzed by Peter Hook (1984). In terms of applicative grammar, this split can be characterized as follows. In some languages, such as Kashmiri or Sumerian, the fundamental syntactic opposition is *primary term:secondary term*, characterized by morphological markers. Thus, in Kashmiri the primary term is indicated by the second person suffix *-akh* (or its allomorphs *-kh* and *-h*), and the secondary term is indicated by the second person suffix *-ath* (or *-th*). Depending on the ergative or nonergative tense/aspect, the opposition *primary term:secondary term* splits as follows: in the ergative tense/aspect, the primary term is absolutive and the secondary term is ergative, but in the nonergative tense/aspect, the primary term is subject and the secondary term is direct object. If the transitive construction is in the ergative tense/aspect, the primary term means patient and the secondary term means agent; if the transitive construction is in the nonergative tense/aspect, the primary term means agent and the secondary term means patient. In order to characterize this split, Hook uses the term *superabsolutive* corresponding to the primary term that means patient in the ergative tense/aspect and agent in the nonergative tense/aspect, and the term *antiabsolutive* corresponding to the secondary term that means agent in the ergative tense/aspect and patient in the nonergative tense/aspect. From the standpoint of applicative grammar, the above split is a very special instance of the Law of Duality:

> The marked term of the syntactic construction with the ergative tense/aspect corresponds to the unmarked term of the syntactic construction

with the nonergative tense/aspect, and the unmarked term of the syntactic construction with the ergative tense/aspect corresponds to the marked term of the syntactic construction with the nonergative tense/aspect; and, vice versa, the marked term of the syntactic construction with the nonergative tense/aspect corresponds to the unmarked term of the syntactic construction with the ergative tense/aspect, and the unmarked term of the syntactic construction with the nonergative tense/aspect corresponds to the marked term of the syntactic construction with the ergative tense/aspect.

The definition of the ergative construction proposed here provides a uniform basis for the explanation of all splits in case marking in ergative languages.

## 10.5 The Class of Ergative Languages

Languages that are represented in current linguistic literature as ergative may be found to be nonergative in the light of the definition of the ergative construction. Thus, Georgian is generally represented as an ergative language (or, more precisely, as a split ergative language). For various reasons, some linguists have questioned whether Georgian is ergative at all (for example, Aronson, 1970). In the light of the Law of Markedness and the Dominance Law, we can characterize Georgian as an ergative language that has undergone a process of the reversal of markedness. Since in Georgian the ergative case has replaced the absolutive in intransitive clauses, the range of the ergative case became greater than the range of the absolutive, and, as a result, the two cases exchanged their places in the markedness opposition: the ergative turned into an unmarked case, and the absolutive into a marked case. With the exception of some traces of ergativity, contemporary Georgian must be considered an accusative language.

A revision of the class of ergative languages in the light of the proposed definitions of the notions 'ergative construction' and 'ergative language' may lead to exclusion of some other languages from this class.

## 10.6 The Practical Results Anticipated

In conclusion, I will say a few words about the practical results anticipated.

The first benefit that can be expected from the proposed theory of ergativity is that it will give an adequate understanding of the already accumulated vast amount of facts on the morphology, syntax, and semantics of ergative languages and will set guidelines for fruitful future field work in this domain.

The last few years have seen a significant increase in the amount of data on ergative languages, in particular on their syntax, but no generally accepted solution to the problem of ergativity has yet evolved. One might argue that the proper way to solve this problem is to increase field research in this area. There is no doubt that further field research on ergative languages is of paramount importance to a deeper understanding of ergativity. But field research cannot be fruitful without an understanding of already accumulated data and a realization of what to look for. In accordance with the proposed theory of ergativity, among the other tasks of future field research in this area, the following can be considered urgent:

1) collection of empirical data concerning different processes in ergative languages that in current linguistic literature are lumped together under the name *passivization;*

2) collection of empirical data concerning the application of the rules Equi-NP Deletion and Subject Raising to ergative constructions. The empirical data so far collected are clearly inadequate. The current view that in most ergative languages these rules apply to absolutives in intransitive clauses and to ergatives in transitive clauses is based on inadequate empirical data. Data from some Caucasian languages present evidence that these rules can be applied freely both to absolutives and ergatives, on the one hand, and to two absolutives, on the other.

3) collection of empirical data concerning the occurrence of ergatives in intransitive clauses. Ergatives occur in intransitive clauses either as a result of special conditions that are to be investigated, or as a result of the reversal of markedness, as in the case of Georgian.

4) collection of data concerning the use of instrumentals and other oblique cases in ergative constructions. It may happen that a theoretical scrutiny of these data will discover that some allegedly ergative constructions are really varieties of the accusative construction.

There are some other important tasks of field research in ergative languages, but I will not discuss them here.

The second benefit that I anticipate is that the proposed research will call for a serious overhaul of existing theories of universal grammar.

In contrast to existing theories of ergativity, which oppose morphological, syntactic, and semantic ergativity and tend to emphasize one of these aspects at the expense of others, the Correspondence Hypothesis underlying the proposed research views ergativity as a unitary phenomenon that presupposes an isomorphism of morphological, syntactic, and semantic levels of ergativity.

The oppositions *absolutive : ergative* and *subject : object* are syntactic oppositions independent of each other. Ergative constructions cannot be defined by accusative constructions, nor can accusative constructions be defined by ergative constructions; rather, both these types of constructions must be defined with respect to a more abstract syntactic level underlying both ergative and accusative syntax. This abstract level is a fundamental component of applicative grammar.

The Law of Duality reveals the interrelation of ergative and accusative constructions in a more general semiotic framework of the opposition of markedness, which is valid not only in syntax but in phonology and semiotics, as well.

One important consequence of the Correspondence Hypothesis is that the morphology of an ergative language corresponds to some of its essential syntactic properties. Only those syntactic properties can be called ergative and have typological significance that have a counterpart in morphology.

With respect to the necessity of an overhaul of the existing theories of universal grammar, the following points are especially important:

a) Since, as was shown above, the notions of subject and direct object cannot be applied to the description of ergative languages, they cannot be considered universal. Therefore, they must be abandoned as primitive syntactic functions of universal grammar and replaced by the concepts of 'primary term' and 'secondary term', which are defined on the basis of the primitive concepts 'operator' and 'operand'.

b) The new theory of ergativity calls for a reformulation of the Accessibility Hierarchy in terms of the concepts 'primary term' and 'secondary term'.

c) Contrary to the common approach to syntax, which disregards or at least underestimates morphological data, the new theory of ergativity calls for a careful study of morphological data.

d) The only theory of universal grammar that at present provides an adequate theoretical framework for the new theory of ergativity is applicative grammar.

## 11. An Informal Theory of Passivization

So far I have taken the notion of the passive voice for granted. In the present section I will give a theoretical analysis of this notion. I will be concerned with difficulties posed by passive constructions and various approaches to these difficulties. As a result of the theoretical analysis, a new theory of passivization will emerge, which will be presented informally here. A formalized theory of passivization will be given later, following the formal description of applicative grammar.

The theory of passivization presented in this book contains much of what was developed in my joint work with Jean-Pierre Desclés and Zlatka Guentchéva (Desclés, Guentchéva, Shaumyan, 1985, 1986) but also introduces new notions and goes beyond what we did in a number of ways.

### 11.1 The Basic Structure of Passive

Although the relation between active and passive seems to be simple, in defining passive we face difficulties, which will be discussed here.

Consider first the sentences in English

(1)     a. *John closed the door.*
        b. *The door was closed by John.*
        c. *The door was closed.*

(1a) is an active sentence; (1b) and (1c) are corresponding passive sentences.
(1a) consists of three parts: the term *John* denoting an agent, the active predicate *closed*, and the term *the door* denoting a nonagent. (1b) consists of three parts: the term *the door* denoting a nonagent, the passive predicate *was closed*, and the term *by John* denoting an agent. (1c) has two parts: the nonagent *the door* and the passive predicate *was closed*—the term *by John*, denoting an agent, is missing.

From now on, I will call sentences such as (1b) *long passive sentences*, and sentences such as (1c) *short passive sentences*.

We observe that sentences (1a) and (1b) correlate with each other. They form an opposition *active : passive*. The correlation between the members of this opposition can be characterized as follows:

The passive predicate *was closed* is the converse of the active predicate *closed*.

The term *John*, which precedes the active predicate, corresponds to the term *by John*, which succeeds the passive predicate. The term *the door*, which succeeds the active predicate, corresponds to the term *the door*, which precedes the passive predicate.

In addition to the opposition *active : passive*, English has another opposition: *long passive : short passive*.

The meaning of passive predicates in short passives is ambiguous. Thus, the predicate *was closed* in (1c) either may imply an unspecified agent or may be simply a synonym of *was not open* without implying any agent. An implication of an unspecified agent is not a formal feature of the passive predicate but depends solely on the context or an opposition with adjectives. Take, for example, the sentence

(2)     *Today the shop is open, but yesterday it was closed all day long.*

In (2) *was closed* is simply a synonym of *was not open*. Unlike *was closed*, the predicate *was opened* usually implies an unspecified agent, only because there is the predicate *was open*. While *opened* is a member of the opposition *opened : open*, there is no corresponding opposition for *closed*.

The ambiguity of passive predicates in short passives can be observed in other languages. For example, in the Russian short passive

(3)     *Ego dom vsegda otkryt dlja každogo.*
        'His house is always open for everybody'.

the passive predicate *otkryt* has the meaning of the adjective 'open'.

In Latin the passive *movetur* means either 'he (she, it) moves' or 'he (she, it) is moved'. Only the second meaning is passive proper; the first one is the meaning of the so-called *middle voice* (Lyons, 1968: 375).

Although some languages, such as Uto-Aztecan ones, have special markers for designating unspecified agents in short passives (Langacker, 1976; Langacker and Munro, 1975), most languages of the world do not have these markers. Nevertheless, the unspecified agent must be considered an integral part of short passive, because short passive is a member of the opposition *short passive:active*. For example, *The door was closed* correlates with a set of active sentences: *John closed the door, The boy closed the door, She closed the door,* and so on. If we abstract from concrete agents in these sentences, we get the notion of the unspecified agent, which must be assigned to the predicate *was closed* of *The door was closed*. In most languages the unspecified agent is a zero term—a 'silent term'—of the predicates of short passives. From a functional point of view, a short passive is a mirror image of an abstract sentence based on the corresponding set of active sentences. Thus, if we abstract from the concrete agents in a set of sentences corresponding to *The door was closed*, we get *[unspecified agent] closed the door,* whose mirror image is *The door was closed [unspecified agent].*

The passive meaning involving the unspecified agent is the inherent function of predicates in short passives. But certain contexts may superpose special functions onto predicates in short passives, as in the superposition of the function of an adjectival predicate onto *was closed* in (2) or onto the Russian *otkryt* in (3), or the function of the middle voice, as in the Latin *movetur.*

The passive predicate of a short passive construction is clearly a one-place predicate, which results from the application of the two-place converse predicate to the zero term denoting an unspecified agent. But what is the passive predicate of a long passive construction? Is the passive predicate of a long passive construction a one-place predicate or a two-place predicate?

If we compare (1b) with (1a), we see that from a functional point of view (1b) is a mirror image of (1a): *The door* in (1b) is a mirror-image counterpart of *the door* in (1a), and *by John* in (1b) is a mirror-image counterpart of *John* in (1a). Actually, *by John* functions as a secondary term of (1b). But can we conclude from this fact that *by John* is a regular secondary term like secondary terms in active sentences? No, we cannot, because normally *by*-phrases are used as oblique complements. Here are some examples:

(4)  a.  *He stood by the window.*
     b.  *John entered the house by the back door.*
     c.  *He walked by me without noticing me.*
     d.  *Be here by this time tomorrow.*
     e.  *He did not play by the rules.*
     f.  *He led the blind man by the hand.*
     g.  *He earns money by writing.*
     h.  *Cats sleep by day and hunt by night.*
     i.  *He is French by birth.*
     j.  *He did it all by himself.*

The function of *by*-phrases in long passive constructions sharply differs from their function as oblique complements. To see that, let us take the sentence

(5)  *Mary was killed by John by the seashore.*

In this long passive construction, *by John* is directly opposed to *Mary* as a secondary term, and it is opposed to *by the seashore* as a nucleus term to a marginal, oblique term. We can replace *by the seashore* with other oblique noun phrases, but that cannot be done with *by John*. The possible replacements are shown in the following example:

(6)  *Mary was killed by John      by the seashore.*
                   *by  Mike      under the bridge.*
                   *by  Peter      in the room.*
                   *by her friend on the roof.*
                      etc.          etc.

(6) shows clearly that *by John* functions as a nuclear secondary term. There is a striking difference between the meanings of the preposition *by* in *by John* and in *by the seashore*. In *by John* the preposition *by* has lost its concrete meaning and has become a marker introducing a secondary term.

We observe a conflict between the normal function of *by*-phrases, which is the role of oblique complements, and the function of *by*-phrases in long passive constructions, which is the role of secondary terms. To resolve the conflict, we must use the notion of functional superposition, which was introduced in section 6.3 of this Chapter.

In the light of the notion of functional superposition, we must distinguish between an inherent syntactic function of *by*-phrases and a syntactic function superposed onto the inherent function. Since the superposed function is special with respect to the inherent function of a syntactic unit, the range of the inherent function is wider than the range of the superposed function. Therefore, the distinction between the inherent and superposed functions of a syntactic unit must be based on the Markedness Law introduced in section 8 of this chapter. As is shown by empirical material, *by*-phrases are normally used as oblique complements—the range of *by*-phrases used as oblique complements is wider than the range of *by*-phrases used as secondary terms of long passive constructions. Consequently, the role of oblique complements is an inherent function of *by*-phrases, and the role of the secondary terms of long passive constructions is their superposed function. Although as a part of a long passive construction a *by*-phrase takes the function of a secondary term, it remains an oblique complement—it modifies the passive predicate, which remains a one-place predicate; the passive predicate in long passive constructions is a one-place predicate having a superposed function of a two-place predicate. Accordingly, the components of long passives in English must be described as follows:

> primary term + one-place passive predicate + *by*-phrase modifier of one-
> place passive predicate

This structure undergoes a functional shift under the pressure of the opposition *active construction : long passive construction.* Since the long passive construction is a mirror image of the active construction, the *by*-phrase takes the function of the two-place predicate: the passive predicate and its *by*-phrase modifier take on the functions of a two-place predicate and its secondary term respectively. Prepositional phrases in active constructions may undergo a similar shift. Compare

(7)              I                                    II
   a. *to sit on the bench*              a. *to agree on the terms*
   b. *to fly over the bridge*           b. *to argue over the plan*
   c. *to be at the office*              c. *to look at the picture*

In both I and II we have one-place predicates. But in II the prepositions have lost their concrete meaning and have become markers introducing a secondary term. Therefore, the prepositional phrases in II have taken the function of secondary terms, which has been superposed onto their inherent function of oblique complements. At the same time, the one-place predicates in II have taken the function of two-place predicates, which is superposed onto their inherent function.

So far I have used examples from English, but a similar analysis of the structure of long passives is supported by diverse languages having long passives. The secondary term of a long passive construction is never an inherently secondary term; it is a prepositional phrase or a noun in an oblique case whose inherent function is the role of an oblique complement.

Here is an example from Latin:

(8)      a. *Magister discipulum laudat.*
            teacher (Nom) student (Acc) praises
            'The teacher praises the student'.
         b. *Discipulus laudatur a magistro.*
            student (Nom) is praised from teacher (Abl)
            'The student is praised by the teacher'.

(8a) is an active sentence, and (8b) is a long passive sentence. In (8b) the phrase *a magistro* consists of the preposition *a* and the noun *magistro* in the ablative. In (8b) *a magistro* has the superposed function of the secondary term, but its inherent function is to be a predicate modifier that means a point of departure; the inherent meaning of *a magistro* is 'from the teacher'.

In Russian the inherent function of the instrumental is to be a predicate modifier that means an instrument. But the instrumental is also used in long passive constructions, where it takes the superposed function of the secondary term. What is the meaning of passive predicates? Is the meaning of passive predicates the same in long passive constructions and in short passive constructions?

The above examples of long passive constructions show clearly that their passive predicates are converses of corresponding active predicates.

To characterize the meaning of passive predicates in short passive constructions, let me first introduce the notion of *derelativization*. This notion, used under different names, has been useful in contemporary logic, and it may turn out to be useful in linguistics, as well. Here is how Quine characterizes derelativization:

> Commonly the key word of a relative term is used also *derelativized*, as an absolute term to this effect: it is true of anything *x* if and only if the relative term is true of *x* with respect to at least one thing. Thus anyone is a brother if and only if there is someone of whom he is a brother. Where the relative term is a transitive verb, the corresponding absolute term is the same verb used intransitively.
>
> Relative terms also combine with singular terms by *application*, to give absolute general terms of a composite kind. Thus the relative term 'brother of' gives not only the absolute general term 'brother' but also the absolute general term 'brother of Abel.' Similarly the relative term 'loves' gives not only the absolute general term 'loves' (intransitive) but also the absolute general term 'loves Mabel.' Again the relative term 'at' gives the absolute general term 'at Macy's.' (Quine, 1960: 106)

Using the notion of derelativization, we can characterize the meaning of the passive predicate in short passive constructions as the *derelativized converse* of the active predicate. When the passive predicate is modified by a *by*-phrase in English or an analogous phrase in other languages, we get long passives in which the passive predicate takes the function of a regular converse predicate, and the phrase modifying the passive predicate takes the function of the secondary term of the converse predicate. The relation between the passive predicate of a short passive and the passive predicate of a long passive—say, between *was closed* in *The door was closed* and *was closed* in *The door was closed by John*—is similar to the relation between *captain* in *He was a captain* and *captain* in *He was the captain of the team*. Derelativization explains why passive predicates in short passive constructions have ambiguous meaning: since passive predicates are one-place predicates, their converse meaning must be supported either by the context or, as in long passive constructions, by agent modifiers; without this support, the converse meaning is lost.

The fact that secondary terms in long passive constructions are not inherent secondary terms but predicate modifiers that have only the function of secondary terms calls for an explanation. To explain this fact, we can advance the following hypothesis:

> The inherent function of passive is the conversion of the active predicate and the derelativization of the converse predicate, which involves the superposition of the function of the secondary term onto the predicate modifier.

This hypothesis is supported by the following facts:

1. In some languages, such as Classic Arabic or Uto-Aztecan languages, long passives are not permitted—only short passives are used. In languages that have short and long passives, short passives are by far more common than long passives. For example, in English approximately 80 percent of all passives are short (Quirk, Greenbaum, Leech, 1972: 807).

Why are long passives either not permitted or much less common than short passives? Because the function of long passives is less important than that of short passives. One of the basic communicative needs is a removal of the agent (denoted by the primary term in the active construction) when the agent is either unknown or unimportant. This need is met by impersonal actives and short passives. Short passives differ from impersonal actives in that they not only remove agents but also topicalize nonagents by changing active predicates into their derelativized converses, and secondary terms (denoting nonagents) into primary terms. In long passives, the agent is mentioned, but the nonagent is topicalized. Compare

(9)     a.  *A golf ball struck the senator.*
        b.  *The senator was struck by a golf ball.*

The long passive (9b) does not remove the agent but topicalizes the nonagent. If we have to tell what happened to the senator, we choose (9b) in order to topicalize *the senator.*

(10)    a.  *Faulkner wrote "The Sound and the Fury."*
        b.  *"The Sound and the Fury" was written by Faulkner.*

If we have to tell who was the author of *The Sound and the Fury*, we choose (10a), because *The Sound and the Fury* must be the topic.

In passive constructions, topicalization of the nonagent is a consequence of the conversion of the active predicate. But topicalization of the nonagent is not necessarily connected with passive constructions. Just as the removal of the agent is not only the function of short passive constructions but also the function of active impersonal constructions, so the topicalization of the nonagent not only is the function of passive constructions but also may be an independent phenomenon that occurs in active constructions. The important thing is to distinguish between two types of topicalization of the nonagent: 1) topicalization of the nonagent by the conversion of the active predicate and 2) regular topicalization of the nonagent, which occurs in active constructions.

Regular topicalization of the nonagent is an important cross-linguistic phenomenon. Here is an example from English:

(11)   a. *John likes wine.*
       b. *Wine, John likes.*

2. Languages, such as English, that have long passives originally had merely short passives. Thus, in Old and Middle English passive sentences, the agent could be marked by the dative case or the prepositions *on, among, at, between, betwixt, by, for, from, mid, of, through, to, with* (Visser, 1963–73: 1988–2000). Noun phrases in the dative case (Old English only) or with these prepositions were mere adverbial modifiers of the passive predicates. It sometimes was not clear whether these noun phrases had an agentive or an instrumental reading. Long passives were introduced into English only in the sixteenth century, when the variety of the agent markers was eliminated and the preposition *by* became the standard marker of the agent in passive sentences.

The above facts support the hypothesis about the inherent and the superposed functions of passive. Let us now turn to further questions concerning the relation of active and passive constructions.

Active is the basic voice, and passive is the derived voice. Passive predicates are derived from active predicates. That can be seen from linguistic data across languages. Thus, in many languages, such as English, Russian, French, Bulgarian, Armenian, Uto-Aztecan languages, etc., the passive predicate consists of *BE + past participle* or *Reflexivization affix + active predicate*. Various morphological processes of passive derivation are described in Keenan, 1975. In very rare cases, such as in Mandarin Chinese, the passive predicate does not differ morphologically from the active predicate, but in these cases passivization is characterized by syntactic symbolic processes. So, in Mandarin Chinese passivization is characterized by the particle *bèi* and a change of word order.

There are many cross-linguistic constraints on the formation of passive constructions. For example, many of the world's languages, probably most, have the following constraint on active sentences: the subject of declarative clauses cannot be referential-indefinite. In order not to violate this *categorial* constraint, the speaker must resort to a special *marked* sentence type, the *existential-presentative* construction (such as English *there is a* . . . , French *il y a un* . . . , etc.). Languages of this type are, for example, Swahili, Bemba, Rwanda (Bantu), Chinese, Sherpa (Sino-Tibetan), Bikol (Austronesian), Ute (Uto-Aztecan), Krio (Creole), all Creoles, and many others (Givón, 1979: 26–27). For example, in Krio (an English-based Creole), one finds the following distribution (Givón, 1979: 27):

(12)    a) *Ge   wan man na di  yad  we   de     -ask fɔ  yu.*
                 have one man in  the yard REL PROG -ask for you
                 'There is a man in the yard who is asking for you'.

        b) *\*Wan man na di yad  de     -ask fɔ  yu.*
                 one man in the yard PROG -ask for you
                 'A man in the yard is asking for you.'

        c) *Di  man na di yad  de     -ask fɔ  yu.*
                 the man in the yard PROG -ask for you
                 'The man in the yard is asking for you'.

In English, the analogues of (12b) occur with extremely low frequency: "About 10% of the subjects of main-declarative-affirmative-active sentences (non-presentative) are indefinite, as against 90% definite" (Givón, 1979: 28, 51–73).

The distribution of definiteness in active and passive constructions is not at all the same. In a transitive active construction, the primary term (denoting an agent) is very often determined, and the object may or may not be determined.

(13)    a)  *John bought a/the book.*
        b)  *The boy bought the book.*
        c)  *?A boy bought the book.*

In a passive construction, the primary term (denoting a patient) is generally determined, while the agent, when it is overt, is often undetermined but may be determined in some contexts (Givón, 1979: 63):

(14)    a)  *?A book was bought by John.*
        b)  *He was beaten to death a minute later by an enraged wino.*

If the secondary term in an active sentence is determined, we can associate a corresponding passive:

(15)    a)  *The boy broke the cup.*
        b)  *The cup was broken by the boy.*

If the secondary term in an active sentence is not determined, we cannot always and unconditionally associate a corresponding passive:

(16)    a)  *The boy broke a cup.*
        b)  *?A cup was broken by the boy.*

Because of various constraints on their formation, passive constructions have a narrower range than active constructions. Therefore, under the Markedness Law, active is the unmarked and passive the marked member of the opposition *active:passive*.

Long passive constructions have passive predicates that function as converses of active predicates in corresponding active constructions. Under the definition of conversion in section 7 above, there must be an equivalence of long passive constructions and corresponding active constructions with respect to their meaning. Equivalence is not identity; it does not mean that long passive constructions can be freely substituted for active constructions—it means only that there are some essential properties of the meaning of long passive constructions and the meaning of corresponding active constructions that are invariant under the operation of the conversion of predicates. Here are some examples:

(17)  a. *John approached Mary.*
      b. *Mary was approached by John.*

(17a) and (17b) are not identical—they are equivalent: the relation between the agent *John* and the nonagent *Mary* is invariant under the conversion of the predicate *approached*. The meaning of (17a) and (17b) is different with respect to topicalization: the topic is *John* in (17a) and *Mary* in (17b).

Differences in topicalization always involve differences in definiteness/indefiniteness. If the sentence *The man stole an automobile* is part of a text, we can conclude that *the man* refers to a person introduced before, while *stole an automobile* conveys new information. The indefinite article is used with the word *automobile* because this word refers to a part of the new information. No matter whether we have an active or a passive construction, the topic is used with the definite article in most cases, because the topic almost always refers to given information. Therefore, the passive sentences *An automobile was stolen by the man* and *The automobile was stolen by a man* differ in meaning from each other and from *The man stole an automobile*, although all three of the sentences have the same underlying invariant—the relation (denoted by the predicates) between the agent *man* and the nonagent *automobile*.

The foregoing shows that the differences in definiteness/indefiniteness of the agent and nonagent in active and passive constructions are logical consequences of the differences in their topicalization.

Another logical consequence of the differences in topicalization of the agent and nonagent is that passive predicates tend to denote a state resulting from a past action. Thus, it is well known that in contemporary English many passive phrases are ambiguous as to whether they refer to a process or a state. *The letter was written* may mean that at a certain moment somebody wrote the letter, or that the letter had already been written. In Russian, passive predicates denoting a process have fallen into disuse—as a rule, only passive predicates denoting the state resulting from past action are used. So, phrases such as *Kniga pročitana* 'The book has been read' (*pročitana* denotes the state resulting from past action) are quite common, while phrases such as *Kniga čitaema* 'The book is read' (*čitaema* denotes the process) are unacceptable in contempo-

rary Russian. This tendency is explained by the fact that in passive constructions the action is presented from the point of view of the nonagent, so that we
focus on the effect of the process rather than on the process itself. The process
relates to the agent rather than to the nonagent. Since the active construction
presents the action from the point of view of the agent, and the passive construction from the point of view of the nonagent, it is natural that the active
construction serves to express the process, and the passive construction serves
to express the effect of the process.

There may be other differences in meaning between active and corresponding passive constructions, but no matter what these differences are, there is
always a certain relation between the agent and nonagent, which is invariant
under the conversion of an active into a passive predicate.

Many languages passivize not only the secondary term but the tertiary term,
as well. For example, we find in English

(18)     a.  *The money was given to John.* (the secondary term passivized)
         b.  *John was given the money.*     (the tertiary term passivized)

In English, the passivization of tertiary terms is not typical; it is an isolated
phenomenon for only a very limited number of predicates. But in some other
languages, such as Malagasy, the passivization of tertiary terms is common. In
these languages, tertiary terms that are passivized may have a variety of meanings (addressee, beneficiary, instrument, place, time, etc.). Here are some examples from Malagasy (Keenan, 1972):

(19)     a.  *Nividy ny    vary ho an'ny ankizy ny  vehivavy.*
             bought the   rice  for the children the woman
             'The woman bought the rice for the children'.
         b.  *Novidyn'ny    vehivavy ho an'ny ankizy ny  vary.*
             bought by the woman     for the children the rice
             'The rice was bought for the children by the woman'.
         c.  *Nividianan'ny vehivavy ny  vary ny ankizy.*
             bought by the woman    the rice the children.
             'The children were bought the rice by the woman'.

(20)     a.  *Nividy ny    vary amin'ny vola   ny  vehivavy.*
             bought the   rice with the money the woman
             'The woman bought the rice with the money'.
         b.  *Nividianan'ny vehivavy ny  vary ny vola.*
             bought by the woman    the rice the money
             'The money was used by the woman to buy the rice'.

In spite of the variety of examples of the passivization of tertiary terms in
different languages, this type of passivization is subordinate to the passivization
of secondary terms. This claim is supported by the following law:

CONDITION ON THE PASSIVIZATION OF TERTIARY TERMS:
Any language that passivizes tertiary terms must passivize secondary terms, but the reverse is not true: the passivization of secondary terms does not presuppose the passivization of tertiary terms.

The passivization of tertiary terms is subordinate to the passivization of secondary terms, and the latter is independent of the former, since the passivization of tertiary terms presupposes the passivization of secondary terms, while the passivization of secondary terms does not presuppose the passivization of tertiary terms.

Now we are ready for a definition of short and long passive constructions.

The *short passive construction* is defined by the following conditions:
1) A one-place passive predicate is derived from a two- or three-place predicate in two steps:
   i) formation of the converse of the active predicate;
   ii) derelativization of the converse predicate by applying it to a zero term denoting an unspecified agent.
2) The passive predicate is applied to a noun phrase that serves as the primary term of the short passive construction.
3) The primary term of the short passive construction denotes a non-agent and is a functional counterpart of the secondary or tertiary term of the corresponding active construction.

The *long passive construction* is defined by the following conditions:
1) The passive predicate is derived in two steps, as in the short passive construction.
2) The passive predicate first is modified by a noun phrase that serves as an oblique term and then is applied to a noun phrase that serves as the primary term.
3) The primary term of the long passive construction denotes a non-agent and is a functional counterpart of the secondary or tertiary term of the corresponding active construction.
4) The function of the secondary term is superposed onto the oblique term, and the function of the two- or three-place converse predicate is superposed onto the passive predicate. As a result of the superposition, the oblique term of the long passive construction turns into a functional counterpart of the primary term of the corresponding active construction.
5) The passive predicate takes on the function of a two- or three-place converse predicate.

The above definition of short and long passive constructions seems to have internal contradictions. Thus:

1) Passive predicates are characterized as having the same form in short and long passive constructions. But while the predicate of a short passive construction is defined as a one-place predicate obtained by applying a converse predicate to a zero term denoting an unspecified agent, the predicate of a long passive construction is defined as a one-place predicate that functions as a two- or three-place converse predicate.

2) The agent term in the long passive construction is defined as an oblique term that functions as a secondary term.

These contradictions show that the passive predicate and the agent in a long passive construction must be viewed as centaurs. The notion of the centaur was introduced in section 1 of chapter 2 in connection with the analysis of the notion of the phoneme. Just as the phoneme is a unity of the sound and the diacritic, the passive predicate in the long passive construction is a unity of the form of a one-place predicate and the function of a two- or a three-place predicate, and the agent in the long passive construction is a unity of the form of an oblique term and the function of a secondary term.

Actually, the paradoxical structure of passive is the result of functional superpositions: in long passive constructions, the function of the two- or three-place converse predicate is superposed onto the one-place passive predicate, and the function of a secondary term is superposed onto an oblique term. These superpositions can be explained as a realization of a potential of natural languages for developing symmetrical constructions. Symmetrical constructions must satisfy two conditions: they must have converse predicates, and they must have the same number of terms converse predicates are applied to. Now, to develop symmetrical counterparts of active constructions, natural languages use short passive constructions with an oblique term used as a modifier of the passive predicate. As was said above, in Old and Middle English passive sentences, the agent could be marked by the dative case or the prepositions *on, at, among, between, betwixt, by, for, from, mid, of, through, to, with*. The passive sentences with an agent expressed by the dative case or a variety of prepositions were short passives rather than long passives proper. Here the meaning of the agent term was rooted in the various concrete meanings of the dative and prepositions, and so indicated a sort of instrument or a source of the action rather than the agent in the strictest sense of the word. These short passives became long passives only when, by the process of grammaticalization, the preposition *by* replaced all the means of expressing the agent and became a grammatical element superposing the function of the secondary term onto the oblique term.

It should be noted that the potential of symmetrical expressions is not necessarily realized in every language. Actually, passive, and especially long passive, constructions are a linguistic luxury, and many languages get by without them. Some languages may have verbal adjectives with passive meaning, but the sentences having these verbal adjectives cannot be considered passive constructions proper. Such was the case in the early stages of the development of Indo-European languages. In languages having passive constructions, the use of passive constructions, and especially of long passives, is connected with the need for a more abstract means of expression.

## 11.2 Impersonal Passive Constructions

In some languages, passive predicates can be derived from intransitive active predicates. Consider the following example from German:

(21)   a. *Die Kinder tanzten.*
          'The children danced'.
       b. *Es wurde von den Kindern getanzt.*
          *'By the children it was danced'.

This example seems to contradict the explanation of passive constructions in terms of conversion. Nevertheless, the difficulty raised by this and similar examples from German and some other languages can be solved by hypothesizing a zero dummy term as follows.

Let us compare (21a) and (21b). The predicates *tanzten* and *wurde getanzt* are oriented in opposite directions. The predicate *tanzten* is directed from the primary term, while *wurde getanzt* is directed to the primary term. The reversal of the orientation of the predicates is what conversion is all about. Therefore, the relation between the terms (21a) and (21b) can be rendered by a proportion:

(22)   *von Kindern : die Kinder* $=$ *es : x*

By substituting a zero dummy term $\emptyset_\Delta$ for $x$, we get

(23)   *von Kindern : die Kinder* $=$ *es : $\emptyset_\Delta$*

We must be cautious in hypothesizing abstract entities. But in our case the hypothesis of zero dummy secondary terms in active intransitive sentences is justified. It is well motivated by directly observable empirical properties of sentences and the operation of conversion.

By introducing a hypothetical zero dummy secondary term into active intransitive sentenes, we establish a well-motivated analogy between the derivation of passive predicates from active one-place predicates and the derivation of passive predicates from active two-place predicates.

One might argue that impersonal passive constructions do not satisfy the conditions implied by the definition of the passive. For these conditions rest upon the assumption that passive sentences are derived from active transitive sentences. It is difficult to imagine that such sentences as Latin *Pugnabatur* 'It was fought' should be derived from active transitive sentences.

To meet this argument, we must take into account the *Principle of Polymorphism*, which can be stated as follows:

There are different ways of constructing the same sentence, and not all ways are possible for every sentence.

For example, the sentence

(24)     *Boris was called by Peter.*

can be constructed in two ways: 1) either we apply the passive predicate *was called* first to *Peter*, then to *Boris;* 2) or we derive (4) from the following sentence:

(25)     *Peter called Boris.*

Not every passive sentence can be constructed by derivation from an active sentence. Such, for example, is the case with impersonal passives having zero terms, such as (21a) or Latin *Pugnabatur* 'It was fought'. The crucial property of passive constructions is not that we can derive them from active constructions but that we can obtain them by applying passive predicates to some terms as their operands. The important thing to notice is that, while it is not always possible to derive a passive construction from an active one, we can always derive a passive predicate from an active predicate.

Generative-transformational grammar and relational grammar admit only one way of characterizing passive constructions—by pointing out how they are derived from active constructions. Thus, they characterize (25) as necessarily obtained from (24). No wonder generative-transformational grammar and relational grammar run into difficulty when they try to characterize impersonal passive constructions that cannot be obtained from active constructions. To solve this difficulty, they have to introduce hypothetical entities that hardly can be justified on empirical grounds.

One of the advantages of the linguistic theory advocated in this book is that it rests on the Principle of Polymorphism, which makes it possible to give a realistic characterization of passive constructions.

One might argue against conversion by pointing out that some languages can sometimes have passive constructions with a patient that is not promoted to the position of the primary term, as in the following example from Polish:

(26)     *a.*          *Zbudowali szkolę.*
                      (they) built          school
                      'They built the school'.
         *b.*                    *Zbudowano szkolę.*
                      by-them was-built      school
                      'The school was built by them'.

In (26a) the noun *szkolę* is in the accusative case, and the predicate *zbudowali* is active in the past tense. In (26b) the impersonal form *zbudowano* has a special suffix *-o*. The noun *szkolę* is in the accusative case.

The impersonal passive construction (26b) differs from the active construction (26a) in that the active predicate *zbudowali* was changed into the impersonal passive *zbudowano*. As to the noun *szkolę*, it remained unchanged.

Do this and similar examples from Welsh, Finnish, and some other languages contravene our definition of the passive construction? To answer this question, we must bear in mind that according to the definition of the two-place predicate, an application of a two-place predicate to a term gives an expression that is equivalent to a one-place predicate. That means that in (26a), *zbudowali szkolę* is equivalent to a one-place predicate, and the whole sentence (26a) can be regarded alternatively either as a transitive sentence with the transitive predicate *zbudowali* and the patient *szkolę* or as an intransitive sentence with the intransitive predicate *zbudowali szkolę*. For the purposes of passivization, the second alternative was chosen by Polish. The possibility of this choice can be explained by the fact that the crucial function of passivization is demotion or suppression of the agent, rather than promotion of the patient to the position of the primary term; passive constructions are used when the agent is either unknown or unimportant. Granted that (26a) is regarded as an intransitive sentence, we can explain (26b) as we explained above the passivization of regular intransitive sentences.

### 11.3  Passive and Antipassive

As was shown in section 10.3, pure ergative languages cannot have a passive voice. What is sometimes called passive in ergative languages is actually a construction resulting from the demotion of ergative. Instead of passive, pure ergative languages can have a so-called antipassive.

While accusative languages have the opposition *active : passive*, pure ergative languages can have the opposition *ergative : antipassive*.

Here is an example of an antipassive construction from Dyirbal (Dixon, 1972):

(27)  Ɖuma     buṛal+ɲa          +ɲʸu yabu+gu.
      father   see +Antipassive+Past mother
      primary,        suffix       secondary,
      agent                        patient
      'Father saw mother'.

      (27) is derived from

(28)  Yabu     ŋuma+ŋgu      buṛa+n.
      mother   father+Agent  see+Past
      primary, secondary     ergative
      patient  agent         predicate
      'Mother was seen by father'.

by: 1) deriving the antipassive predicate *buṛal+ɲa+ɲʸu* from the ergative predicate *buṛa+n* (*ɲa* is a phonetically conditioned variant of the antipassive suffix *-ŋay*); 2) changing the original secondary term *ŋuma+ngu* in the ergative case into the primary term *ŋuma* in the absolutive case; and 3) changing the original primary term *yabu* in the absolutive case into the secondary term *yabu+gu* in the dative case.

Note that although I translated (27) by an English active construction, this translation is a crude device, for want of a better one, used to show the contrast between the passive and the antipassive constructions. Although an antipassive construction reminds one superficially of an active construction, there is a fundamental difference between them. As was said above, the active construction is fundamental and normal, while the antipassive construction is derived and stylistically marked.

It should be noted that most ergative languages lack antipassive constructions; they have only ergative constructions. This fact has a counterpart in accusative languages: some of these languages lack passive constructions. The only difference between ergative and accusative languages in this respect is that the lack of antipassive constructions is a much more common phenomenon than the lack of passive constructions.

Why are antipassive constructions less common in ergative languages than are passive constructions in accusative languages? Antipassive constructions are used to topicalize the agent; therefore, they make sense when in corresponding ergative constructions the topic is the nonagent rather than the agent, as can be seen in Dyirbal and in some ergative languages—these languages have antipassive. But, as was shown in section 10, in most ergative languages the function of the primary term is superposed onto the secondary term—which results in the topicalization of the secondary term by changing word order: now the topicalized secondary term precedes and the primary term follows the ergative predicate. Since the secondary term denotes an agent, ergative languages that topicalize the agent by changing word order do not need antipassive. Neither do they need passive, because they can get an analogue of passive constructions simply by denoting the agent without the conversion of the ergative predicate, as was shown in section 10.3.

There are two types of antipassive constructions: *short antipassive constructions* and *long antipassive constructions*. Antipassive constructions, which are mirror images of passive constructions, are defined as follows:

The *short antipassive construction* meets the following conditions:

1) a one-place antipassive predicate is derived from a two- or three-place ergative predicate in two steps:

    i) formation of the converse of the ergative predicate;

    ii) derelativization of the converse of the ergative predicate.

2) The antipassive predicate is applied to a noun phrase that serves as the primary term of the short passive construction.

3) The primary term of the short passive construction denotes an agent and is a functional counterpart of the secondary term of the corresponding ergative construction.

The *long antipassive construction* meets the following conditions:

1) The antipassive predicate is derived in two steps, as in the short anti-passive construction.

2) The antipassive predicate is first modified by a noun phrase that serves as an oblique term and is then applied to a noun phrase that serves as a primary term.

3) The primary term of the long antipassive construction denotes an agent and is a functional counterpart of the secondary term of the corresponding ergative construction.

4) The function of the secondary term is superposed onto the oblique term; the function of the two- or three-place converse predicate is superposed onto the antipassive predicate. As a result of the superposition, the oblique term of the long antipassive construction turns into a functional counterpart of the primary term of the corresponding ergative construction.

## 12. Alternative Theories of Passivization

To appreciate the implication of the abstract theory of passivization presented in section 11, one must compare it with alternative theories of passivization. I will consider the theories of passivization in generative-transformational and relational grammar and the demotion theory of passivization.

### 12.1 Generative-Transformational Grammar

Generative-transformational grammar defines the rules of passivization in terms of word order. For example, the rule of passivization in English is characterized as follows: the passive transformation has as input a string of the form

(1)    $NP_1 + V + NP_2$

(where *NP* denotes a noun phrase and *V* denotes a verb), interchanges the two NPs, puts the verb in the passive form, and marks $NP_1$ by the preposition *by*, yielding the string of the form

(2)    $NP_2 + V_{pass} + by + NP_1$

as (3) illustrates:

(3)    *John ate the banana → The banana was eaten by John.*

The definition of the rules of passivization in terms of word order raises a series of problems.

In the first place, as was shown in section 1 of this chapter, there are languages, such as Russian, in which active and passive sentences may have the same word order, because word order is irrelevant for passivization.

Second, this approach runs into difficulties even when word order is relevant for passivization. Since different languages have different word order, we have to formulate distinct rules for each language where the order of the relevant words is different. Therefore, we have to treat functionally identical rules in two languages as distinct rules; as a result, we will miss the essential features of passivization and focus on its superficial aspects.

Third, granted that the transformational approach precludes the formulation of the universal rules of passivization, one might expect that, at least within the limits imposed by a highly specific nature of word order in various languages, this method could be valuable for understanding specific features of passivization in individual languages. But transformational theory falls short even of these modest expectations. Generative-transformational grammar rests upon the *Autonomous Syntax Hypothesis,* which claims that grammatical morphemes are for the most part meaningless and are inserted for purely formal purposes. In our case, the grammatical morphemes marking the passive constructions— *by, be,* and the perfect participial inflection—are considered meaningless entities with a purely formal function. Generative-transformational grammar claims that passive constructions can be produced only by deriving them from active sentences. But this claim is false. As a matter of fact, English passives frequently lack a *by*-phrase, because a *by*-phrase is not an intrinsic part of the English passive construction. Counterparts of English *by*-phrases, that is, agentive phrases, are not permitted at all in many languages. As a matter of fact, passive constructions with an agentive phrase are based on passive constructions without an agentive phrase, rather than vice versa. That can be stated as the following law:

> If a language has passive constructions with agentive phrases, it must have passive constructions without agentive phrases, but the reverse is not true: if a language has passive constructions without agentive phrases, it may or may not have passive constructions with agentive phrases.

It is wrong to treat the preposition *by* as a tool of transformation of active constructions into passive constructions. The correct approach is to treat *by*-phrases as normal modifiers of intransitive passive predicates. The preposition *by* is a binary operator whose first operand is a term and whose second operand is a predicate. *By*-phrases are constructed in two steps: first, we apply *by* to a term, and then we apply the result of this application to a predicate. That means that *by* is a *transposer* of a term into a modifier of a predicate.

Passive constructions are not necessarily derived from active constructions. Rather, they are produced by the successive accretion of smaller components. That is possible because every component has its own meaning.

## 12.2 Relational Grammar

Relational grammar (henceforth RG) is a model of syntactic description suggested and developed by Perlmutter and Postal since about 1972. Perlmutter and Postal characterize RG as a new linguistic theory that is directly opposed to generative-transformational grammar (henceforth GTG). True, RG has many attractions in comparison with the standard version of GTG. But at the same time, RG shares with GTG many essential features, which gives us good reason to regard RG as a new type of GTG.

The basic feature that RG shares with GTG is the notion of an abstract underlying syntactic structure. This abstract structure is called *deep structure* in GTG and *initial stratum* in RG. True, there are significant technical differences between these notions, but with respect to their essence, these notions are alike: both are fictitious entities from which the empirical structure (called *surface structure* in GTG and *final stratum* in RG) is derived.

The derivation of surface structure from deep structure is described in GTG by means of a dynamic meta-language—in terms of *transformations*. The derivation of final stratum from initial stratum is described in RG by means of a static meta-language—in terms of static grammatical *relations* between successive strata, starting with initial stratum and ending with final stratum. But we should not be misled by the differences between the two meta-languages. The essential point is that both GTG and RG operate with a fictitious abstract structure from which they derive the empirical structure, no matter what they call all these things.

What really sets RG apart from classic GTG is the claim that grammatical relations such as 'subject of', 'direct object of', 'indirect object of', and others are needed to achieve three goals of linguistic theory: 1) to formulate linguistic universals; 2) to characterize the class of grammatical constructions found in natural languages; and 3) to construct adequate and insightful grammars of individual languages.

Another basic claim of RG is that grammatical relations cannot be defined in terms of other notions, such as word order, phrase structure configurations, or case markings. Rather, they must be taken as primitives of linguistic theory.

RG correctly criticizes classic GTG for its failure to provide cross-linguistically viable notions of grammatical relations to achieve the goals of linguistic theory; GTG is unable to do that because it states transformations in terms of the linear order of constituents.

One must be in sympathy with these important proposals of RG. But at the same time, RG is committed to the framework of multilevel structure in the spirit of classic GTG, which has grave consequences.

Before discussing the RG theory of passivization, I want to make a few terminological comments.

RG calls such notions as 'subject of', 'object of', etc. *grammatical relations*. These are binary relations. The question arises, What are the members of these binary relations? RG does not give a direct answer to this question. Neither can one find an unequivocal answer. Thus, we can regard the members of these relations as noun phrases and sentences. For example, given a sentence S and two noun phrases A and B, we can define the relations between them as follows: A is the subject of S, B is the direct object of S. Or we can regard the members of these relations as noun phrases and predicates. For instance, given a sentence S, a binary predicate P, and two noun phrases A and B, we can define the relations between them as follows: A is the subject of P, B is the direct object of P.

Under both interpretations, *subject-of* and *direct-object-of* are relations in a very trivial sense. By adding the preposition *of* to the words *subject* and *direct object*, we get the relational terms *subject-of* and *direct-object-of*. But these relational terms do not characterize the essence of the notions of 'subject' and 'direct object'.

By adding the preposition *of* to any noun, we can produce a variety of relational terms: *house-of, heart-of, leg-of, tail-of*, etc., etc.

Obviously the notions of subject, direct object, and indirect object cannot be understood as relations in an interesting, nontrivial sense, which would make it possible to draw an essential distinction between these notions and other syntactic notions.

With respect to these notions, the key word must be *function* (taken in a nonmathematical sense as a synonym of the word *role*) rather than *relation*. The essential feature that distinguishes them from other syntactic relations is the notion of *syntactic function*. Subject, direct object, and indirect object are basic functional units of the sentence, and as such they are essentially distinct from all other syntactic entities.

We have to look for a nontrivial notion of relation elsewhere. If we define a relation $R_n$ (where $n=2,3, \ldots$) as an entity that combines $n$ elements, called the members of $R_n$, into a whole, then the basic relational syntactic notions are the notions of binary and ternary predicates, which connect two or three noun phrases of a sentence. Subject, direct object, and indirect object are the members of these relations. Binary and ternary predicates are relations in an interesting, nontrivial sense, because, as was shown above, by treating predicates as relations we can develop a rich variety of revealing relation-changing operations.

Since binary and ternary predicates are special instances of operators, the fundamental notion of linguistic relation in a nontrivial, significant sense must be 'binary operator of' and 'ternary operator of'.

As was shown above, subject, direct object, and indirect object are not valid universal notions and must be replaced by the theoretical constructs *primary term, secondary term,* and *tertiary term.*

Let us now turn to the RG theory of passivization (Perlmutter, Postal, 1977).

RG starts with a basic universal assumption about the nature of clause structure. This assumption is stated informally as follows:

1)—A clause consists of a network of grammatical relations—among them are 'subject of', 'direct object of', and 'indirect object of'.

On the basis of this assumption, RG states the universals of passivization as follows:

2)—A direct object of an active clause is the superficial subject of the corresponding passive clause.

3)—The subject of an active clause is neither the superficial subject nor the superficial direct object of the corresponding passive.

2) and 3) together have the following consequence:

4)—A passive clause is an intransitive clause.

2), 3), and 4) are called *universals of passivization*. Consider the following English active-passive pair:

(4)    a.  *Louise reviewed that book.*
       b.  *That book was reviewed by Louise.*

The simplified network of grammatical relation for (4a) is

(5)

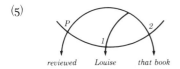

where *p* means predicate, *1* means subject, and *2* means object.
    The simplified diagram for (4b) is

(6)

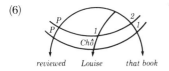

Here two horizontal curves show that the structure of the passive consists of two strata: 1) an initial stratum (indicated by the upper curve) and 2) a final stratum (indicated by the lower curve). RG claims that in any human language, every possible clause has a noun phrase that is an object in the initial stratum and a subject in the final stratum. (4b) includes (4a) as its initial stratum and in this way represents the correspondence stated in 2). Symbol *Chô* means *chômeur*; this term denotes a noun phrase that is neither a superficial subject or direct object nor an oblique.

The universals of passivization 2), 3), and 4) are based on the following laws (which are stated here in nontechnical terms) (Perlmutter, Postal, 1978):

> *The Oblique Law.* Any noun phrase that bears an oblique relation to a clause must bear it in the initial stratum.

In nontechnical terms, the Oblique Law means that a subject, direct object, or indirect object cannot be converted into an oblique.

> *The Stratal Uniqueness Law.* No stratum can contain more than one subject, one direct object, or one indirect object.

Let us now turn to a special condition that follows from the Oblique Law and the Stratal Uniqueness Law.

What relation does *Louise* bear in the second stratum of (6)? Since *that book* is the subject in this stratum, it follows from the Stratal Uniqueness Law that *Louise* cannot be the subject in the second stratum. RG claims that the relation borne by *Louise* in the second stratum is an additional primitive relation called the *chômeur* relation. The term *chômeur* is a French word meaning 'unemployed' or 'idle'. A noun phrase that is a chômeur in a given stratum is a subject, direct object, or indirect object in a higher stratum (the term *chômeur* reflects an earlier conception of RG, when chômeur was a nominal that lost its grammatical relation).

> *The Chômeur Condition.* If some noun phrase $NP_a$ bears a given term relation in a given stratum $S_i$, and some other noun phrase $NP_b$ bears the same relation in the following stratum $S_{i+1}$, then $NP_a$ bears a *chômeur* relation in $S_{i+1}$.

So, since *Louise* in (6) is the subject in the first stratum, and *that book* is the subject in the second, the Chômeur Condition stipulates that *Louise* be the chômeur in the second stratum.

The Chômeur Condition follows from the above laws. So, *Louise* cannot be an oblique in the second stratum, because it is not an oblique in the first stratum (that follows from the Oblique Law), and it cannot be a subject in the second stratum, because no stratum can contain more than one subject, direct object, or indirect object (that follows from the Stratal Uniqueness Law).

> *The Final 1 Law.* Every basic clause contains a final stratum subject.

This law claims that there is no basic clause without a subject. The subject may not appear on the surface, as in the following examples:

(7)     a. *Kiss one salamander, and people say you are a pervert.*
        b. *Try and tickle yourself.*
        c. *John went home and then called Betty.*

Many languages have basic clauses that do not appear to have subjects. Take Russian, for instance:

(8)   *a. Morozit.*
           'It's freezing.'
      *b. Menja tošnit.*
           me       nauseates
           'I feel nauseated'.

Or French:

(9)   *a. Voilà Pierre.*
           'There's Pierre'.
      *b. Le voici.*
           'Here he is'.

RG claims that these sentences have a dummy subject. The dummy may appear on the surface, as in French

(10)   *Il pleut.*

or in its English counterpart

(11)   *It is raining.*

There are also dummy objects, as in the following sentences:

(12)   *a. Terry made it clear that he would resign.*
       *b. I hate it very much for you to scream like that.*

To define a class of possible sentences with dummy terms, the following law is advanced:

   *The Nuclear Dummy Law.* Only subjects and objects can be dummy terms.

This law predicts, among other things, that chômeurs cannot be dummy terms. RG recognizes the following hierarchy of grammatical relations:

(13)

| Highest | *1* | *= Subject* |
|---------|-----|-------------|
|         | *2* | *= Direct object* |
|         | *3* | *= Indirect object* |
| Lowest  | *Nonterm Relations = (chômeur, oblique relations, etc.)* | |

RG recognizes a class of rules called *advancements* and a class of structures produced by these rules. An advancement is a rule that moves a noun phrase up the hierarchy. A noun phrase undergoing an advancement is called an *advancee*.

The rules of passivization belong to the class of advancements. Here are some examples:

(14)    a.  *Harriet gave a new bowling ball to Ted.*
        b.  *Harriet gave Ted a new bowling ball.*
        c.  *Ted was given a new bowling ball by Harriet.*

In (14a) *Ted* bears the initial 3-relation to the clause. In (14c) *Ted* is an advancee, because it is advanced from the initial 3-relation first to the 2-relation, as in (14b), and then through passivization to the 1-relation. It can be seen from (14c) that a single noun phrase can undergo more than one advancement.

What can be said about the RG theory of passivization?

This theory marks an essential progress in comparison with the theory of passivization of GTG. The critical point is that RG explains passivization in terms of relational, or, better, functional, units—subject, direct object, indirect object—rather than in terms of the linear order of constituents.

Another significant advantage of this theory is that it builds on a body of universal laws. These laws are important not because they are definitive but because they have heuristic power: they direct linguists towards fruitful empirical research and raise significant theoretical issues.

RG has already stimulated interesting empirical research on a variety of typologically different languages and has given impetus to a discussion of some intriguing problems of linguistic theory. It should be noted, however, that the results of RG are far from conclusive. It must be given credit for raising novel theoretical problems rather than for solving them. As a matter of fact, the RG theory of passivization meets substantial difficulties when it is applied to accusative languages, and it breaks down with respect to ergative languages.

The difficulty with RG is that it conflates subject with the agent and object with the patient in transitive sentences. But if we take subject and object as purely syntactic terms, subject may be a patient and object an agent. Subject as a purely syntactic term is what I call the primary term. Object as a purely syntactic term is what I call the secondary term. RG is unable to accept the notion of transitive subject as a patient and the notion of object as an agent. Therefore, RG interprets the ergative case as a transitive subject, and the absolutive case in transitive sentences as a transitive object, although the reverse is true: in ergative languages the ergative case denotes a transitive object rather than a transitive subject, and the absolutive denotes a transitive subject rather than a transitive object.

Since RG conflates subject with the agent and direct object with the patient, it conflates the notion of the active construction, characteristic for accusative languages, with the notion of the ergative construction, characteristic for ergative languages. This conflation involves a conflation of the notion of passive voice with the notion of antipassive voice. RG regards antipassive constructions in ergative languages simply as passive constructions.

The label *antipassive* is sometimes used in RG, but in a completely different sense from that established for ergative languages. The term *antipassive* is proposed to be a label for constructions that are produced as a result of converting the direct object into a chômeur which can be omitted (Postal, 1977). This definition is applied to ergative and accusative languages. According to this definition, we obtain the following correspondences in accusative languages:

(15)    Active constructions   Antipassive constructions
   *The woman sewed the dress.*  *The woman sewed on the dress.*
              *The woman sewed.*
   *The hunter shot the bear.*  *The hunter shot at the bear.*
              *The hunter shot.*

The notion of antipassive in RG clearly has nothing in common with the current notion of the antipassive construction used to characterize specific constructions of ergative languages that are the reverses of the passive constructions in accusative languages.

The RG theory of passivization is rooted in the syntax of accusative languages, where the transitive subject denotes the agent and the direct object denotes the patient. Therefore, RG rules for passive constructions can work only for accusative languages, but even there some serious difficulties arise.

Consider the impersonal passives.

RG correctly regards passives and impersonal passives as the same phenomenon. Using the concept of the dummy term, RG correctly states that impersonal passives involve an advancement of 2 to 1. The dummy subject in impersonal passives can be represented either by zero or by a pronoun.

Examples of a dummy subject represented by zero:
German:

(16) *Hier wurde den ganzen Abend getanzt.*
   'It was danced here all evening'.

Turkish:

(17) *Burada çalişilir.*
   'Here it was worked'.

Example of a dummy subject represented by a pronoun from German:

(18) *Es wurde getanzt.*
   'It was danced (There was dancing)'.

But how about impersonal passives with a direct object, as in the following examples from Polish:

(19)    *Stefana   poslano        do doma.*
        Stephen sent+PASSIVE to home
        'Stephen was sent home'.


and Welsh (Xolodovič, 1974: 367):

(20)    *Llodwid        Jones gan Williams.*
        killed+PASSIVE Jones by  Williams
        'Jones was killed by Williams'.


*Stefana* in (19) and *Jones* in (20) are direct objects rather than subjects. The direct object is marked in Polish by the accusative case suffix, and in Welsh by the syntactic environment.

These examples illustrate passive constructions without an advancement of 2 to 1. They contravene the claim of RG that any passive construction must involve an advancement of 2 to 1.

To solve the difficulty, RG resorts to such an ad hoc contrivance as a claim that although *Stefana* and *Jones* in the above examples are marked as direct objects, they must be interpreted as chômeurs from the relational point of view, because here a dummy allegedly is inserted as 2, putting 2 *en chômage*, and then is advanced from 2 to 1 (Perlmutter and Postal, 1984).

As a matter of fact, a satisfactory explanation of the above impersonal passive constructions can be given only by reference to universals that follow from the definitions of predicates and terms based on the *Applicative Principle*. These universals in terms of RG are:

1) A transitive predicate plus a direct object is syntactically equivalent to an intransitive predicate.

2) A ditransitive predicate plus an indirect object is syntactically equivalent to a transitive predicate.

In view of universal 2), impersonal passive constructions with a direct object can be regarded simply as impersonal passive constructions without a direct object. Accordingly, rules that apply to impersonal passive constructions without a direct object apply to impersonal passive constructions with a direct object.

RG has raised an interesting question: What syntactic type of intransitive predicates can be passivized?

It has been observed cross-linguistically that some intransitive predicates can never be passivized, while other predicates can. For example, the following intransitive predicates can never be passivized cross-linguistically (Perlmutter, 1978):

1. predicates expressed by adjectives in English: predicates describing sizes, shapes, weights, colors, smells, states of mind, etc.;

2. predicates whose initial nuclear term is semantically a patient, such as *burn, fall, float, tremble, roll, flow, soar*, etc.;

3. predicates of existing and happening: *exist, happen, occur, vanish*, etc.;
4. nonvoluntary emission of stimuli that impinge on the senses (light, noise, smell, etc.): *shine, sparkle, jingle, smell, stink*, etc.;
5. aspectual predicates: *begin, start, continue, end*, etc.;
6. duratives: *last, remain, stay, survive*, etc.

And here is the list of intransitive predicates whose passivization is possible cross-linguistically:

1. predicates describing willed or volitional acts: *work, play, speak, quarrel, walk, knock*, etc.;
2. certain involuntary bodily processes: *cough, snore, weep*, etc.

The question is: How is the semantic difference between these two classes characterized syntactically? Can we state a syntactic hypothesis predicting a cross-linguistic possibility of the passivization of intransitive predicates?

RG answers affirmatively to these questions. It advances a syntactic hypothesis called the *Unaccusative Hypothesis*, meant to predict the cross-linguistic possibility of the passivization of intransitive predicates.

The Unaccusative Hypothesis is stated as follows:

Certain intransitive clauses have an initial 2 but not an initial 1.

This hypothesis means that certain intransitive clauses have an underlying structure with a direct object that corresponds to the subject of the surface structure. For example, the underlying structure of

(21)    *Gorillas exist.*

must be

(22)    *Exist gorillas.*

*Gorillas* in (22) is the direct object of *exist*, and it corresponds to *gorillas* in (21), which is the subject of *exist* in (21).

This correspondence is presented by the following relational network:

(23)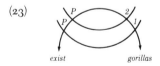

*Gorillas* is initial 2 but final 1.

The advancement in (23) is called *unaccusative*. The following terminology facilitates the discussion:

A *transitive stratum* contains a 1-arc and a 2-arc.
An *unaccusative stratum* contains a 2-arc but no 1-arc.
An *unergative stratum* contains a 1-arc but no 2-arc.

In current terminology, a transitive stratum contains a subject and an object; an unaccusative stratum contains a direct object but not a subject; an unergative stratum contains a subject but no object.

The Final 1 Law predicts that clauses with *final unaccusative strata* will not be well formed in any language. Taken together with certain other proposed linguistic universals, it has the following consequence:

Every clause with an unaccusative stratum involves an advancement to 1.

Under the Unaccusative Hypothesis, then, a class of intransitive clauses with an initial unaccusative stratum contrasts with a class of intransitive clauses with an initial unergative stratum. Impersonal passive clauses can be obtained from the second class of clauses. This syntactic class of clauses are semantically characterized by the list given above of the intransitive predicates whose passivization is possible cross-linguistically.

Is the Unaccusative Hypothesis correct?

What empirical facts support this hypothesis?

The fact that the class of intransitive clauses that can be passivized follows from the Unaccusative Hypothesis cannot be regarded as supporting this hypothesis: it is a basic principle of logic that true statements can follow from false statements. In view of this principle of logic, the truth of the Unaccusative Hypothesis cannot be confirmed by the prediction of the facts it was constructed to explain. The Unaccusative Hypothesis, like any other scientific hypothesis, can be considered plausible only if we can find facts that follow from it on independent grounds.

The trouble with the Unaccusative Hypothesis is that it cannot be tested on independent grounds.

The Unaccusative Hypothesis is unacceptable not in the sense that there are counterexamples to it; rather, it is unacceptable because it is consistent with any conceivable set of empirical data. There is a possibility always open to assign an initial unaccusative stratum to intransitive clauses that cannot be passivized and an initial unergative stratum to intransitive clauses that can be passivized. The trouble with the Unaccusative Hypothesis is that it is impossible to construct even potential counterexamples to it. As a matter of fact, only those hypotheses can have an empirical import to which potential counterexamples can be constructed.

The Unaccusative Hypothesis assumes an abstract stratum, called the unaccusative stratum, which contains an object and no subject, and it assumes an advancement of the object to the position of the subject. But there is no way of constructing counterexamples to these assumptions. These assumptions are gratuitous, because they make no empirical claims.

As an alternative to the Unaccusative Hypothesis, I propose a hypothesis that is free of assumptions to which counterexamples cannot be constructed. I call this hypothesis the *syntactic neutralization hypothesis*.

The Syntactic Neutralization Hypothesis claims that any intransitive clause is a result of the neutralization of transitive clauses containing a binary predicate applied to two terms, one of which becomes a primary term and another one, a secondary term. The terms in a transitive clause are always assigned a definite meaning: in accusative languages, the primary term denotes an agent and the secondary term a patient. In ergative languages the reverse is true: the primary term denotes a patient, and the secondary term denotes an agent. But in both accusative and ergative languages, the primary term in an intransitive clause may denote either an agent or a patient, because the primary term in an intransitive sentence represents the opposition *primary term: secondary term* and so can be identified with either member of this opposition.

The Syntactic Neutralization Hypothesis predicts that the primary term in an intransitive clause may denote either an agent or a patient, and in some languages, called active languages, this prediction is reflected in different case markings for terms denoting agents and terms denoting patients in intransitive clauses. In accordance with this prediction, intransitive clauses can be divided into two classes: a class of intransitive clauses that cannot be passivized, and a class of intransitive clauses that can be passivized cross-linguistically.

Both the Unaccusative Hypothesis and the Syntactic Neutralization Hypothesis predict the same facts, but the latter has two advantages over the former: 1) it is free of the assumptions of an underlying stratum, that is, a deep structure, which cannot be tested empirically; and 2) it can be tested on independent grounds, because it is a particular case of the Neutralization Hypothesis, which stands out as one of the pillars of linguistic theory and semiotics.

Let us now turn to the problems connected with the passivization of indirect objects.

Consider the sentence

(24)    *Peter gave money to Nancy.*

In this sentence *Peter* is the subject, *money* is the direct object, and *Nancy* is the indirect object.

RG claims that the indirect object *Nancy* cannot be passivized by advancing it to *1*. Rather, it is passivized in two steps: first, *Nancy* is advanced to *2*, and *money* is put en chômage, which yields

(25)    *Peter gave Nancy money.*

This sentence can be represented by the following stratal diagram:

(26)

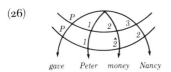

gave    Peter    money    Nancy

In (26) *Nancy* is the direct object and *money* is a chômeur.

The second step is advancing *Nancy* to *1* and putting *Peter* en chômage, which yields

(27)     *Nancy was given money by Peter.*

This sentence can be represented by the following diagram:

(28)
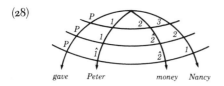

As these examples show, RG claims that indirect objects can be promoted to subjects only via promotion to direct object and putting the direct object en chômage.

There are two groups of counterexamples to this claim.

In some languages, such as Dutch, an indirect object can be promoted to direct object but cannot be promoted to subject (Dik, 1978: 125):

(29)     a. *Jan  gaf  het boek aan Piet.*
            John gave the book to   Peter
            'John gave the book to Peter'.
         b. *Jan  gaf  Piet  het boek.*
            John gave Peter the book
            'John gave Peter the book'.
         c. *\*Piet   werd het boek gegeven door Jan.*
            Peter was   the book given    by   John
            'Peter was given the book by John'.

On the other hand, in some languages an indirect object can be promoted to subject, although it cannot be promoted to direct object. Here is an example from Achenese (Lawler, 1977):

(30)     a. *Gɔpnyan ka    gi-bre  buku nyan ki-kamo.*
            he          perf. he-give book that to-us
            'He gave that book to us'.
         b. *Buku nyan ka    gi-bre  ki-kamo le-gɔpnyan.*
            book that perf. he-give to-us     by-him
            'That book was given to us by him'.
         c. *Kamo ka    gi-bre  buku nyan le-gɔpnyan.*
            we    perf. he-give book that by-him
            'We were given that book by him'.
         d. *\*gɔpnyan ka    gi-bre  kamo buku nyan.*
            he          perf. he-give us    book that
            'He gave us that book'.

Another group of counterexamples conflicts with the claim of RG that promotion of an indirect object to direct object puts the initial direct object en chômage. So, in some dialects of the English language, it is possible to passivize both *Nancy* and *money* in (24). These dialects can have

(31)  a. *Peter gave Nancy money.*
      b. *Nancy was given money.*
      c. *Money was given Nancy.*

(31c) conflicts with the claim of RG that *money* in (31a) is a 2-chômeur. As a matter of fact, (31a) is a stylistic variant of (24) rather than the result of the promotion of *Nancy* from 3 to 2; therefore, the passive construction (27) must be regarded as derived from both (24) and (25).

We can advance strong arguments also against the notion of the *1-chômeur.* Consider the following passive sentences:

(32)  *Mary was led by the hand.*

(33)  *Mary was led by John.*

RG claims correctly that *by John* in (33) is syntactically different from the oblique *by the hand* in (32) and at the same time has something in common with the subject in the active construction

(34)  *John led Mary.*

That raises the problem, What is *by John* in (33), if it is different from a regular oblique?

To solve this problem, RG posits two levels for the passive construction (33), and the chômeur relation *by John* is considered a chômeur on the final level and a subject on the initial level.

This solution is not satisfactory for the following reason:

The claim of RG that *by John* in (33) is syntactically different from the oblique *by the hand* in (32) is correct. But that is only half of the story. The other half is that *by John* also has something syntactically in common with *by the hand*. RG recognizes only the difference between the two prepositional phrases, but it fails to see that these prepositional phrases are syntactically identical from a structural point of view.

The crucial fact is that the two prepositional phrases are identical in their syntactic function of modifying predicates: both are predicate modifiers. But that is what can be called their inherent function. To see the difference between the two phrases, let us consider the meaning of *by.*

There is a striking difference between the meaning of the preposition *by* in (32) and in (33). In *by the hand* the preposition has a concrete meaning: it denotes a mode of action. In *by John* the preposition *by* has lost its concrete meaning, and *by John*, which is an oblique, has taken on the function of the secondary term—it has become a functional counterpart of the primary term of the corresponding active sentence.

Linguistic theory can dispense with both chômeur relations and strata in explaining passive constructions. The crucial thing is to distinguish between the inherent and superposed functions of the terms. It must be stressed that the inherent and superposed functions of oblique terms in passive constructions are not ad hoc notions. The distinction between the inherent and superposed functions concerns any syntactic, morphological, and phonological unit—a syntaxeme, a word, a morpheme, a phoneme. The distinction between inherent and superposed functions of linguistic units pervades any natural language and must be a cornerstone of universal grammar.

### 12.3 The Demotion Theory of Passivization

Some linguists have recently advanced a claim that passivization is essentially a *demotion of the subject* in a sentence (Keenan, 1975; Comrie, 1977; Jain, 1977). This claim is based on the syntax of impersonal passives.

True, passivization of active constructions involves the demotion of the subject. But the demotion of the subject is not characteristic only with respect to passivization; it is also involved in producing impersonal active sentences. Two kinds of demotion of the subject must be distinguished: a demotion connected with passivization, and a demotion connected with producing active impersonal constructions. Compare in Russian

(35)     *a. Pulja       ubila  bojca.*
             bullet-Nom. killed soldier-Acc.
             'The bullet killed the soldier'.
         *b. Boec        byl ubit  pulej.*
             soldier-Nom. was killed bullet-Instr.
             'The soldier was killed by the bullet'.
         *c. Pulej       ubilo           bojca.*
             bullet-Instr. killed-Impersonal soldier-Acc.
             Literally: *'It killed the soldier with the bullet'.

(35c) has no counterpart in English. It is an impersonal construction that was obtained by the demotion of the subject.

Similar examples can be found in other languages. They are crucial: by comparing passive constructions with impersonal active constructions, it becomes clear that the demotion of the subject that accompanies passivization is a part of the operation of conversion.

Consider now the following expression from Russian:

(36)     *Oni govorjat.*
         'They speak'.

By demoting and eliminating the subject, we get an impersonal active construction

(37)    *Govorjat*
        'It is said'

rather than an impersonal passive construction.

The demotion theory of passivization is motivated by a desire to avoid abstractions, such as the zero or dummy subject. Of course, we must avoid unnecessary abstract entities. But to explain impersonal passive constructions, we need the notion 'dummy subject'. By introducing this notion, we can see that the passivization of the sentence with a one-place predicate is analogous to the passivization of the sentences with two-place predicates. Otherwise the mechanism of the passivization of the sentences with a one-place predicate remains a mystery.

I have considered the most important alternative theories of passivization— the transformational theory, the theory of relational grammar, and the demotion theory. In view of the foregoing discussion, none of these theories is acceptable for one or another reason. All of them are inferior to the theory of passivization based on applicative grammar.

## 13. The Formalism of Applicative Grammar

### 13.1 The Formal System of Applicative Grammar

The formalism of applicative grammar is related to the formalism of categorial grammars, but at the same time there is an essential difference between the two formalisms.

Y. Bar-Hillel, C. Gaifman, and E. Shamir proved the formal equivalence of phrase structure grammars (immediate constituent grammars) and categorial grammars (Bar-Hillel, 1964). Since categorial grammars are equivalent to phrase structure grammars, categorial grammars are inadequate for the description of natural languages in the same way as are phrase structure grammars.

To have a grammar that could be adequate for the description of natural languages, I unified categorial grammar and the system of the combinators of combinatory logic into an integrated whole; the linguistic theory based on the resulting formalism I call *applicative grammar*. The relation of applicative grammar to categorial grammar is similar to the relation of generative-transformational grammar to phrase structure grammar. Just as it would be a mistake to identify generative-transformational grammar with phrase structure grammar, so it would be a mistake to identify applicative grammar with categorial grammar.

I now turn to the formalism of applicative grammar.

A language, by definition, must have three kinds, or *categories*, or *types* of expressions (henceforth I will use the term *type* as a synonym of the term *category*):

1) *terms*, or names of objects;

2) *sentences;*

3) *operators*, that is, expressions that combine expressions to form other expressions.

In applicative grammar, operators are connected with one another by a network of formal definitions, which eventually reach the ultimate definientia—term and sentence. Let us take, for instance, the operators *one-place predicate* $(p_1)$, *two-place predicate* $(p_2)$, and *three-place predicate* $(p_3)$ and see how their definitions are interrelated with one another and with the ultimate definientia, the *sentence* $(s)$ and the *term* $(t)$. Consider the following example:

(1)     *showed*                          $— (p_3)$
        *showed Nancy*                    $— (p_2)$
        *showed Nancy pictures*    $— (p_1)$
        *Jim showed Nancy pictures* $— (s)$

The first expression *showed* is a three-place (or ditransitive) predicate of type $p_3$. Applying it to an expression of type $t$ produces *showed Nancy*, an expression of type $p_2$, that is, a transitive predicate of the same type, as, for example, *took*. Applying *showed Nancy* to *pictures* produces *showed Nancy pictures*, an intransitive predicate of the same type $p_1$, as, for example, *took the book* or *walked*. Applying *showed Nancy pictures* to *Jim* produces *Jim showed Nancy pictures*, an expression of type $s$.

By *type* I mean a class of operators. For the sake of generality, I conceive of sentences and terms as zero-place operators. This approach is convenient not only from the formal point of view; it is empirically justified, too. Thus, *Jim walks* or *Jim takes the book* is equivalent to the Latin impersonal *Ningit* 'It snows', which is nothing but a zero-place predicate. The English term *the blind man* is equivalent to *the blind*, which is nothing but a zero-place attribute.

Since I used the term *type* only in the sense of a class of operators, I will henceforth replace it with the term *O-type*.

The combinatory properties of predicates and terms can be expressed in a series of definitions:

(2)     1)   $sA \equiv p_1B \ \ tC$
        2)   $p_1B \equiv p_2B^1 \ \ tC^1$
        3)   $p_2B^1 \equiv p_3B^2 \ \ tC^2$
             .    .    .    .
             .    .    .    .
             .    .    .    .

The symbol $\equiv$ indicates identity by definition. The juxtaposition of O-type symbols with the expression symbols indicates that a given expression belongs to a given type. The blanks between expressions are meant to divide them. The left expression is applied to the right one.

The above definitions read:

1) Expression $A$ of $O$-type $s$ is identical by definition with expression $B$ of $O$-type $p_1$ applied to expression $C$ of $O$-type $t$.
2) Expression $B$ of $O$-type $p_1$ is identical by definition with expression $B^1$ of $O$-type $p_2$ applied to expression $C^1$ of $O$-type $t$.
3) Expression $B^1$ of $O$-type $p_2$ is identical by definition with expression $B^2$ of $O$-type $p_3$ applied to expression $C^2$ of $O$-type $t$.

We face a conceptual problem: How do we dispose of $p_1$, $p_2$, and $p_3$ by reducing them to the ultimate definientia $t$ and $s$?

To solve this problem, I will construct a formal definition of $O$-type.

Consider an expression $XY$ where $X$ is an operator and $Y$ is an operand. It is obvious that if expression $XY$ belongs to a certain type $v$, and expression $Y$ belongs to a certain type $u$, expression $X$ must belong to a type of expressions that change expressions of type $u$ into expressions of type $v$. Let us designate this type as

(3)     $Ouv$

where the symbol $O$ stands for *operationality*, that is, for the general notion of the type of operators. I call it the *operationality primitive*.[5] This formula reads: 'the type of operators from $u$ into $v$'.

We can formulate a rule for classifying the above expression $XY$:

(4)     If $X$ is in $Ouv$ and $Y$ is in $u$, then $XY$ is in $v$.

Now we can have a formal calculus of operators.

We postulate certain primitive $O$-types: $c_1, c_2, \ldots$ .

We define the formal concept of $O$-type as follows:

RULE T:  a.  Primitive types $c_1, c_2, \ldots$ are $O$-types;
         b.  if $u$ and $v$ are $O$-types, then $Ouv$ is an $O$-type.

Rule T can be represented by the following tree diagram:

(5)     $\dfrac{u \quad v}{Ouv}$

Then we introduce notation for the relation 'belongs to':

(6)     $yX$

Formula (6) reads: 'expression $X$ belongs to type $y$'.

Next we adopt the above rule (5) and present it as a tree diagram:

RULE E: $\dfrac{OuvX \qquad uY}{v(XY)}$

Here the horizontal line is meant to indicate that resultant $v(XY)$ follows from the application of operator $X$ to operand $Y$. I want to stress the relativity of the concepts 'operand' and 'resultant': the three expressions $X$, $Y$, and $XY$ are all operators. But besides, $Y$ is an operand and $XY$ is a resultant of $X$.

Rule E reads: 'if expression $X$ belongs to $O$-type $Ouv$, and expression $Y$ belongs to $O$-type $u$, then expression $XY$ belongs to $O$-type $v$'.

It should be noted that formula $Ouv$ could be presented in a different form, say as $(u \rightarrow v)$, if we adopted a convention that the arrow designates '$O$-type'. But the notation with prefix $O$ is more convenient than the notation with infix $\rightarrow$, since the former is bracketless and the latter involves the use of brackets, as in the case with any mathematical notation using infixes instead of prefixes. Besides, the arrow might involve conceptual ambiguity, since usually this symbol does not designate abstract objects.

We can deduce the following two rules from Rule E:

RULE E1: $\dfrac{v(XY), \qquad uY}{OuvX}$

This rule reads: 'if the resultant of the application of expression $X$ to expression $Y$ belongs to $O$-type $v$, and expression $Y$ belongs to $O$-type $u$, then expression $X$ belongs to type $Ouv$.'

Rule E1 is a straightforward consequence of Rule E, and the proof is obvious: let $X$ belong to $O$-type $z$; then, according to Rule E, since $y$ belongs to $O$-type $u$ and $XY$ belongs to $O$-type $v$, $z$ must be identical with $Ouv$.

Rule E1 defines the $O$-type of an operator in terms of the $O$-types of its operand and resultant.

The reverse of Rule E1 is this:

RULE E2: $\dfrac{XY, \qquad OuvX}{uY, v(XY)}$

This rule reads: if expression $XY$ is the resultant of the application of operator $X$ to its operand $Y$, and $X$ belongs to $O$-type $Ouv$, then $Y$ belongs to $O$-type $u$ and $XY$ belongs to $O$-type $v$.

The proof of Rule E2 is no less obvious: if expression $XY$ is constructed by Rule E, and operator $X$ belongs to $O$-type $Ouv$, then $Y$ must belong to $O$-type $u$ and $XY$ must belong to $O$-type $v$.

Rule E2 defines the $O$-types of an operand and of a resultant in terms of the $O$-type of their operator.

Let us now turn to our problem. By applying Rule E1 to the above set of definitions, we can define $p_1$, $p_2$, and $p_3$ in terms of the ultimate definientia $t$ and $s$. That is done in three steps: first, we define $p_1$ as $Ots$, then we define $p_2$ as $OtOts$, and finally we define $p_3$ as $OtOtOts$. As a result, we get a new set of definitions:

(7)  1') $\quad\quad sA \equiv \quad\quad OtsB\ tC$
     2') $\quad OtsB \equiv \quad OtOtsB^1\ tC^1$
     3') $OtOtsB^1 \equiv OtOtOtsB^2\ tC^2$

$$\begin{matrix} \cdot & \cdot & \cdot & \cdot \\ \cdot & \cdot & \cdot & \cdot \\ \cdot & \cdot & \cdot & \cdot \end{matrix}$$

Reducing the definitions of all $O$-types to their ultimate definientia makes it possible to determine clearly to which $O$-types given expressions must belong if they are to combine into well-formed expressions. As a matter of fact, Rule E formalizes the concept of well-formedness with respect to type.

I call an expression $X$ *well-formed with respect to type* if it is constructed from expressions $Y_1, \ldots, Y_n$ by Rule E.

We can construct applicative tree diagrams to represent various type analyses of expressions. For example, a type analysis of the sentence *Jim showed Nancy pictures* can be represented by the following diagram:

(8) $\quad$ *OtOtOts* $\quad$ *showed* $\quad\quad$ *t Nancy*

$\quad\quad\quad$ *OtOts* $\quad$ *(showed Nancy)* $\quad\quad\quad\quad$ *t pictures*

$\quad\quad\quad\quad$ *Ots* $\quad$ *((showed Nancy) pictures)* $\quad\quad$ *t Jim*

$\quad\quad\quad\quad\quad$ *s (((showed Nancy) pictures) Jim)*

Let us now apply the calculus of $O$-types to other conceptual problems. We will be concerned with problems arising from conceptual ambiguity and vagueness. It is obvious that conceptual ambiguity and vagueness are highly disadvantageous for any science. The history of science abounds in examples where an increase in the conceptual clarity of a theory through careful clarifications and specifications of meaning had a significant influence on the progress of science, as, for example, the emergence of the theory of special relativity depended upon the recognition and subsequent reduction of conceptual ambiguity and vagueness within a particular domain.

We will be able to construct precise definitions for syntactical concepts either that are used undefined or whose definitions are of little avail because of their ambiguity and vagueness.

I start with the definition of the *syntactic system* of applicative grammar. This system is defined by six sorts of notions, as follows:

1. primitive *O*-types: *t, s;*
2. rules for constructing composite types from the primitives:
   a. primitive *O*-types *t, s* are *O*-types,
   b. if *x* and *y* are *O*-types, then *Oxy* is an *O*-type;
3. expressions belonging to *O*-types;
4. rules for constructing expressions: Rule E, Rule E1, Rule E2;
5. nine combinators (or *combinatory operators*): I, C, C$_*$, W, B, S, K, Φ, Ψ;
6. rules for applying combinators: reduction rules and expansion rules;
7. replacement rules;
8. deductive processes: expansion and reduction.

I introduce a few definitions:

DEFINITION 1.   If expression *XY* belongs to type *s*, expression *Y* belongs to type *t*, and expression *X* belongs to type *Ots*, I call *X* a *one-place predicate* and *Y* a *primary term.*

DEFINITION 2.   If expression *XY* belongs to type *Ots*, expression *Y* belongs to type *t*, and expression *X* belongs to type *OtOts*, I call *X* a *two-place predicate* and *Y* a *secondary term.*

DEFINITION 3.   If expression *XY* belongs to type *OtOts*, expression *Y* belongs to type *t*, and expression *X* belongs to type *OtOtOts*, I call *X* a *three-place predicate* and *Y* a *tertiary term.*

The opposition of a primary and a secondary term constitutes the *nucleus* of a sentence. These terms I call *nuclear.*

It follows from definitions 1 and 2 that primary terms occur both in the opposition *primary term : secondary term* (with two-place predicates) and outside this opposition (with one-place predicates). Therefore, the position with a one-place predicate must be regarded as the point of neutralization of the opposition *primary term : secondary term,* which is represented by the primary term in this position. The secondary term is the positive (marked) member of this opposition, and the primary term is its neuter-negative (unmarked) term.

DEFINITION 4.   Let *AB* be a well-formed expression. It follows from Rule E that *A* belongs to *O*-type *Oxy*, *B* belongs to *O*-type *x*, and *AB* belongs to *O*-type *y*. Either *A* or *B* can be considered the main constituent of expression *AB*, called its *head:* if $x \equiv y$, the head is *B*, and if $x \not\equiv y$, the head is *A*.

If *B* is the head, *A* is called a *modifier of the head*. If *A* is the head, *B* is called a *complement of the head*. The term *dependent* denotes modifiers and complements together.

Example: The expression *Bill bought new books* is represented by the following tree diagram:

(9)

$$Ott\ new \qquad t\ books$$

$$OtOts\quad bought \qquad\qquad t\,(new\ books)$$

$$Ots\ \ (bought\ (new\ books)) \qquad t\ Bill$$

$$s\,((bought\ (new\ books))\,Bill)$$

*books* is the head of *(new books)*, and *new* is its modifier; *bought* is the head of *(bought (new books))*, and *(new books)* is its complement; *(bought (new books))* is the head of *((bought (new books)) Bill)*, and *Bill* is its complement.

DEFINITION 5. A type symbol is called *adjoined* if it is introduced into the syntactic system by a definition of the form
$$z = Oxy,$$
where *z* denotes an adjoined type symbol and *Oxy* denotes an *O*-type where *x* and *y* are either other adjoined type symbols or *t*, or *s*.

It follows from this definition that we can introduce adjoined type symbols only in stages. At the first stage we can define only four adjoined type symbols for which arbitrary letters can be used:

(10)    $a = Ott, \qquad m = Oss, \qquad p_1 = Ots, \qquad c = Ost$

By substituting these adjoined type symbols for their definientia used as components of complex categories, we can introduce new adjoined type symbols, for example:

(11)    $p_2 = Otp_1, \qquad d = Op_1p_1$

By substituting new adjoined type symbols for their definientia used as components in more complex types, we can introduce further adjoined type symbols, and so on.

It is obvious that any adjoined type symbol introduced at later stages can be defined in terms of the ultimate definientia $t$ and $s$ by a series of definitions. I call this series of definitions a *definitional reduction*.

Example of definitional reduction:

(12)     $p_3 = Otp_2 = OtOtp_1 = OtOtOts$

The concept of adjoined type symbols and their definitional reduction is important, because by introducing adjoined type symbols, we can present the system of types in a compact form.

Here is a table of adjoined type symbols denoting some basic syntactic types:

(13)

| Adjoined Type Symbols | Definitional Reduction | Meaning |
|---|---|---|
| $p_1$ | $= Ots$ | One-place predicate |
| $p_2$ | $= Otp_1 = OtOts$ | Two-place predicate |
| $p_3$ | $= Otp_2 = OtOtOts$ | Three-place predicate |
| $a$ | $= Ott$ | Modifier of a term |
| $d$ | $= Op_1p_1 = OOtsOts$ | Modifier of a one-place predicate |
| $d'$ | $= Op_2p_2 = OOtp_1Otp_1$ $= OOtOtsOtOts$ | Modifier of a two-place predicate |
| $p_1^{+1}$ | $= Op_1p_2 = OOtsOtp_1$ $= OOtsOtOts$ | Operator increasing the valence of a one-place predicate |
| $p_1^{-1}$ | $= Op_1s = OOtss$ | Operator decreasing the valence of a one-place predicate |
| $p_2^{+1}$ | $= Op_2p_3 = OOtp_1Otp_2$ $= OOtOtsOtOtp_1$ $= OOtOtsOtOtOts$ | Operator increasing the valence of a two-place predicate |
| $p_2^{-1}$ | $= Op_2p_1 = OOtp_1Ots$ $= OOtOtsOts$ | Operator decreasing the valence of a two-place predicate |

We can introduce as many adjoined type symbols as we need.

I will close this section by suggesting an alternative method of constructing applicative tree diagrams.

The above examples presented the construction of tree diagrams in accordance with a convention that an operator must be placed before its operand and that the tree diagram must be constructed from top to bottom, starting with the smallest units.

Sometimes, however, it is convenient to construct a tree diagram from bottom up, starting with a sentence. We take a sentence and treat it as the node, extract the operator from the sentence, and write the operator on the left and the operand on the right above the horizontal line. The same procedure is repeated over new nodes from left to right until we reach the ultimate constituents of the sentence. To illustrate how that is done, let us take the sentence *Bill bought new books* in the above example. We will construct an applicative tree diagram in steps.

Our first step is to take the sentence, draw a horizontal line over it, extract the operator from it, and form two new nodes over the horizontal line:

(14)     $\overline{Ots\ bought\ new\ books\quad t\ Bill}$

         *s Bill bought new books*

Our second step is to apply this procedure to the new nodes from left to right. We get

(15)     $\overline{OtOts\ bought\qquad t\ new\ books}$

         $\overline{Ots\ bought\ new\ books\quad t\ Bill}$

         *s Bill bought new books*

By applying the same procedure to the new nodes, we complete the construction:

(16)                      $\overline{Ott\ new\quad t\ books}$

         $\overline{OtOts\ bought\qquad t\ new\ books}$

         $\overline{Ots\ bought\ new\ books\quad t\ Bill}$

         *s Bill bought new books*

There is no need to use brackets in this type of diagram.

Here is a tree diagram without brackets for the sentence *Jim showed Nancy pictures:*

(17)     $\overline{OtOtOts\ showed\quad t\ Nancy}$

         $\overline{OtOts\ showed\ Nancy\quad t\ pictures}$

         $\overline{Ots\ showed\ Nancy\ pictures\quad t\ Jim}$

         *s Jim showed Nancy pictures*

The syntactic system provides the means for transposing one syntactic function into another. For example, the type *OOttOts* is a class of operators that transpose a modifier of a term into a one-place predicate; the type *OtOtt* is a class of operators that transpose a term into a modifier of a term. Sentences also can be transposed into different syntactic functions: for example, the type *Ost* is a class of operators that transpose a sentence into a term, and so on.

## 13.2 Superposition of Types

Now we are ready to formalize the notion of functional superposition. From a formal point of view, functional superposition amounts to superposition of types. *Superposition of types* is to be defined as follows:

DEFINITION 6.  Let $E$ be an expression of type $x$, and let $E$ take on type $y$ on type $x$. Then $E$ shall be said to belong to a type $z$, such that $z$ is stratified into $y$ superposed onto $x$. Type $z$ is represented by the formula

$$\langle y/x \rangle,$$

where the slash (/) indicates the stratification of type $z$ into $y$ superposed onto $x$, which are enclosed in angle brackets.

Let us define the notion of the *superposer*.

DEFINITION 7.  An operator $R$ of type $Ox\langle y/x \rangle$ shall be called a *superposer*.

As an example of superposition, let us consider the derivation of the English gerund from the finite forms of the verb. In English, the gerunds derived from the finite form of verbs are assigned a stratified type:

(18)      $\langle t/Ot^k s \rangle$

The suffix *-ing* in English gerunds is a superposer of type

(19)      $OOt^k s \langle t/Ot^k s \rangle$

(Formula $Ot^k s$, where $k=1$, 2, 3, indicates intransitive, transitive, and ditransitive predicates.)

Here are examples illustrating (18). The English gerund *leaving*, in the context of the expression *John proposed our immediately leaving the office*, belongs to type $t$, because it is modified by *our* of type $Ott$; also it belongs to type $OtOts$ because it takes the secondary term *the office* of type $t$ and is modified by the adverb *immediately* of type $OOt^k sOt^k s$.

There are six rules of combination of expressions belonging to stratified types:

Rule S1: $\dfrac{Ox\langle y/x \rangle A \quad xB}{\langle y/x \rangle AB}$

Rule S2: $\dfrac{OxyA \quad \langle x/z \rangle B}{yAB}$

Rule S3: $\dfrac{OxyA \quad \langle z/x \rangle B}{\langle z/y \rangle AB}$

Rule S4: $\dfrac{\langle Oxy/z \rangle A \quad xB}{yAB}$

Rule S5: $\dfrac{\langle z/Oxy\rangle A \quad xB}{\langle z/y\rangle AB}$

Rule S6: $\dfrac{\langle Oxy/z\rangle A \quad \langle x/u\rangle B}{yAB}$

Here is an explanation of the notation and meaning of rules S1-6. Symbol *A* is a variable indicating an operator, and *B* is a variable indicating an operand. Expressions enclosed in angle brackets indicate stratified types.

Rule S1 is interpreted as follows. Let *A* be an expression of type $Ox \langle y/x\rangle$ (which means that *A* is a superposer). Then, if *A* is applied to *B* of type *x*, we obtain a combination *AB* of a stratified type $\langle y/x\rangle$. Rule S1 is a version of Rule E given in section 13.1. Rule S1 is illustrated by the derivation of a gerund:

(20) $\dfrac{OOtOts\langle t/OtOts\rangle \text{ -ing} \quad OtOts \text{ leave}}{\langle t/OtOts\rangle\text{-ing leave}}$

Rule S3 is illustrated by the combination *immediately leaving*:

(21) $\dfrac{OOtOtsOtOts \text{ immediately} \quad \langle t/OtOts\rangle \text{ leaving}}{\langle t/OtOts\rangle \text{ immediately leaving}}$

Rule S5 is illustrated by the combination *immediately leaving the office*:

(22) $\dfrac{\langle t/OtOts\rangle \text{ immediately leaving} \quad t \text{ the office}}{\langle t/Ots\rangle \text{ immediately leaving the office}}$

Rule S2 is illustrated by the combination *our immediately leaving the office*:

(23) $\dfrac{Ott \text{ our} \quad \langle t/Ots\rangle \text{ immediately leaving the office}}{t \text{ our immediately leaving the office}}$

If we consider the above expressions as parts of the sentence *John proposed our immediately leaving the office*, we get the following tree diagram:

(24)
$$OOtOtsOtOts \text{ immediately} \quad \langle t/OtOts\rangle \text{ leaving}$$
$$\langle t/OtOts\rangle \text{ immediately leaving} \qquad t \text{ the office}$$
$$Ott \text{ our} \qquad \langle t/Ots\rangle \text{ immediately leaving the office}$$
$$OtOts \text{ proposed} \qquad t \text{ our immediately leaving the office}$$
$$Ots \text{ proposed our immediately leaving the office} \qquad t \text{ John}$$
$$s \text{ proposed our immediately leaving the office} \quad \text{John}$$

Rule S4 is illustrated by combinations of participles with nouns in Russian. Thus, in Russian, participles are assigned the stratified type $Ott/Ot^ks$. When we apply the Russian participle *spjaščij* 'who is sleeping' to *maľčik* 'boy', we obtain *spjaščij maľčik* 'the boy who is sleeping':

(25)     *‹Ott/Ots› spjaščij    t maľčik*

        *t spjaščij maľčik*

Rule S6 can be illustrated by the long passive construction. As will be explained in section 13.7, in long passive constructions passive predicates, which are intransitive, take on the function of transitive predicates, and the term denoting an agent, which is a modifier of the passive predicate, takes on the function of a secondary term. Therefore, we assign the stratified type *‹OtOts/Ots›* to the passive predicate and the stratified type *‹t/OOtsOts›* to the term denoting the agent. As an example, let us take the passive sentence *This hypothesis was advanced by Einstein*. Its structure is represented by the following tree diagram:

(26)     *‹OtOts/Ots› was advanced    ‹t/OOtsOts› by Einstein*

        *Ots was advanced by Einstein        t this hypothesis*

          *s was advanced by Einstein this hypothesis*

A more detailed discussion of the formal structure of long passive constructions will be given below.

Let us now turn to functional superposition among terms. Every term can take on the function of another term. Here are some examples from Russian.

In the sentence

(27)     *Otcu          xolodno.*
     to-father(dat) is-cold
     'Father is cold'.

the function of the primary term is superposed onto the tertiary term *octu* 'to father'. In the sentence

(28)     *Ivana          tošnit.*
     John(acc) it-nauseates
     'John is nauseated'.

the function of the primary term is superposed onto the secondary term *Ivana* 'John (acc)'. In the sentence

(29)  *Petru       nužna       kniga.*
      to-Peter(dat) is-needed(adj) book(nom)
      'Peter needs the book'.

the function of the primary term is superposed onto the secondary term *Petru* 'to Peter', and the function of the secondary term is superposed onto the primary term *kniga* 'the book (nom)'.

In most ergative languages, among them Basque and Tongan, the ergative, which is the secondary (marked) term of a clause, is treated under some syntactic rules as if it were the primary (unmarked) term of a clause. As was shown in section 9 above, the paradoxical syntactic behavior of the ergative must be explained by functional superposition resulting from the conflict between the semantic hierarchy *agent-patient* and the syntactic hierarchy *absolutive-ergative*. Being syntactically a secondary term, the ergative is semantically a chief term, since it designates an agent. The conflict between the syntactic function and the meaning is resolved by the superposition of the function of the primary term onto the ergative. Thus, in the Basque sentence

(30)  *Gizonak   gozokia jandu.*
      man(erg) pie(abs) has-eaten
      'The man has eaten the pie'.

the secondary term, ergative *gizonak* 'the man', has taken the function of the primary term, and the primary term, absolutive *gozokia* 'the pie', has taken the function of the secondary term. But the ergative has not lost its secondary function, nor has the absolutive lost its primary function.

All terms belong to type $t$. Primary, secondary, and tertiary terms belong to subtypes of $t$, which we will distinguish by symbols $t_1$, $t_2$, and $t_3$ respectively. Superposition of term functions amounts to superposition of a subtype $t_i$ upon a subtype $t_j$; for example, $\langle t_1/t_2 \rangle$, $\langle t_2/t_1 \rangle$, $\langle t_3/t_2 \rangle$, and so on.

From a point of view of functional superposition, all predicates must be divided into two groups: regular predicates and *predicates-superposers*. Regular predicates do not affect the syntactic function of terms to which they are applied, while predicates-superposers, being applied to given predicates, superpose onto them syntactic functions of other terms. For example, the English predicate *is cold* is a regular predicate, since, being applied to a term, say to *John* (as in *John is cold*), it does not change the function of *John* as a primary term. On the other hand, the Russian counterpart of *is cold*, the predicate *xolodno*, is a superposer, since, being applied to a tertiary term *Ivanu* (dative), it superposes onto it the function of the primary term.

In terms of subtypes $t_1$, $t_2$, and $t_3$ of $t$, a regular one-place predicate $P_1$ belongs to type $Ot_1s$, a regular two-place predicate $P_2$ belongs to type $Ot_2Ot_1s$, and a regular three-place predicate $P_3$ belongs to type $Ot_3Ot_2Ot_1s$.

Note that the order of $t$-subtypes in the above formulas reflects the order of the application of the predicates to their terms: first, a predicate is applied to a tertiary term (if there is one); second, a predicate is applied to a secondary term (if there is one); and last, a predicate is applied to a primary term; a one-place predicate, naturally, can be applied only to a primary term.

Taking the correspondence between the order of the application of regular predicates to their terms and the order of the terms in the above formulas as our starting point, we can compute all possible types of predicates-superposers by computing all possible replacements of $t$-types in these formulas. Our computation can be represented in the following table:

(31)    Regular predicates                  Predicates-superposers

$Ot_1s$                          $Ot_2s$, $Ot_3s$

$Ot_2Ot_1s$                       $Ot_3Ot_1s$, $Ot_2Ot_3s$

$Ot_3Ot_2Ot_1s$                    $Ot_2Ot_3Ot_1s$, $Ot_1Ot_2Ot_3s$, $Ot_3Ot_1Ot_2s$,
                               $Ot_3Ot_1Ot_2s$, $Ot_1Ot_3Ot_2s$

In computing possible types of predicates-superposers, a constraint was imposed that a predicate cannot be applied to two terms of identical types. Therefore, types such as $Ot_1Ot_1s$ or $Ot_3Ot_1Ot_3$ were crossed out.

We face the problem, How are the above types realized in various natural languages, and what are the constraints on their realization? This problem will be considered elsewhere. Here I will confine myself to representing the above examples of sentences with predicates-superposers on tree diagrams.

The Russian sentence (27) is represented as follows:

(32)    $Ot_3s$ xolodno    $t_3$ otcu
        _____
           s xolodno otcu

The Russian sentence (28) is represented as follows:

(33)    $Ot_2s$ tošnit    $t_2$ Ivana
        _____
           s tošnit Ivana

The Russian sentence (29) is represented as follows:

(34)    $Ot_1Ot_3s$ nužna    $t_1$ kniga
        _____
           $Ot_3s$ nužna kniga     $t_3$ Petru
           _____
              s nužna kniga Petru

The Basque sentence (30) is represented as follows:

(35)    $Ot_1Ot_2s$ jandu    $t_1$ gozokia
        _____
           $Ot_2s$ jandu gozokia     $t_2$ gizonak
           _____
              s jandu gozokia gizonak

## 13.3 Combinators in Applicative Grammar

Let us turn to abstract operators that, following H. B. Curry (Curry and Feys, 1958), I call *combinators*.

Applicative grammar uses the following basic combinators: $C$, $I$, $W$, $B$, $S$, $K$, $C_*$, $\Phi$, $\Psi$.

Combinators can be represented by the so-called *reduction rules*, which have the form

(36)    $X \triangleright Y$

The infix $\triangleright$ in (36) designates the reduction relation. (36) reads: '*X* reduces to *Y*'.

Let us now consider combinators and their reduction rules.

Combinator $I$ is called the *identificator*. Let *X* be an expression; the result of applying $I$ to *X* is identical with *X*, which is represented by the reduction rule

(37)    $IX \triangleright X$

Identificator $I$ is used to define other combinators and some purely formal operations, as will be seen below.

Combinator $C$ is called the *permutator*. One possible interpretation of permutation is *conversion*: if $R$ is a two-place relation, $CR$ is the converse relation connected with $R$ by the reduction rule

(38)    $CRXY \triangleright RYX$

The notion of converse relation can be used to explain passive constructions. The predicate in a passive construction can be conceived of as the converse of the predicate in the respective active construction. The converse of the predicate involves the exchange of positions between the primary and the secondary terms. (By a position I mean a node in the applicative tree diagram.) For example, *was bought* in

(39)    *This book was bought by Peter yesterday.*

is the converse of *bought* in

(40)    *Peter bought this book yesterday.*

And *was bought* involves the exchange of the positions between *Peter* and *this book*: with respect to the active sentence (40), in the passive sentence (39) *this book* is in the position of *Peter* and *Peter* is in the position of *this book*.

Here I give a simplified account of passivization for the sole purpose of illustrating conversion as a possible interpretation of permutation. As was seen above, to produce an adequate theoretical characterization of passive, we had to solve a number of difficulties. Thus, in (39) the predicate *was bought* has the meaning of a two-place predicate but the form of a one-place predicate; the expression *by Peter* has the meaning of a secondary term but the form of an adverbial modifier. An adequate theory of passivization must explain the above and other contradictions between the form and meaning of passive constructions. But for the present purpose, we leave these difficulties aside.

Conversion is not the only possible interpretation of permutation, but here we will not discuss other possible interpretations.

The theory of passive constructions must be viewed as a part of the *theory of valence*. Within the framework of applicative grammar, the theory of valence is concerned with the following operations: 1) *relativization*, 2) *derelativization*, and 3) *transrelativization*. Relativization is an increase in the number of the relations that a predicate contracts with its terms, that is, an increase of the valence of a predicate. Derelativization is a decrease in the number of relations that a predicate contracts with its terms, that is, a decrease of the valence of a predicate. Transrelativization is a change in the relational nature of a predicate, that is, the operation of getting the converse of a predicate.

To provide means for constructing a complete theory of valence, applicative grammar has generalized the operation of conversion so as to apply it to $n$-place predicates. Applicative grammar uses a *generalized permutator* $C_k$, which is defined as follows: if $R_n$ is an $n$-place relation, then $C_k R_n$ is a converse relation connected with $R_n$ by the definition

$$(41) \quad C_k R_n X^1 \ldots X^k X^{k+1} \ldots X^n \equiv R_n X^1 \ldots X^{k+1} X^k \ldots X^n$$

Here $X^1$, $X^k$, $X^{k+1}$, and $X^n$ are terms of the relation $R_n$ and its converse $C_k R_n$. The superscript index $k$ shows the number of the term that permutates with the following term; that is, $X^k$ permutates with $X^{k+1}$. We get all possible conversions of $n$-place relation.

The generalized permutator $C_k$ permits the formalization of the notion of *generalized passive*. Under the rules of generalized passive, passivization involves not only the conversion between the primary and the secondary terms but also the conversion between the primary and the tertiary terms, which occurs in many languages.

Applicative grammar also has a complete set of operators decreasing or increasing the valence of predicates. For example, operator $E_{OOtsOtOts}$ increases the valence of an intransitive verb; that is, it changes an intransitive verb into a transitive verb. Operator $E_{OOtOtsOts}$ decreases the valence of a transitive predicate; that is, it changes a transitive verb into an intransitive predicate, etc.

Combinator $W$ is called the *duplicator*. If $R$ is a two-place relation, then $WR$ is a one-place relation associated with the relation $R$ by the reduction rule

$$(42) \quad WRX \triangleright RXX$$

One possible interpretation of the duplicator **W** is the coreferentiality relation. Let the formula $P_2TT$ be interpreted as *John shaves himself*; then the formula $WP_2T$ must be interpreted as *John shaves*. The term $T^1$ is not deleted (or canceled); the duplicator **W** involves the fusion of the term $T^1$ with its coreferential counterpart, the term $T$. As a part of the formula $WP_2T$, the term $T$ must be interpreted as a combination of primary and secondary terms: in *John shaves*, *John* is both the agent and the patient of the predicate *shaves*.

The combinator **W** can be generalized as combinator $W_k$. If $R_n$ is an $n$-place relation, then $W_kR_n$ is a relation one of whose terms is a result of the fusion of its coreferential terms. $W_kR_n$ is connected with $R_n$ by the reduction relation

(43) $\quad W_kR_nX^1 \ldots X^kX^{k+1} \ldots X^n \triangleright R_nX^1 \ldots X^kX^kX^{k+1} \ldots X^n$

The term $X^k$ in the left part of the formula is the result of the fusion of the two coreferential terms $X^kX^k$ shown in the right part of the formula.

By using the combinator $W_k$, applicative grammar provides formal means for presenting the analysis of the decrease of the valence of predicates involved in processes resulting from coreference.

The combinator **B** is called the *compositor*. Let $F$ be some one-place operator, and let the operand of the operator $F$ be the resultant of some other one-place operator $G$ having $X$ as its operand, which can be written as $F(GX)$. By means of the combinator **B** we can obtain, instead of two operators $F$ and $G$, one complex operator $BFG$, which can be applied to $X$. The operator $BFG$ is related to the operators $F$ and $G$ by the definition

(44) $\quad BFGX \triangleright F(GX)$

The complex predicate $BFG$ is obtained as follows: first, **B** is applied to $F$, as a result of which we get the operator $BF$, which has the operator $G$ as its operand. Then we apply $BF$ to $G$ to get the operator $BFG$, which has $X$ as its operand. When we apply $BFG$ to $X$, we get the combination $BFGX$, which is identical by definition to the combination $F(GX)$.

It should be noted that there are four initial components in the first combination: $B$, $F$, $G$, and $X$, and only two in the second: $F$ and $(GX)$. If we reconstruct the parentheses in the first combination according to the notational rule of association to the left, it will have the form $(((BF)G)X)$, or (if we do not restore the outer parentheses) $((BF)G)X$.

The compositor **B** can have different important interpretations on the empirical level. One possible interpretation is this: the compositor **B** can be thought of as an operator that changes predicates with subordinate object clauses into the constructions of the forms 'accusative+infinitive'. When we consider the operation of the composition, we must bear in mind that subordinate object clauses can be formed not only by applying conjunctions (for example, English *that*) to independent clauses and then applying predicates to the result of application, but also by directly applying predicates to independent clauses (in which case the independent clause is considered to be one of the operands of the predicate). Following the first method for forming subordinate object clauses, we get in English, for example, sentences with the conjunction *that: I have known that he paints*, and following the second method, we get sentences without *that* (with the same meaning): *I have known him to paint*.

Let $F$ be a two-place predicate $P_2$ which is interpreted: *have known*. If we apply this predicate to the sentence $P_1T$, we get:

(45)    $P_2(P_1T)$

to which the predicate *have known that he paints* may correspond. If we apply (45) to $T^1$, we get:

(46)    $P_2(P_1T)T^1$

to which the sentence *I have known that he paints* corresponds.

Using the combinator **B**, we can get the following two reductions:

(47)    $\mathbf{B}P_2P_1T \triangleright P_2(P_1T)$

(48)    $\mathbf{B}P_2P_1TT^1 \triangleright P_2(P_1T)T^1$

The left-hand part of (47) corresponds to the phrase *have known him to paint*, and its right-hand part corresponds to the phrase *have known that he paints*. The left-hand part of (48) corresponds to the sentence *I have known him to paint*, and its right-hand part corresponds to the sentence *I have known that he paints*.

The term $T$ in the left-hand parts of (47) and (48), which corresponds to the pronoun *him* in the English sentences, must be interpreted as the fusion of the agent and the patient: it is the patient of $p_2$ and the agent of $p_1$. On the level of the empirical interpretation, in *I have known him to paint* the pronoun *him* is the patient of *have known* and the agent of *to paint*.

The combinator **S** will be called the *confluentor*. Let $F$ be a two-place operator with $X$ as its first operand and the resultant of the one-place operator $G$, which also has $X$ as its operand, as its second operand. That can be written $FX(GX)$.

If we apply **S** to $F$ and **S**$F$ to $G$, we get the complex one-place operator **S**$FG$, which is connected with the operators $F$ and $G$ by the reduction rule

(49)    $\mathbf{S}FGX \triangleright FX(GX)$

We see that when we introduce the operator **S**$FG$, a fusion into a single operand takes place between the two identical operands to which operators $F$ and $G$ are applied.

The confluentor can be interpreted on the empirical level, for instance, as an operator that changes constructions *order, permit,* and similar predicates plus a subordinate clause into constructions 'accusative+infinitive'.

Let *F* be a predicate *order,* denoted by the symbol *Ord.* When applied to the term *T* and sentence $(P_1T)$, Ord gives a complex predicate

(50)    $OrdT(P_1T)$

which can be interpreted as *orders that the boy take a walk.* Applying (50) to the term $T^1$, we get

(51)    $OrdT(P_1T)T^1$

which can be interpreted as *Mother orders the boy that the boy take a walk.*

Using the confluentor **S**, we can get the following two reductions:

(52)    $SOrdP_1T \triangleright OrdT(P_1T)$

(53)    $SOrdP_1TT^1 \triangleright OrdT(P_1T)T^1$

The expression *orders the boy to take a walk* corresponds to the left-hand part of (52), and the expression *orders the boy that the boy take a walk* corresponds to its right-hand part. The sentence *Mother orders the boy to take a walk* corresponds to the left-hand part of (53), and the sentence *Mother orders the boy that the boy take a walk* corresponds to its right-hand part.

The term *T* in the left-hand parts of (52) and (53), which corresponds to the noun *boy* in the English sentences, must be interpreted as the fusion of the primary term and the secondary term: it is the secondary term of *Ord* and the primary term of $p_1$. On the level of empirical interpretation, in *Mother orders the boy to take a walk,* the noun *boy* is the patient of *orders* and the agent of *to take a walk.*

The combinator **K** introduces a *pleonastic operand.* If *F* is an *n*-place operator, then **K***F* is an $(n+1)$-place operator connected with *F* by the reduction rule

(54)    $KFX \triangleright F$

By using the combinator **K**, we can get the following identity:

(55)    $KP_2TT^1T^2 \triangleright P_2T^1T^2$

Let *F* be a two-place predicate *hate* whose patient is *that man* $(T^1)$ and whose agent is I $(T^2)$. Let the application of the combinator **K** to $P_2$ be interpreted as the introduction of the pleonastic agent $(T)$ with the simultaneous stress on *that man.* Then we get

(56)    *That man, I hate him* $\triangleright$ *I hate that man.*

The combinator $C_*$ makes an operator and an operand *exchange* their roles. Let $F$ be a one-place operator with $X$ as its operand. Then $C_*F$ is an operator related to $F$ by the reduction rule

(57)    $C_*XF \triangleright FX$

Example:

(58)    *the redness of light* $\triangleright$ *red light*

In the right-hand part of this identity, *red* $(F)$ is an operator and *light* $(X)$ is its operand. The application of the combinator $C_*$ to $X$ must be interpreted in this case as a structural change that makes $F$ and $X$ exchange their roles: *red* becomes an operand (*redness*), and *light* becomes its operator (*of light*).

The combinator $C_*$ is connected with the combinator $C$ by the reduction rule

(59)    $C_*XY \triangleright CIXY$

This reduction is derived as follows:

(60)    $C_*XY \triangleright YX \triangleright I(YX) \triangleright I(IYX) \triangleright IYX \triangleright CIXY$

The reduction (59) facilitates the analysis of the exchange of roles between agents and intransitive predicates. Consider the following sentence:

(61)    $P_1T$

which can be interpreted as *John works.*

The subject *John* and the predicate *works* cannot exchange their roles directly. But they can do so indirectly. Since $IP \equiv P$ (by definition of identity), we can change (61) into

(62)    $IP_1T$

In (62) $P_1$ is an operand of $T$, which is the predicate of this sentence. Now $P_1$ must be interpreted as a term rather than a predicate, and I must be interpreted as a copula that is the predicate of this sentence. We interpret (62) as

(63)    *John does work.*

Applying $C$ to $I$, we get

(64)    $CITP_1$

which must be interpreted in our case as

(65)     *Work is done by John.*

Thus we get the reduction

(66)     *John works* ▷ *John does work* ▷ *Work is done by John.*

There are two combinators denoted by Greek letters: Φ and Ψ.

Let us consider Φ first. Let $F$ be a two-place operator, and let its first operand be the resultant of a one-place operator $G$ whose operand is $X$, and let its second operand be the resultant of a one-place operator $H$ whose operand is also $X$. That can be represented by the formula $F(GX)(HX)$.

With the combinator Φ we get, instead of three operators and $X$, a single complex operator Φ$FGH$, which can be applied directly to $X$. The operator Φ$FGH$ is connected with the operators $F$, $G$, and $H$ by the reduction rule

(67)     Φ$FGHX$ ▷ $F(GX)(HX)$

The relationship between Φ and two-place operators is the same as that between B and one-place operators.

Let us now turn to the combinator Ψ. Let $F$ be a two-place operator, and let its first operand be the resultant of a one-place operator $D$ whose operand is $X$, and let its second operand be the resultant of the same one-place operator $D$ whose operand is $Y$. That can be represented by the formula $F(DX)(DY)$.

With the combinator Ψ we get, instead of the two operators $F$ and $D$, a single complex operator Ψ$FD$, which is applied directly to $X$ and $Y$. The operator Ψ$FD$ is connected with the operators $F$ and $D$ by the reduction rule

(68)     Ψ$FDXY$ ▷ $F(DX)(DY)$

On the empirical level, combinators Φ and Ψ can be interpreted as operators used for the direct construction of conjoined structures without using the transformations of conjunction reduction.

The reduction with combinator Φ can be interpreted as

(69)     *John finished his work and* ▷ *John finished his work, and*
         *went home.*                    *John went home.*

where $F \equiv and$, $G \equiv (finished\ his\ work)$, $H \equiv (went\ home)$, $X \equiv John$, and Φ$FGH$ combines these three operators into one complex operator.

The reduction with combinator Ψ can be interpreted as

(70)     *John and Peter like coffee.* ▷ *John likes coffee, and Peter*
                                          *likes coffee.*

where $F \equiv and$, $D \equiv (like\ coffee)$, $X \equiv John$, $Y \equiv Peter$, and Ψ$FD$ combines $F$ and $D$ into one complex operator.

The combinators considered above constitute an open set, which can be extended by adjoining new combinators if need be.

## 13.4 Assignment of Types to Combinators

The question arises as to which types can be assigned to the combinators. Since combinators are specified with respect to functions that are regarded as variables to be replaced by concrete functions of the genotype language, it is not concrete types that can be assigned to combinators but abstract type formulae containing variables to be replaced by concrete types. For convenience, the abstract type formulae will be called abstract types. That means that the question posed at the beginning of this section has to be rephrased thus: Which abstract types can be assigned to the combinators?

The following method will be used for determining the assignment of abstract types to combinators. First, we take the formula in the right-hand part of the definition of a combinator and assign this formula an arbitrary abstract type $z$. The formula together with the abstract type is treated as the root of a tree diagram for the construction of expressions, and the tree diagram is built up by the decomposition of the formula into its elementary components. As the tree diagram is constructed, each component is assigned an abstract type in accordance with Rule E for the construction of expressions. This rule says that if a formula $X$ with an abstract type $v$ is decomposed into an operator $A$ and an operand $B$, then, the operand $B$ having been assigned the abstract type $u$, it must be concluded that the operator $A$ should be assigned the abstract type $Ouv$.

After obtaining a tree diagram for the formula in the right-hand part of the definition of the combinator, we construct the corresponding tree diagram for the formula in the left-hand part of the definition, making use of the information obtained for the first tree diagram. That brings us to a specification of the appropriate abstract type for the combinator.

By way of illustration, suppose we wish to specify the abstract type that should be assigned to the combinator B. We begin as follows. Let the abstract type $z$ be assigned to the expression $F(GX)$. In accordance with Rule E for the construction of expressions, it can be supposed that $GX$ has the abstract type $v$, and $F$ the abstract type $Ovz$. That is shown in the tree diagram

$$(71) \qquad \frac{Ovz F \quad v(GX)}{zF(GX)}$$

If the expression $(GX)$ has the type $v$, the above-mentioned Rule E for the constructions of expressions allows us to suppose that $X$ has the type $u$, and $G$ the type $Ouv$. That yields the tree diagram

(72)
$$\frac{OuvG \quad uX}{\dfrac{OvzF \quad v(GX)}{zF(GX)}}$$

We shall now construct the tree diagram for the formula **B**FGX. If the formula F(GX) has been assigned the abstract type z, the formula **B**FGX must also be assigned z. We know from tree diagram (72) that expression X is assigned the abstract type u and that the first stage in the construction of the new tree diagram will be

(73)
$$\frac{OuzBFG \quad uX}{zBFGX}$$

We know from tree diagram (72) that the expression G is assigned the abstract type Ouv and that the second stage in the construction of the new tree diagram is

(74)
$$\frac{OOuvOuzBF \quad OuvG}{\dfrac{OuzBFG \quad uX}{zBFGX}}$$

We know from tree diagram (71) that the expression F is assigned the abstract type Ovz and that the final stage in the construction of the tree diagram is

(75)
$$\frac{OOvzOOuvOuzB \quad OvzF}{\dfrac{OOuvOuzBF \quad OuvG}{\dfrac{OuzBFG \quad uX}{zBFGX}}}$$

It is obvious from tree diagram (75) that the combinator **B** must be assigned the abstract type

(76)     OOvzOOuvOuz

Let us consider the combinator **W**. Let the expression FXX be assigned the abstract type z. According to Rule E for the construction of expressions, it is supposed that the expression X has the abstract type v; then the expression FX must have the abstract type Ovz. It follows that F must have the abstract type OvOvz. That yields the tree diagram

(77)
$$\frac{OvOvzF \quad vX}{\dfrac{OvzFX \quad vX}{zFXX}}$$

Using this tree diagram, it is easy to specify the abstract type that must be assigned to the combinator **W**. It is

(78)      $OOvOvzOvz$

The operation of the combinator **W** is shown in the tree diagram below:

(79)      $$\frac{\dfrac{OOvOvzOvzW \quad OvOvzF}{OvzWF \quad vX}}{zWFX}$$

Consider now the combinator $C_*$. Let the expression $YX$ have the tree diagram

(80)      $$\frac{OvzY \quad vX}{zYX}$$

From this tree diagram it is clear that $C_*$ has to be assigned the abstract type

(81)      $OOvzOvz$

The operation of the combinator $C_*$ is shown in the following tree diagram:

(82)      $$\frac{\dfrac{OvOOvzzC_* \quad vX}{OOvzzC_*X \quad OvzY}}{zC_*XY}$$

The combinator **I** must have the abstract type

(83)      $Ozz$

That is obvious if we suppose that the expressions I$X$ and $X$ are assigned the abstract type $z$.

From these examples of the assignment of abstract types to combinators, the reader should be able to assign abstract types to other combinators.


### 13.5 Construction Rules, Replacement Rules, and Structure-Changing Rules

Applicative grammar has three basic types of rules: construction rules, replacement rules, and structure-changing rules.

*Construction rules* are those that combine primitive objects into complex ones. Thus, in constructing $O$-types, we start with the primitive $O$-types $t$ and *s* and with the operationality primitive *O*, and, using two construction rules, combine them into complex *O*-types, such as *Ots*, *OOtsOts*, and so on (Rule T). In constructing sentences, we start with primitive expressions, that is, with words having various syntactic functions, combine them into syntactic word groups, and finally combine syntactic word groups into sentences (Rule E). The basic syntactic rule of applicative grammar is Rule E, stated in section 13.1 of this chapter.

*Replacement rules* are those of the following type: given a component *A* of an expression *B*, we can substitute an expression *C* for *A* according to some specified conditions. The basic replacement rule of applicative grammar is the *definitional replacement rule*:

> DEFINITION 8. *The Definitional Replacement Rule.*
> Given a component *A* of an expression *B*, we can substitute an expression *C* for *A* if *C* and *A* are identical by definition.

An example of definitional replacement: Given an expression *OOtsOts*, we can replace *Ots* with $p_1$, because these expressions are identical according to the definition of adjoined type symbols (section 2). Thus, replacing *Ots* in *OOtsOts* with $p_1$, we get $Op_1p_1$ from *OOtsOts*.

The name *structure-changing rules* clearly indicates what these rules are all about: they apply to the structure of a whole expression and convert it into some new structure. All reduction rules representing combinators are structure-changing rules. The relation converse to the reduction relation $\triangleright$ is the expansion related designated by the infix $\triangleleft$. The rules representing combinators by means of expansion relations are called *expansion rules* and have the form

(84)    $X \triangleleft Y$

(84) reads: '*X* expands to *Y*'.
Examples of expansion rules:

(85)    $F(GX) \triangleleft \mathsf{B}FGX$

(86)    $FX(GX) \triangleleft \mathsf{S}FGX$

The expansion rules (85) and (86) are counterparts of the reduction rules

(87)    $\mathsf{B}FGX \triangleright F(GX)$

(88)    $\mathsf{S}FGX \triangleright FX(GX)$

## 13.6 Deductive Processes: Reduction and Expansion

We posit a primitive language $L_p$ to be a sublanguage of the genotype language $L_g$. And we posit $L_g$ to be an extension of $L_p$. The relationship between $L_p$ and $L_g$ can be expressed by notation:

(89)    $L_p \subseteq L_g$

The infix $\subseteq$ means '. . . is included in . . . .'. (89) reads: '$L_p$ is included in $L_g$.'

The sentences of $L_p$ are called *normal forms*. The sentences of $L_g$ are mapped onto normal forms, that is, the sentences of $L_p$, by means of reduction rules. In order to test whether a given sentence belongs to $L_p$, that is, whether it is a normal form, we must use the reducibility test: if the sentence is a normal form, it does not have a part to which a reduction rule can be applied.

The deductive process of mapping sentences of $L_g$ onto normal forms is called *reduction*. Reduction is defined as follows:

> DEFINITION 9.    A sentence $U$ *directly reduces* to a sentence $V$ if $V$ is obtained from $U$ by application of one reduction rule.

To designate *direct reduction*, the infix $\models$ will be used. The expression

(90)    $U \models V$

means that the sentence $V$ is directly reduced to the sentence $U$. If there are $n$ reduction rules, there are $n$ types of direct reduction.

> DEFINITION 10.    If there is a sequence of sentences $U^0$, $U^1$, . . . , $U^n$ in which each preceding sentence $U^k$ directly reduces to the successive sentence $U^{k+1}$, $U^0$ *reduces* to $U^n$, the sequence $U^0$, $U^1$, . . . , $U^n$ is called the *reduction* of $U^0$ to $U^n$.

Reduction will be designated by the infix $\vdash$, and the expression

(91)    $U^0 \vdash U^n$

will be read: 'sentence $U^0$ reduces to $U^n$'

The following assumptions specify the properties of reduction:

(92)    a.  $U \vdash U$      for any sentence
        b.  $U \vdash V$ and $V \vdash Z \rightarrow U \vdash Z$
        c.  $U \models V \rightarrow U \vdash V$

(The infix $\rightarrow$ in (92b) and (92c) means 'if . . . , then . . . .') (92a) asserts that reduction is reflexive, (92b) that reduction is transitive, and (92c) that direct reduction is a particular instance of reduction.

Applying the reduction rules to the sentences of $L_g$, we obtain a set of reductions.

A corollary from (92a) is that each normal form can reduce to itself, and thus $L_p$ must be regarded as reducible to itself.

The linguistic sense of reductions is as follows.

One of the basic goals of any theory, and in particular of a linguistic theory, is to reduce complex theoretical concepts to primitive theoretical concepts, because such reduction leads to unification and simplification of the theory's premises. Einstein once said:

> New theories are first of all necessary when we encounter new facts which cannot be 'explained' by existing theories. But this motivation for setting up new theories is, so to speak, trivial, imposed from without. There is another, more subtle motive of no less importance. This is striving toward unification and simplification of the premises of the theory as a whole. (Einstein, 1973: 332–33)

What is the significance of the notion of the normal form?

In order to answer this question, let us start with the following assumptions about the properties of the normal forms in $L_g$:

(93) a. Every sentence X is reducible to a normal form Z.
   b. If a sentence X is a normal form, then X is reducible to X.
   c. If a sentence X is reducible to normal form Y, then the normal form Y is unique; that is, if X is reducible to Y and X is reducible to Z, then Y and Z are identical.

Taking these assumptions as axioms, we generate the relation ‹R› by introducing the following rule:

(94) X‹R›Y, if X and Y are reducible to the same normal form Z.

Let us now prove that the relation ‹R› is the equivalence relation.

As a consequence of (93a), if X shares the property of reducibility to a normal form with Y, then X shares this property with X; that is, X‹R›X. Hence, ‹R› is reflexive.

As a consequence of (93a), if X shares the property of reducibility to a normal form with Y, then Y shares this property with X; that is, X‹R›Y → Y‹R›X. Hence, ‹R› is symmetric.

If X‹R›Y and Y‹R›Z, then, under (93a), X and Y are reducible to the same normal form, but under (93c) Y is not reducible to a normal form different from a normal form for Z. Therefore, X‹R›Z. Hence, ‹R› is transitive.

That completes the proof that ‹R› is the equivalence relation.

The equivalence relation ‹*R*› defines the classes of sentences in $L_g$ called *semantic fields* or *families of sentences* (Shaumyan, 1977; Desclés, Guentchéva, Shaumyan, 1985).

In applicative grammar, assumption (93c) is taken as an axiom. But in a wider framework of combinatory calculus, this assumption must be considered a consequence of the Church-Rosser theorem, which is central to lambda-calculus and combinatory calculus.

The Church-Rosser theorem is formulated as follows (Hindley, Lercher, and Seldin, 1972: 9):

(95)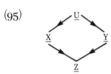

If $U \triangleright X$ and $U \triangleright Y$, then there exists a Z such that $X \triangleright Z$ and $Y \triangleright Z$.

The proof of this theorem is very long and complicated. For various versions of the proof, see Curry and Feys, 1958; Curry, Hindley, and Seldin, 1972; Rosser, 1984; Hindley and Seldin, 1986.

The normal form of a semantic field is the simplest sentence that is taken to represent an invariant under the replacement of one member of the semantic field by another one in a changing context.

Any semantic field has a hierarchical structure: all its members are ordered with respect to the degree and the type of complexity. The normal form does not comprise any combinator, while the other members of the field do have one or more combinators. One way of measuring the degree of the complexity of a sentence is to determine the number of combinators: the more combinators in a sentence, the more complex it is.

Here is an example of a semantic field (for the sake of simplicity, here I will not use combinators and will present the semantic field informally; examples of the formal presentation of semantic fields will be given below).

Let us consider the following family of sentences:

(96)     a.  *John sent a letter to Mary.*
        b.  *John sent Mary a letter.*
        c.  *A letter was sent to Mary by John.*
        d.  *John, he sent a letter to Mary.*
        e.  *John, he sent Mary a letter.*
        f.  *Mary was sent a letter by John.*
        g.  *Mary, she was sent a letter by John.*

These sentences have the same invariant meaning. (96a) is considered the normal form representing the invariant meaning of the other sentences. By reduction rules the sentences (96b–g) are mapped onto (96a), and by expansion rule (96a) is mapped onto (96b–g).

Why is (96a) considered to be the normal form of the other sentences? Because, by definition, a normal form of a family of semantically related sentences is a sentence having the simplest structure, and (96a) is exactly the sentence with the simplest structure in the above family of sentences. Thus, (96a) is simpler than (96c), because the active structure is simpler than the passive one; (96a) is also simpler than (96b), because (96b) involves the so-called dative shift; (96a) is simpler than (96d), as well, because (96d) involves topicalization.

Here is a graph of the complexity hierarchy for the sentence family (96):

(97)

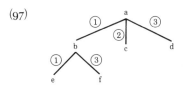

The circled numbers in the diagram indicate different sorts of complexity: ① is the dative shift, ② is passivization, ③ is topicalization. The diagram shows that (96a) is structurally the simplest sentence among the other sentences.

The counterpart of the semantic field in lambda-calculus and combinatory calculus is the notion of the superstructure on the normal form. Rosser writes:

> The lambda-formulas of interest mostly have normal forms. These normal forms constitute a foundation, on which is erected an elaborate superstructure. Each normal form has its own individual superstructure, however, not overlapping the superstructures of the other normal forms. Because formulas of the LC can be identified with formulas of combinatory calculus and vice versa, there are superstructures in the combinatory logic corresponding to those of the LC. (Rosser, 1984: 341)

(*LC* in this quote stands for 'lambda-calculus'.)

Through the notion of the normal form, we can define an important notion which I call *R-structure*.

> DEFINITION 11. Given a reduction $U^0, U^1, \ldots, U^n$ where $U^n$ is the normal form of the sentence $U^0$, the R-structure of the sentence $U^0$ is the set of structures $S(U^0), S(U^1), \ldots, S(U^n)$ of the sentences $U^0, U^1, \ldots, U^n$.

The *R*-structure of a sentence contrasts with its *S-structure*, or *superficial structure*. The true structure of a sentence is its *R*-structure rather than its *S*-structure. The relation of the *S*-structure to the *R*-structure is similar to the relation of the tip of an iceberg to its body immersed in water.

The deductive process converse to reduction is expansion. We start from the sentences of $L_p$, that is, from the sentences that are normal forms, and, by introducing various combinators, expand normal forms into sentences of $L_g$. Since $L_p$ is part of $L_g$, we use identificator I for presenting the *identical* expansion, that is, the expansion in which no change occurs: a sentence expanded by I is the same as when it does not have I.

> DEFINITION 12.  A sentence $U$ *directly expands* to a sentence $V$ if $V$ is obtained from $U$ by application of one expansion rule.

To designate direct expansion, the infix $\dashv$ will be used. The expression

(98)     $U \dashv V$

means that the sentence $V$ directly expands to the sentence $U$. If there are $n$ expansion rules, there are $n$ types of direct expansion.

> DEFINITION 13.  If there is a sequence of sentences $U^0, U^1, \ldots, U^n$ in which each preceding sentence $U^k$ directly expands to the successive sentence $U^{k+1}$, $U^0$ *expands* to $U^n$, and the sequence $U^0, U^1, \ldots, U^n$ is called the *expansion* of $U^0$ to $U^n$.

Expansion will be designated by the infix $\dashv$, and the expression

(99)     $U^0 \dashv U^n$

will be read: 'sentence $U^0$ expands to $U^n$'.

Like reduction, expansion has the properties of reflexivity and transitivity, and direct expansion is a particular instance of expansion, which can be presented by the following formulas:

(100)     a.  $U \dashv V$
          b.  $U \dashv V$ and $V \dashv Z \rightarrow U \dashv Z$
          c.  $U \dashv V \rightarrow U \dashv V$

Let us now turn to the technique of presenting deductive processes. Deductive processes will be presented according to the technique developed by Fitch (1952, 1974). This technique can be traced back to natural deduction, proposed by Gerhard Gentzen (1934), and to the rules of suppositions by Stanislaw Jaśkowski (1934).

The deduction of a normal form will be presented as a sort of formal deduction, that is, as a sequence of sentences such that each sentence is either a hypothesis of the sequence or a direct consequence of preceding sentences. The formal deduction consists of steps. We will number each step on the left and draw a vertical line between the numbers and the list of items. To the right of each sentence we will write the reason for its inclusion in the formal deduction: each sentence is either a hypothesis or a direct consequence from the preceding sentence(s) under some rule. In the latter case we will write the numbers of the preceding sentences in point. We will designate given sentences by writing *hyp* after each of them, and we will draw a short horizontal line separating them from other sentences of the formal deduction. In addition to hypotheses and to rules of direct consequence, we will also state formal laws of equivalence and formal laws of reduction, and we will use the schema of modus ponens for coimplication (as in Fitch, 1952: 38):

$$(101) \quad
\begin{array}{c|ll}
1 & p & \text{hyp} \\
2 & [p=q] & \text{hyp} \\ \hline
3 & q & 1,2
\end{array}$$

where $p$ and $q$ are symbols designating sentences. This schema reads: 'if $p$ and $[p=q]$, then $q$'; that means: if $p$ is asserted (in the proof) and $[p=q]$ is also asserted, then $q$ is asserted. Here the symbol = designates coimplication. $[p=q]$ reads: '$p$ coimplies $q$', which amounts to saying that $p$ and $q$ imply each other. Thus, coimplication is a sort of equivalence. We will generalize the meaning of $[p=q]$ and use it simply as a formula of equivalence.

Here is an example of a proof. Consider the sentence

(102)    *Mary likes to dance.*

The component of (102) *likes to dance* is a complex predicate, which we will represent by $P'$. *Mary* will be represented by $T$. We will represent *like* by $F$ and *dance* by $G$.

Applicative grammar posits the following equivalence relation:

(103)    $[P' = \mathsf{W B} F G]$

This relation gives an analysis of the simple complex predicate $P'$ in terms of the simple predicates $F$ and $G$.

Positing $P'T$ as a given sentence of $L_g$, we obtain the following reduction of $P'T$ to its normal form $F(GT)T$:

$$(104) \quad
\begin{array}{c|ll}
1 & P'T & \text{hyp} \\ \hline
2 & [P'=\mathsf{BWF}G] & \text{the equivalence relation} \\
3 & \mathsf{WB}GT & 1, 2, \text{coimp elim} \\
4 & \mathsf{B}FGTT & 3, \text{W-elim} \\
5 & F(GT)T & 4, \text{B-elim}
\end{array}$$

The deduction (104) is to be interpreted as follows. The sentence of step 5 is in a normal form. It represents the meaning of the infinitive construction of step 1. Step 2 introduces the equivalence relation. Step 3 is deduced from steps 1 and 2 by applying the rule of coimplication elimination (designated by the symbols 'coimp elim'). Step 4 is deduced from step 3 by applying the rule of W-elimination (designated by 'W-elim'). Step 5 is deduced from step 4 by applying the rule of B-elimination (designated by B-elim'). The terms W-elimination' and 'B-elimination' are synonymous with the terms 'W-reduction' and 'B-reduction'.

If we substitute concrete words for the abstract symbols in (104), we will get a concrete instance of the equivalence relation and a concrete instance of (104), as follows:

(105) 

| | | |
|---|---|---|
| 1 | *likes to dance Mary* | hyp |
| 2 | *likes to dance* = BW'likes' 'dance' | an instance of the equivalence relation |
| 3 | WB'like' 'dance' 'Mary' | 1, 2, coimp elim |
| 4 | B'like' 'dance' 'Mary' | 3, W-elim |
| 5 | *like(dance Mary)Mary* | 4, B-elim |

(Single quotes are used in (105) to differentiate the elements of formulas.)

### 13.7 Sample Formalization: A Formal Theory of Passive and Antipassive[6]

In section 11 I presented a conceptual framework of a theory of passivization based on semiotic principles. Now we are ready to formalize this theory using the formal apparatus of applicative grammar. The formalization of the theory will increase our understanding of passivization, and in addition it will serve as an example of applicative grammar in action, of how its formal apparatus can help to solve knotty linguistic problems.

Let us turn to our topic.

#### 13.7.1 Short and Long Passive Constructions

From an active transitive predicate $P_2$ (such as *killed*) of the type $OtOts$, we derive the converse predicate $CP_2$ of the same type. We apply this converse predicate $CP_2$ to a term $\emptyset_0$ of the type $t$, thus obtaining a one-place passive predicate $CP_2\emptyset_0$ (such as *was-killed*) of the type $Ots$. Finally, we apply the passive predicate $CP_2\emptyset_0$ to a term $T$ (*the-deer*) to obtain a short passive construction $(CP_2\emptyset_0)T$ (*The-deer was-killed*). The above construction is represented by the following derivational tree:

(106)

$$
\begin{array}{ll}
OOtOtsOtOts\ \mathsf{C} \quad OtOtsP_2 \\
\hline
\quad OtOts\ CP_2 \quad t\emptyset_0 \\
\hline
\quad\quad Ots\ (CP_2\emptyset_0) \quad tT \\
\hline
\quad\quad\quad s\ (CP_2\emptyset_0)T
\end{array}
$$

In the long passive construction, the introduced agent is considered a modifier of the passive predicate. The predicate modification is analyzed in terms of the operator ω (realized by means of *by* in English, *par* in French, *ot* in Bulgarian, instrumental case in Russian, oblique cases in other languages, etc.), which is a transposer, with a term $T^1$ (e.g., *John*) as its operand. The resultant of the action of ω on $T^1$ is a modifier of the predicate, that is, an operator whose operand is a predicate and whose resultant is also a predicate. The type of ω is

(107)    *OtOOtsOts*

The type of the resultant '$\omega T^1$' is

(108)    *OOtsOts*

The resultant '$\omega T^1$' (*by-John*) applies to the passive predicate '$CP_2\emptyset_0$' (e.g., *was-killed*) yielding the 'modified passive predicate' $(\omega T^1)(CP_2\emptyset_0)$ ('*was-killed-by-John*'). As in short constructions, this (modified) passive predicate applies to a term $T^2$ (e.g., *the-deer*), yielding the long passive construction

(109)    $((\omega T^1)\,(CP_2\emptyset_0))T^2$
         (*The-deer was-killed-by-John*)

The above construction is represented by the following derivational tree:

(110)

$$OOtOtsOtOts \quad C \quad OtOtsP_2$$
$$OtOOtsOts \quad [\omega \quad tT^1 \qquad OtOtsCP_2 \quad t\,\emptyset_0$$
$$OOtsOts \quad [(\omega T) \qquad Ots] \quad CP_2\emptyset_0$$
$$Ots(\omega T^1)\,(CP_2\emptyset_0) \qquad t]\quad T^2$$
$$s] \quad ((\omega T^1)\,(CP_2\emptyset_0)T^2$$

Let us compare the structures of short and long passive constructions:

(111)    short:        $(CP_2\emptyset_0)T^2$
         long:         $((\omega T^1)(CP_2\emptyset_0)T^2$

We have complete parallelism between the two constructions, since the long passive construction is obtained from the short by modifying the basic passive predicate $CP_2\emptyset_0$. The analysis of the two constructions shows clearly why the short construction is basic, the long derived, and how the modifier is introduced into the long passive construction.

More generally, the passive (short or long) construction is obtained by application of the passive predicate (either not modified, or modified by a term denoting an agent) to a term.

Unlike other linguistic works that use such vague notions as 'optional choice' or such irrelevant concepts as 'deletion', this analysis and its representation afford a unified view of the two kinds of passive construction, thus making it possible to solve many problems involved in passivization.

The term $\emptyset_0$ is called an *unspecified term*. The unspecified term is defined here as a term concerning which no specific statement is made beyond the fact that it is a term. As was shown in section 11.1, a passive predicate is a derelativized converse of the active predicate. The converse of an active predicate is derelativized by being applied to an unspecified term. Depending on the context, an unspecified term may denote an unspecified agent or may have an empty meaning, in accordance with the analysis of short passive constructions in section 11.1. An unspecified term is essentially a means of derelativizing converse predicates by saturating one place of the construction.

### 13.7.2 Formal Reduction from the Long Passive Construction

The tree diagrams in section 13.7.1 correctly represent the s-structure, that is, the superficial structure, of short and long passive constructions. But they do not capture the phenomenon of functional superposition. As was demonstrated in section 11 above, the agent term in long passive constructions is not merely a modifier of the passive predicate but takes on the function of the secondary term. The passive predicate in long passive constructions is not merely an intransitive predicate but takes on the function of the two-place converse predicate.

In order to capture the phenomenon of functional superposition in long passive constructions, I will posit the following equivalence relation for predicates of long passive constructions (*eq pas*):

(112)     $[\omega T(CP_2\emptyset_0) = (CP_2\emptyset_0)(\omega T)]$

(112) involves functional superpositions, which can be shown on the following tree diagram:

(113)     $$\dfrac{OOtsOts(\omega T) \quad Ots(CP_2\emptyset_0)}{Ots(\omega T)(CP_2\emptyset_2)} = \dfrac{\langle OtOts,Ots\rangle(CP_2\emptyset_0) \quad \langle t,OOtsOts\rangle(\omega T)}{Ots(CP_2\emptyset_0)(\omega T)}$$

The components of the right part of (113) are assigned stratified types in accordance with the method of the formalization of functional superposition proposed in section 13.1 above.

I posit the following definition:

(113a)     $(CP_2\emptyset_0)(\omega T) \equiv CP_2T$

Now we can relate the long passive construction to its normal form by the following deduction:

(114)

| | | | |
|---|---|---|---|
| 1 | $'\omega T^1 (CP_2\emptyset_0)T^2$ | | hyp |
| 2 | $[\omega T^1 (CP_2\emptyset_0) = CP_2\emptyset_0(\omega T^1)]$ | | eq pas |
| 3 | $CP_2\emptyset_0(\omega T^1)T^2$ | | 1, 2, coimp elim |
| 4 | $CP_2 T^1 T^2$ | | 3, rep, def |
| 5 | $P_2 T^2 T^1$ | | 4, C elim |

Step 1 presents the S-structure of long passive. Step 2 presents the equivalence relation for predicates of long passive constructions (designated by *eq pas*). Step 3 is deduced from steps 2 and 3 by the rule of coimplication elimination (designated by *coimp elim*). The reason for step 4 is repetition and definition. That means merely that step 3 is being repeated, but in a form in which $CP\emptyset_0(T)T$ is replaced by an expression that is, by definition, identical with it. Step 5 is deduced from step 4 by the rule of C elimination. Step 5 is in the normal form because no reduction rules can be applied to it.

In accordance with deduction (114), we posit the following relation:

(115)    $((\omega T^1)(CP_2\emptyset_0))T^2 \vdash P_2 T^2 T^1$

where $\vdash$ means 'reduces to'. $P_2 T^2 T^1$ is the normal form of the long passive construction.

Let us now turn to the normal form of the short passive construction. It is shown in the right part of the formula:

(116)    $(CP_2\emptyset_0)T \vdash P_2 T\emptyset_0$

Symbol $\vdash$ in (116) means 'reduces to'. The unspecified term $\emptyset_0$ in the active construction $P_2 T\emptyset_0$ is to be correlated with so-called impersonal pronouns in some languages such as French:

(117)    *Le livre est lu.* $\vdash$ *On lit le livre.*

or German:

(118)    *Das Buch wird gelesen.* $\vdash$ *Man liest das Buch.*

Both (117) and (118) correspond to English

(119)    *The book is read.* $\vdash$ *They read the book.*

Although *they* is a personal pronoun, in (119) it is used in the sense of an impersonal pronoun, such as French *on* or German *man*. Therefore, the unspecified agent $\emptyset_0$ can also be correlated with English *they* when it is used in the sense of an impersonal pronoun as in (119).

### 13.7.3. *Impersonal Passive Constructions*
How to explain impersonal passive constructions?
Let us take examples from German:

(120)    a) *Er tanzt.*
            'He dances'.
         b) *Es wird getanzt.*
            lit.: 'It is being danced'.

(121)    a) *Alle Kinder tanzen.*
            'All children dance'.
         b) *Es wird von allen Kindern getanzt.*
            lit.: 'It is being danced by all children'.

To explain this kind of passive construction, we must first explain impersonal active constructions for the purpose of relating impersonal passive constructions to general passive constructions, on the one hand, and to impersonal active constructions, on the other hand.

Let us consider an impersonal active construction denoting an atmospheric situation, such as

(122)    It is raining.

We call *it* in this sentence a 'dummy term' $\varnothing_\Delta$. *Es* in (120b) and (121b) is also a dummy term $\varnothing_\Delta$. We define *dummy term* as follows:

> DEFINITION 14.    A dummy term $\varnothing_\Delta$ is a term with a null meaning. It
>                   is used only in place of a full term in a construction.

Dummy terms are used for purely structural reasons. For example, in English, as in some other languages, every sentence must have a subject (primary term, in our terminology). But, from a semantic point of view, impersonal predicates do not need subjects; the meaning of impersonal constructions excludes subjects (that is why these constructions are called impersonal). Dummy terms serve to resolve the conflict between syntactic and semantic requirements: since dummy terms have a null meaning, they do not change the semantic context of an impersonal sentence, and at the same time they allow satisfaction of the structural requirement that every sentence must have a subject. Being necessary from a syntactic, structural point of view, dummy terms are redundant, pleonastic expressions with respect to the semantic content of impersonal sentences.

The dummy term is introduced in a construction by the combinator **K**, whose function is precisely the *introduction of a pleonastic term Y*:

(123)    **K***XY* = *X*

We can thus replace an occurrence of $X$ with $\mathsf{K}XY$ where $Y$ is a pleonastic term of the operator $\mathsf{K}X$.

To relate the impersonal construction represented in genotype language as

(124)    $P_1'\varnothing_\triangle$

to a normal form, we introduce the following equivalence relation, called an *impersonal relation (I-rel)*:

(125)    $P_1' = \mathsf{K}P_0$

which expresses a one-place predicate $P_1'$ as a complex predicate $\mathsf{K}P_0$, where $P_0$ denotes a situation, such as *there-is-rain* (or in French: *il-y-a-pluie*). Indeed, $P_0$ is a zero-place operator, that is, a sentence.

Now, we can relate the impersonal construction to its normal form using the following derivation:

(126)  $\quad$ 1 $\ \Big|\ $ $P_1'\varnothing_\triangle$ $\qquad$ hyp
$\qquad\ \ $ 2 $\ \Big|\ $ $[P_1' = \mathsf{K}P_0]$ $\quad$ I-rel
$\qquad\ \ $ 3 $\ \Big|\ $ $\mathsf{K}P_0\varnothing_\triangle$ $\qquad$ 1, 2, coimp elim
$\qquad\ \ $ 4 $\ \Big|\ $ $P_0$ $\qquad\qquad$ 3, $\mathsf{K}$ elim

We have the following relation for the impersonal construction:

(127)    $P_1'\varnothing_\triangle \vdash P_0$

as for the above example:

(128)    $\quad$ *It rains* $\vdash$ 'there-is-rain'
$\qquad\quad$ *Il pleut* $\vdash$ 'il-y-a-pluie' (French)

Now we can analyze sentence (120b) in the above example from German by means of the following representation:

(129)    $\mathsf{C}(\mathsf{K}P_1)\varnothing_0\varnothing_\triangle$

where $\varnothing_0$ is an unspecified term denoting 'the place of an agent', $\varnothing_\triangle$ is a dummy term, and $\mathsf{C}(\mathsf{K}P_1)\varnothing_0$ is the passive predicate for this kind of passive construction.

This impersonal passive construction is related to the corresponding active by means of the following derivation:

(130)  $\quad$ 1 $\ \Big|\ $ $\mathsf{C}(\mathsf{K}P_1)\varnothing_0\varnothing_\triangle$ $\quad$ hyp
$\qquad\ \ $ 2 $\ \Big|\ $ $\mathsf{K}P_1\varnothing_\triangle\varnothing_0$ $\qquad$ $\mathsf{C}$ elim
$\qquad\ \ $ 3 $\ \Big|\ $ $P_1\varnothing_0$ $\qquad\qquad$ $\mathsf{K}$ elim

The passive predicate $\mathsf{C}(\mathsf{K}P_1)\varnothing_0$ is the resultant of the application of the converse predicate $\mathsf{C}(\mathsf{K}P_1)$ to the unspecified term $\varnothing_0$ denoting an agent. The predicate $C(KP_1)$ is the converse of the predicate $KP_1$ (step 1). As $KP_1$ is a two-place predicate, there is a second term, which is the dummy term $\varnothing_\Delta$; hence step 2. This two-place predicate is a complex predicate involving the combinator $K$. By means of the combinator $K$, we eliminate the dummy term $\varnothing_\Delta$ and obtain the active construction with an unspecified term $\varnothing_0$, denoting an agent.

We then have the relation

(131)      $C(KP_1)\varnothing_0\varnothing_\Delta \vdash P_1\varnothing_0$

relating the passive construction to its corresponding active. With respect to the German examples, the above relation (131) holds between the passive (120b) and its corresponding active (120a): (120b) $\vdash$ (120a).

Thus, we can see how the impersonal passive construction is related to other impersonal constructions by the impersonal predicate $KP_1$, and to other passive constructions by the one-place predicate $C(KP_1)\varnothing_0$ with the combinator $C$ and the unspecified term.

The important thing to notice is that while the dummy term $\varnothing_\Delta$ in $C(KP_1)\varnothing_0\varnothing_\Delta$ corresponds to a real dummy term in German, it is hypothetical in $KP_1\varnothing_\Delta\varnothing_0$, as can be seen if we compare this abstract expression with (120b). The hypothetical dummy term captures a subtle structural parallelism between passive predicates derived from transitive active predicates (as in regular passive constructions) and passive predicates derived from intransitive active predicates (as in impersonal passive constructions). The derivation of passive predicates is based on the conversion operation by analogy with the derivation of passive predicates from transitive active predicates, and the hypothetical dummy term reflects this analogy because it is motivated by the fact that in impersonal passive constructions, intransitive predicates are treated as if they were transitive ones.

Sometimes the dummy term $\varnothing_\Delta$ can be zero, as is shown by the following example from German:

(132)      *Hier wurde den ganzen Abend getanzt.*
           'There was dancing here all evening'.

This sentence has a dummy *es*, which is denoted by zero. Zero dummy terms should not be confused with hypothetical dummy terms; zero dummy terms are determined by the opposition *nonzero dummy terms : zero dummy terms* (as a special case of the opposition *nonzero sign : zero sign*)—this opposition can be observed by comparing (132) with other impersonal passives where nonzero *es* occurs. As to hypothetical dummy terms, they cannot be determined by an opposition of sentences; they are motivated by purely theoretical considerations.

For impersonal passive constructions where the agent is expressed, as in (121b), we have the following representation:

(133)    $((\omega T)\ (C(KP_1)\emptyset_0))\emptyset_\triangle$

and the relation between the passive and its corresponding active:

(134)    $((\omega T)\ (C(KP_1)\emptyset_0))\emptyset_\triangle \vdash P_1 T$

as in German: (121b) $\vdash$ (121a). This relation is obtained through the following deduction:

(135)
|   |   |   |
|---|---|---|
| 1 | $((\omega T^1)(C(KP_1)\emptyset_0))\emptyset_\triangle$ | hyp |
| 2 | $[(\omega T^1)(C(KP_1)\emptyset_0)) = C(KP_1)(\omega T^1)]$ | eq pas |
| 3 | $C(KP_1)(\omega T^1)\emptyset_\triangle$ | 1,2, coimp elim |
| 4 | $C(KP_1)T^1\emptyset_\triangle$ | 3, rep, def |
| 5 | $KP_1\emptyset_\triangle T^1$ | C elim |
| 6 | $P_1 T^1$ | K elim |

### 13.7.4. *Impersonal Passive Constructions with Transitive Predicates*

Let us now consider impersonal passive constructions with transitive predicates. This type of passive construction occurs in Polish, Finnish, Welsh, French, and a few other languages. Here are examples from Polish:

(136)    a. *Oni zbudowali szkolę.*
            'They built a school'.
         b. *Zbudowano szkolę.*
            'There was built a school'.

Both in (136a) and (136b) *szkolę* is in the accusative case; in (136a) *oni* is in the nominative, case, while (136b) is an agentless sentence.

In French we also have

(137)    a. *Cette année, il a été vendu beaucoup de livres dans ce rayon.*
            lit.: 'This year there were sold a lot of books in this area'.
         b. *Il sera dansé, cette nuit, un quadrille par toutes les jeunes filles de la pension.*
            lit.: 'There will be danced, tonight, a quadrille by all the young girls of this boarding house'.

In these examples the patient is not promoted to the position of a primary term, since in (136) *szkolę* is clearly a secondary term in both active and passive constructions, just like *livres* in (137a) and *un quadrille* in (137b). Some languages (Finnish, Welsh, etc.) have this type of passive construction. For instance, in Welsh we have (Comrie, 1977: 55)

(138)    *Lladdwya          dyn  gan ddraig.*
         killed+PASSIVE man by   dragon
         'A man was killed by a dragon'.

Since, as was shown above, an application of a transitive predicate to a term gives an intransitive predicate, we can treat impersonal passive constructions with transitive predicates as impersonal passive constructions with complex intransitive predicates incorporating terms. Hence, two types of impersonal passive constructions must have a similar structure.

So, sentences (137a), (137b), and (138) are represented by

(139)    $\mathsf{C}(\mathsf{K}(P_2T^2))\varnothing^1{}_0)\varnothing^3{}_\Delta$

The normal form of the above representation is provided by the following deduction:

(140)    1 | $\mathsf{C}(\mathsf{K}(P_2T^2))\varnothing^1{}_0)\varnothing^3{}_\Delta$
         2 | $\mathsf{K}(P_2T^2)\varnothing^3{}_\Delta\varnothing^1{}_0$        C elim
         3 | $P_2T^2\varnothing^1{}_0$              K elim

The normal form $P_2T^2\varnothing^1{}_0$ is the representation of the corresponding active, hence

(141)    $\mathsf{C}(\mathsf{K}(P_2T^2)\varnothing^1{}_0)\varnothing^3{}_\Delta \vdash P_2T^2\varnothing^1{}_0$

Thus, in French we have

(142)    *il a    été   vendu des livres* $\vdash$ *on    a    vendu des livres*
         'it has been sold  the books'    Imp. 'has sold   the books'
                                          Pron.

The normal form $P_2T^2\varnothing^1{}_0$ is an active construction with an unspecified term (denoting 'a place of agent').

This passive construction is related to other passive constructions by the complex passive predicate

(143)    $\mathsf{C}(\mathsf{K}(P_2T^2))\varnothing^1{}_0$

where $\mathsf{C}(\mathsf{K}(P_2T^2))$ is the converse predicate of the two-place predicate $\mathsf{K}(P_2T^2)$ derived from the one-place predicate $P_2T^2$, which incorporates the term $T^2$.

In Polish, *-o* is the linguistic marker of the impersonal construction; in French, *il* is the marker of the dummy term $\varnothing_\Delta$, and the passive verb *a été vendu des livres* is the realization of the passive predicate $\mathsf{C}(\mathsf{K}(P_2T^2))\varnothing_0$.

In Russian

(144)   a.  *Molnija ubila korovu.*
        '(The) lightning killed (the) cow'.
     b.  *Korova ubita molniej.*
        '(The) cow has been killed by (the) lightning'.
     c.  *Korovu ubilo molniej.*
        lit.: 'There was killed (the) cow with (the) lightning'.

we have the same explanation for the transitive passive construction (144b) and the impersonal passive construction (144c).

### 13.7.5 *Passivization of the Tertiary Term*

How to explain the passive constructions where the indirect object is passivized?

Let us consider the following examples:

(145)   a.  *Mary gives the money to John.*
     b.  *The money is given to John (by Mary).*
     c.  *John was given the money (by Mary).*

We must consider the three-place predicate in (145a) as a two-place predicate that incorporates either the tertiary term $T^3$ (in (145b)) or the secondary term $T^2$ (in (145c)).

Sentence (145b), without an agent, is represented by

(146)    $C(P_3T^3)\emptyset_0T^2$

The relation of (145b) to (145a) is explained by the following deduction:

(147)    
$$
\begin{array}{ll}
1 & C(P_3T^3)\emptyset_0T^2 \quad\quad \text{hyp} \\
2 & P_3T^3T^2\emptyset_0 \quad\quad\quad 1, C \text{ elim}
\end{array}
$$

If the agent is expressed, then (145a) is represented by

(148)    $((\omega T^1)\,(C(P_3T^3)\emptyset_0))T^2$

Thus, we deduce the relations

(149)   a.  $C(P_3T^3)\emptyset_0T^2 \vdash P_3T^3T^2\emptyset_0$
     b.  $((\omega T^1)\,(C(P_3T^3)\emptyset_0))T^2 \vdash P_3T^3T^2T^1$

Now, for the passive sentence (145c), we have the following representations:

(150)   short:  $C\,(CP_3T^2)\,\emptyset_0T^3$
      long:   $((\omega T^1)\,(C(CP_3T^2)\,\emptyset_0))T^3$

For example, the long passive construction is related to its corresponding active of the normal form by the following deduction:

(151)

| | | |
|---|---|---|
| 1 | $((\omega T^1)\,(C(CP_3T^2)\,\emptyset_0))T^3$ | hyp |
| 2 | $[(\omega T^1)\,(C(CP_3T^2)\,\emptyset_0) = C(CP_3T^2)\,\emptyset_0(\omega T^1)]$ | eq pas |
| 3 | $C\,(CP_3T^2)\emptyset_0(\omega T^1)T^3$ | 1, 2, coimp elim |
| 4 | $C(CP_3T^2)T^1T^3$ | 3, rep, def |
| 5 | $CP_3T^2T^3T^1$ | 4, C elim |
| 6 | $P_3T^3T^2T^1$ | 5, C elim |

We then have the following relations:

(152)
$$C(CP_3T^2)\,\emptyset_0T^3 \vdash P_3T^3T^2\emptyset_0$$
$$((\omega T^1)\,(C(CP_3T^2)\,\emptyset_0))T^3 \vdash P_3T^3T^2T^1$$

And we have the following hierarchy of incorporations:

(153)  i) $(P_3T^3)T^2T^1$
      ii) $(CP_3T^2)T^3T^1$

The incorporation (ii) is possible only with the derived predicate $CP_3$ from $P_3$; $CP_3$ is always a three-place predicate. When this converse predicate is constructed, we can incorporate the term $T^2$ into it and thus obtain the two-place predicate $CP_3T^2$. We can then consider the converse of this complex two-place predicate and construct the corresponding passive predicate

(154)    $C(CP_3T^2)\,\emptyset_0$

Hence, the two passive predicates correspond to $P_3$:

(155)  i) $C(P_3T^3)\,\emptyset_0$
      ii) $C(CP_3T^2)\,\emptyset_0$

This hierarchy of incorporation explains why we have the following law across natural languages:

> If a language uses passivization for the tertiary term, then this language also uses passivization for the secondary term.

Now, there exist languages where passivization of the tertiary term is forbidden. For instance, in French, the following sentence is inadmissible:

(156)    *Jean est donné un livre (par Pierre).
       'John is given a book (by Pierre)'.

However, in French, we can have

(157)  *Jean s'est vu donner*          *un livre (par Pierre).*
       'John has seen himself being given a book (by Pierre)'.

That is, in French, we cannot derive the predicate $CP_3T^3$ directly from the predicate $P_3$.

The hierarchy of incorporation is related to a hierarchy of predicates:

(158)    $P_3 \Rightarrow P_3T^3$
         $\Downarrow$
         $CP_3 \Rightarrow CP_3T^2$

where the vertical arrow denotes the derivation of $CP_3$ from $P_3$, and the horizontal arrows the mechanisms of incorporation of a term (tertiary term or secondary term).

### 13.7.6 Passive and Antipassive Predicates and Constructions
Now, we can consider all passive predicates:

(159)

|  | short | long |
|---|---|---|
| a) | $CP_2\emptyset_0$ | $(\omega T^1)\,(CP_2\emptyset_0)$ |
| b) | $C(KP_1)\emptyset_0$ | $(\omega T^1)\,(C(KP_1)\emptyset_0)$ |
| c) | $C(KP_2T^2)\,\emptyset_0$ | $(\omega T^1)\,(C(KP_2T^2)\,\emptyset_0)$ |
| d) | $C(P_3T^3)\emptyset_0$ | $(\omega T^1)\,(C(P_3T^3)\,\emptyset_0)$ |
| e) | $C(CP_3T^2)\,\emptyset_0$ | $(\omega T^1)\,(C(CP_3T^2)\emptyset_0)$ |

where the above formulas represent:
a)  transitive constructions
b)  impersonal constructions
c)  impersonal constructions with incorporation of a term
d)  passivization with incorporation of the tertiary term (passivization of the secondary term)
e)  passivization with incorporation of the secondary term (passivization of the tertiary term).

All these passive predicates are characterized by (i) a *converse predicate* that applies to (ii) an unspecified term $\emptyset_0$. When the agent is expressed, it is represented by a modifier of the passive predicate. We can then posit the following schemata for all passive predicates (without or with an agent):

(160)    $C\pi_2\emptyset_0$          —short passive

(161)

$$\boxed{(\omega T)(C\pi_2\emptyset_0)}$$  —long passive

where $\pi_2$ is one of the two-place predicates: $P_2$, $KP_2$, $KP_2T^2$, $P_3T^3$, $CP_3T^2$.

The notions of converse predicate and unspecified term are the universal concepts required for a definition of passivization.

Now we shall propose mirror-image representations for ergative and anti-passive constructions.

The *ergative construction* is represented by

(162)     $P'_2U^2_{erg}U^1_{abs}$

where $P'_2$ is a two-place predicate and $U^2_{erg}$ and $U^1_{abs}$ are respectively a secondary and a primary term with ergative and absolutive case markers.

The *absolutive construction* is represented by

(163)     $P'_1U_{abs}$

where $P'_1$ is a one-place predicate and $U_{abs}$ is a term with an absolutive case marker.

In ergative constructions, $U^2_{erg}$ and $U^1_{abs}$ denote respectively an agent $(a)$ and a patient $(p)$, while in absolutive constructions, the opposition *agent: patient* is neutralized.

Comparing active and ergative constructions, we arrive at the following equivalence between marked and unmarked terms:

(164)

|          | marked         | unmarked       |
|----------|----------------|----------------|
| agents   | $U^2_{erg} =$  | $T^1_{nom}$    |
| patients | $T^2_{acc} =$  | $U^1_{abs}$    |

The accusative case is marked in accusative languages, while the ergative case is marked in ergative languages. In both constructions (accusative and ergative), the primary term ($T^1_{nom}$ or $U^1_{abs}$) is never marked.

The antipassive construction is analogous to the passive construction, since we have antipassive constructions with and without overtly expressed patients.

The structure of antipassive constructions with an overt patient is constructed from the antipassive without a patient, the antipassive predicate ($CP'_2\emptyset_0$) being derived from a more basic two-place predicate $P'_2$.

The antipassive construction with an overt patient is represented by the following:

(165)     $((\omega U^1)_{obl}(CP_2\emptyset))U^2_{abs}$

where the subscript *obl* indicates an oblique case—instrumental or dative. The antipassive construction is related to a corresponding ergative construction by means of an equivalence relation for passive-antipassive (*eq pas antipas*):

(166)    $(\omega U^1)_x(CP_2\emptyset) = (CP_2\emptyset)\,(\omega U^1)_x$

The subscript $x$ in $(\omega U^1)_x$ is a variable that can be replaced by constant subscripts $a$ (agent) or $p$ (patient).

We have the following deduction in ergative languages:

(167)

| | | |
|---|---|---|
| 1 | $((\omega U^1)_{obl}(CP_2\emptyset))U^2_{abs}$ | hyp |
| 2 | $((\omega U^1)_p(CP_2\emptyset))U^2_a$ | 1, rep, def |
| 3 | $[(\omega U^1)_p(CP_2\emptyset)=(CP_2\emptyset)\,(\omega U^1)_p]$ | eq pas antipas |
| 4 | $(CP_2\emptyset)\,(\omega U^1)_p U^a$ | 2, 3, coimp elim |
| 5 | $CP_2 U^1_p U^2_a$ | 3, rep, def |
| 6 | $P_2 U^2_a U^1_p$ | 5, C elim |
| 7 | $P_2 U^2_{erg} U^1_{abs}$ | 6, rep, def |

In accusative languages, we have an analogous deduction:

(168)

| | | |
|---|---|---|
| 1 | $((\omega U^1)_{obl}(CP_2\emptyset))U^2_{nom}$ | hyp |
| 2 | $((\omega U^1)_a(CP_2\emptyset))U^2_p$ | 1, rep, def |
| 3 | $[(\omega U^1)_a(CP_2\emptyset)=(CP_2\emptyset)\,(\omega U^1)_a]$ | eq pas antipas |
| 4 | $(CP_2\emptyset)\,(\omega U^1)_a U^2_p$ | 2, 3, coimp elim |
| 5 | $CP_2 U^1_a U^2_p$ | 3, rep, def |
| 6 | $P_2 U^2_p U^1_a$ | 5, C elim |
| 7 | $P_2 U^2_{acc} U^1_{nom}$ | 6, rep, def |

At this point we introduce the *general law of reduction by conversion* (for accusative and ergative languages), which is a counterpart of the Law of Duality:

(169)    $C\pi_2 X^1_\beta X^2_\alpha \triangleright \pi_2 X^2_\alpha X^1_\beta$

where $\beta$ is the corresponding marked case of the case $\alpha$. In accusative languages, $\beta$ is the accusative case and $\alpha$ is the nominative case; in ergative languages, $\beta$ is the ergative case and $\alpha$ is the absolutive case.

The two deductions (167) and (168) above must be viewed as analytic presentations of (169). They show that the general law of reduction by conversion involves the processes of functional superposition.

The present comparison of structures of accusative and ergative languages is compatible with explanations of the diachronic shift of ergative and passive, on the one hand, and antipassive and active, on the other hand, for Proto-Indo-European (Schmalstieg, 1982).

A comparison of clause structures in accusative and ergative languages can be presented by the following table:

(170)

| Accusative languages | Ergative languages |
|---|---|
| 1) Active constructions | 2) Ergative constructions |
| $P_2 T^2_{acc} T^1_{nom}$ <br> $p \quad a$ | $P'_2 U^2_{erg} U^1_{abs}$ <br> $a \quad p$ |
| $P_1 T^0_{nom}$ <br> $a/p$ | $P'_1 U^0_{abs}$ <br> $p/a$ |
| 2) Passive constructions | 2) Antipassive constructions |
| $(CP_2 \varnothing_0) T^2_{nom}$ <br> $p$ | $(CP'_2 \varnothing_0) U^2_{abs}$ <br> $a$ |
| $((\omega T^1)_{obl}(CP_2 \varnothing_0)) T^2_{nom}$ <br> $a \qquad p$ | $((\omega U^1)_{obl}(CP'_2 \varnothing_0)) U^2_{abs}$ <br> $p \qquad a$ |

### 13.8 Sample Formalization: Reflexive Constructions[7]

In many languages, reflexive markers have passive meaning in addition to their basic reflexive meaning. The passive meaning of reflexive markers can be illustrated by a Russian sentence such as

(171)    *Rebenok kupaet-sja.*
         child     is bathing-self

On one reading (171) is an ordinary reflexive and means 'The child is bathing'; on the other, it is a reflexive passive and means something like 'One is bathing the child'.

The dual reading—reflexive and passive—of reflexive markers is a cross-linguistic phenomenon that can be observed not only in genetically related languages, such as German and French, but also in genetically unrelated and structurally sharply distinct languages, such as the Uto-Aztecan family of American Indian and Slavic languages. Obviously, that cannot be considered an accident; rather, it is rooted in some fundamental universal property of human languages. In order to explain the passive use of reflexive markers, we have to search for an invariant underlying the reflexive and passive meanings of reflexive markers.

Reflexive markers are operators that intransitivize predicates. For example, the Russian two-place predicate *myt'* 'to wash' is reduced to the intransitive predicate *myt'sja* 'to wash (oneself)':

(172)    a.  *Rebenok moet  sebja.*
             'A child washes himself'.
         b.  *Rebenok moetsja.*
             'A child washes'.

In (172a) the reflexive pronoun *sebja* is the secondary term of the two-place predicate *moet*, while in (172b) there is no secondary term—*moetsja* is an intransitive predicate.

The Russian three-place predicate *zapasti* 'to store' is reduced to the intransitive predicate *zapastis'*:

(173)  a.  *On zapas sebe          ugol'.*
           he stored himself-DAT coal-ACC
           'He stored coal for himself'.
       b.  *On zapassja      uglem.*
           he stored(Refl.) coal-INST
           'He stored coal for himself'.

(173a) and (173b) have the same meaning, but in (173a) the pronoun *sebe* is the tertiary term of the three-place predicate *zapas*, while in (173b) the pronoun *sebe* is eliminated and the secondary term *ugol'* turns into the tertiary term *uglem*.

In order to explain why reflexive predicates can have a dual meaning—active and passive—I advance a hypothesis that under special conditions, reflexivization involves a conversion of active predicates.

A key to understanding reflexivization is the notion of neutralization. The application of the reflexive marker to a transitive active predicate involves neutralization of the syntactic opposition *primary term : secondary term*. While in a transitive active construction the primary term denotes an agent, and in a passive construction the primary term denotes a patient, in the reflexive constructions the primary term is unmarked with respect to the denotation of the agent or patient—depending on the context, the primary term of a reflexive construction can denote either an agent or a patient.

The use of the notion of neutralization and the related notions 'marked' and 'unmarked' for explaining syntactic phenomena can be traced back to the works of Roman Jakobson and other linguists of the Prague School (Jakobson, 1971). An attempt to explain reflexivization by using the notion of neutralization has been made by Ronald Langacker in his monograph on nondistinct arguments in Uto-Aztecan (Langacker employs the term *non-distinctness* for *neutralization*). He writes:

> The concept of non-distinctness is familiar from phonology, but little use of it has been made in syntactic studies. To be sure, the relevance of non-distinctness to syntax cannot be taken for granted but must be demonstrated. (Langacker, 1975:5)

Recently, the relevance of the notion of neutralization for an explanation of reflexivization was demonstrated by Alexander M. Schenker in his papers on reflexive markers in Polish and Russian (Schenker, 1985; 1986).

Granted that the notion of neutralization is relevant for explaining reflexivization, one may wonder whether the choice between the 'agent' and the 'patient' interpretation of the unmarked primary term in reflexive constructions depends entirely on the context or whether there is a covert syntactic process that predicts the 'patient' interpretation.

To answer this question, the hypothesis is proposed that the 'patient' interpretation of the primary term in a reflexive construction is predicted by the *conversion of the reflexive predicate*—a covert syntactic process associated with neutralization.

The primary term in a reflexive construction is an analogue of an archiphoneme in phonology. An archiphoneme can function alternatively as one or the other term of a phonological opposition. For example, in the Russian word *rok* the segment *k* is an archiphoneme *k/g* which functions as one of the members of the phonological opposition *k:g*. When this archiphoneme functions as *k, rok* means 'fate'; when it functions as *g, rok* means 'horn'. In the process of the neutralization of the phonological opposition *k:g*, the members of this opposition behave differently: *k* remains unchanged, while *g* changes into *k*. Just as in the neutralization of a phonological opposition the archiphoneme functions as one or the other member of the opposition, so in the syntactic neutralization realized by reflexivization the primary term functions as either the primary term or the secondary term of the opposition *primary term:secondary term*. Depending on whether it functions as the primary or the secondary term of this opposition, it denotes an agent or a patient. In the same way, just as in the process of the neutralization of a phonological opposition one of its members remains unchanged while another changes so that it coincides with the first member, so in the syntactic neutralization realized by reflexivization, the primary term (denoting an agent) of the neutralized syntactic opposition remains unchanged, while the secondary term (denoting a patient) changes so that it coincides with the primary term. This change is realized by means of the covert conversion of the predicate.

To see how reflexivization involves the covert conversion of predicates, let us take some examples.

Consider the Russian sentence

(174)     *Mat' branit syna.*
          mother scolds son
          'Mother scolds (her) son'.

If we apply the reflexive marker *-sja* to the transitive active predicate *branit*, we get the reflexive intransitive predicate *branitsja*, as in

(175)     *Mat' branitsja.*
          'Mother scolds'.

In (174) the transitive predicate *branit* affects the patient denoted by the secondary term *syna*. But in (175) the secondary term is eliminated; now the predicate is related only to the primary term (denoting an agent), which remains unchanged. The reflexive predicate stresses the involvement of the agent in the action. I have translated (175) as *Mother scolds*, with a nonreflexive, but then there is a subtle difference of meaning between the English and Russian sentences. In the English sentence we have an unspecified secondary term (denoting a patient) which can be replaced by some concrete secondary term. In the Russian sentence, however, the reflexive predicate excludes the possibility of adding a secondary term, because it is a formally intransitive predicate. A more precise, though awkward, translation of the Russian sentence would be 'Mother is involved in scolding'.

Compare now the following Russian sentences:

(176)    a.  *Devočka moet   sebja.*
            'The girl washes herself'.
        b. *Devočka   moet-sja.*
            'The girl washes-Refl'.
        c.  *Devočka moet   kuklu.*
            'The girl washes the doll'.
        d. *Kukla     moet-sja.*
            'The doll is washed-Refl'.

In (176b) the primary term *devočka* is a functional counterpart of *devočka* in (176a). In (176b) reflexivization eliminated the secondary term *sebja*, but it did not affect the primary term—that remained unchanged. In (176d) the primary term *kukla* is a functional counterpart of the secondary term *kuklu* in (176c). Therefore, we posit that there is a covert conversion of the predicate underlying the reflexive construction in (176d); we posit that the primary term *kukla* in (176d) is originally a secondary term, which changes into a primary term as a result of the conversion associated with reflexivization.

Let us now compare (176b) with the sentence

(177)    *Mat'    moet   devočku.*
        Mother  washes girl
        'Mother washes (her) girl'.

*Devočka* in (176b) is a functional counterpart of *devočku* in (177) and, as was said above, a functional counterpart of *devočka* in (176a). Therefore, the reflexive predicate *moet-sja* must be regarded as the intransitivized converse of *moet*, with *devočka* denoting an agent.

Although the operation of conversion may be associated with reflexive predicates, there is an essential difference between reflexive and passive predicates. From the point of view of conversion, reflexive and passive predicates constitute a markedness opposition *reflexive predicate : passive predicate*. The first term is unmarked, and the second one is marked. The passive predicate, as the marked term of this opposition, always is the converse of the corresponding

active predicate, while the reflexive predicate as the unmarked term of the opposition may or may not be the converse of the corresponding nonreflexive active predicate.

The markedness opposition *reflexive predicate : passive predicate* is valid also
from the point of view of the reference to an unspecified agent. While the passive predicate always implies an unspecified agent, the converse reflexive
predicate may or may not imply it. Consider the Russian sentences

(178)     a. *Derev'ja    lomajut-sja.*
                 trees      break-themselves
              'The trees break'.
          b. *Dver' otkryvaetsja.*
                 door   opens  -  itself
              'The door opens'.

Although the primary terms *derev'ja* and *dver'* denote patients, the corresponding reflexive predicates do not imply unspecified agents.

Now we are ready to define the invariant of reflexive predicates. *The invariant of reflexive predicates is the signalization of obligatory intransitivity involving a nondistinction of agents and patients and of plain and converse relations.*

There are some cross-linguistic phenomena that apparently contradict the
proposed definition of the invariant of reflexive predicates. Thus, in some languages reflexive predicates have nonreflexive counterparts that are also intransitive; for example, Russian has the reflexive *svetit'-sja* 'shine' and nonreflexive
*svetit'* 'shine'—both are considered to be intransitive, and both are synonymous. In Russian the impersonal nonreflexive predicate *govorjat* 'they say' has
a reflexive impersonal counterpart *govoritsja* 'it is said'—both are intransitive,
and both are synonymous. In general, every language has such predicates as
the English *work, run,* or *sleep* that are intransitive although they do not have
a reflexive marker as a sign of their intransitivity.

These are only apparent counterexamples to the claim that reflexive markers
signalize obligatory intransitivity. The word *obligatory* is crucial. As a matter of
fact, in English as in many other languages, there is no obligatory distinction
between intransitive and transitive verbs; there is no formal difference between
the intransitive verbs *run, sleep,* and *work* and the transitive verbs *eat, see,*
and *take.* The fact that *run, sleep,* and *work* do not have a secondary term,
while *eat, see,* and *take* do have a secondary term, depends on the lexical
meaning of these verbs, rather than on a formal grammatical distinction between the two groups of verbs. Depending on the variation of the lexical meaning, intransitive verbs may get a secondary term, and, conversely, transitive
verbs may be used without a secondary term (cf. *The children run races, He
eats well, He sees well*). On the other hand, reflexive verbs never take a secondary term, because reflexive markers as a formal device signalize an obligatory
absence of the secondary term.

As was shown above, reflexive predicates involve the nondistinction of the agent and the patient. But this nondistinction of the agent and the patient must be a specific characteristic of only obligatory intransitive predicates. In languages such as Russian or Polish, which have an opposition of reflexive predicates and their nonreflexive counterparts, only reflexive predicates involve the nondistinction of the agent and patient. Analyzing Polish material, Schenker states correctly that the reflexive verb *świecić się* 'shine' differs from its nonreflexive counterpart *świecić* 'shine' in that *świecić* refers to a subject (primary term in our terminology) denoting an agent that emits light, while *świecić się* refers to a subject that does not signalize an agent. Therefore, the typical context for *świecić się* and other reflexive verbs that refer to the emission of light is reflected or internal light (Schenker, 1985).

Tesnière introduced the notion of recessive diathesis, whose function is to decrease the valence of predicates. He considered reflexive markers as a morphological realization of recessive diathesis. Under this characterization, reflexive markers are viewed as a morphological device that is used to decrease the valence of predicates (Tesnière, 1966: 272–75). A similar view is expressed by Dowty, who regards reflexive markers essentially as a grammatical device for the reduction of the number of the arguments of a predicate (Dowty, 1982). The characterization of reflexivization given above shows that the view of reflexive markers as a grammatical device for the reduction of the valence of predicates is untenable. The true function of reflexive markers is the signalization of obligatory intransitivity and the neutralization of the opposition *agent : patient*. True, when the signalization of obligatory intransitivity involves a change of transitive predicates into intransitive ones, we observe a decrease of the valence of predicates, but this decrease is only a consequence of the signalization of obligatory intransitivity—as was shown above, reflexive markers, when applied to intransitive predicates, do not decrease their valence.

Reflexivization can be formalized as follows.

We introduce a reflexivization operator *R*, which is an abstract analogue of reflexive markers used in different contexts.

Our next step is to assign a category (or type) to the operator *R*. In accordance with what was said above about reflexive markers, no matter what is the valence of a predicate, when *R* is applied to it, it becomes a one-place predicate. Therefore, we assign the category *OπOts* to *R*. The symbol π in *OπOts* is a variable for which we can substitute categories *Ots* for a one-place predicate, *OtOts* for a two-place predicate, and *OtOtOts* for a three-place predicate.

To show the action of the operator *R*, let us present tree diagrams illustrating the derivation of Russian reflexive predicates:

*Svetit'-sja* from *svetit'* 'shine' (a one-place predicate):

(179)     $\underline{OOtsOts\ R \qquad\qquad Ots\ svetit'}$

         *Ots R svetit'*

*Branit'-sja* from *branit'* 'scold' (a two-place predicate):

(180)    $\underline{OOtOtsOts\ R \qquad OtOts\ branit'}$

                $Ots\ R\ branit'$

*Razdobyt'-sja* from *razdobyt'* 'to procure (for somebody)' (a three-place predicate):

(181)    $\underline{OOtOtOtsOts\ R \qquad OtOtOts\ razdobyt'}$

                $Ots\ R\ razdobyt'$

These tree diagrams show that the operator $R$ does not necessarily reduce the valence of predicates. In (179) the valence of the predicate has not been reduced; in (180) the valence of the predicate has been reduced by one term; in (181) it has been reduced by two terms.

Let us now formulate the *Hypothesis of Reflexive Neutralization:*

> The application of operator $R$ to a two-place predicate neutralizes the opposition *primary term : secondary term* so that either the primary or the secondary term is eliminated. If the primary term is eliminated, the secondary term changes into the primary term, and the predicate is replaced by its converse. If the secondary term is eliminated, the primary term and the predicate remain unchanged.

Reflexive neutralization can be illustrated by the following examples from Russian:

If the reflexive marker *-sja* is applied to the predicate *kusat'* 'to bite', the secondary term (denoting a patient) is eliminated, and the reflexive predicate *kusat'sja* can be applied only to a primary term (denoting an agent) so that we get sentences such as *sobaka kusaet-sja* 'the dog bites'. If, on the other hand, *-sja* is applied to *čitat'* 'to read', the primary term (denoting an agent) is eliminated; the secondary term (denoting a patient) is changed into the primary term, and the predicate is replaced by its converse, so that we get sentences such as *kniga čitaet-sja* 'the book is read'. The application of *-sja* to some predicates, such as, *brit'* 'to shave', allows an alternate elimination of the secondary and primary terms, so that we get sentences such as *on breet-sja*, which can mean either 'he shaves' or 'he is shaved'—the difference between the two meanings is due to different covert syntactic processes: to the elimination of the secondary term in the first case, and to the elimination of the primary term, the change of the secondary term into the primary one, and the replacement of the predicate by its converse in the second case. It is to be noted that an alternate elimination of the primary and secondary terms is characteristic of predicates whose primary and secondary terms may be identical: thus, the elimination of the secondary term of the predicate *brit'* is possible only when we have sentences such as *on breet sebja* 'he shaves himself'.

There is an analogy beteween reflexive neutralization and phonological neutralization. Thus, in Russian we have the phonological opposition *voiceless
consonant:voiced consonant*, which is analogous to the syntactic opposition
*primary term:secondary term* with respect to the markedness relation: the
voiceless consonant, like the primary term, is unmarked, while the voiced consonant, like the secondary term, is the marked member of the opposition. At
the end of the word before a pause, the opposition *voiceless consonant:voiced
consonant* is neutralized, so that this opposition is represented by the unmarked member—the voiceless consonant—just as reflexive neutralization of
the opposition *primary term:secondary term* is represented by the unmarked
member of this opposition—the primary term. Now, the neutralization of the
opposition *voiceless consonant:voiced consonant* is realized in two ways: 1) if at
the end of the word the voiceless consonant occurs rather than the voiced consonant, then the voiceless consonant remains unchanged, just like the primary
term of the syntactic opposition *primary term:secondary term* when the secondary term is excluded; and 2) if at the end of the word the voiced consonant
occurs rather than the voiceless, the voiced consonant changes into the voiceless consonant, just as the secondary term of the syntactic opposition *primary
term:secondary term* changes into the primary term when the secondary term
is excluded. The first way is exemplified by the Russian word *rot* 'mouth'—at
the end of this word the voiceless consonant *t* cannot be in opposition to the
voiced consonant *d*, and it remains unchanged. The second way is exemplified
by the word *sad* 'garden'—at the end of the word the voiced consonant *d* cannot
be in opposition to the voiceless consonant *t*, and it changes into *t*, so that *sad*
becomes /sat/.

Now we are ready to define exactly the operator *R*.

Proposition. Reflexive markers are considered to be linguistic traces of
an abstract operator *R* called *the operator of reflexiveness*.

Definition. The syntactic function of the reflexive operator $R_n$ is to
change an *n*-place predicate $\pi_n$ into a one-place predicate $\pi_1'$.
We call $\pi_1'$ a *reflexive predicate*, and we posit the following
equivalence between the predicates:

$$\pi_1' = R_n \pi_n$$

From this definition, it follows that if *n*=2, the type of $R_2$ is
*OOtOtsOts*; if *n*=1, the type of $R_1$ is *OOtsOts*.

In each construction where an operator $R_n$ occurs, its action is given
by an explicit equivalence between constructions. Each equivalence is
of the following form:

(182)    $c[\pi_1'] = c[U_1]$

The predicate $\pi_i'$ is a *definiendum*, and the predicate $[U_n]$ is the *definiens* of $\pi_i'$ in the *context c of the construction.*

From this equivalence relation between constructions, it follows that we can replace $\pi_i'$ with $U_i$ in the context $c$ of the specific construction. This replacement defines the action of the operator $R_n$ in the construction. From it we can deduce the grammatical meaning of this construction by obtaining its normal form.

Now we are able to determine the formal laws of the action of $R_n$ (called *R-laws*) in different constructions where it occurs. These laws generate immediate equivalence relations (called *R-relations*) between predicates.

*Laws of the action of the operator R:*

A reflexive predicate $\pi_i'$ is replaced with another predicate $U_i$ according to different contexts:

*when n=2*

(183)  a. $T_a[P_i'] = T_a[RP_2]$
      b. $T_p[P_i'] = T_p[BRCP_2]$
      c. $T[P_i'] = T[RP_2]$

In (183) $T_a$ denotes an agent, and $T_p$ denotes a patient. Depending on different contexts, $T_a$ or $T_p$, the same predicate $P_i'$ is replaced with $RP_2$ or $BRCP_2$. In (183c) $T$ denotes a term irrespective of whether it is an agent or a patient.

When $n=2$, the rule of R-elimination is introduced:

(184)  $RP_2 T \equiv P_2 \emptyset_0 T$

If a reflexive construction is synonymous with a transitive construction with a reflexive pronoun (as in Russian, *on breet-sja* 'he shaves' is synonymous with *on breet sebja* 'he shaves himself'), then $RP_2 = WP_2$, and by rule of W-elimination we get

(185)  $WP_2 T \equiv P_2 TT$

The condition for $RP_2 = WP_2$ is called here *the pronoun connection.*
From the above R-laws, we deduce the following reductions:

For reflexive constructions with $T_a$: $P_i' T_a = RP_2 T_a \triangleright P_2 \emptyset_0 T_a$
For reflexive constructions with $T_a$ and the synonymy condition:
    $P_i' T_a = RP_2 T_a \triangleright P_2 TT_a$
For reflexive constructions with $T_p$: $P_i' T_p = BRCP_2 T_p \triangleright R(CP_2) T_p \triangleright$
    $P_2 T_p \emptyset_0$

Here the reflexive predicate is defined in terms of 1) other predicates $P_2$ or $P_1$, 2) combinators B and C and 3) the unspecified term $\emptyset_0$.

Let us now turn to other types of reflexive constructions.

Consider the Russian sentence

(186)   *Otec branit-sja.*
        'Father is scolding'.

This sentence is represented on the genotype level by the expression

(187)   $P_1'T_a$

The normal form of (187) is given by the following derivation:

(188)
| | | |
|---|---|---|
| 1 | $P_1'T_a$ | hyp |
| 2 | $T_a[P_1'] = T_a[RP_2]$ | R-law |
| 3 | $RP_2T_a$ | 1,2, coimp elim |
| 4 | $P_2\emptyset_0T_a$ | R elim |

Here is the explanation of this derivation. In step 1 we posit the genotype sentence $P_1'T_a$ (representing the above Russian sentence *Otec branit-sja* 'Father is scolding' and similar empirical sentences in Russian and other languages). In step 2 we posit an R-law stating the equivalence $P_1' = RP_2$ in the context of the term $T_a$ (denoting an agent). In step 3 we obtain $RP_2T_a$ from 1 and 2, substituting $RP_2$ for $P_1'$ in $P_1'T_a$ by the coimplication scheme. By the elimination of R we arrive at step 4, which is a normal form, since reduction cannot be applied any further.

Let us now take a Russian reflexive construction that is synonymous with a transitive construction having a reflexive pronoun as its secondary term.

(189)   *Otec breet-sja.*
        'Father is shaving'.

This sentence is synonymous with

(190)   *Otec breet sebja.*
        'Father shaves himself'.

(189) is represented on the genotype level by the expression

(191)   $P_1'T$

The normal form of (191) is represented by the derivation

(192)
| | | |
|---|---|---|
| 1 | $P_1'T$ | hyp |
| 2 | $T[P_1'] = T[RP_2]$ | R-law |
| 3 | $RP_2T$ | 1, 2, coimp elim |
| 4 | $[RP_2 = WP_2]$ | Pronoun connection |
| 5 | $WP_2T$ | 3, 4, coimp elim |
| 6 | $P_2TT$ | W-elimination |

In step 1 we posit an expression corresponding to sentences such as (189). In step 2 we posit an $R$-law stating the equivalence $P_1' = RP_2$ in the context of the abstract term $T$. In step 3 we obtain $RP_2T$ from 2 and 3 by the coimplication scheme. In step 4 we posit the equivalence $[RP_2 = WP_2]$ under the condition that above was called the pronoun connection. In step 5 we obtain $WP_2T$ from 3 and 4 by the coimplication scheme. By elimination of $W$ we come to step 6, which is a normal form because it cannot be reduced any further.

The term $T$ in (189) can also be interpreted as a patient, so that (189) turns synonymous with the passive construction *the father is being shaved*. In this case (189) is represented by the genotype sentence

(193)      $P_1'T_p$

The normal form of (193) is derived as follows:

(194)    1 | $P_1'T_p$                         hyp
         2 | $T_p[P_1'] = T_p[BRCP_2]$         $R$-law
         3 | $BRCP_2T_p$                       1,2, coimp elim
         4 | $R(CP_2)T_p$                      B elim
         5 | $(CP_2)Ø_0T_p$                    R elim
         6 | $P_2T_pØ_0$                       C elim

The explanation of derivation (194) is similar to the explanation of derivations (192) and (188): in step 1 we posit an abstract sentence, in step 2 we posit an $R$-law, then in step 3 we obtain a new expression from 1 and 2 by applying the coimplication scheme; the expressions in steps 4, 5, and 6 are obtained by a successive elimination of B, R, and C. Expression 6 is a normal form, because it cannot be reduced any further.

In conclusion, let us examine the use of reflexive markers in impersonal constructions.

As was shown above, the operator $R$ changes an $n$-place predicate into a one-place predicate. In particular, $R$ changes a one-place predicate into a one-place predicate. The operator $R$ does not seem to have a special impersonal function. An impersonal construction is obtained by applying an intransitive predicate to an unspecified term $Ø_0$, no matter whether an intransitive predicate is non-reflexive or reflexive. Compare the following Russian sentences:

(195)    a.  *Tak delajut.*
             'They do so'.
         b.  *Tak delaet-sja.*
             'It is done so'.

Both (195a) and (195b) are impersonal constructions: (195a) is a nonreflexive and (195b) a corresponding reflexive impersonal construction. Both *delajut* in (195a) and *delaet-sja* in (195b) are intransitive predicates and are applied to an unspecified term $Ø_0$ to form an impersonal sentence. The essential difference between (195a) and (195b) is that the unspecified term of (195a) is clearly interpreted as an unspecified agent, while there is no clear interpretation of the specified term in (195b): as a matter of fact, it may be interpreted as both an unspecified agent and an unspecified patient. Owing to the latter possibility, we can substitute the pronoun *èto* 'this' for the unspecified term in (195b), which is impossible in (195a):

(196)    *Tak èto ne delaet-sja.*
         'This is not said so'.

### 13.9 Sample Formalization: Causative Constructions

Consider

(197)    *John is opening the door.*

which is represented at the genotype level by the expression

(198)    $P_2T^2T^1$

Where $T^1$ and $T^2$ denote respectively an agent and a patient, and $P_2$ denotes a causative predicate. Since we interpret (198) as a causative construction, it must be interpreted by the following derivational tree:

(199)

$$\frac{OsOts\ CAUSE \quad \dfrac{Ots\ P_1 \qquad t\ T^2}{s(P_1T^2)}}{\dfrac{Ots\ (CAUSE(P_1T^2)) \qquad\qquad t\ T^1}{s\ (CAUSE(P_1T^2))T^1}}$$

The expression $\langle CAUSE(P_1T^2))T^1$ is well-formed; its type is $s$. The interpretation of this expression is: '$T^1$ causes the situation $P_1T^2$'. For example: 'John causes the situation "the door is open"', or 'John causes the situation "the dog walks"'. These interpretations are grammatical meanings of the sentences *John is opening (or opens) the door; John is walking (or walks) the dog.*

The normal form of $P_2T^2T^1$ is then expressed in terms of the grammatical operator *CAUSE* and a lexical one-place operator $P_1$, whose meaning is related to that of $P_2$. This normal form is given by the following derivation:

(200)    1  | $P_2T^2T^1$              hyp
         2  | $B'CAUSE'P_1T^2T^1$      Since $[P_2 = B'CAUSE'P_1]$
         3  | $'CAUSE'(P_1T^2)T^1$     B elim

The above analysis enables us to explain the linguistic data in sentence pairs such as the following:

(201)    a.  *The door opens.*            a.  *The dog walks.*
         b.  *John opens the door.*        b.  *John walks the dog.*

In applicative grammar we use the tools of combinatory logic to describe how the one-place predicate $P_1$ coalesces with the operator $CAUSE$ by means of the combinator $\mathbf{B}$. For this purpose, we present the following deduction:

(203)  

| | | | |
|---|---|---|---|
| | 1 | $CAUSE(P_1T^2)T^1$ | hyp |
| | 2 | $\mathbf{B}`CAUSE`P_1T^2T^1$ | B-introduction |
| | 3 | $[\mathbf{B}`CAUSE`P_1]=P_2$ | `CAUSE`-relation |
| | 4 | $P_2T^2T^1$ | 2, 3, coimp elim |

The first step is a normal form that gives directly the underlying grammatical meaning of the sentence whose representation is given by the fourth step. The second step is obtained by the introduction of the combinator $\mathbf{B}$. That is the rule of $\mathbf{B}$ introduction, which can be represented as

(204)     $(x(yz)) \lhd \mathbf{B}xyz$

The action of $\mathbf{B}$ eliminates the brackets; that is, $\mathbf{B}`CAUSE`P_1$ is now considered a two-place analytic complex predicate derived from the lexical predicate $P_2$ by means of the composition of $P_1$ with the grammatical operator $CAUSE$. For this analytic complex predicate $\mathbf{B}`CAUSE`P_1$ we substitute a two-place syntactic predicate $P_1$, given the relation $[P_2=\mathbf{B}`CAUSE`P_1]$, which is described in a dictionary. To relate the two meanings of *move* or *walk*, a dictionary interprets these verbs either as denoting the situations '$x$ moves' and '$x$ walks', or the situations '$x$ causes y to move', '$x$ causes y to walk'.

In the fourth step we obtain synthetic causative construction by substituting the synthetic predicate $P_2$ for $\mathbf{B}`CAUSE`P_1$ in $\mathbf{B}`CAUSE`P_1T^2T^1$ in accordance with the rule Coimplication Elimination.

Let us now turn to some theorems concerning causative constructions (Desclés, Guentchéva, Shaumyan, 1986).

Theorem 1: If $P_2 = \mathbf{B}`CAUSE`P_1$, then $P_2T^2T^1 \rhd `CAUSE`(P_1T^2)T^1$

| | | |
|---|---|---|
| 1 | $P_2T^2T^1$ | hyp |
| 2 | $[P_2=\mathbf{B}\ `CAUSE`\ P_1$ | `CAUSE`-relation |
| 3 | $\mathbf{B}\ `CAUSE`\ P_1T^2T^1$ | 1, 2, Coimp. Elim. |
| 4 | $`CAUSE`(P_2T^2)T^1$ | B elim |

Theorem 2: If $P_3 = \mathbf{B}^2\ `CAUSE`\ P_2$, then $P_3T^3\ T^2T^1 \rhd `CAUSE`$ $(P_2T^3T^2)T^1$

| | | |
|---|---|---|
| 1 | $P_3T^3T^2T^1$ | hyp |
| 2 | $[P_3=\mathbf{B}^2`CAUSE`P_2]$ | CAUSE-relation |
| 3 | $\mathbf{B}^2`CAUSE`P_2T^3T^2T^1$ | 1, 2, coimp elim |
| 4 | $\mathbf{B}\ `CAUSE`(P_2T^3)T^2T^1$ | B elim |
| 5 | $`CAUSE`(P_2T^3T^2)T^1$ | B elim |

The meaning of the normal form $`CAUSE`(P_2T^2)T^1$ is: '$T$ causes the situation $P_2T^2$'. The meaning of the normal form $`CAUSE`(P_2T^3T^2)T^1$ is: '$T$ causes the situation $P_2T^3T^2$'. The situation $P_2T^3T^2$ can be interpreted as any clause with a transitive predicate, for example, *John writes the letter*. The symbol $\mathsf{B}^2$ means $\mathsf{B}$ applied twice, that is, $\mathsf{B}^2 = \mathsf{BB}$. Thus, given $x((yz)w)$, we can eliminate parentheses in two steps: first we get $\mathsf{B}x(yz)w$, then we get $\mathsf{B}(\mathsf{B}x)yzw = \mathsf{B}^2 xyzw$.

Causative predicates are transitive, but not all transitive predicates are causative; there are causative and noncausative transitive predicates. They differ in that a causative transitive predicate can be reduced to an analytic complex predicate consisting of the operator *CAUSE* and a predicate denoting the situation brought about, while a noncausative transitive predicate cannot. Thus, *John melted the glass* can be represented as *John made the glass melt* (where *made = CAUSE*), while *John saw the glass* cannot be represented by a construction with *saw* reduced to *CAUSE* plus a more primitive predicate, because *to see* is a noncausative transitive predicate.

The fact that any synthetic causative predicate can be reduced to an analytic causative predicate does not mean that, from a morphological point of view, any causative predicate is derived from a noncausative one. The above formal deductions of causative predicates and constructions represent only the relation between synthetic and analytic causative predicates and do not involve morphological considerations. From a morphological point of view, three possibilities are open: 1) a causative predicate is derived from a noncausative one, as in Armenian *xmel* 'drink'→*xm-e-c-n-e-l* 'to give to drink'; the suffix -*c*- means 'cause'; 2) a noncausative predicate is derived from a causative one, as Russian *varit'* 'to cook (causative)'→ *varit'-sja* 'to cook (noncausative, intransitive)'; 3) the causative and noncausative predicates are morphologically independent, as in Georgian *i-γ-eb-a* '(it)opens' ↔ *a-γ-eb-s* '(he, she) opens (causative)'. English predicates, such as *open, close, burn, cook,* and *run*, are morphologically neutral; depending on the context, they can have either noncausative or causative meaning.

In analyzing causative and noncausative predicates and constructions, the important thing is not to confuse the relational and morphological analyses.

## 13.10 Sample Formalization: Sentence Nests

We are ready to consider a useful notion, 'sentence nests'. This notion, which corresponds to the notion 'semantic field' (in Shaumyan, 1977: 103–113), makes it possible to present in a single picture a hierarchy of syntactic interconnections between sentences (Desclés, Guentchéva, Shaumyan, 1986).

A sentence nest is a set of derivations from a basic predicate and can be represented by a labeled tree. The root of the tree corresponds to a given basic predicate, and each branch corresponds to a syntactic derivation. The node on each branch corresponds to the predicates and sentences that are derived: the initial node, i.e., the root, corresponds to the basic predicate and the basic sentence; the intermediate nodes, to the intermediate predicates and sentences; and the final node, to the final derived predicate and sentence. The lines joining the nodes correspond to the steps in the derivation and can be labeled with the symbols for the rules by whose application the predicate and sentence corresponding to each node have been obtained. The tree of a sentence nest can also display information about its interpretation in a natural language. Assuming that there is an accompanying description of the sentences in a natural language, that is done by taking the numbers of the appropriate examples in that description and assigning them to the nodes that correspond to the genotype sentences whose interpretation is to be indicated. Each branch is called a subnest of the sentence nest.

Each sentence nest in the genotype language is paralleled by a sentence nest in the phenotype language, the latter being a class of related sentences that interpret the genotype sentence nest. A subnest of the phenotype sentence nest is a set of sentences that interpret a genotype sentence subnest.

In order to present a sample of a sentence nest, I will consider the following set of sentences in Russian:

(205)    a.  *Vanna polna.*
             'The bath is full'.
         b.  *Mat' napolnjaet vannu.*
             'Mother is filling the bath'.
         c.  *Vanna byla napolnena.*
             'The bath was filled'.
         d.  *Vanna napolnjaet-sja.*
             1)  'The bath is filling'.
             2)  'The bath is being filled'.

From the root *POLN-* 'full' we construct the different predicates given below:

(206)

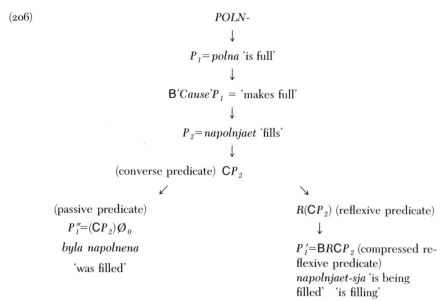

$$POLN-$$
$$\downarrow$$
$$P_1 = polna \text{ 'is full'}$$
$$\downarrow$$
$$B'Cause'P_1 = \text{ 'makes full'}$$
$$\downarrow$$
$$P_2 = napolnjaet \text{ 'fills'}$$
$$\downarrow$$
(converse predicate) $CP_2$

(passive predicate)                                        $R(CP_2)$ (reflexive predicate)
$P_1'' = (CP_2)\emptyset_0$                                        $\downarrow$
*byla napolnena*                                        $P_1' = BRCP_2$ (compressed reflexive predicate)
'was filled'                                        *napolnjaet-sja* 'is being filled'  'is filling'

Here is the explanation of tree (206). The predicate $P_1$ (*polna* 'is full') denotes a stative property, hence (205a). From $P_1$ we derive the analytic two-place causative predicate $B\,{}^cCause'P_1$. This predicate has a direct realization in English (where $B\,{}^cCause' = make$), but not in Russian. The analytic causative predicate changes into a synthetic causative predicate $P_2$ (*napolnjaet* 'fills'); hence the sentence (205b). From $P_2$ we derive its converse $CP_2$ and the passive predicate $P_1'' = (CP_2)\emptyset_0$, which is a one-place predicate; hence the sentence (205c). From the converse of the synthetic predicate $CP_2$ we derive the reflexive predicate $R(CP_2)$, which is compressed into $P_1' = BRCP_2$; hence the sentence (205d). It should be noted that (205d) is ambiguous: depending on the context, it means that either the bath fills by itself or one fills it. This ambiguity is a consequence of the grammatical structure of reflexive constructions: unlike passive predicates, which are one-place predicates owing to the application of converse predicates to unspecified terms, reflexive predicates derived from converse two-place predicates become one-place predicates by a derelativization through reflexive markers; unspecified terms are not part of reflexive predicates but are determined solely by the context.

A comparison of the above sentence family in Russian with the corresponding sentence family in English shows that Russian does not have an analytic causative predicate, while English does. On the other hand, English does not distinguish between transitive and intransitive predicates: *to fill* is used both as an intransitive and as a synthetic causative transitive predicate. English does not distinguish between reflexive and nonreflexive predicates, while Russian does.

The above tree of a sentence family and the comments on it are not meant as a generalization concerning the typological similarities and differences between Russian and English. They serve only as an example of the method of presenting sentence families by means of tree diagrams. If carried out in a systematic way, this method is important both for understanding the inner structure of a given language and for typological studies.

## 14. A Comparison of Applicative Grammar and Montague Grammar

The dimensions and significance of any theory in linguistics, as well as of any theory in other sciences, can be understood and appreciated properly only by comparing it with alternative theories. Therefore, I have to compare applicative grammar with alternative linguistic theories.

I will compare applicative grammar with four alternative theories: Montague grammar, relational grammar, the functional-lexical grammar of Bresnan, and generative-transformational grammar.[8] In this section I will consider Montague grammar.

Montague syntax is a version of categorial grammar which the logician Richard Montague first presented in 1970 (Montague, 1970a and 1970b), five years later than the complete version of applicative grammar was presented in my book *Structural Linguistics* (Shaumyan, 1965; English translation: Shaumyan, 1971). Montague grammar is not a linguistic theory; rather, it is a logical theory. Just as with any logical theory, truth is the central notion in Montague grammar, while this notion is peripheral to any linguistic theory. Characterizing his theory, Montague wrote:

> I regard the construction of a theory of truth—or rather, of the more general notion of the truth under an arbitrary interpretation—as the basic goal of serious syntax and semantics; and the developments emanating from the Massachusetts Institute of Technology offer little promise towards that end. (Montague, 1974: 188)

It is clear from this passage that Montague understands syntax and semantics not in a linguistic sense but rather in the sense of logical syntax and logical semantics in the tradition of Carnap, Reichenbach, Quine, and other logicians who studied language from a logical point of view.[9] In Montague grammar, the denotation of a sentence is its truth-value. But from a linguistic point of view, the truth-value is irrelevant to linguistic analysis (with the exception of peripheral cases when it is expressed by linguistic means). Logic deals with thought proper, but linguistics is interested only in communicated thought. A distinction between thought proper and communicated thought is crucial. A witness may say: "I saw John in the store this morning." But that may be a lie, not the truth. The basic fact of semiotics is that any system of signs is neutral to truth. Signs have their own meaning, and this meaning may conflict with the thought of the speaker who uses the signs. As a matter of fact, fiction writing is possible only because signs are neutral to truth.

For the purposes of logical analysis of language, Montague grammar uses a complicated logical formalism, including the formalism of intensional logic, which is irrelevant from a linguistic point of view.

There is nothing wrong in constructing a logical theory of natural languages. On the contrary, the study of natural languages from a logical point of view may provide new insights that can be of benefit to linguists. What is wrong with the logical grammar proposed by Montague is that he regarded it as an alternative to linguistic theories proper, in particular to generative-transformational grammar, which Chomsky had been developing at the Massachusetts Institute of Technology since about 1955.

In what follows I will argue that the claim of Montague and his followers that their logical grammar is a linguistic theory is unjustified.

The basic goal of any serious linguistic theory must be the discovery of language universals. Montague called his grammar universal, but he understood the term *universal grammar* in a quite different sense from that used by linguists. Montague used the term *universal* as synonymous with the term *general*. Accordingly, he used the term *universal grammar* to denote simply a mathematical description of language, since a mathematical description of language is much more general than a usual linguistic description.

In this connection I would like to quote R. Thomason, a well-known exponent of Montague grammar, who writes the following about its relation to the study of linguistic universals:

> Such universals have no interest for Montague. They are mentioned nowhere in his paper, nor does he ever suggest that his work should be applied to topics such as the psychology of language acquisition. Where the term "universal" appears in his writings, as in "Universal Grammar," the title of chapter 7, it has reference to the mathematician's natural tendency to generalize. A theory that is intuitive and mathematically elegant, and that comprehends all special cases of a certain topic, can be termed a universal theory of that topic. In this sense topology is a universal theory of geometry, and Montague's theory of universal grammar is a universal theory of grammar. (Thomason, 1974:3)

As a matter of fact, Montague grammar cannot be used as a universal grammar in the sense of linguistics, because its rules are stated in terms of the linear order of constituents.

As was shown above (sec. 12 this chapter), a grammar that states its rules in terms of linear order of constituents fails to provide cross-linguistically valid notions for formulating linguistic universals, because it makes it necessary to formulate distinct rules for languages with different word order for phenomena that could be considered identical in terms of relational rules.

The syntax of a language in Montague grammar is a simultaneous recursive definition of all of the syntactic categories of a language. The formalism used for the recursive definitions is similar to the formalism used for the recursive definitions of syntactic categories in applicative grammar. But there is a crucial difference between the lists of syntactic categories in both grammars. Let us compare these lists.

Montague confines his list to the following eleven syntactic categories (Montague, 1974:249):

1) $e$, or a category of entity expressions.

2) $t$, or a category of truth-value expressions.

3) $IV$, or the category of intransitive verb phrases. Symbol $IV$ is an abbreviation for symbol $e/t$, which, in terms of applicative grammar, must be interpreted as a category of operators (Montague's term *function* corresponds to the term *operator* in applicative grammar) that, when applied to their operands of category $e$, form an expression of category $t$, such as *run, walk*, etc.

4) $T$, an abbreviation for $t/IV$, or the category of terms that consists of operators that, when applied to intransitive verbs, form an expression of category $t$, such as *John, Mary, ninety, he*. Montague uses the label *term* to denote proper nouns and similar expressions.

5) $TV$, an abbreviation for $IV/T$, or the category of operators that, when applied to terms, form intransitive verbs.

6) *IAV*, an abbreviation for *IV/IV*, or the category of operators that, when applied to intransitive verbs, form intransitive verbs.

7) *CN*, an abbreviation for *t//e*, or the category of operators that, when applied to expressions of category *t*, form expressions of category *e*, such as *man*, *park*, *fish*, etc.

8) *t/t*, the category of sentence-modifying adverbs, such as *necessarily*, etc.

9) *IAV/T*, the category of *IAV*-making prepositions, such as *about*, etc.

10) *IV//t*, the category of sentence-taking verb phrases, such as *believe that*, *assert that*, etc.

11) *IV//IV*, the category of *IV*-taking verb phrases, such as *try to*, *wish to*, etc.

Double slashes (*//*) in some of the above names of categories are used to distinguish between two types of the same category; for example, to distinguish between two types of the same predicate: *t/e*, or intransitive verbs, and *t//e*, or common nouns.

This list of syntactic categories oriented towards purely logical analysis of a sentence conflicts with some well-justified principles of linguistics.

First, Montague considers intransitive verbs and common nouns to be two types of the same category of predicate. That conforms to the treatment of common nouns in logic but contravenes the treatment of common nouns in any linguistic theory. From a linguistic standpoint, common nouns, like any nouns in general, are not primarily predicates. They are opposed to predicates as the operands of predicates, or, in another terminology, as arguments of predicates. Nouns can be used as predicates, but that is their secondary function. By contrast, the primary function of a verb is to be a predicate, and its secondary function is to be a noun. The phenomena of nominalization and predicativization are based precisely on the basic opposition of nouns and verbs in their primary functions and their capacity for exchange of their functions. By treating common nouns and intransitive verbs as predicates alike, Montague grammar precludes the description of the processes of nominalization and predicativization in natural languages: these processes do not make sense in the framework of this grammar.

Logic does not distinguish between nouns and intransitive verbs; it lumps them together under the label 'predicate'. This approach is consistent with a principle of logic according to which only variables can be arguments of a predicate, never nouns, which are constants. That is one of the points where a logical and linguistic analysis of the sentence cannot be reconciled.

Second, Montague considers proper nouns and similar expressions to be secondary predicates whose arguments are primary predicates—intransitive verbs. This approach is consistent with the type of logical semantics espoused by Montague but has nothing whatsoever to do with linguistics.

Third, Montague introduces a mysterious syntactic category denoted by the symbol *e* and called *entity*. This category is empty; *entity* means nothing. By introducing this empty category, Montague had in mind two things: first, to justify the treatment of common nouns as predicates; and second, to use this category for a certain purpose in the semantic part of his grammar. The use of this category in semantics will be discussed below. Here I will explain its use in syntax.

Montague utilizes the categorial calculus whose rules require that any predicate must have an argument. In ordinary logic, arguments of predicates are individuals. But since Montague espouses a type of logic in which individuals cannot be arguments of predicates, he runs into a difficulty with his calculus. To solve this difficulty, he introduced the empty category, which is used as an empty argument of predicates. And, as we shall see, the empty category is also helpful in the semantic part of Montague's grammar.

Montague grammar has seventeen syntactic rules for the fragment of the English grammar he describes. As a matter of fact, most of these rules are concrete instances of one syntactic rule:

If $\alpha$ is of category $C_1$ and $\beta$ is of category $C_2$, then $\gamma$ is of category $C_3$, where $\gamma = F_k(\alpha, \beta)$.

One reason that Montague does not use this generalized syntactic rule is that he wants to specify word order. Since different functions can involve different word order, different syntactic rules involving the operation of concatenation are formulated to represent different word order.

The semantic part of Montague grammar consists of the rules of the translation of syntactic structures into sentences in a particular formalized language of intensional logic; this process is followed by laying down the conditions for truth of a sentence with respect to a given language. There is a one-one correspondence between syntactic and semantic rules. The semantic categories of intensional logic are called *types*.

The role of the category *e* in semantics is explained as follows. In standard logical interpretation, this category must denote individuals. Montague wants to establish semantic parallelism between proper names and quantifier phrases, for instance, between expressions such as *John* and *every man* in

(1)    *John walks.*
(2)    *Every man walks.*

To establish this parallelism, one can try to construe the quantifier phrase as an individual and assign both the quantifier phrase and the proper name to category *e*, but it is questionable whether the quantifier phrases should be construed as individuals. The standard logic approach is to treat quantifier phrases as a kind of second-order predicates whose arguments are first-order predicates. Montague has chosen to elevate proper names from the category *e* to the category *T*, that is, to treat proper names not as individuals but as a set of properties that are used as second-order predicates with respect to first-order predicates. In ordinary logical interpretation, sentence (1) must be presented as

(3)     *Walks (John).*

But according to Montague's interpretation, this sentence must be represented as

(4)     *John (walks).*

As a result of the elevation of proper names from category *e* to category *T*, category *e* becomes empty in semantics, as it was in syntax.

Montague's treatment of proper names and quantifier phrases may seem ingenious from a logical point of view, but one may wonder whether this approach is justified from a linguistic standpoint. A linguistic explanation of the parallelism between proper names and quantifier phrases must be based on an analysis of the structural properties of the sentences rather than on a logical analysis.

Montague's semantics has nothing whatsoever to do with linguistic analysis of meaning. That is a logical theory based on notions of intensional logic. The central notion in this theory is the notion of the intension of a sentence. The intension of a sentence is defined as a function from possible worlds to truth values: to each possible world the function assigns the truth value of that sentence in that world. The term *possible world* means 'situation' or 'case' in everyday language. In terms of the notion 'possible world', we can define the meaning of some predicates, for instance,

(5)     *possible ≡ true in some possible world*
        *certain ≡ true in all possible worlds*

There is no doubt that a translation of expressions of a natural language into intensional logic may be interesting from a logical standpoint, but one may wonder whether this translation can be viewed as an alternative to a linguistic analysis of meaning.

Since the formalism of Montague grammar is roughly equivalent to the formalism of an immediate constituent grammar, Montague grammar encounters all the difficulties encountered by an ordinary immediate constituent grammar. Therefore, Barbara Partee recently suggested extending Montague grammar in the same way as Chomsky extended the immediate constituent grammar, that is, to enrich it by a system of transformations. Now an ordinary Montague grammar is going to be replaced by a transformational Montague grammar (Partee, 1975).

I will not discuss Partee's contribution to Montague grammar. Suffice it to say that Partee suggests neither conceptual nor formal changes in Montague grammar. What she does is simply to add a few transformations taken from the standard version of generative-transformational grammar.

Partee's version of Montague grammar combines all the limitations of ordinary Montague grammar with the limitations of generative-transformational grammar.

Montague grammar cannot be an alternative either to generative-transformational grammar or to any other linguistic theory, simply because Montague grammar is not a linguistic theory.

Let me hasten to add that I do not mean to reject any work that has been done in the framework of Montague grammar. Thus, recently Dowty (1982a, b) made a serious attempt to rid Montague grammar of some of its fundamental faults. He suggests distinguishing two levels of grammar corresponding to the genotype and phenotype levels of applicative grammar, and he makes some other constructive suggestions. Nevertheless, this attempt and some other serious work done in the framework of Montague grammar cannot change our principled evaluation of Montague grammar as a conceptually unsound theory, since it lumps together logical and linguistic concepts and so creates a linguistically illicit, inherently heterogeneous system.

The case of Montague grammar is an interesting illustration of the crucial role of ideas and concepts in constructing linguistic theory. The same mathematical calculus can be combined with very different conceptual systems, which may be opposed to each other. The ideas and concepts constitute the essence of a theory, not mathematical calculus. A mathematical calculus must be combined with an appropriate system of ideas and concepts. Otherwise, a mathematical calculus is more than worthless: it may do harm as an instrument of the promotion of the products of immature thinking.

## 15. A Comparison of Applicative Grammar and Generative-Transformational Grammar

The first version of generative-transformational grammar was published in 1957 (Chomsky, 1957). Generative-transformational grammar was created to solve the difficulties encountered by the immediate constituent model called *phrase structure grammar* by Chomsky.

Phrase structure grammar accounts for the structure of a sentence in terms of three important aspects:

1) linear order of words in a sentence;

2) categorization of words into morphological word classes (called *parts of speech*);

3) grouping of words into structural constituents of the sentence.

These three types of structural information can be encoded into a diagram called a *tree diagram*, or a *phrase marker*. Here is an example of a tree diagram:

(1)

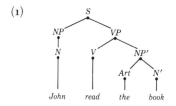

Tree (1) is a coding of the above structural information. The various parts of the sentence are shown in a fixed word order. Each word is assigned a morphological category: *N, N'* (nouns), *V* (verb), *Art* (article). And different parts of the sentence are shown as grouped into successively larger constituents of the sentence: *Art* and *N'* make up a noun phrase *NP'*; *V* and NP' make up a verb phrase *VP*; *N* makes up a noun phrase *NP*; *NP* and *VP* make up a sentence *S*.

Chomsky conceives of phrase structure grammar as a logical device that generates the phrase markers by phrase structure rules of the following sort:

(2)      *1) S → NP VP*
          *2) NP → N*
          *3) VP → V NP'*
          *4) NP' → Art N'*
          *5) N → John, Bill, . . .*
          *6) V → read, bought, ate, . . .*
          *7) Art → the, a, . . .*
          *8) N' → book, orange, . . .*

These phrase structure rules may generate phrase marker (1). Each rule is a formula that specifies the relation between the constituents in the phrase marker. For example, rule 1) tells us that sentence *S* can consist of sequence *NP VP*. The other rules tell us that *VP* can consist of sequence *V NP'*, *NP'* can consist of sequence *Art N'*, etc.

The term *generation* is conceived of as an enumeration of possible phrase markers by means of rules.

Chomsky discovered that the phrase structure model meets a number of serious difficulties. One grave difficulty is that phrase markers cannot represent discontinuous constituents. Consider, for example, the following pair of sentences:

(3)      *a. Peter gave up smoking.*
        *b. Peter gave smoking up.*

Both sentences contain a construction known as 'verb+particle' construction in English. In constructions of this type, the particle can occur separated from its verb. Clearly, *gave up* is a single constituent in sentence (3a), because it has a single meaning, it is synonymous with *stopped*. Although the particle *up* goes with the verb *gave*, it is separated from it by *smoking* in sentence (3b). That creates the following difficulty for phrase structure grammar.

Sentence (3a) can be naturally represented by phrase marker (4):

(4)

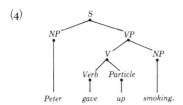

But when we address sentence (3b), we have to represent discontinuous constituents. It turns out that phrase markers are completely inadequate in representing discontinuous connections between parts of a sentence. Thus, sentence (3b) can be represented by phrase marker (5):

(5)

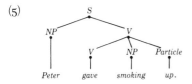

But phrase marker (5), though accurate in representing the linear word order, is essentially inadequate in another way: it does not show the affinity, the syntactic connection, between *gave* and *up*. And this example illustrates a general essential inadequacy of phrase markers: no matter which sentence with discontinuous constituents we have, a phrase marker may represent the linear order of the constituents of this sentence, but it will fail to represent the syntactic constituents of the sentence.

How to account for discontinuous connections between the constituents of a sentence?

One way to solve this problem is to devise a grammar that will be able to relate two or more phrase markers by means of special operations called *transformations*. This grammar was devised by Chomsky, and it is widely known under the name *generative-transformational grammar.*

To illustrate what is meant by transformation, let us turn again to the pair of sentences in (3).

We assume, as before, that sentence (3a) is assigned the phrase marker shown in (4). We assume further that phrase marker (5) is derived from phrase marker (4). Call phrase marker (4) the *underlying structure* for phrase marker (5).

Now we will introduce a transformation, which can be stated informally as follows:

Particle Movement Transformation:
In a *verb + particle* construction, the particle may be shifted away from the verb and moved to the immediate right of the noun phrase that is a constituent of the verb phrase.

By applying the Particle Movement Transformation to phrase marker (4), we get the derived phrase marker (5). The derived phrase marker (5) is called the *surface structure* of sentence (3b), and the underlying phrase marker (3) is called the *deep structure* of sentence (3b). Now sentence (3b) is characterized by two markers, and the relation between them is defined by the Particle Movement Transformation. That is an example of how discontinuous connections can be accounted for. Phrase marker (5) correctly represents the surface structure of sentence (3b), but now we can claim that *gave* and *up* are really contiguous, since phrase marker (5) is derived from phrase marker (4).

Let us turn to a formal definition of a transformational rule. A transformational rule consists of two parts: a *structural description (SD)*, which is an instruction to analyze a phrase marker into a sequence of constituents, and the *structural change (SC)*, which is an instruction to modify the structural description. Thus, the formal definition of the above particle movement transformation can be stated as follows:

(6)      SD: $X$ — $Verb$ — $Particle$ — $NP$ — $Y$
$$1 - 2 - 3 - 4 - 5 \Rightarrow$$
$$SC: 1 - 2 - \emptyset - 4{+}3 - 5$$

The variables $X$ and $Y$ indicate that the constituents to the left of the verb and to the right of the $NP$ are irrelevant for this transformation—they can represent anything. The sign $\emptyset$ indicates that *Particle*, which occupies the third place from the left, is shifted away from the verb; the signs $4{+}3$ indicate that the particle is moved to the immediate right of the $NP$. The remaining parts of the $SD$ are left unchanged, which is indicated by repeating the same numbers in the $SC$.

Consider the passive transformation in another example. Let us take the following pair of sentences:

(7)      a. *Mary dropped the glass.*
         b. *The glass was dropped by Mary.*

Sentence (7a) can be represented by phrase marker (8):

(8)

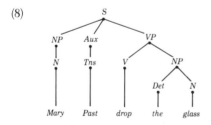

Symbol *Aux* indicates an auxiliary element, *Tns* means tense, *Det* means a determiner.

To get a derived phrase marker from (8), we postulate the following transformation:

(9)    SD: $NP - Aux - \quad V \quad - NP - \quad X$
    $\quad\quad 1 - \quad 2 \quad - \quad 3 \quad\quad - 4 - \quad\quad 5 \quad \Rightarrow$
    $\quad SC: 4 - \quad 2 \quad - be+en+3 - \varnothing \quad - 5+by+1$

Informally speaking, the phrase marker of a passive sentence can be derived from the phrase marker of an active sentence by making three changes: first, moving the subject noun phrase to the end of the sentence and inserting *by* before it; second, moving the noun phrase following the verb into subject position; and third, inserting the appropriate form of *be* before the verb and putting the verb in the past participial form. In the above formula of the passive transformation rule, symbols *be+en* are a conventional representation of the past participial form.

Applying rule (9) to phrase marker (8), we get phrase marker (10):

(10)

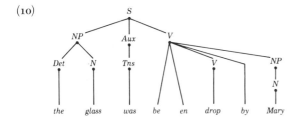

The passive sentence (7b) is represented by two phrase markers: phrase marker (8) as its deep structure and phrase marker (10) as its surface structure.

Generative-transformational grammar has two levels of representations of syntactic structure: 1) the level of syntactic structure generated by phrase structure rules (called *deep structure*), and 2) the level of syntactic structure generated by transformational rules (called *surface structure*). Therefore, generative-transformational grammar has two components: 1) the *base component* and 2) the *transformational component*.

The base component consists of two elements: the phrase structure rules (called *rewriting* rules) and the lexicon to which all the syntactic, semantic, and phonological properties of the lexical items are assigned. The base component generates deep structure.

The transformational component transforms deep structure into a sequence of other structures. The final term of this sequence is a surface structure.

Generative-transformational grammar has two interpretive components: the *phonological* component and the *semantic* component.

The standard theory of generative-transformational grammar can be visualized through the following diagram (Chomsky, 1965):

(11)

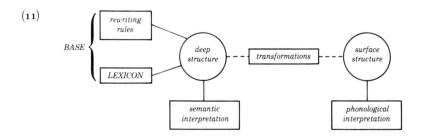

Chomsky has conclusively shown the inadequacy of phrase structure grammar. Besides discontinuous constituents, whose syntactic connection this grammar cannot represent at all, there are many other kinds of structures that it represents very awkwardly at best. Generative-transformational grammar was devised as a means for overcoming the inadequacies of phrase structure grammar.

Granted that we accept Chomsky's analysis of the inadequacies of phrase structure grammar, does that mean that we have to accept the assumption that a formal grammar must necessarily have a transformational component?

I do not think so. The assumption that a formal grammar must have a transformational component is just one possibility to remedy the inadequacies of the constituency model. This assumption leads to new difficulties. Let me point out two main difficulties encountered by generative-transformational grammar.

The difficulties I am going to discuss are consequences of conceptual unclarities. By conceptual unclarity I do not mean lack of a clear formal definition of a concept: a concept can be taken as a primitive, that is, as an undefined, notion and yet be clear; on the other hand, we can construct a clear formal definition of a concept, and yet this concept will be unclear. By conceptual unclarity I mean a lack of clear correspondence between concepts and real objects to which concepts apply. Our concepts must clearly match their objects, or else we can get into trouble. True, as the history of science shows, some degree of vagueness in a concept is probably uneliminable; it sometimes may even happen that some small measure of vagueness is a positive bonus, since less precise concepts can often be more readily applied to new domains of investigation than can more precise ones. Still, the increase of the conceptual clarity of a theory through careful analysis of how its concepts relate to real objects is one of the most important ways in which science progresses. The history of science shows that many significant revolutions in science, such as the emergence of the theory of relativity in physics, have largely been consequences of the recognition and subsequent reduction of the conceptual vagueness of theories in particular domains.

Let us now turn to an analysis of conceptual unclarities in generative-transformational grammar. I will argue that unclear concepts are the chief troublemakers that cause insurmountable difficulties for generative-transformational grammar. And I will show that applicative grammar is free from these difficulties.

The chief troublemaker is the notion of *constituency* as conceived by Chomsky. Chomsky confounds constituency structure with linear word order; he regards linearity as an inherent property of constituency. But, as was demonstrated in section 3, constituency is independent of linearity; the notion of the constituent was defined there independently of linearity. Turning to our example with discontinuous constituents represented by phrase marker (5), we can replace (5) with phrase marker (12), where the constituency relations are separated from their linear representation:

(12)

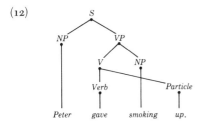

Another example of separating constituency from its linear representation is tree diagrams (6) and (7) in section 2.

The result of confounding constituency with linear word order is that transformations are stated in terms of linear order of constituents, which makes it necessary to formulate distinct rules for languages with different word order for what is the same phenomenon from a relational point of view.

By contrast, since applicative grammar defines constituency independently of linear word order, it is able to state significant cross-linguistic generalizations in relational terms, which makes it possible to formulate identical rules for cross-linguistically identical phenomena.

Why does Chomsky confound constituency with linear word order? Because he does not see that constituency and linear word order belong to different levels of abstraction. Constituency structure is a system of part-whole relations that constitutes a higher level of abstraction than linear word order, but Chomsky does not distinguish between these two levels of abstraction. Considering an early version of applicative grammar presented in a book that I coauthored with P. A. Soboleva (Shaumyan, Soboleva, 1963), Chomsky argues against a distinction of both levels as follows:

> They propose, in essence, that in place of such rules as (69), the categorial component should contain the corresponding rules (70), where the element on the right is a set rather than a string:
> (69)  S→ NP⌣VP
>        VP→ V⌣NP
> (70)  S→ {NP,VP}
>        VP→ {V,NP}
> In (70), no order is assigned to the elements on the righthand side of the rule; thus {*NP,VP*} = {*VP,NP*}, although *NP⌣VP* ≠ *VP⌣NP*. The rules (70) can be used to

define grammatical relation in exactly the way indicated for the rules (69). The rules (69) convey more information than the corresponding rules (70), since they do not only define an abstract system of grammatical relations but also assign an abstract underlying order to the elements. The Phrase-marker generated by such rules as (69) will be representable as a tree-diagram with labeled nodes and labeled lines; the Phrase-marker generated by such rules as (70) will be representable as a tree-diagram with labeled nodes and unlabeled lines.

Proponents of *set-systems* such as (70) have argued that such systems are more 'abstract' than *concatenation-systems* such as (69), and can lead to a study of grammatical relations that is independent of order, this being a phenomenon that belongs only to surface structure. The greater abstractness of set-systems, so far as grammatical relations are concerned, is a myth. Thus the grammatical relations defined by (70) are neither more nor less 'abstract' or 'order-independent' than those defined by (69); in fact, the systems of grammatical relations defined in the two cases are identical. A priori, there is no way of determining which theory is correct; it is an entirely empirical question, and the evidence presently available is overwhelmingly in favor of concatenation-systems over set-systems, for the theory of the categorial component. In fact, no proponent of a set-system has given any indication of how the abstract underlying unordered structures are converted into actual strings with surface structures. Hence, the problem of giving empirical support to this theory has not yet been faced. (Chomsky, 1965: 124–25)

First of all, let us define our terms. Chomsky assigns the applicative model to the class of abstract set systems. That is simply incorrect. The example (70) used by Chomsky has nothing to do with generation in the applicative model. In the latter, *NP* and *VP* are not some unordered set of elements that can be written down in the formula {*NP,VP*}, as in set theory; they are elements hierarchically related to each other as constituent parts of a single whole: *VP* is the operator for *NP*. In the same way, *VP* does not split up into an unordered set of elements {*V,NP*}, as Chomsky says, but consists of the operator *V* and its operand *NP*. In general, all the objects in the applicative model form a hierarchical system whose elements are connected by the hierarchical relation *operator: operand*. Thus, the applicative model belongs not to the class of abstract set systems but to the nonlinear type of constructive systems.

Mistakenly identifying the applicative model as an abstract set system, Chomsky maintains that the rules of the transformational model, a concatenation system, contain more information than the rules of the applicative model, since the former convey information as to how the constituent elements of the generated objects are ordered (he means the linear ordering of these elements), but the latter supposedly do not. This assertion is incorrect: in actual fact, both the rules of the generative-transformational model and the rules of the applicative model contain information about the ordering of these elements, but not the same information. The former are concerned with the linear concatenative ordering of elements, the latter with the hierarchical ordering of elements connected by the relation *operator: operand*.

Thus, the applicative model is a *relational system,* and the generative-transformational model is a *concatenation system.* Hence, we must reformulate Chomsky's arguments quoted above, since we are not comparing an abstract set system with a concatenation system, but a relational system with a concatenation system.

Now that we have defined our terms, we can return to the question posed by Chomsky and reformulate it thus: Which system should be considered more abstract, a relational system or a concatenation system?

Leaving aside a discussion of this question from a logical point of view and taking only purely linguistic criteria into consideration, we must agree with Chomsky that this question is completely empirical and therefore cannot be decided a priori.

What are the empirical data relating to this question?

It seems to me that when discussing this question, we must take into account the following:

1) In each sentence there are two planes: the expression plane and the content plane, or, which comes to the same thing, the sign plane and the meaning plane.

2) The linear order of morphemes belongs to the expression plane. From that it is obvious that differences in the order of morphemes in some languages correspond to the differences in the phonological composition of morphemes in other languages. Take, for example, the sentences

(13)     a. *Ann teaches Peter.*
         b. *Peter teaches Ann.*

and the corresponding Russian sentences

(14)     a. *Anna učit Petra.*
         b. *Annu učit Petr.*

Sentence (14a) is equivalent in meaning to sentence (13a), and sentence (14b) is equivalent in meaning to sentence (13b). Comparing (13a) and (13b), we see that the difference in meaning is connected only with a difference in the order of the morphemes in (13a) and (13b). As for the similar difference in meaning between (14a) and (14b), it is connected not with the order of the morphemes but with their phonological shape. If the difference in meaning between (13a) and (13b) is equivalent to the difference in meaning between (14a) and (14b), the difference in the order of morphemes between (13a) and (13b) is equivalent to the difference in phonological shape between (14a) and (14b).

3) Grammatical relations are invariant in relation to the means by which they are expressed. That is evident from a comparison of the above sentences. One and the same subject-object relation (13a) and (14a) is expressed in the former by a definite order of morphemes and in the latter by a definite phonological composition of morphemes. The same holds for (13b) and (14b). Mor-

pheme order in the one and the phonological composition of morphemes in the other express the same subject-object relation.

If these empirical assertions are accepted as correct, it follows that, from an empirical point of view, the more abstract model is the one that abstracts from the expression plane and deals directly with invariant grammatical, and in the broadest sense semantic, relations. It is clear that invariants are more abstract than the realization of invariants.

We have already noted that the rules of the applicative model contain information about a hierarchical system of elements connected by the relation *operator: operand,* whereas the rules of the generative-transformational model contain information about the linear ordering of morphemes based on concatenation. From that it is clear that the generative-transformational model is concerned with the realization of the content plane on the expression plane, whereas the applicative model isolates the pure invariant *operator: operand* relation. Because of this empirical fact, the applicative model must be considered more abstract than the generative-transformational model.

It goes without saying that a complete description of a language must include a full description of both the content and the expression planes. The question as to whether the generative-transformational model should or should not include a description of the expression plane is not worth discussion, because it is clear to every linguist that there cannot be a complete description of a language without a description of the expression plane. What is worth discussing is this: What is an adequate method of describing the correlations between the content and expression planes?

Two solutions are available: 1) either we describe the content and expression planes jumbling the two together, 2) or we first describe the content plane as such and then study how the linguistic invariants we have revealed are realized by various means of the expression plane.

The generative-transformational model follows the first course, the applicative model the second.

If it is true that linguistics, like any science, must first and foremost set itself the goal of discovering invariants, then it is the second way of describing language that is productive. In fact, it is difficult to see how it is possible to discover linguistic invariants if the content plane is not clearly distinguished from the expression plane.

As a matter of fact, the concatenation system used by Chomsky precludes the detection of word order universals. It will be shown below that word order universals can be detected only on the basis of the study of syntactic relations.

The foregoing discussion shows that there must be two levels of abstraction in grammar: the abstract level—a system of grammatical functions and relations; and the concrete level—a system of linearly ordered morphological units (morphemes and words). The abstract level I call the *genotype level,* and the concrete level—the *phenotype level.* In accordance with this distinction, we must distinguish between genotype structure and phenotype structure.

The distinction between genotype and phenotype structures, that is, relational structures and linear structures, is an alternative to the distinction between deep structure and surface structure. The notions of deep structure and surface structure are direct consequences of confounding the notion of constituency with linear word order. Transformations were devised to remedy phrase structure grammar defined in terms of the mistaken notion of constituency as conceived by Chomsky. If we abandon the mistaken notion of constituency and the definition of phrase structure grammar based on this mistaken notion, we have to abandon the notion of transformations; and if we abandon this notion, we must abandon the distinction of deep and surface structure.[10]

## 16. A Comparison of Applicative Grammar and Relational Grammar

Relational grammar has been developed by Perlmutter and Postal since about 1972 (Perlmutter, Postal, 1974). The goals of relational grammar are similar to the goals of applicative grammar. However, both grammars use very different means of achieving their goals.

The essential features of relational grammar, as presented in a recent paper (Perlmutter, 1980), are as follows.

Relational grammar has the following three goals:

1) to formulate linguistic universals;
2) to characterize the class of grammatical constructions;
3) to construct adequate and insightful grammars of individual languages.

The basic claim of relational grammar is that *grammatical relations*, such as 'subject of', 'direct object of', 'indirect object of', and others, are needed to achieve the goals of linguistic theory.

Another basic claim of relational grammar is that grammatical relations cannot be defined in terms of other notions, such as word order, phrase structure configurations, or case markings. Rather, they must be taken as primitives of linguistic theory.

Three things must be specified in syntactic representations:

1) which elements bear grammatical relations to which elements;
2) which grammatical relations each element bears to other elements;
3) levels at which each element bears grammatical relations to other elements.

To represent this information, the following types of primitive linguistic elements are introduced:

1) a set of nodes representing linguistic elements;
2) a set of R-signs, which are the names of grammatical relations that elements bear to other elements;
3) a set of coordinates, which are used to indicate the levels at which elements bear grammatical relations to other elements. Two equivalent notations are introduced:

(1)    *a.*

b.  $[GR_x(a,b){\langle}c_i{\rangle}]$

The object in (1) is called an *arc*. The interpretation of (1) is that the primitive linguistic element $a$ bears the relation whose name is $GR_x$ to the primitive linguistic element $b$ at the $c_i$ level. Thus, if $GR_x$ is '2', the name of the direct relation, and $c_i$ is $c_1$, then the arc in (2) indicates that $a$ bears the 2-relation to $b$ at the first, or $c_1$, level of $b$.

(2)    *a.*                     *b*

$$2 \quad \big\downarrow \quad c_i$$

$$a$$

b.  $[2(a,b){\langle}c_1{\rangle}]$

(1a) and (2a) are pictorial representations of (1b) and (2b) respectively; $a$ in the arc is called the *head* of the arc, and $b$ the *tail*. The R-signs '1', '2', '3', and *Chô* are the names of the subject, direct object, indirect object, and chômeur relations respectively. As an example of a representation of clause structure in these terms, consider the passive clause

(3)    *Sally was criticized by Marcia.*

The structure of (3) can be represented by *relational network* (4):

(4)

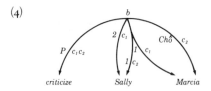

As indicated by (4), the structure of (3) has two levels. *Marcia* bears the 1-relation at the first level and the chômeur relation at the second level. The fact that *Marcia* bears the 1-relation at the first level and the chômeur relation at the second level is indicated by the fact that *Marcia* heads a 1-arc with coordinate $c_1$ and a Chŏ-arc with coordinate $c_2$. The fact that *Sally* bears the 2-relation at the first level and the 1-relation at the second level is indicated by the fact that *Sally* heads a 2-arc with coordinate $c_1$ and a 1-arc with coordinate $c_2$. The fact that *criticize* bears the predicate relation to $b$ at both the first and the second levels is indicated by the fact that *criticize* heads a *P*-arc with coordinates $c_1c_2$.

The notion of linguistic level can be reconstructed in terms of the notion of *stratum*. The $c_{ith}$, or *i*th, stratum of $b$, where $b$ is a node and $c_i$ is an arbitrary coordinate, is the set of all arcs with tail $b$ and coordinate $c_i$. Thus, the relational network (4) has two strata, the first, or $c_1$, stratum consisting of the arcs in (5), and the second, or $c_2$, stratum consisting of the arcs in (6):

(5)

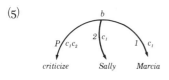

(6)

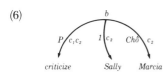

The relational network can be represented in the form of *stratal diagrams*. The stratal diagram of (4) is represented in (7):

(7)

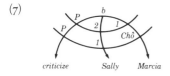

Sometimes symbols '*î*', '*2̂*', and '*3̂*' are used to represent the notions '1-chômeur', '2-chômeur', and '3-chômeur' respectively. An '*n-chômeur*' in a stratum $c_i$ is a nominal heading a *Chô*-arc in the $c_i$ stratum and an *n*-arc in the stratum immediately before the first stratum in which it heads a *Chô*-arc. So, in (7) the symbol '*Chô*' in the second stratum could be replaced by '*î*'.

I now turn to comments on relational grammar as a linguistic theory.

As was said in discussing the concept of passivization in relational grammar (sec. 12.2 above), 'subject of', 'direct object of', and 'indirect object of' can be called grammatical relations only in a trivial sense. These are essentially grammatical functions, rather than grammatical relations. Some grammatical functions, such as two-place or three-place predicates, are at the same time grammatical relations in a nontrivial sense, but owing to a perverse understanding of grammatical relations, relational grammar is not interested in predicates as grammatical relations.

Contrary to relational grammar, applicative grammar claims that in a clause, say, with a two-place predicate, subject and direct object are not relations but members of a binary relation which is the two-place predicate. Whether we regard subject, direct object, and indirect object as relations is not a terminological question. That is a confusion of concepts, which has an immediate consequence: relational grammar represents predicates as identical in all strata and is concerned only with those changes that affect subject, direct object, or indirect object. That can be seen, for example, in (4). In this diagram *criticize* is shown to be identical on both linguistic levels; only terms are assigned different relations on the two levels. That is a perverse representation of linguistic facts: a passive predicate cannot be identical with an active predicate; passivization changes an active predicate into a passive predicate, and this change in its turn involves a change in the grammatical functions of the terms.

Contrary to relational grammar, which changes the grammatical status of terms and leaves the grammatical status of predicates unchanged, applicative grammar conceives of grammatical rules primarily as predicate-changing rules and views the changes of the grammatical status of terms as a consequence of the changes of a predicate; applicative grammar requires that predicate-changing rules apply to a predicate before the predicate applies to its terms.

Linguistic facts contravene the relational grammar conception of the grammatical rule and support the applicative grammar conception of the grammatical rule. Consider the following consequences of the applicative grammar conception of the grammatical rule:

1) Applicative grammar predicts that morphemes that signify the change of relations must be part of a verb rather than part of nouns.

2) Applicative grammar predicts that sentences with changed grammatical relations can be obtained independently of sentences with unchanged grammatical relations. For instance, a passive sentence can be obtained directly by applying a passive predicate to its terms, rather than by transforming an active sentence into a passive sentence. This prediction follows from the requirement that predicate-changing rules must be applied to a predicate before the predicate is applied to its terms. An important consequence of this prediction is that linguistic levels and strata postulated by relational grammar are gratuitous: since sentences with changed predicates can be obtained directly by applying changed predicates to their terms, we can dispense with linguistic levels in the sense of relational grammar.

3) Applicative grammar predicts that in sentences with changed grammatical relations, the grammatical status of terms can be governed only by verbs, as, for instance, in sentences with converse or causative predicates.

Linguistic facts support these predictions of applicative grammar and contravene relational grammar, which conceives of predicates as unchangeable entities.

Let us now turn to other aspects of relational grammar.

Relational grammar postulates subject, direct object, indirect object, chômeur, and other relations as primitives rather than as defined notions. There is nothing wrong with this approach. The important thing is not whether or not we define these concepts but whether or not they correctly match linguistic facts. Unfortunately, these concepts, as they are understood by relational grammar, are either ambiguous or simply incorrect. In discussing passivization (sec. 12.2 above), it was shown that the concept of subject in relational grammar is ambiguous: relational grammar confounds two different notions—the notion of salience and the notion of agentivity. When relational grammar speaks about a transitive subject, it means an agent, but when relational grammar speaks about an intransitive subject, it means simply a salient term of a sentence. That leads to further confusion. Thus, in active sentences of Dyirbal the term in the absolutive is a patient, and it is salient; the term in the ergative is an agent, and it is nonsalient. In accordance with the terminology of relational grammar, we must call the term in the ergative a transitive subject, but then we will have two subjects in a sentence, since the term in the absolutive, being salient, has a similar functional status to that of the term in an intransitive sentence.

As was shown in previous sections on ergative languages and the Keenan-Comrie Accessibility Hierarchy (secs. 9–10 above), the notions of subject, direct object, and indirect object are not valid universal concepts; they can be applied only to accusative languages. Therefore, these notions must be abandoned as theoretical constructs.

Arguments for the rejection of the notion of chômeur and the Unaccusative Hypothesis were already presented in the section on the treatment of passivization in relational grammar (sec. 12.2 above).

Here are some additional arguments.

Let us turn to the notion of 2-chômeur, represented by symbol $\hat{2}$. Perlmutter illustrates this notion using the following examples.

To illustrate the 2-chômeur relation, Perlmutter (1980) gives two examples from Indonesian based on a work by Chung (1976) and one example concerning verb agreement in Swahili.

Chung has shown that direct objects in Indonesian can be relativized in a construction with the complementarizer *yang*, as in (9):

(8)   *Ali membawa     surat   ini kepada saya.*
        TRANS/bring letter this  to    I
        'Ali brought this letter to me'.

(9)   *surat yang Ali bawa kepada saya*
        letter that      bring   to    I
        'the letter that Ali brought to me'

These examples illustrate the general condition of relativizing final 1s and 2s. But in Indonesian there is a grammatical sentence synonymous with (8) in which *surat* cannot be relativized with *yang*:

(10)   *Ali   memba wakan saya surat ini.*
         'Ali brought me this letter'.

(11)     *surat yang Ali bawakan saya
         'the letter that Ali brought me'

The question arises, Why is (9) possible while (11) is not?
Consider now two synonymous passive sentences:

(12)     Surat ini  dibawa kepada saya oleh Ali.
         letter this PASS/bring to    I   by
         'This letter was brought to me by Ali'.

(13)     Saya dibawakan  surat ini   oleh Ali.
         I     PASS/bring letter this by
         'I was brought this letter by Ali'.

Again, a similar question arises: Why can surat be relativized with yang in
(14) but not in (15)?

(14)     surat yang dibawa kepada saya oleh Ali
         'the letter that was brought to me by Ali'

(15)     *surat yang saya dibawakan oleh ali
         'the letter that I was brought by Ali'

RG explains the above contrasts by means of the following hypothesis:

(16)     a.  In sentences (10) and (13) initial 3 is advanced to 2.
         b.  In the stratum in which the initial 3 is advanced to 2, the initial 2 becomes a
             chômeur.
         c.  Only a nominal that is a final 1 or 2 can be relativized with yang in Indonesian.

Under this hypothesis, (8) is associated with the relational network in (17),
while (10) is associated with the relational network in (18).

(17)

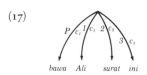

bawa    Ali    surat    ini

(18)

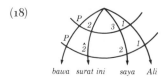

bawa  surat ini    saya    Ali

(18) represents advancement of the 3 to 2 and the chômage of 2 in the final
stratum.

The passives in (12) and (13) are represented by the following stratal diagrams:

(19)

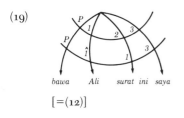

*bawa    Ali    surat ini  saya*

$[=(12)]$

(20)

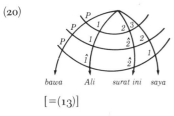

*bawa    Ali    surat ini  saya*

$[=(13)]$

The essential difference between (19) and (20) is that in (19) *surat ini* is *1* in the final stratum, while in (20) *surat ini* is $\hat{2}$ in the final stratum.

The notion of conversion and the distinction of primary and secondary functions of terms make it possible to dispense both with the chômeur relation and with strata. As a matter of fact, there is a conversion of tertiary terms and secondary terms in the above examples. The crucial fact is that the secondary terms can and the tertiary terms cannot be relativized. When a conversion takes place between the tertiary term and the secondary term, the tertiary term functions as the secondary term and therefore can be relativized, while the secondary term functions as the tertiary term and therefore loses its ability to be relativized.

In view of that, the correct formulation of hypothesis (16) is:

    a.  Sentences (10) and (13) involve conversion of the secondary and tertiary terms.
    b.  As a result of the conversion, the secondary term functions as the tertiary term, and the tertiary term functions as the secondary term.
    c.  Only the terms that function either as a primary or a secondary term can be relativized.

A similar argument based on the notion of conversion and the interplay of primary and secondary functions can be presented for data from Swahili.

Swahili has the following verb agreement rule (in terms of the notions of subject and direct object):

(21)    The verb agrees with the noun class of the direct object.

For example:

(22)   *Msichana a-li - (u) - fung-a    mlango.*
         girl 1-PST -2- open -INDC door
       'The girl opened the door'.

Here -*u*- is the direct object agreement marker that agrees with the noun class of *mlango*.

Swahili has sentences that seem to be counterexamples to this rule: the verb agrees with the indirect object rather than with the direct object. For example:

(23)   *Johni a - li    - m - p - a    mkunga zawadi.*
           1 -PST-    2 -give-INDC nurse    present
       'John gave the nurse the present'.

Here the agreement marker -*m*- indicates agreement with *mkunga*, which belongs to the human class of the indirect object.

Further, the indirect object *mkunga* passivizes naturally, while the direct object *zawadi* cannot be passivized.

Perlmutter explains these counterexamples away by stating that sentence (23) involves advancement of 3 to 2; that is, *mkunga*, which is an initial 3, has advanced to 2, which entails the chômage of *zâwadi*, which is initial 2.

This explanation is plausible in the framework of RG, but again we can propose a better explanation based on the notion of conversion and an interplay of primary and secondary functions.

In terms of these notions, the above rule of the verb agreement must be formulated as follows:

(24)   The verb agrees with the noun class that has the function of the secondary
       term.

We posit the conversion between the secondary and tertiary terms. In (23) the verb agrees with *mkunga* rather than with *zawadi*, because *mkunga* is the tertiary term converted into the secondary term, while *zawadi* is the secondary term converted into the tertiary term.

The notions of the chômeur relation and strata are fictions that are not necessary for linguistic theory.

As an alternative to the Unaccusative Hypothesis, we propose to explain the relevant facts by deducing them from the Markedness Law in conjunction with the statement that primary terms have a wider range than secondary terms. (This law and the statement were explained in the previous section.)

Applicative grammar is a linguistic theory whose cornerstone is the notion of linguistic relations. The basic linguistic relation is the relation *operator : operand*. In terms of this relation and the Applicative Principle, all basic linguistic relations and functions can be defined. Some laws of relational grammar, such as the Stratal Uniqueness Law, the Oblique Law, and the Final *1* Law, automatically follow from the Applicative Principle and the notion of valence. The important thing to notice is that the laws of applicative grammar are obtained deductively, and therefore the possibility of their falsification is of great significance for this linguistic theory, because rejection of some of these laws on empirical grounds will throw doubt on the Applicative Principle; the laws of relational grammar, on the other hand, are simply empirical generalizations that are logically independent of each other, and therefore linguists who espouse relational grammar are free to abandon some of these laws, and still their theory remains intact.

In summary, a comparison of applicative grammar and relational grammar reveals an overwhelming superiority of applicative grammar.

### 17. A Comparison of Applicative Grammar and the Lexical-Functional Grammar of Bresnan

The lexical-functional grammar of Bresnan (1978, 1982) assigns two levels of syntactic description to every sentence of a language: a constituent structure and a functional structure. The constituent structure is a conventional phrase-structure tree, while the functional structure provides a characterization of such notions as subject, object, complement, and adjunct.

The difference between constituent and functional structures can be illustrated by the following example (Kaplan and Bresnan, 1982):
Consider the sentence

(1)      *A girl handed the baby a toy.*

Given the rules

(2)      a.      S → NP   VP
         b.      NP → Det   N
         c.      VP → V   NP   NP

the following constituent structure can be assigned to sentence (1):

(3)

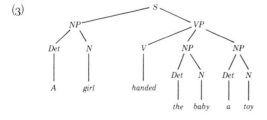

The functional structure for (1) would indicate that the noun phrase *a girl* is the grammatical subject, *handed* conveys the semantic predicate, the noun phrase *the baby* is the grammatical object, and the noun phrase *a toy* serves as the second grammatical object.

According to Bresnan, the minimal semantic information about verbs that must be represented in the lexicon is their logical predicate-argument structure. For example, the intransitive verb *to walk* is represented by a one-place relation (or a one-place predicate), the transitive verb *to eat* is represented by a two-place relation (or a two-place predicate), and the ditransitive verb *to hand* must be represented by a three-place relation (or a three-place predicate).

So *to walk* and *to eat* can be described as follows:

(4)    a.  *walk*   $V, [\underline{\qquad}]$,    $NP_1$   WALK
       b.  *eat*    $V, [\underline{\qquad}]$,    $NP_1$   EAT $NP_2$
                    $V, [\underline{\qquad}]$,    $\exists y\ NP_1$ EAT $y$

These formulas include immediate constituent syntactic contexts for the lexical insertion of verbs and functional structures for *walk* and *eat*. The syntactic contexts are given in the left column of (4), and the functional structures are represented by formulas in the right column.

Functional structures cannot be regarded as sentences as long as lexical items are not inserted. Functional structures turn into sentences only after the lexical insertion takes place.

By drawing a distinction between two levels—the level of constituent structures and the level of functional structures—Bresnan has taken a step towards the concept of genotype language.

Nevertheless, Bresnan's system of functional structures cannot be compared with genotype language. While genotype language is a universal system, Bresnan's system of functional structures with inserted lexical items depends on these lexical items and is, therefore, not universal. The essential difference between genotype grammar and Bresnan's grammar is that genotype grammar is concerned with purely abstract linguistic objects, which allows one to discover universal relations between sentences, while Bresnan's grammar operates with functional structures with inserted lexical items that stand in language-specific, rather than universal, relations to one another. To see that, let us consider how this grammar handles passive constructions:

(5)    a.  *eat:*       $V, [\underline{\qquad} NP]$,        $NP_1$ EAT $NP_2$
       b.  *eat+en*    $V, [be \underline{\qquad}]$,        $(\exists x)\ x$ EAT $NP_1$
       c.  *eat+en*    $V, [be \underline{\qquad}[_{pp} by\ NP]]$,   $(\exists x)\ (x$ EAT $NP_1$ & $x{=}NP_{by})$

As was said above about this framework, the material in square brackets represents syntactic contexts for lexical insertion of verbs. The formulas on the right are functional structures. (5a) represents an active construction, (5b) a short passive construction, and (5c) a long passive construction. The active-passive relation is described by operations of two types: one relating syntactic contexts, and the other relating functional structures of active and passive verbs. Examples of rules relating functional structures of active and passive verbs are: 'Eliminate $NP_1$' or 'Replace $NP_2$ by $NP_1$'. Such rules used in conjunction with rules of lexical insertion cannot capture universal laws of passivization. These laws must be expressed in terms of language-independent universal relations between active and passive constructions, as is done in genotype grammar.

## 18. The Place of Applicative Grammar among Other Semiotic Systems

The term *applicative grammar* has two senses: it denotes a special kind of mechanism stored in speakers' brains and not open to direct inspection; or it denotes a model that is a hypothesis about the structure and the functioning of this mechanism. Likewise, the term *genotype language* has two senses: it denotes the common semiotic basis of natural languages that exists in objective reality but is not open to direct inspection; or it denotes an artificial, specially constructed language that is a hypothesis about the objective semiotic basis.

The genotype language in the sense of a hypothesis about the common semiotic basis of natural languages is an artificial language that belongs to a class of applicative languages. The class of applicative languages includes the lambda-calculus, the combinatory calculus, the high-level programming language LISP, used in artificial intelligence, and low-level computer languages.

The lambda-calculus originated for the purpose of a more careful study of mathematical functions. As Frege (1893) maintains, any function can be reduced to a sequence of functions of a single argument. Thus, for binary functions we write $f(a, b)$ and use, in some cases, infixes, for example $+$ in $a+b$. But we can reduce binary functions to a sequence of two functions of a single argument. In order to do so, we replace the function $f$, which is an operation, by an abstract object $F$, which is, so to say, a nominalized operation, a sort of noun denoting the binary function $f$. As a result of this replacement, we obtain a new object $F$ in addition to the initial two objects $a$ and $b$. To combine these three objects, we introduce the application operation. We apply $F$ first to $x$ and obtain $(Fa)$, then we apply $(Fa)$ to $b$ and obtain $(Fa)b$. In the case of $a+b$, we replace the binary function $+$ ('plus') with a sort of noun $A$ ('addition', 'sum'), denoting the binary function $+$, and apply $A$ first to $a$ and then to $b$, so that we get $(Aa)b$. The difference between $+$ and $A$ is comparable to the difference between an adjective and a noun: while $a+b$ reads '$a$ plus $b$', $(Aa)b$ reads: 'the sum of $a$ and $b$'.

The method of reducing functions to functions of a single argument was brought into prominence by the works of Haskell B. Curry. That is why it is sometimes called *currying*. Although this method was originally introduced into mathematics for purely theoretical purposes, it gained wider significance in connection with the development of more sophisticated computer languages. Thus, Rosser writes:

> This is the way computers function. A program in a computer is a function of a single argument. People who have not considered the matter carefully may think, when they write a subroutine to add two numbers, that they have produced a program that is a function of two arguments. But what happens when the program begins to run, to produce the sum $A + B$? First $A$ is brought from memory. Suppose that at that instant the computer is completely halted. What remains in the computer is a program, to be applied to any $B$ that might be forthcoming, to produce the sum of the given $A$ and the forthcoming $B$. It is a function of one argument, depending on the given $A$, to be applied to any $B$, to produce the sum $A + B$. It is Frege's intermediary function $\oplus(A)$. (Rosser, 1984:337–38)

George W. Petznik (1970) showed that it is possible to design a computer to work exclusively with combinatory formulas stored as trees. The combinatory calculus has been successfully applied to the analysis of programming languages by Backus (1978) and other researchers in computer science (Stoy, 1977; Abelson and Sussman, 1985). Pointing out the advantages of the combinatory method of programming as opposed to the old von Neuman style, Backus gave a characteristic title to his paper: "Can Programming Be Liberated from the von Neuman Style?"

My attempt to use combinatory calculus for constructing genotype language as a model simulating the common basic semiotic properties of natural languages can be viewed as an expansion of the above method into a new domain—linguistic science. Recently, Jean-Pierre Desclés brought to my attention an interesting passage from the book *The Development of Logic* (1962) by W. Kneale and M. Kneale. Presenting the primitive formalism of Schönfinkel (1924), which was developed by Curry and his followers—Rosser and others—into combinatory calculus, W. Kneale and M. Kneale write:

> But it has never been claimed that combinatory logic, as this study is now called, provides formulae of great intuitive clarity. So far, Schönfinkel's technique is important chiefly for the light it throws on the role of variables and the notion of substitution in the symbolism of mathematical logic. Conceivably it may prove useful also in the exact analysis of patterns in natural languages, but at present that is mere conjecture. (Kneale and Kneale, 1962:524)

There is a close relationship between combinatory calculus and lambda-calculus. In order to understand this relationship, we must compare application—the fundamental primitive concept in combinatory calculus, and functional abstraction—the fundamental primitive concept in lambda-calculus.

Application and functional abstraction are two processes that are inverses of each other. Application is a process of finding the value of a function, given the function and an argument of the function: we apply the function to its argument in order to find the value of the function for that argument. Functional abstraction is a process of finding a function, given relevant information about the values of the function for all its arguments: let $x$ indicate any argument of the function, and let $M$ containing $x$ be an expression indicating the value of the function for its argument $x$; then

(1)    $\lambda x.M$

designates the function itself.

The operation of forming (1) from $x$ and $M$ is called functional abstraction. Symbol $\lambda$ is called the lambda operator (or $\lambda$-operator).

An example of functional abstraction: $\lambda x.x^2$ is the square function, that is, the function whose value is $x^2$ for the value of its argument $x$.

A natural extension of (1) is an $n$-fold functional abstraction:

(2)    $\lambda^n x \ldots x_n M$

which means 'the function whose value is $M$ if its arguments are $x_1, \ldots, x_n$'.

Combinatory calculus does not have the operation of functional abstraction, because it takes functions as primitive abstract objects. The abstract objects are called combinators. Schönfinkel, who, independently of Frege, came up with the idea of reducing functions to a function of a single argument, discovered that all functions can be built up of only two basic functions—K and S. Combinators are K and S and all other functions built from K and S by application. Combinatory calculus studies the use and properties of combinators.

Combinators are taken as primitive in combinatory calculus. But we can define combinators in terms of the operation of functional abstraction, if we so desire (Curry and Feys, 1958:152–54). For example:

(3)    $I \equiv \lambda x.x$

(4)    $C \equiv \lambda fxy.fyx$

(5)    $B \equiv \lambda fgx.f(gx)$

(6)    $S \equiv \lambda fgx.fx(gx)$

(7)    $W \equiv \lambda fx.fxx$

The operation of functional abstraction is basic in lambda-calculus, but it also has the application operation. Combinatory calculus has only the application operation. Curry calls combinatory calculus an applicative system, and he calls lambda-calculus a quasi-applicative system (Curry and Feys, 1958:84). According to Curry's definition, an *applicative system* is a system with application as its sole operation, and a *quasi-applicative system* is a system that has application in combination with other operations.

The theories of combinators and λ-calculus are now a hot topic in computer science and artificial intelligence, because they can be viewed as abstract proto-types of powerful functional programming languages. Hindley and Seldin write:

> The theories of combinators and λ-calculus both have the same purpose; to de-scribe some of the most primitive and general properties of operators and com-binations of operators. In effect they are abstract programming languages. They contain the concept of computation in full generality and strength, but in a pure 'distilled' form with syntactic complications kept to a minimum. (Hindley and Seldin, 1986:VI)

Some basic ideas of lambda- and combinatory calculus are worked into LISP. The creator of this computer language, John McCarthy, recognized procedures as functions of one argument.

LISP is an acronym for LISt Processing. This name refers to the notion of the list, the fundamental structure underlying most LISP programs and data.

The LISP community has been expanding rapidly since the inception of this language in 1950. As a result of its expansion, LISP has evolved into a number of dialects, so that there is no such thing as standard LISP. Although LISP dia-lects share many basic features, they differ from one another in substantial ways. A version of LISP called Common LISP is one of the LISP dialects (Winston and Horn, 1984). The most widely used dialects of LISP today are MacLISP, developed at MIT, and INTERLISP, developed at Bolt, Beranek, and Newman and Xerox Palo Alto Research Center.

The examples given below are taken from a dialect called Franz LISP, devel-oped at the University of California at Berkeley and available under the name Berkeley UNIX. This dialect, closely related to MacLISP, has the advantage of a lucid notation, revealing the applicative structure (Wilensky, 1984).

The primary data of LISP are *atoms*, wordlike objects. Combinations of atoms form objects called *lists*, which are sentencelike objects. A list is just a sequence of objects inside a pair of parentheses; combinations of lists give higher-level lists. Atoms and lists together constitute symbolic expressions called *s-expressions*.

The process of taking an *s*-expression and performing a computation on it is called *evaluation*. The result of evaluating an *s*-expression is called the *value* of that expression. For example, if we want to compute 9+4, we type the following:

(8)      → (plus 9 4)
         13
         →

The arrow in Franz LISP signals that it is waiting for an input. In (8), *plus* is the name for the addition operator, 9 and 4 are arguments of their operator, and 13 is the value of the *s*-expression.

Here is the LISP Evaluation Rule: *Look at the outermost list first. Evaluate each of its arguments. Use the results as arguments to the outermost operator* (Wilensky, 1984: 3).

This rule is a counterpart of the Combination Rule in combinatory calculus and applicative grammar: *Apply primitive operators to their operands, and use the results of the application as operands to the outer operator.*

By using the LISP Evaluation Rule, we can compute *s*-expressions of arbitrary complexity. For example, to compute $(6+4)\cdot(5+(7\cdot3))$, we would type

(9)     → (times (plus 6 4)(plus 5(times 7 3)))
260
→

The first argument in (9) is (*plus* 6 4). Evaluating it, LISP gets 10. The second argument is (*plus* 5(*times* 7 3)). That argument itself contains an argument, namely, (*times* 7 3). LISP evaluates first (*times* 7 3) and gets 21. Then LISP evaluates the second argument and gets 26. Having completed the evaluation of the two arguments of the entire *s*-expression, LISP applies *times* to the results of the evaluation of the two arguments, namely, to 10 and 26, and gets 260.

For simplicity, LISP may omit some parentheses. But an omission of parentheses reflects only specific conventions concerning their use in a given dialect of LISP, and in no way compromises the Applicative Principle. No matter which conventions concerning the use of parentheses was adapted, the underlying structure of an *s*-expression is always binary. Lists are represented in LISP by using binary trees. Characterizing the binary structure of LISP, Rosser writes:

> John McCarthy worked several ideas of the LC [lambda-calculus] into LISP. He clearly recognized procedures as functions of one argument. In the LC, such functions can be applied to each other and give such functions when applied. In LISP, it is possible to apply one procedure to another, and on occasion get another procedure. (Rosser, 1984:339)

In addition to the applicative operation, LISP also uses the operation of functional abstraction represented by lambda notation. Therefore, LISP must be classified as a quasi-applicative system, in Curry's terminology.

LISP is used largely as a programming language for artificial intelligence research. It is one of the important bridges between the combinatory and lambda calculi and computer science.[11]

# IV.

# *Phenotype Grammar*

## 1. The Task of Phenotype Grammar

In chapter 3, section 1, it was shown that two levels must be distinguished in a sentence: a functional level and a syntagmatic level. The functional level is called the *genotype level*, because it underlies the world's languages as their universal semiotic basis; language universals are part of the genotype level. The syntagmatic level is called the *phenotype level*, because it is different in different languages; the same functional structure can be represented by a variety of different syntagmatic structures.

In accordance with the distinction of the genotype and the phenotype levels, applicative grammar consists of two parts: *genotype grammar* and *phenotype grammar*. An outline of genotype grammar was given in the foregoing chapter. In this chapter I will present an outline of phenotype grammar.

The basic sign of the phenotype level is the *word*. Every combination of words is called a *word syntagm*. The *sentence* as a functional unit is usually represented by a word syntagm, and sometimes it is represented by one word.

The task of phenotype grammar is the study of the structure of the word and of the syntagmatic structure of the sentence. What is called *morphology* constitutes only a part of phenotype grammar; phenotype grammar studies not only the structure of the word but the structure of word groups, as well. An important part of phenotype grammar is the *theory of word order*.

## 2. The Word

The notion of the *word* is common in current linguistic literature. But in defining this notion, one runs into difficulties.[1]

In Bloomfield's classic formulation, forms such as *-ess* [es] in *countess, lioness, duchess*, etc.; *-ish* [ɪʃ] in *boyish, childish*, and *greenish*; and *-s* [s] in *hats, books*, and *cups*, are *bound* forms, because they can appear only as part of a larger form or larger sequence of morphemes. However, *big lioness, childish games*, and so on are all *free* forms—capable, that is, of appearing on their own. A free form that consists of two or more free forms is called a *phrase*. Thus, *big lioness* and *childish games* are phrases, because they can be divided into smaller

284

free forms. But *lioness* and *childish* cannot themselves be so divided: they are *minimal free forms*. Bloomfield defines the word as a free form that cannot be divided into smaller free forms. The word is a minimal free form (Bloomfield, 1933).

Bloomfield's definition of the word is not satisfactory for several reasons.

First, Bloomfield conceives of his definition as an explication of what modern linguists normally call the word. But this definition conflicts with the normal use of the term *word*. For example, the pronoun *my* and the articles *a* and *the* are normally called words, but they cannot appear on their own.

Second, Bloomfield confounds the phonological representation of the word with the grammatical notion of the word. Thus, the phonological word *lɪkt* and the corresponding orthographic word *licked* represent a particular grammatical word that can be characterized as the past tense of *lick*. But the phonological word *ʃʌt* and the corresponding orthographic word *shut* represent three different grammatical words: the present tense of *shut*, the past tense of *shut*, and the past participle of *shut*.

Third, it follows from Bloomfield's definition that *table* and *tables* are different words rather than two forms of the same word. By the same token, he considers *do, does, did,* and *done* as four different words rather than four forms of the same word. Bloomfield, like many other modern linguists, condemns the abstract notion of the word.

In search of an adequate definition of the word, as well as of other linguistic notions, we must recognize the fact that concepts are defined within the context of a particular theory, and this context changes as different theories are advanced. The same term may signify different things within the context of different theories. Concepts change constantly as theories change. The terms *space* and *time* do not signify in the theory of relativity what they meant in classical physics. The evolution of a concept may involve a radical break with established ideas in a particular domain.

Our problem is to define the notion of the word within the theoretical matrix of applicative grammar.

I will advocate a functional approach to the morphological notion of the word. I mean that the main classes of words are morphological crystallizations of the basic syntaxemes: predicates crystallize into verbs, terms crystallize into nouns, modifiers of predicates crystallize into adverbs, modifiers of terms crystallize into adjectives. And subclasses of words are crystallizations of their different paradigmatic functions. A definition of the word must be independent of the notion of the morpheme. The word must be defined through the notion of syntactic function.

I propose the following definition of the word, which is independent of the notion of the morpheme and is based on the notion of syntactic function.

A *word* is a minimal linguistic sign that is capable of having various syntactic and paradigmatic functions either (1) by itself or (2) together with a word of type (1) meeting in the latter case the condition of separability. 'Minimal' means that a word contains no other word.

A word of type (1) I call an *autonomous* word; a word of type (2) I call a *nonautonomous* word.

Let us take some examples. *Run, runs, ran, run,* and *running* are different forms of the same autonomous word *RUN*, because they signify different syntactic or paradigmatic functions, and the symbolic function of *RUN* is invariant of changes in its syntactic and paradigmatic functions and forms. (The capital letters of *RUN* mean that it signifies an abstract word, that is, a class of different forms of a word.) On the other hand, *runner* and *runners* are forms of the autonomous word *RUNNER* rather than forms of the word *RUN*, because *RUN* and *RUNNER* have different symbolic functions. Since *RUNNER* is derived from *RUN*, these different words are related derivationally.

*Book* and *books* are different forms of the autonomous word *BOOK*, whose symbolic function is invariant of these forms signifying its different paradigmatic functions.

The Russian word *KNIGA* 'book' has the following forms: *kniga* ('book', nominative singular), *knigi* ('of the book', genitive singular), *knige* ('to the book', dative singular), *knigu* ('the book', accusative singular), *knigoj* ('with the book', instrumental singular), [*o*] *knige* ('[about] the book', prepositional singular), *knigi* ('books', nominative plural), *knig* ('of the books', genitive plural), *knigam* ('to the books', dative plural), *knigi* ('the books', accusative plural), *knigami* ('with the books', instrumental plural), and [*o*] *knigax* ('[about] the books', prepositional plural).

Let us compare these forms with their English equivalents, for example, genitive singular *knigi* and the English prepositional phrase *of the book*. Although the English preposition *of* corresponds to the genitive singular suffix *-i* of *knigi*, *of* cannot be considered a suffix because it is separable from *the book*. Owing to separability, the preposition *of*, like other prepositions, assigns syntactic function not only to nouns but to noun phrases, as well: compare *of the book*, *of the large book*, *of a very interesting large book*. By contrast, inseparable case suffixes assign syntactic functions only to the words they are an integral part of. The preposition *of* is a word of type (2), that is, a nonautonomous word.

Under the above definition of the word, autonomous words are verbs, nouns, adjectives, adverbs, pronouns, and interjections; nonautonomous words are prepositions, articles, and conjunctions.

According to the sign functions described in chapter 1, section 1, autonomous words are classified into words having a representational function— verbs, nouns, adjectives, adverbs, pronouns—and words having an expressive or vocative function—interjections (such as *oh, wow,* or *hey*).

Autonomous words having a representational function are classified into words having a symbolic function (verbs, nouns, adjectives, adverbs) and words having a deictic function (pronouns).

The classification of autonomous words according to sign functions can be represented by the following tree diagram:

(1)  *Autonomous word:*

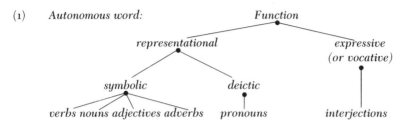

The above definition of the word has the following advantages:

1) It conceives of the autonomous word as an abstract unit with all its syntactic and paradigmatic functions expressed by its different forms. For example, *walk, walks, walking,* and *walked* are not four different words but four different forms of one word, *WALK.*

2) It establishes correlations between autonomous words and syntactic functional units, or syntaxemes. This correlation has significant typological implications; one of the basic questions of linguistic typology must be: How are primary syntactic functions of words transposed into secondary syntactic functions? To answer this question, we must a) describe forms of words having primary syntactic functions, and b) describe formal processes that serve to transpose primary syntactic functions of words into secondary syntactic functions.

3) Since the word is defined independently of the notion of the morpheme, it is conceived as the central unit of morphology. That makes it possible to regard morphemes not as sequentially organized units but as properties of each word as a whole. This insight increases our understanding of the word.

### 3. The Structure of the Word and Morphological Formatives

In post-Bloomfieldian linguistics, only the utterance and the morpheme were taken for granted. The word was no longer considered a theoretical concept. Since the word was denied a theoretical status, the division between morphology and syntax could not have a theoretical status anymore, either. Morphology, which was traditionally defined as the branch of grammar that is concerned with the structure of the word, was to go into limbo.

This neglect of morphology—characteristic not only of post-Bloomfieldian structural linguistics but of generative-transformational grammar, as well—cannot be justified. If we accept the notion of syntactic functional units, we must accept the word as the basic morphological unit that can serve as a syntactic functional unit. Morphemes in themselves cannot serve as syntactic functional units. A morpheme can have syntactic functions solely as a part of a word. Only a word or a combination of words can serve as a syntactic functional unit.

Every word can be analyzed into smaller units, customarily referred to as *morphs*. For example, the English word *renewable* is made up of three morphs: *re*, *new*, and *able*. The morph is a minimal unit that comprises a minimal sign represented by a phoneme sequence or one phoneme and its meaning. A class of morphs with the same meaning but different phonemic shapes is called a *morpheme*, and the morphs representing the same morpheme are called the *allomorphs*, or *variants*, of that morpheme.

The difference between the variants of a morpheme can be conditioned phonetically or phonologically.

An example of phonetically conditioned variants of a morpheme is the alternation resulting from the neutralization of the opposition *voiced consonant: voiceless consonant*. In Russian at the end of a word or before a voiceless consonant, *b, d, g, v, z, ʒ*, etc. are replaced by *p, t, k, f, s, ʃ*, etc.; for instance,

(1)     *sad* [sat] 'garden': *sadu* [sád-u] 'garden (Dat.)'
        *gudok* [gud-ók] 'whistle': *gudka* [gut-ká] 'whistle (Gen.)'

Before voiced consonants, *p, t, k, f, s, ʃ*, etc. are replaced by *b, d, g, v, z, ʒ*, etc.; for instance,

(2)     *molotit'* [məlat'-ít'] 'to thresh': *molot'ba* [məlad'-bá] 'threshing'
        *kosit'* [kas'-ít'] 'to mow': *kos'ba* [kaz'-bá] 'mowing'.

An example of morphologically conditioned variants of a morpheme is the alternations of the back vowels *a, o, u*, and *au* and the respective front vowels *ä, ö, ü*, and *äu* in German; for instance,

(3)     *Bad: Bäder* 'bath: baths'
        *Wort: Wörter* 'word: words'
        *Haus: Häuser* 'house: houses'

It is common to distinguish between *lexical* and *grammatical* morphemes and between *free* and *bound* morphemes.

Lexical morphemes are units such as *big, walk*, and *table*; grammatical morphemes are units such as *of, for*, and *with*, or Russian 'genitive', 'dative', and 'instrumental'. A lexical morpheme indicates a fundamental concept, a concept of subject matter (*lexical meaning*). A grammatical morpheme indicates a subsidiary, usually a more abstract concept (*grammatical meaning*). Grammatical morphemes comprise *closed-set* items. The sets of items are closed in the sense that, as a rule, no new items can be created to extend these sets. Lexical morphemes comprise *open-set* items. The sets of items are open in the sense that new items can be created to extend these sets. A list of grammatical morphemes is limited; it can take a few pages of a book on the grammar of a particular language. By contrast, lexical morphemes of a language belong to a lexicon that may comprise thousands of items and is open to further extension.

There are two types of grammatical morphemes: *functional* morphemes and *derivational* morphemes. Functional morphemes (also called *inflectional* morphemes) indicate different functions of a word. Derivational morphemes are used to derive new words from a given word. For instance, *s, ed, ing* in *works, worked, working* are functional morphemes, because they indicate different functions of the word *(to) work*. But *er* in *worker* is a derivational morpheme, because it is used to derive the word *worker* from the word *work*. The morpheme *s* in *boys* is a functional morpheme, because it indicates a paradigmatic function of the word *boy*, while the morpheme *hood* in *boyhood* is a derivational morpheme, because it is used to derive the word *boyhood* from the word *boy*.

Derivational morphemes modify the meaning of lexical morphemes. A lexical morpheme unmodified by a derivational morpheme is called a *root*. Roots modified by one or more derivational morphemes are called *stems*. For instance, *work* is a root and *worker* is a stem in *workers*.

Grammatical morphemes are also called *affixes*. Derivational affixes serve to derive new words, and inflectional affixes serve to differentiate different forms of the same word.

Affixes are only one type of morphological formative, even though they are the most frequently used.

A *morphological formative* is an elementary linguistic unit that, being a part of a word, is not a root. Given a root $X$ and a meaning $Y$ that is not expressed by a root, the question is: In what ways can $X$ be combined with $Y$ so that the meaning of $X$ and the meaning of $Y$ constitute the meaning of a single word $W$, and how should the forms of $X$ and $W$ differ?

For example, let the meaning of $X$ be *dog* and the meaning of $Y$ be 'plural'. To obtain a word that means *dogs*, we can use two types of morphological processes: 1) adding to $X$ a separate unit $Z$ whose meaning is $Y$; this unit is an affix; or 2) changing $X$ in a certain way; as a result, we obtain a unit that I call a *suprafix*.

We can distinguish five types of suprafixes:

1) A suprafix whose meaning is correlated with a shift of a prosodic feature. For example, when in English nouns are derived from verbs of two syllables, the stress is sometimes shifted from the second to the first syllable. Thus, the nouns *mísprint, récord,* and *ábstract* are derived from the verbs *misprínt, recórd,* and *abstráct* (Quirk, Greenbaum, and Leech, 1972: 1018)

2) A suprafix whose meaning is correlated with subtraction. For example, in French, the masculine adjectives are said to be derived from the feminine adjectives by a process of subtraction. Thus, the masculine *blanc* [blã] is derived from the feminine *blanche* [blã:ʃ] by the subtraction of final ʃ; *long* [lõ] is de-

rived from *longue* [lɔ̃ːg] by the subtraction of g; *bon* [bɔ̃] is derived from *bonne* [bɔn] (with accompanying nasalization of ɔ). One may wonder whether we could treat the relation between French masculine and feminine adjectives as a reverse process: an expansion of the stems of the masculine adjectives by the respective consonants. We could, but in that case we should posit as many rules as there are final consonants in feminine adjectives, while the adopted description requires only one rule: subtract the final consonant. This process can be generalized in one direction, but not in the other (Matthews, 1974:134).

3) A suprafix whose meaning is correlated with an alternation of phonemes. Examples: *take:took, man:men, foot:feet.* In Rumanian: [lup] *lup* 'wolf':[lup'] *lupi* 'wolves', [kopák] *copac* 'tree':[kopač'] *copaci* 'trees'. In English: the verb *hauz* from the noun *haus* (*house*).

4) A suprafix whose meaning is correlated with reduplication. Reduplication may be partial, as in Latin *tango* 'I touch':*tetigi* 'I have touched', *cado* 'I fall':*cecidi* 'I have fallen', or complete, as in Malaysian *orang* 'man':*orang-orang* 'men, people'.

5) A suprafix whose meaning is correlated with transference (meaning converting change of the context of the word). For example, in English, the noun *play* is derived from the verb *play* by combining *play* with the articles: *a play, the play.* By changing the context, we obtain the transitive verb *stop* from the intransitive *stop:the train stopped:John stopped the train.*

A word is a root plus a bundle of formatives—affixes and suprafixes. Affixes are linearly ordered, but suprafixes are not. Therefore, derivational analysis of a word cannot be reduced to an analysis of immediate constituents of its stem. The partial nonlinearity of the formation of a word is a problem for linguists who attempt to study the structure of the word in the framework of generative grammar, which regards the word structure as a system of internally bracketed immediate constituents. Thus, Aronoff writes:

> According to our theory of morphology, every new word, if it is derived by a regular rule, must have a cyclic structure: that is, it must be bracketed internally. However, [proəbišən] has been shown not to have cyclic structure. This seems to be a problem for our theory. According to it, shouldn't all complex words be derived cyclically? (Aronoff, 1976:26)

It is difficult to see how the conflict between the partial nonlinearity of the word structure and the linearity of the linguistic model of generative grammar can be resolved satisfactorily.[2]

## 4. Agglutination and Fusion

Morphological formatives may differ with respect to two types of affixation, called *agglutination* and *fusion*. To see the difference between the two types of affixation, let us compare parallel case forms of the Russian word *konec* 'end' and the Turkish word *son* 'end'.

(1)

|  | Russian | Turkish |
|---|---|---|
| nominative, singular | *konec* | *son* |
| dative, singular | *konc-u* | *son-a* |
| nominative, plural | *konc-y* | *son-lar* |
| dative, plural | *konc-am* | *son-lar-a* |

We can see the following difference between the Russian and Turkish word forms:

1) In Russian the phonemic shape of the root may change: in the nominative singular, the root of the word *konec* has the vowel *e*, which is lost in other forms of this word.

In Turkish the phonemic shape of the root does not change.

2) In Russian, affixes may have more than one meaning; for instance, the inflectional suffix -*am* signifies both the dative and the plural.

In Turkish, there is a one-one correspondence between affixes and their meanings; that is, each affix has only one meaning: -*a* signifies the dative, and -*lar* signifies the plural; therefore, to represent the dative and the plural, these affixes constitute a linear sequence -*lar-a*.

3) In Russian the affixes are nonstandard; that is, to express a grammatical meaning, we cannot use one and the same affix that fits all contexts: in our example the dative singular is expressed by the suffix -*u*, and the dative plural by the suffix -*am*.

In Turkish, affixes are standard; that is, one and the same affix is used for expressing a given grammatical meaning. In our example, the affix -*a* indicates the dative both in the singular and in the plural; the affix -*lar* indicates the plural in all cases.

4) In Russian, affixes are combined with a stem that normally is not used without these affixes: in our example, *konc*- is not used by itself without suffixes.

In Turkish, affixes are combined with a stem that can be used as an autonomous word.

Affixation in Russian involves a blend, a fusion, of affixes and roots, while affixation in Turkish is a mechanical process of combining monosemantic standard affixes with regular stems that can be used as autonomous words.

In view of these differences, the type of affixation represented by Russian examples is called *fusion*, and the type of affixation represented by Turkish examples is called *agglutination*.

Both types of affixation can occur in one language. For example, the formalization of plural nouns in English normally involves agglutination, as in *book-s*, *head-s*, etc. But the plural forms, such as *feet* or *mice*, involve fusion, because these forms simultaneously signify both some lexical concepts and the grammatical meaning 'plural'. Similarly, the past tense forms of English verbs such as *(he) walk-ed, (he) cover-ed,* etc. involve agglutination, while the past tense forms such as *(he) took, (he) came,* etc. involve fusion.

Depending on which type of affixation prevails in a given language, the world's languages are classified into fusional and agglutinating languages. Indo-European languages belong to fusional languages (although they may use agglutination, as in the above English examples). Asiatic, African, Malayo-Polynesian, and Australian languages belong to agglutinating languages.

## 5. Syntagmatic Formatives

The term *grammatical formatives* covers the morphological formatives, which were considered in the foregoing sections, and formatives that can be called syntagmatic formatives.

Morphological formatives are units that indicate grammatical meanings inside of a word. By contrast, syntagmatic formatives are units that express grammatical meanings outside of words. Morphological formatives are internal and syntagmatic formatives are external in regard to words.

Morphological formatives synthesize grammatical meanings and lexical meanings inside of a word, while syntagmatic formatives separate grammatical meanings from lexical meanings—grammatical meanings are indicated by three types of formatives: 1) prepositions and other nonautonomous words, 2) word order, and 3) sentence intonation.

The nonautonomous words and word order can be called *segmental* syntagmatic formatives, and sentence intonation can be called a *suprasegmental* syntagmatic formative.

Depending on whether morphological formatives play the chief part in a language or a language employs nonautonomous words and word order for expressing grammatical meanings, the language is called *synthetic* or *analytic*.

In synthetic languages, isolated words taken out of a sentence retain their grammatical characteristics. For instance, the Latin word *lupum* has the lexical meaning 'wolf', and besides, it has signs that indicate that it is 1) a noun, 2) singular, 3) in the accusative case, 4) a secondary term depending on a transitive verb, etc. The word in synthetic languages is independent of environment; it has a full value both lexically and grammatically and requires a morphological analysis in the first place, and its syntactic properties are direct consequences of its morphological structure.

The word in analytic languages expresses solely a lexical meaning; it acquires grammatical characteristics only as a part of a sentence. In English, *play* signifies solely a certain general notion. Only in syntactic contexts can we distinguish different words: *the play was good, children play,* etc. But the Russian words *igra* 'the play', *igrat'* 'to play', etc. are clear outside of their contexts, and therefore they are incommensurate with the English *play,* although they have the same lexical meaning.

Analytic languages use word order as a means for expressing grammatical meanings, while in synthetic languages word order normally is used not for expressing grammatical meanings but mainly for stylistic purposes, as a means for expressing different shades of the same grammatical meaning. Compare the English sentence

(1)     *John frightened Mary.*

with the Russian synonymous sentence

(2)     *Ivan ispugal Mariju.*

In (1) the agent is expressed by the primary term *John*, which precedes the verb *frightened*, and the patient is expressed by the secondary term *Mary*. If we exchange the positions of both terms, we will get

(3)     *Mary frightened John.*

The meaning of (3) is opposite to the meaning of (1), because of the change of the word order.

By contrast, in Russian the exchange of the positions of the primary and secondary terms in (2) does not change its meaning:

(4)     *Mariju ispugal Ivan.*

The difference between (2) and (4) is stylistic; in (4) the emphasis is on *Mariju*.

Typical synthetic languages are Greek, Latin, Old Slavonic, Russian, German, and some others. Typical analytic languages are English, French, Danish, Modern Greek, Bulgarian, and others.

Some languages synthesize words that are equivalent to parts of sentences, or even to whole sentences, in regular analytic languages. For example, in Chukchee the following words occur (Uspenskij, 1965:99):

(5)     a.  *ny-lk'yt-k'inet*
            walk
        b.  *ny- jyk' -y-lk'yt-k'inet*
            quickly - walk
        c.  *ny-gytg-y- jyk' -y-lk'yt-k'inet*
            lake - quickly - walk

In these words, *ny-* . . . *-k'inet* is a confix that signifies third person plural, present tense.

(5a), (5b), and (5c) are equivalent to the sentences *They walk, They walk quickly*, and *They walk quickly to the lake*.

Languages of the Chukchee type are called *polysynthetic* languages. Polysynthetic languages are found among the Indian languages of North America and the Paleosiberian languages of Russia (Chukchee is one of them).

## 6. Concord and Government

In some languages the connection between words constituting a syntagm is characterized by an obligatory repetition of some grammatical meanings. Compare the Russian sentence

(1)     *Malen'kie deti pridut.*

with its English translation

(2)     *The small children will come.*

In the Russian sentence, plural is expressed three times: in the noun *det-i,* in the adjective *malen'k-ie,* and in the verb *prid-ut,* while in the English translation, plural is expressed only once, in *childr-en.*

We say that in the Russian example the adjective *malen'k-ie* and the verb *prid-ut* are in *concord,* or *agree,* with respect to number with the noun *det-i.*

The connection between words characterized by an obligatory repetition of some grammatical meanings is called *concord,* or *agreement.*

Concord is characteristic of synthetic languages; analytic languages have relatively little concord. This difference can be explained as follows: since synthetic languages have a free word order, they need a formal means to indicate connections between words separated by other words, and concord serves this purpose; it is a formal means indicating connections between words. Concord is much less important for analytic languages, where words that are grammatically connected normally are not separated from one another, and the connections between words are indicated by the fact that they are adjacent.

Here are some examples of concord in English:

(3)     a. *this (that) man : these (those) men*
      b. *he walks : I (you, we, they) walk*
      c. *he has walked : I (you, we, they) have walked*
      d. *he is walking : you (we, they) are walking : I am walking*
      e. *he (I) was walking : you (we, they) were walking*

In (3a) the demonstrative pronouns agree with the nouns with respect to number.

In (3b) and (3c), the verb is third person singular; and if the primary term is not third person singular, the verb has an unmarked form.

In (3d), besides third person singular concord, there is also first person singular concord (*I am walking*).

In (3e) the verb is singular when the primary term is singular and plural when the primary term is plural. There is no concord with respect to person here, because first person singular and third person singular fall together.

Another type of formal connection between words is a phenomenon called *government*.

Government is a connection between two words that belong to two different grammatical classes, with the grammatical class of one word determining the grammatical class of another word.

Examples of government: In many languages the verb governs a noun in a particular case: in the Russian sentences

(4)  a. *Ja beru karandaš.*
       'I take a pencil'.
     b. *Ja pišu karandašom.*
       'I write with a pencil'.

the opposition *karandaš* versus *karandašom*—accusative versus instrumental—is governed by the opposition of the verbs *beru* versus *pišu*.

In Russian, Latin, German, etc., not only verbs but prepositions can govern a noun. Compare Latin *ad urbem* 'to the city' (*ad* governs the accusative: *urbem*) versus *ab urbe* 'from the city' (*ab* takes the ablative: *urbe*).

In current linguistic literature, concord and government are treated as phenomena that correspond to syntactic dependencies between functional units. But as a matter of fact, concord and government are morphologically conditioned connections between words that do not necessarily reflect dependencies between syntactic functional units.

Morphologically conditioned dependencies between words may conflict with syntactic dependencies between functional units. For example, in Latin and Russian, the predicate is characterized by morphological markers of agreement with the primary term. So, from a morphological point of view, the predicate depends on the primary term, but from a syntactic point of view, the reverse is true: the predicate is the head, and the primary term is its dependent. In Abkhaz, a Caucasian language, the verb may agree not only with the primary term but also with the secondary and tertiary terms. So, from a morphological point of view, the Abkhazian verb may depend simultaneously on three nouns. But from a syntactic point of view, it is not the verb that depends on the nouns but the nouns that depend on the verb.

In the Turkish syntagm

(5)  *talebelerin odalarī*
     'the rooms of the students'

*odalarī* 'rooms' is the head, and *talebelerin* 'of the students' is its dependent. But from the standpoint of Turkish morphology, both the head and the modifier depend on each other, since both the head and the dependent have morphological markers of dependency: the dependent is marked by the genitive suffix *-in,* and the head is marked by the third person possessive suffix *-ī.*

Given a syntagm *A + B* where *A* is the head and *B* is its dependent, there are the following possibilities of morphological marking: 1) only the head is morphologically marked; 2) only the dependent is morphologically marked; 3) both the head and its dependent are morphologically marked; 4) neither the head nor its dependent is morphologically marked. All of these possibilities are realized in the world's languages.

Syntactic connections between functional units, on the one hand, and concord and government, on the other hand, are completely independent of each other.

We cannot explain either syntactic connections between functional units by facts of concord and government, or concord and government by syntactic connections between functional units.

Confounding the level of syntactic connections between functional units and the level of morphologically conditioned connections between words can have grave consequences. Here are two examples:

Some linguists question the validity of the word as a theoretical notion, because they explain syntagmatic connections between words in terms of connections between functional units. Thus, J. Kuryłowicz considers prepositional phrases such as French *sur la table* or English *on the table* to be one word rather than a group of words. He writes:

> A prepositional phrase such as, for example, *sur la table*, is a word rather than a group of words. If it were a group, the member which governs the group could be put to the same syntactic use as the group itself. But *sur* cannot be put to this use. Therefore the preposition is not a word, but rather a morpheme (and sometimes a sub-morpheme which constitutes a unit with a case marker). (Kuryłowicz, 1973: 47)

Kuryłowicz confounds the functional unit with the word—a morphological unit. True, the English prepositional phrase *of the wolf* has the same syntactic function as its Latin synonym *lupi,* but from a morphological point of view, *lupi* is one word and *of the wolf* consists of three words. By lumping syntactic functional units and words together, Kuryłowicz disregards the fundamental contrast between analytic languages, such as English, and synthetic languages, such as Latin or Russian.

A. Martinet draws another conclusion from the functional equivalence of prepositional phrases, such as English *of the wolf,* and words such as Latin *lupi.* He rejects the word as a theoretical notion and claims that the real meaningful units of language are so-called *monemes.* (The moneme is nothing but a refined notion of the morpheme. Martinet seems to have chosen the term *moneme* because in the French linguistic tradition the term *morpheme* means what is called *grammatical morpheme* in linguistic science of other countries, while

French linguists use the term *semanteme* for what is called *lexical morpheme* in other countries.) Martinet writes:

> Since we are not inclined to salvage the concept of word, we must operate with 'minimal significant units' and therefore my definition of morphology will have to be couched in terms involving this concept. Now what sort of minimal significant units should we retain? Both in Europe and America, the minimal significant unit has been called a morpheme. For a number of reasons, I was led to choose for it another designation, namely 'moneme.' (Martinet, 1975 : 154)

By eliminating the notion of word and introducing the notion of moneme as the basic significant unit of language, Martinet blends the main part of morphology with syntax and restricts morphology to the study of formal variants of morphemes.

## 7. Linguistic Categories

The term *category* generally denotes a class of objects that share a common feature. The term *linguistic category* can be defined as a class of expressions that share a common meaning or function denoted by common morphological or syntagmatic formatives.[3] Thus, the words *book-s, citi-es, hous-es, glass-es,* etc. belong in the category of the plural number; this category is denoted by a common morphological formative, a suffix having variants: *s, z, ɪz*. The words (*he*) *walk-ed, danc-ed, explain-ed, extend-ed,* etc. belong in the category of the past tense; this category is denoted by a common morphological formative, a suffix having variants: *t, d, ɪd*.

Forms such as *feet, lice,* etc., on the one hand, and (*he*) *wrote, bought, went,* etc., on the other hand, are also members of the category of the plural or the past respectively, since the relation between *foot* and *feet,* etc. is the same as that between *book* and *books,* and the relation between *write* and *wrote,* etc. is the same as that between *walk* and *walked.* What is crucial is proportions, such as *foot:feet=book:books* and *write:wrote=walk:walked.* It follows that the plural category is denoted in English by two morphological formatives: a plural suffix having variants *s, z, ɪz,* and apophonies.

The categories of primary and secondary terms are denoted in English by a syntagmatic formative of word order—primary terms precede the verbs, and secondary terms follow the verbs. In Russian and Latin, categories of primary and secondary terms are denoted by morphological formatives—primary terms are denoted by a set of nominative case markers, and secondary terms are denoted by a set of accusative case markers.

The category of modifiers of a term is denoted in English by two syntagmatic formatives: the preposition *of* and word order. Compare

(1)  a. *the wall of stone*
     b. *the stone wall*

Both *of stone* in (1a) and *stone* in (1b) belong in the category of modifiers of terms.

A word can be a member of different categories. Thus, in English, the word *writes* is a member of the category of the present tense, the category of the third person, and the category of the singular number.

Phonological units, such as phonemes or syllables, also constitute categories. There are categories of vowels, categories of consonants, categories of voiced and voiceless consonants, etc.

In accordance with the distinction of derivational and inflectional morphemes, we must distinguish derivational and inflectional grammatical categories. Since the range of occurrence of inflectional categories is wider than that of derivational categories, the latter are subordinated to the former.

The essential changes of the grammatical system of a language result from the shifts between related inflectional and derivational categories. The change of an inflectional category into a derivative category is called *lexicalization*. The opposite change of a derivational category into an inflectional category is called *grammaticalization*.

## 8. The Category of Case

By *case* I understand systematic differences in the forms of nouns, adjectives, and participles corresponding to the differences between their roles as functional units in a sentence.

There are three basic types of case systems: a) the *active* system, b) the *ergative* system, and c) the *accusative* system.

### a) The Active System

The active system is based on case markings for the contrasting syntactic functions *agent : nonagent*.

Agent terms are expressed in the *active* case. Nonagent terms are expressed in the *inactive* case.

One finds the following distinction of the active and inactive case:

(1)     *Active case*                           *Inactive case*
        *Mary*$_{agent}$ *walked.*                   *Mary*$_{nonagent}$ *is beautiful.*
        *Mary*$_{agent}$ *deceived Bill*$_{nonagent}$.   *Mary*$_{agent}$ *deceived Bill*$_{nonagent}$.

In the active system, verbs are divided into *active* verbs and *stative* verbs rather than into transitive and intransitive verbs, as in the ergative and the accusative systems.

In Dakota, the prefix *wa* marks the first person singular agent, while *mā* marks the first person singular nonagent, as in

(2)  *wa-kaśka*  'I bind him'
    *mā-waste*  'I am good'
    *mā-kaśka*  'he binds me'

## b) The Ergative System

In the ergative system, the choice of cases is determined by the contrast between *transitive* and *intransitive* verbs.

The primary terms of transitive and intransitive verbs are denoted by the *accusative* case, and the secondary term of the transitive verb is denoted by the *ergative* case.

## c) The Accusative System

As in the ergative system, the choice of cases in the accusative system is determined by the contrast between *transitive* and *intransitive* verbs.

The primary terms of transitive and intransitive verbs are denoted by the *nominative* case, and the secondary term of the transitive verb is denoted by the *accusative* case.

The ergative and accusative systems relate to each other as mirror images. If we compare transitive sentences in both systems, we find that the accusative corresponds to the absolutive and the nominative corresponds to the ergative.

I will focus on the analysis of case in the accusative system.

The cases of the accusative system are divided into two classes: 1) *grammatical* cases and 2) *concrete* cases. Grammatical cases are the nominative, the accusative, and the genitive. There are four basic concrete cases: the instrumental, the allative, the ablative, and the locative. Both grammatical and concrete cases have primary and secondary functions.

The primary function of the nominative is to denote the primary term in a sentence; the primary function of the accusative is to denote the secondary term in a transitive sentence. The primary function of the genitive is to serve as an instrument of the transposition of a sentence into a nominal group, for example, in Russian

(3)  *Ivan priexal* 'John arrived' → *priezd Ivana*(Gen.) 'John's arrival'
    *Ivana ubili* 'They killed John' → *ubijstvo Ivana*(Gen.) 'the murder of John'

The primary functions of concrete cases are as follows: the locative means 'lack of movement', the ablative means 'movement from', the allative means 'movement to', and the instrumental means 'movement across'.

The important thing is a distinction of central and marginal positions in the case system. The grammatical cases occupy central positions, while the concrete cases occupy marginal positions. The hierarchy of positions can be represented by the following scheme:

(4)     *Verb > Grammatical Case > Concrete Case > Adverb*

This hierarchy is purely relational and is independent of the linear order of words. Concrete cases are intermediary categories between grammatical cases and adverbs.

To understand the meaning of the positional hierarchy of cases, consider the following sentence in Russian:

(5)     *On čitaet knigu v sadu.*
        'He is reading the book in the garden'.

The accusative in *knigu* is a mere exponent of a syntactic dependency of the noun, while the prepositional group *v sadu* in the locative has a concrete meaning. The expressions *knigu* and *v sadu* cannot be substituted one for another. If we omit *knigu* in the above sentence, we will get a structure with one free position:

(6)     *On čitaet _____ v sadu.*

The secondary function of grammatical cases is to serve as concrete cases. By contrast, the secondary function of concrete cases is to serve as grammatical cases. Here are some examples from Russian:

(7)     *On pisal pis'mo čas.*
        'He was writing the letter for an hour'.

In this sentence there are two accusatives, *pis'mo* and *čas*. The second accusative has the secondary function of a concrete case and therefore occupies a marginal position.

(8)     *On upravljaet zavodom.*
        'He manages the factory'.

The instrumental *zavodom* has a secondary function here. It functions as a grammatical case equivalent to an accusative.

An understanding of the interplay of the primary and secondary functions of the grammatical and concrete cases is of paramount importance for explaining many synchronic and diachronic syntactic phenomena, in particular the phenomena relating to passivization.

The agentive term in the instrumental or other concrete cases in passive constructions can be explained as a secondary term resulting from the use of the instrumental or other concrete cases in their secondary function of a grammatical case equivalent to the accusative.

# V.

# *Linguistic Methodology*

## 1. Empirical and Conceptual Problems in Linguistics

Linguistics, like any science, is essentially a problem-solving activity. The goal of linguistic methodology is to classify and evaluate linguistic problems and methods of their solution.

The first step in classifying linguistic problems is to distinguish between empirical and conceptual linguistic problems. *Empirical* linguistic problems are first-order questions about the substantive entities of language. *Conceptual* linguistic problems are higher-order questions about the well-foundedness of the conceptual structures that have been devised to answer the first-order questions. To illustrate the difference between the two types of problems, I will consider an example from phonology.

A phonological description of a language must start with setting up a list of its phonemes. Setting up a list of phonemes of a given language is an empirical problem of phonology. Now, although linguists describing a given language may have different notions of the phoneme and belong to different schools of linguistic thought, they come to results that are, for practical purposes, the same: lists of phonemes arrived at by linguists of different linguistic schools are the same, or, at any rate, they do not differ very much.

Why do linguists who espouse very different, even opposing phonological theories come to the same results when they try to determine the number of phonemes in a given language?

The answer is this: because all phonological theories have the same or nearly the same predictive power.

The radical differences between different theories of the phoneme result not from the above empirical problem but from problems of an essentially different type: problems that are generated by conceptual difficulties in phonology.

The basic fact about language sounds is that they are used to distinguish different words; that is, they are diacritics. Language sounds, as diacritics, are members of distinctive oppositions. An analysis of the semantic properties of distinctive oppositions results in the discovery of the Law of Phonemic Identity, which was stated in chapter 2, section 1. The following consequence can be deduced from this law:

No matter how sounds change in different positions in the speech flow, the phonological oppositions whose members they are remain intact as long as the sounds do not merge.

We can imagine a theoretical situation where vowels in a position $X$ become more open by one degree than they are in a position $Y$. This theoretical situation obtained deductively can be represented by the following diagram:

(1)     *Position X*                *Position Y*
              A          $\longleftrightarrow$          B
              B          $\longleftrightarrow$          C
              C          $\longleftrightarrow$          D
              D          $\longleftrightarrow$          E

As a result of this imaginary experiment, we discover that the same vowels, say $C$ in position $X$ and $C$ in position $Y$, must be considered different phonemes; and, conversely, completely different vowels, such as $A$ and $B$, must be considered variants of the same phoneme. This discovery generates a problem for available phonological theories, which hesitate to separate completely the functional aspect of sounds from their physical aspect. The phonological theories that claim that the physical properties of speech sounds are somehow relevant for defining their functional identity have to answer this question: If the physical properties of sounds are relevant for determining their functional identity, why must the same sounds be considered different phonemes, and, conversely, why must completely different sounds be considered the same phonemes?

This problem, which arose as a result of a deduction, can be called a conceptual problem.

In chapter 2 this conceptual problem was resolved as follows: an assumption was made that language sounds have a dual nature—physical and functional—and that the identity of concrete phonemes is logically independent of their physical properties. On the basis of this assumption, a dual classification was proposed: we must construct two types of classes, 1) classes of physically equivalent sounds and 2) classes of functionally equivalent sounds as concrete phonemes.

The solution to the above conceptual problem is a significant step towards a deeper understanding of the phonological phenomena; it leads to a radically new phonological theory, which views language sounds from the angle of their dual nature. But the new phonological theory does not differ very much in its predictive power even from the most primitive phonological theories, which view the phoneme as a class of physically related sounds.

Why is that so?

Because the function, the semiotic essence, of language sounds is veiled by their nearly permanent but extraneous properties. A nearly permanent property of functionally equivalent sounds is their physical equivalence. The coincidence of the functional and physical equivalences of sounds leads to the notion of the phoneme as a class of physically related sounds. But linguists who espouse this notion of the phoneme do not see that the coincidence of the physical and functional equivalences is a phenomenon extraneous to the semiotic essence of sounds; they simply do not suspect the existence of the above conceptual problem. True, the above imaginary theoretical situation obtained by way of deduction predicts the possibility of real situations in real languages when the same sounds must be interpreted as different phonemes, and different sounds must be interpreted as variants of the same phoneme. This possibility is sometimes realized in concrete languages and is known in current phonological literature under the name of phonemic overlapping; but the linguists who think of the phoneme as a class of physically related sounds discard phonemic overlapping as a marginal phenomenon, because they do not see any serious problem in it.

To illustrate how extraneous but permanent, or quasi-permanent, features of an object can be confounded with its essential features, I will take an example from zoology. For a long time, a common view in zoology has been that mammae are an essential property of any mammal. This view was based not on theoretical considerations but on the empirical fact that all known mammals have mammae. This view, well supported by empirical observation, broke down when platypuses—small egg-laying animals—were discovered in Australia. Platypuses are mammals that have no mammae. It became clear that, although almost all mammals have them, mammae are an accidental rather than an essential property of mammals.

The history of science abounds with striking examples of when absolutely permanent properties of an object that cannot be separated from it by an experiment are extraneous to its essence and veil its essence from the eye of the mind.

The foregoing discussion leads to the following conclusions: 1) there are two types of linguistic problems: empirical linguistic problems and conceptual linguistic problems; 2) solving conceptual linguistic problems may lead to radically new, very abstract linguistic theories; and 3) the new linguistic theories do not necessarily have a stronger predictive power than the old theories; the predictive power of new theories may be the same or nearly the same.

In comparing and evaluating different linguistic theories, current linguistic literature attaches a lot of importance to a comparison of their predictive powers. It seems that the significance of the predictive power of a linguistic theory is overstated. True, the evaluation of the predictive power of a new linguistic theory is important. Thus, in our example the two-level theory of the phoneme has a stronger predictive power than the theory of the phoneme as a class of physically related sounds: the two-level theory does predict the phenomenon of phonemic overlapping, while the theory of the phoneme as a class of physically related sounds does not. Still, what is crucial in evaluating the two theories is not their predictive power but their capacity for discovering and solving the above conceptual problem generated by a deduction of consequences from the facts concerning the basic semiotic properties of language sounds.

The history of science shows that major debates about theories in different scientific domains were focused not on discussing the predictive power of theories, not on their capacity for solving empirical problems, but on conceptual matters, on the capacity of theories to solve conceptual problems that had nothing to do with the predictive power of theories. To illustrate that, I will quote an illuminating passage from a recent book on the philosophy of science:

> Even the briefest glance at the history of science makes it clear that the key debates between scientists have centered as much on nonempirical issues as on empirical ones. When, for instance, the epicyclic astronomy of Ptolemy was criticized (as it often was in antiquity, the Middle Ages and the Renaissance), the core criticisms did *not* deal with its adequacy to solve the chief empirical problems of observational astronomy. It was readily granted by most of Ptolemy's critics that his system was perfectly adequate for "saving the phenomena." Rather, the bulk of the criticism was directed against the conceptual credentials of the mechanisms Ptolemy utilized (including equants and eccentrics, as well as epicycles) for solving the empirical problems of astronomy. Similarly, the later critics of Copernican astronomy did not generally claim it was empirically inadequate at predicting the motions of celestial bodies; indeed, it could solve some empirical problems (such as motions of comets) far better than the available alternatives. What chiefly troubled Copernicus' critics were doubts about how heliocentric astronomy could be integrated within a broader framework of assumptions about the natural world—a framework which had been systematically and progressively articulated since antiquity. When, a century after Copernicus, Newton announced his "system of the world," it encountered almost universal applause for its capacity to solve many crucial empirical problems. What troubled many of Newton's contemporaries (including Locke, Berkeley, Huygens, and Leibniz) were several conceptual ambiguities and confusions about its foundational assumptions. What was absolute space and why was it needed to do physics? How could bodies conceivably act on one another at-a-distance? What was the source of the new energy which, on Newton's theory, had to be continuously super-added to the world order? How, Leibniz would ask, could Newton's theory be reconciled with an intelligent deity who designed the world? In none of these cases was a critic pointing to an unsolved or anomalous empirical problem. They were, rather, raising acute difficulties of a *nonempirical kind.* Nor is it merely "early" science which exhibits this phenomenon.
>
> If we look at the reception of Darwin's evolutionary biology, Freud's psychoanalytic theories, Skinner's behaviorism, or modern quantum mechanics, the same pattern repeats itself. Alongside of the rehearsal of empirical anomalies and solved empirical problems, both critics and proponents of a theory often invoke criteria of theoretical appraisal which have nothing whatever to do with a theory's capacity to solve the empirical problems of the relevant scientific domain. (Laudan, 1977: 46–47)

Now the fact that major debates about theories have so far focused not on discussing the predictive power of theories but on conceptual matters that have nothing to do with their predictive power can be viewed as a methodological fault, as a sign of methodological immaturity. Such is the view of Carnap, Popper, Kuhn, and other proponents of empiricist philosophies of science who imagine that theory choice in science should be governed exclusively by empirical considerations (Carnap, 1962; Popper, 1959; Kuhn, 1962).

Philosophers of science of the younger generation sharply criticize this view. Thus, Laudan writes that philosophers of science holding this view "simply fail to come to terms with the role of conceptual problems in science, and accordingly find themselves too impoverished to explain or reconstruct much of the actual course of science." He writes further:

> Such empiricist theories of science exhibit particularly awkward limitations in explaining those historical situations in which the empirical problem-solving abilities of competing theories have been virtually *equivalent*. Cases of this kind are far more common in science than people generally realize. The debates between Copernican and Ptolemian astronomers (1540–1600), between Newtonians and Cartesians (1720–1750), between wave and particle optics (1810–1850), between atomists and anti-atomists (1815 to about 1880) are all examples of important scientific controversies where the empirical support for rival theories was essentially the same. Positivistically inspired accounts of these historical encounters have shed very little light on these important cases: this is scarcely surprising since the positivist holds empirical support to be the only legitimate arbiter of theoretical belief. These controversies must, by the strict empiricist, be viewed as mere *querelles de mots*, hollow and irrational debates about issues which experience cannot settle.
>
> A broader view concerning the nature of problem solving—one which recognizes the existence of conceptual problems—puts us in a position to understand and to describe the kind of intellectual interaction that can take place between defenders of theories which are equally supported by the data. Because the assessment of theories is a multi-factorial affair, parity with respect to one factor in no way precludes a rational choice based on disparities at other levels. (Laudan, 1977: 47–48)

There is a widely held fallacy that the ability to predict is a necessary consequence of having a good explanation. But the well-known fact that both Ptolemian and Copernican astronomies were able to predict correctly the same facts and similar examples from other sciences shows that we can make correct predictions without being able to understand.

Why can we make correct predictions without being able to understand? A reasonable answer to this question is given by Abraham Kaplan in his book *The Conduct of Inquiry* (1964). He writes:

> An explanation rests on a nomological or theoretical generalization, or on an intelligible pattern, but a prediction need not have such a basis. I am not speaking

of guesses, even of those that rest on knowledge of which the guesser is unaware. A prediction, as distinct from a guess, is reasoned—a basis is put for-
ward, some premise from which what is predicted is being inferred. The point is
that the basis may be a merely empirical generalization. We can give a reason for
making some specific prediction rather than another, but we may be able to give
no reason other than past successes for expecting the prediction to come true.
Analyses of voting behavior, for example, may have identified certain counties or
states as barometers of the political weather, thereby allowing the computer to
make early predictions; but making predictions from them is very different from
having an explanation of the vote.

In short, explanations provide understandings, but we can predict without
being able to understand, and we can understand without necessarily being able
to predict. (Kaplan, 1964: 350)

Linguistics has been dominated for a long time by empiricist views of science:
most linguists consciously or unconsciously follow the empiricist pattern of research, which ignores true conceptual problems of linguistics. My analysis of
linguistic concepts throws new light on the above controversy between proponents and opponents of empiricist philosophies of science. The time has come
to adopt a broader, a more realistic pattern of linguistic research than that
which dominates the contemporary linguistic scene.

There are different kinds of conceptual problems. The most important is
when a theory $T_1$ conflicts with another theory or doctrine $T_2$. In our example,
the statement that the same sounds can belong to different phonemes, and, conversely, that different sounds can be variants of the same phoneme, was in conflict with the well-founded assumption of phonetics that the same sounds belong to the same class of sounds and different sounds belong to different classes
of sounds. That generated tension, a conflict between phonology and phonetics. To resolve this conceptual problem, it was necessary to modify phonological theory by introducing into it a principle of the dual nature of sounds,
which meant dual classification of sounds into classes of functionally equivalent
sounds and classes of physically equivalent sounds.

Another good example of conceptual problems between two theories is the
conceptual problems generated by a conflict of Montague grammar with the
well-founded assumption of linguistics about the nature of language. Examples
of this conflict were given above (chap. 3, sec. 14). It affects the very founda-
tion, the very heart, of Montague grammar. This conflict is so serious that it
cannot be resolved by a modification of Montague grammar; Montague grammar must be rejected, not modified.

Another type of conceptual problem is generated by ambiguity or unclarity
of scientific concepts. The increase of the conceptual clarity of a linguistic theory through a careful analysis of the meanings of its concepts is an important
condition of the progress in linguistics. The notions of subject, direct object,
and indirect object in relational linguistics are an example of the conceptual

problems generated by conceptual ambiguity. The trouble with these concepts as they are used by relational grammar is not that they are not defined—a formal definition of scientific concepts is not required; what is important is that they must be clearly matched with the objects of the domain of research—the trouble is that these concepts are ambiguous. As was shown above, the notion of subject in relational grammar confounds the syntactic concept of the pivot of a sentence with the semantic concept of the agent.

Conceptual problems also arise from circularity. A striking example of circularity in linguistics is provided by Chomsky's explanation of deep structure. Chomsky explains deep structure through the notion of competence. But because we know nothing about competence, the notion of competence is supported only by the notion of deep structure. Therefore, an explanation of deep structure in terms of competence is entirely circular.

Every ad hoc hypothesis creates circularity in explanation; that is why ad hoc hypotheses are unacceptable. For example, the Unaccusative Hypothesis of relational grammar discussed above (chap. 3, sec. 12.2) is unacceptable because it creates circularity; this hypothesis does not give rise to observable consequences relating to facts lying outside the facts of impersonal passives, for explanation of which it was devised. It turns out that the necessary condition for the facts of impersonal passives is the Unaccusative Hypothesis, the necessary condition for which is the facts of impersonal passives being explained.

Still another example of circularity is provided by the concept of 'psychological reality' used by Chomsky. He needs this concept to give independent evidence for the theoretical constructs of generative-transformational grammar. He writes:

> We impute existence to certain mental representations and to the mental computations that apply in a specific way to these mental representations. . . . We attribute psychological reality to the postulated representations and mental computations. In short, we propose (tentatively, hesitantly, etc.) that our theory is true. (Chomsky, 1978: 206)

Since we know no more about psychological reality than we know about linguistic evidence for it, the notion of psychological reality cannot be used to give independent psychological evidence for validity of linguistic constructs. As a matter of fact, Chomsky uses the term *psychological reality* as a label for the notion 'truth in the linguistic domain'. Therefore, the notion of psychological reality is vacuous.[1]

## 2. The Analytical-Deductive Method and Imaginary Experiments

The goals of linguistic theory formulated in chapter 1, section 2 come down to one thing: a quest for the essence of language. What are the methods of achieving the goals of linguistic theory? What are the methods of unveiling the essence of language?

Linguistics has developed a variety of more or less sophisticated methods of research in different domains of the study of human language. A discussion of these methods is outside the scope of this book; it is appropriate in treating special branches of linguistics. Here I will consider the basic method that must be at the heart of basic theoretical research in linguistics—this method I call the *analytical-deductive method*.

The analytical-deductive method can be characterized as a principle consisting of four steps:

1) We analyze human language and formulate principles that define its semiotic properties. These principles are universal, because they apply to any human language. They can be called initial principles or axioms of linguistic theory.

2) We deduce necessary consequences from the axioms of linguistic theory. These consequences can be called linguistic laws.

3) We test linguistic laws by using them for the explanation and prediction of the facts of concrete languages.

4) Testing linguistic laws may generate empirical or conceptual problems. The resolution of these problems may lead to modification of the theory. The modifications may affect any part of the linguistic theory: its concepts, laws, and axioms.

The four steps of the analytical-deductive method can be illustrated by the above example concerning the birth of the two-level theory of phonology.

Our first step was to analyze language sounds and define their semiotic property of being members of distinctive oppositions. The statement that language sounds are members of distinctive oppositions is an axiom of phonology that defines the basic semiotic property of sounds. This axiom I call the *diacritic principle*.

Our second step was to deduce the Law of Semiotic Variability of Sounds from the Diacritic Principle.

Our third step was to test the Law of Semiotic Variability of Sounds. By deducing necessary consequences from this law, we set up an imaginary experiment that created a hypothetical situation in which the same sounds must be interpreted as belonging to different phonemes, and, conversely, different sounds must be interpreted as variants of the same phoneme.

Our fourth step was to consider the conceptual problem that was generated by our imaginary experiment. To solve this problem, the notion of equivalence of sounds was split into two contrasting notions: functional equivalence and physical equivalence. An extension of this contrast to all objects of phonology— distinctive features, prosodical units, etc.—led to the two-level theory of phonology.

The above account of the use of the analytical-deductive method calls for a definition of the *imaginary experiment*.

DEFINITION:

The *imaginary experiment* is a deductive inference from a set of principles or laws of theoretically possible situations that lay bare the covert essential properties of an object.

By 'theoretically possible situation' I mean a situation that may not be actually realizable but is a necessary consequence of some set of principles and laws.

Instead of the term *imaginary experiment*, such terms as *thought experiment* and *mental experiment* are also used. In accordance with the above distinction, the imaginary experiment must be understood as a special type of deductive reasoning that makes it possible to discover essential features of an object.

### 3. The Special Role of Linguistic Anomalies

In making cross-linguistic generalizations, a linguist may run into facts that do not fit into the conceptual framework in terms of which cross-linguistic generalizations are stated. These facts do not make sense; they are considered *anomalous*. Anomalous facts are important for the linguist, because they generate empirical problems. He must be on the lookout for such facts, because they make it necessary for him to trim and shape his ideas further, so that within the reshaped conceptual framework, the anomalous facts can become intelligible and cease to be anomalous. So long as everything proceeds according to his prior expectations, the linguist has no opportunity to improve on his linguistic theory. Improvements on a linguistic theory result from searching for the explanations of anomalous facts.

The statement about the importance of anomalous facts for improvement on linguistic theories needs to be qualified. Not all anomalies are equally important for a linguistic theory. For instance, irregular plurals in English, such as *mice* from *mouse*, are anomalous, but they are not crucial for a theory of English grammar: these facts belong in the lexicon. Only if *significant* anomaly can be demonstrated will there be a genuine theoretical issue to face.

A fact that is a significant anomaly for a given linguistic theory I call a *linguistic phenomenon*.

It follows from the definition of the linguistic phenomenon that this concept is relative to a given theory. A fact that is anomalous from the standpoint of one theory may be regular from the standpoint of another theory.

To explain a linguistic phenomenon is to subsume it under a conceptual framework from whose point of view it ceases to be anomalous and is considered regular.

In testing a linguistic theory, it is important to find out whether it can make sense of linguistic phenomena that there is no way of accounting for using the currently accepted theories, and, in addition, of all those phenomena that contravene these theories.

A rich source of significant anomalies for linguistic theories that use the concepts of subject and object, such as relational grammar or generative-transformational grammar, is ergative languages.

No matter how well these theories fit the accusative languages, they run into difficulties when applied to the ergative languages.

There are two ways of solving these difficulties: either to demonstrate that ergative languages have the same syntactic structure as accusative languages, or, if that cannot be done and rather the opposite can be demonstrated, to abandon the notions of subject and object as universal concepts and develop a new conceptual framework.

In chapter 3 it was demonstrated that *ergative vs. accusative* is a fundamental typological syntactic dichotomy. This view opposes theories that claim that from a syntactic standpoint ergative languages are organized in the same way as accusative languages. The nature and dimensions of this dichotomy can be explained and understood properly only by relating the ergative system and the accusative system to a more abstract underlying system, which is presented in applicative grammar.

Applicative grammar claims that *ergative* and *accusative* cannot be defined in terms of *subject* and *object* but rather must be distinct primitive syntactic functions, and therefore *subject* and *object* cannot be considered valid universal concepts. Both series of concepts must be related to a more abstract series of concepts defined in terms of the relation *operator : operand*.

The crucial test in favor of applicative grammar is presented by the Keenan-Comrie Accessibility Hierarchy. As was shown in chapter 3, section 10.2, this hypothesis formulated in terms of subject and object breaks down with respect to the facts of ergative languages. It turns out that this hypothesis is too narrow; it is valid only for accusative languages. In order to make it universal, we must generalize it in terms of the 'primary term', 'secondary term', and 'tertiary term' of applicative grammar and view it as an instance of a more general principle—the Applicative Hierarchy. Facts that are anomalous from the standpoint of the Keenan-Comrie Accessibility Hierarchy have become regular from the standpoint of applicative grammar.

## 4. The Complementarity Principle and the Centaur Concepts

Language is an instrument of communication and an instrument of cognition. We can apply to language what Bohr has said about the interaction between the objects under investigation and the measuring instruments necessary for the definition of the experimental arrangements (Bohr, 1958). If language is viewed as an instrument, then, speaking of its impact upon the formation of our concepts, we can make an analogy with the impact of a measuring instrument on the results of measurements in the microworld.

Science is a symbolic representation of experience. The improvements in experimental technique bring into the scope of science new aspects of nature that come into obvious conflict with the conventional means of expression. Kant's notion of space and time as innate categories that are not given to us in experience is, from a semiotic point of view, nothing more than a guess about space and time having a linguistic nature. Relativistic physics, which came into conflict with the language of classical physics, created a semiotic problem that was solved by finding a new language for the description and interpretation of the new experience.

Viewing language as an instrument of cognition, linguistics must study the impact of language on the results of cognitive processes.

In a natural science, the object of cognition is a particular aspect of nature. But the object of linguistics is languages. So, linguistics creates languages for the description of languages. The languages used for such description are called *meta-languages,* and languages described by meta-languages are called *object languages.*

The basic question of linguistic theory must be: What factors contribute to the similarities and differences between natural languages? To answer this question, linguistics must create a meta-language in terms of which it is possible to present correct cross-linguistic generalizations, to state universal laws explaining these generalizations, and to provide an insightful linguistic typology and adequate descriptions of individual languages.

Since a meta-language of linguistic theory is an instrument for the cognition of the languages of the world, the structure of the meta-language must interfere with the structure of the description of the object languages: the limits of the meta-language mean the limits of the description of the object languages. One of the important tasks of linguistics is the search for ways of reducing to a minimum the interference of the meta-language with the description of the object languages.

The present crisis of generative-transformational grammar is partly due to the serious limitations of its meta-language. This meta-language was shaped under the influence of the structure of the English language, which has the linear order of constituents. The meta-language of generative-transformational grammar is inadequate as an instrument of linguistic theory, because transformations stated in terms of the linear order of constituents make it necessary to formulate distinct rules for languages with different word order for what can be characterized as the same phenomenon in relational terms.

Another example of an inadequate meta-language of linguistic theory is the meta-language of relational grammar. This meta-language, which treats the terms *subject, direct object,* and *indirect object* as primitives of linguistic theory, gets into serious difficulties when applied to ergative languages. The notions denoted by these terms cannot be regarded as universal categories. In this case, the construction of the meta-language has been shaped under the influence of the syntactic categories of accusative languages.

A different kind of an inadequate meta-language is presented by Montague grammar. The meta-language of Montague grammar has been shaped under the influence of the language of formal logic. Hence, this meta-language imposes on the description of natural languages various logical characteristics that are either alien or irrelevant to their structure.

Semiotics is able to solve the problem of constructing an adequate meta-language for linguistic theory. The way to the solution of this problem might be as follows.

The construction of a meta-language of linguistic theory is necessarily limited by the Principle of Linguistic Relativity, which can be traced back to W. von Humboldt but was most clearly formulated and applied by B. L. Whorf and E. Sapir. According to the Principle of Linguistic Relativity, any one language will give a relative picture of the world. It follows that since languages of the world are object languages for a meta-language of linguistic theory, we cannot construct an adequate universal grammar no matter which meta-language we use. That creates a serious difficulty for universal grammar. But we can solve this difficulty by introducing the Principle of Semiotic Invariance into universal grammar. Since it is indeed indisputable that any one language will give only a relative picture of the world, relativity and invariance may seem incompatible with each other. But, as a matter of fact, they complement each other (Shaumyan, 1980). The relativity principle applies to relativity itself. Relativity is relative. The complementarity of linguistic invariance and linguistic relativity has its counterpart in physics. The concept of invariant is central to the theory of relativity. The theory of relativity is concerned with finding out those things that remain invariant under transformations of coordinate systems.

I propose the concept of the meta-language of linguistic theory as an invariant under all possible transformations of one language system into another. This invariant meta-language of linguistic theory I call the *genotype language*.

Modern linguistics faces a semiotic problem that arises from situations defined by Bohr's Complementarity Principle. Originally this principle was formulated for quantum mechanics, but soon it became clear that it can be applied to other fields of human knowledge, as well. This principle precludes the simultaneous use of classical concepts that in different connections are equally necessary for the explanation of a given phenomenon. For example, once we have decided to describe a certain event in terms of the wave concept, we cannot *at the same time* make use of the particle concept *for the same purpose*. If we mix these two interpretations, we get into difficulties. These difficulties are in the last resort due to the rules of the language we are accustomed to using.

Here is an example of the situations in linguistics that can be characterized by the Complementarity Principle. As was shown in chapter 2 (also see Shaumyan, 1968), every speech sound splits into two objects: a physical object and a functional object. Both types of objects are logically independent. Functional and physical identity are complementary and at the same time mutually exclusive concepts. A sound as a member of a class of physically identical objects is a sound proper, but as a member of a class of functionally identical objects, it is a fundamentally new object—a phoneme. As a unity of contradictory objects—physical and functional—a speech sound is a combined object: a sound-diacritic. The notion of the phoneme as a unity of the sound and the diacritic is reminiscent of such notions as the wave-particle in physics, the commodity as a unity of use-value and exchange-value in economics, etc. I use the metaphorical term *centaur concepts*, or, simply, *centaurs* to denote this type of notions, or objects, because the structure of these notions reminds one of centaurs, the fabulous creatures of Greek mythology, half men and half horses.

Objects created by functional superposition are a special type of centaurs. Consider, for example, long passive constructions. As was shown in section 2 of chapter 3, both passive predicates and agent terms in long passive constructions have a contradictory nature. Thus, in a long passive construction, the predicate has the form of a one-place predicate and, by functional superposition, the function of a two- or a three-place predicate; and the agent has the form of a modifier of the passive predicate (that is, the form of an oblique term) and the function of a secondary term. In the long passive construction, the predicate is a centaur *one-place predicate/n-place predicate,* and the agent is a centaur *oblique term/secondary term.* Other centaur concepts in linguistics are functional segmentation-physical segmentation of speech flow, linearity-nonlinearity of word sequences, and constituent structure-dependency structure. The treatment of these pairs of contradictory notions as centaur concepts makes it possible to solve the difficulties that result either from mixing these notions or from exaggerating the significance of one notion at the expense of the notion that is complementary to it.

It should be stressed that difficulties that are solved by the Complementarity Principle are not due to the nature of the phenomena; these difficulties arise from the choice of concepts, a choice dictated by semiotic requirements, by the need for simple symbolic models, and by the desire for visualization. The dualism inherent in human language makes it impossible to represent the contradictions inherent in the nature of an object in terms of a single concept. In the beginning of quantum theory, attempts were made to interpret the phenomena in terms of a single concept 'wavicle', but they did not lead to success. It is impossible to make a model of such a wavicle, because we cannot make use of the customary rules of our language. Only by creating a centaur concept 'wave-particle' can we present a reasonably clear picture of the phenomenon. Only by creating the centaur concepts 'sound-diacritic', 'constituency-dependency', 'linearity-nonlinearity,' 'form-function,' etc. can we get a reasonably clear picture of linguistic reality.

## 5. Static and Dynamic Meta-languages

The Principle of Semiotic Invariance must be regarded as a constraint on linguistic relativity: although the classification of the elements of reality is arbitrary, there are limits to the arbitrariness of the classification. Different languages present different pictures of reality, but these pictures may be isomorphic with respect to their cognitive value. Let me give an example of cognitive isomorphism between two languages.

There are two ways of describing reality. We can describe it as a system of coexisting things or as a system of changing things. In terms of ontological categories, we can describe reality as Being or as Becoming. These two means of describing reality can be traced to Greek philosophy. Parmenides advocated the description of reality as Being, and Heraclitus advocated the description of reality as Becoming.

Two different languages correspond to the two types of the description of reality; I call them *static language* and *dynamic language*. A static language is used to describe reality as Being, and a dynamic language is used to describe reality as Becoming. Static language is used by Lamb's stratificational linguistics and by relational grammar; dynamic language is used by applicative grammar and by generative-transformational grammar.

As a matter of fact, both a static language and a dynamic language give only relative pictures of reality. In many cases, the choice between one or the other type of description is merely a choice between two metaphors. Which type of description is chosen is often simply a matter of convenience.

Static and dynamic languages are used in physics as alternative languages for the description of physical reality. A. Einstein and L. Infeld point out that these two languages can be equivalent:

> We picture the motion as a sequence of events in the one-dimensional space continuum. We do not mix time and space, using a *dynamic* picture in which positions *change* with time.
> But we can picture the same motion in a different way. We can form a *static* picture, considering the curve in the two-dimensional time-space continuum. Now the motion is represented as something which *is*, which exists in the two-dimensional time-space continuum, and not as something which changes in the one-dimensional space continuum. Both these pictures are exactly equivalent and preferring one to the other is merely a matter of convention and taste. (Einstein, Infeld, 1938: 205)

It is to be noted that cybernetics, which has been defined by Wiener as "the science of control and communication in the animal and machine," makes a study of mechanism from a purely functional (that is, synchronic) point of view, and it describes the work of the mechanism in dynamic terms, that is, in terms of the relation *operator : operand*, in terms of *change*. There is an analogy between natural language as a mechanism used for communication and other types of mechanisms. Just as we speak of the behavior of a mechanism, we can speak of the behavior of language. Characterizing cybernetics, Ashby writes:

> Many a book has borne the title "Theory of Machines", but it usually contains information about *mechanical* things, about levers and cogs. Cybernetics, too, is a "theory of machines", but it treats, not things but *ways of behaving*. It does not ask "what *is* this thing?" but "*what does it do?*" Thus it is very interested in such a statement as "this variable is undergoing a simple harmonic oscillation", and is much less concerned with whether the variable is the position of a point on a wheel, or a potential in an electric circuit. It is thus essentially functional and behaviouristic. (Ashby, 1956: 1)

Like cybernetics, synchronic linguistics is essentially functional and behavioristic. Why, then, should synchronic linguistics shun dynamic concepts? I repeat, though, that the choice between dynamic and static terms is basically a matter of convenience.

What is important is not which language for description we choose, but rather which hypothesis about the nature of reality we combine with the language we have chosen. In order to obtain a correct description of reality, we must choose a correct hypothesis about the nature of reality. Two descriptions presented in different languages have the same invariant cognitive structure if they are combined with identical hypotheses about the nature of reality. Under this condition, two descriptions in different languages must be regarded as two variants, or two realizations, of the same cognitive structure.

The distinction between a synchronic and a diachronic description of a language should not be confused with the distinction between a static and a dynamic meta-language. A synchronic description of a language can be presented not only in a static meta-language but in a dynamic meta-language, as well; a diachronic description of language can be presented not only in a dynamic meta-language but also in a static meta-language.

The choice of a dynamic or a static meta-language for a synchronic or diachronic linguistic description has nothing to do with a confusion of synchrony and diachrony. Thus, both generative-transformational grammar and applicative grammar use dynamic meta-languages, but generative-transformational confounds synchrony with diachrony, and applicative grammar does not.

Generative-transformational grammar confounds synchrony and diachrony not because it uses a dynamic meta-language but because it disregards fundamental functional properties of language as a sign system used as an instrument of communication and cognition.

In summary, two languages can be used for the description of reality—a static meta-language and a dynamic meta-language. One can always translate statements from one language into another without loss of information. The choice between the two meta-languages is a matter of convenience. The essential thing is not a choice of meta-language but a choice of the right hypothesis about reality.

## 6. The Role of Analogies in the Semiotic Theory of Language

The Semiotic Theory of Language rests on the assumption that semiotic phenomena exhibit various forms of an underlying single semiotic reality; therefore, semiotic principles and laws, such as the Principle of Semiotic Relevance and the Markedness Law, hold in both the grammatical and the phonological systems of a natural language, and they hold in other semiotic systems, as well.

There is a deep analogy between various semiotic systems. In using the word *analogy*, I do not assert that semiotic systems are like one another in all respects. The relation of analogy between different semiotic systems means that they are similar only in some fundamental properties that can be regarded as essential.

Of course, one semiotic system may have important properties that are not found in other semiotic systems and that are essential for the functioning of this particular semiotic system. There is a hierarchy of essential properties: properties that are essential for any semiotic system, properties that are essential for a particular class of semiotic systems, and, finally, properties that are essential for an individual semiotic system.

The important thing about thinking in terms of analogy is that analogy has a heuristic value: if we find that some semiotic systems have some analogous properties, we can expect that a further analysis will lead to a discovery of new, hitherto unknown analogous properties of these properties.

Other things being equal, our choice between rival hypotheses must be governed by the considerations of analogy: if a hypothesis is valid in a particular semiotic domain and, in addition, is valid in some other semiotic domains owing to analogous properties of all these semiotic domains, while a rival hypothesis is valid only in this particular semiotic domain, then we have to choose the first hypothesis as more plausible.

Of particular importance is the search for analogies between the grammatical and the phonological systems of language. A systematic comparison of the phonological and grammatical domains must throw light both on the general theory of the sign and on the basic properties of the structure of language. Let me give some examples.

In chapter 3, section 9, I proposed the Law of Duality, which characterizes the relation between accusative and ergative constructions. The Law of Duality is valid in phonology, as well. Consider, for instance, the opposition $d:t$ in Russian and the opposition $d:t$ in Danish. On the surface these two oppositions are the same. But, as a matter of fact, the Russian $d:t$ is a case of the opposition *voiced:voiceless*, and the Danish $d:t$ is a case of the opposition *lax:tense*.

In Danish, the neutralization of the opposition $d:t$ results in $d$, which can represent either $d$ or $t$. So, $d$ is a neutral-negative (unmarked) member of the opposition $d:t$, and $t$ is a positive (marked) member of this opposition. That can be represented by the following diagram:

(1)

In Russian, the neutralization of the opposition *d:t* results in *t*, which can represent either *d* or *t*. So, *t* is a neutral-negative (unmarked) member of the opposition *d:t*, and *d* is a positive (marked) member of this opposition. That can be represented by the following diagram:

(2)

We come up with the opposition *unmarked phoneme:marked phoneme* in phonology. On the basis of this opposition, we establish the following correspondence between members of the oppositions *lax:tense* and *voiced:voiceless:*

(3)

| Opposition of markedness | Lax:Tense | Voiced:Voiceless |
|---|:---:|:---:|
| Unmarked phoneme | *d* | *t* |
| Marked phoneme | *t* | *d* |

Now we can apply the Law of Duality in phonology:

The marked term of the opposition *lax:tense* corresponds to the unmarked term of the opposition *voiced:voiceless*, and the unmarked term of the opposition *lax:tense* corresponds to the marked term of the opposition *voiced:voiceless*; and, vice versa, the marked term of the opposition *voiced:voiceless* corresponds to the unmarked term of the opposition *lax:tense*, and the unmarked term of the opposition *voiced:voiceless* corresponds to the marked term of the opposition *lax:tense*.

Another example of a fruitful comparison of the phonological and grammatical systems is the explanation of reflexivization (chap. 3, sec. 13.8). This explanation is based on the notion of neutralization. There is a deep analogy between phonological neutralization and the neutralization of the opposition *primary term:secondary term* in syntax.

The markedness relation and the notion of neutralization dominate the whole of language—both its grammatical and its phonological systems. Therefore, if I intended to give further examples of analogies between grammar and phonology, I would have to review a considerable part of this book. The reader may find further examples himself.

The lesson from the foregoing is this: a linguist who in studying grammar ignores phonology does so at his peril. The peril is that he may be deprived of insights into grammar that phonology is able to provide.

## 7. The Use and Abuse of Mathematical Formalism

Mathematics plays an important part in contemporary science, and it is important for linguistics, as well. Mathematical language, as a meta-language for the description of natural languages, is employed for constructing *calculi*—special artifacts used to organize our linguistic experience.

A calculus has many functions. First, it is a tool for expressing our ideas in a rigorous and precise form. Second, it provides methods for arranging our linguistic hypotheses in a deductive system. Third, it has a great heuristic power; it enables us to explore all logical possibilities that follow from initial fundamental ideas and to discover concrete facts that realize these possibilities.

It is true that ideas, not formulas, constitute the essence of any linguistic theory, and of any scientific theory. But mathematical language is an important aid for expressing ideas; not everything that is easily expressed in a mathematical language can be readily translated into an ordinary language of science. To see that, let us try to translate the formulas of grammatical categories in applicative grammar into an ordinary language of linguistics. Take the formula

(1)      *OtOtOts*

An exact translation of this formula into the ordinary language of linguistics is this: 'an operator which applied to a term yields an operator which applied to a term yields an operator which applied to a term yields a sentence'. That is a formal definition of the three-place predicate.

Why, then, not translate formula (1) simply as 'three-place predicate'? Because it lays bare the internal structure of the three-place predicate; it shows that a three-place predicate applied to a term is equivalent to a two-place predicate, that a two-place predicate applied to a term is equivalent to a one-place predicate, and that a one-place predicate applied to a term is equivalent to a sentence. All of this information will be lost if we translate formula (1) merely by the expression 'three-place predicate'.

Take the formula

(2)      *OOtsOts*

An exact translation of this formula into the language of ordinary linguistics is this: 'an operator which applied to an operator which applied to a term yields a sentence which yields an operator which applied to a term yields a sentence'.

That is a formal definition of the modifier of a one-place predicate. It lays bare its internal structure; it shows that the modifier of a one-place predicate applied to a one-place predicate is equivalent to a one-place predicate, and that a one-place predicate applied to a term is equivalent to a sentence. All of this information will be lost if we translate the above formula simply as 'the modifier of a predicate'.

The above examples show that a mathematical language can have an enormous power for compressing information into a perspicuous symbolism that lays bare internal structure and relations between elements of a system. Information compressed by a mathematical language is not readily translatable into an ordinary scientific language.

At the present stage of the development of linguistics, no serious linguistic theory can dispense with mathematical formalism. On the other hand, mathematical formalism should not be confused either with a meta-language of linguistics or with linguistic theory.

Linguistic theory deals with concepts, principles, and laws that are independent of mathematical formalism. The basic problems of linguistic theory, such as the relation between the sound and the phoneme, functional and physical identity of sounds, functional and physical segmentation of the speech flow, the stratification of language, the basic units of morphology and syntax, etc., have nothing to do with mathematical formalism. Mathematical formalism is only a tool for expressing ideas of linguistic theory, and ideas must depend on an analysis of facts of real languages rather than on mathematical formalism. Besides, mathematical formalism is not adequate for expressing all ideas of linguistic theory. Basic ideas of linguistic theory, such as those relating to the above problems, must be expressed in an ordinary meta-language of linguistics. True, mathematical formalism is an important means for expressing ideas, but it is only a part of the language of science. Neither linguistics nor any science can do without the use of terminologically refined ordinary language. Linguistic theory cannot dispense with mathematical formalism, but it cannot dispense with terminologically refined ordinary language, either. The basic tool for expressing ideas of linguistic theory is ordinary language rather than the language of mathematics. Mathematical formalism is only an extension of the ordinary meta-language of linguistics.

It should be noted that uninterpreted mathematical formalism cannot be considered a language of science, because the symbols of an uninterpreted formalism have no meaning and therefore cannot be regarded as signs of a language. Only an interpreted formalism becomes a language of science.

The same formalism can have very different interpretations depending on the ideas of different theories. A mathematical formalism with two different interpretations constitutes not one language but rather two different languages, in spite of the formal similarity of the symbols used.

An example of how two different interpretations of a similar mathematical formalism constitute two different meta-languages of different linguistic theories is the categorial part of the meta-languages of applicative grammar and Montague grammar. In spite of their formal similarities, the categorial calculus of applicative grammar and the categorial calculus of Montague grammar constitute two very different meta-languages.

A meta-language must be tailored to the goals and conceptual system of a given linguistic theory. Different meta-languages can have different expressive power. Therefore, not everything that is expressed in one meta-language can be translated into another meta-language. For example, applicative grammar posits a rich class of operators, functions, and relations. Statements about these concepts cannot be translated from the meta-language of applicative grammar into the meta-language of generative-transformational grammar. That is impossible, because the meta-language of generative-transformational grammar can express some of these notions awkwardly and cannot express most of them at all.

Mathematical formalism is a powerful tool of cognition. Mathematics is a sort of energy whose function is to stimulate our imagination and help us to gain new insights into the nature of reality. But any kind of energy gives man power only when it is put to a right use. Electricity does a lot of good for man, but it also kills. A misuse of mathematics can be dangerous.

The major danger involved in the use of mathematical apparatus is this: Intoxicated by the power of mathematical formalism, we may be tempted to confound specific properties of mathematical formalism with properties of real objects.

As to a mathematical formalism used in a linguistic theory, we may be tempted to confound rules that we are able to posit within the framework of our mathematical formalism with rules of a language that we describe.

In chapter 1, section 8, I gave examples of a wrong use of mathematical formalism, when deductive necessity implied by mathematical rules is confounded with empirical necessity. It was shown that the failure of generative-transformational grammar is the result of a confusion of deductive and empirical necessity.

What I have said about generative-transformational grammar equally applies to Montague grammar and relational grammar. All of these linguistic theories confound logical necessity with empirical necessity; they cultivate formalization for the sake of formalization. By making a fetish of formal systems, they replace an empirical analysis of semiotic properties of human language with an exquisite play with symbols.

A confusion of mathematical formalism with reality is not a phenomenon that is found only in linguistics. In a chapter on mathematics as a language in his book on semiotics, the Russian mathematician V. Nalimov gives striking examples of the abuse of mathematical formalism in different sciences. He concludes:

> The use of mathematical language by itself does not eliminate absurdities from publications. It is possible "to dress scientific brilliancies and scientific absurdities alike in the impressive uniform of formulae and theorems" (Schwartz, 1962). Mathematics is not the means for correcting errors in the human genetic code. Side by side with mathematization of knowledge, mathematization of nonsense also goes on; the language of mathematics, strange as it seems, appears fit for carrying out any of these problems. (Nalimov, 1981)

The abuse of mathematical formalism annoys J. Schwartz so much that he calls his paper "The Pernicious Influence of Mathematics on Science" (Schwartz, 1962). Among other publications that warn against the abuse of mathematics in science, papers by Doyle (1965), Shannon (1956), Box (1966), and Leontiev (1971) can be mentioned.

As an instrument of cognition, mathematical language has a specific function—to be a tool of deduction. The word *deduction* is important. The use of mathematical language as a tool of deduction makes sense when the initial ideas from which we deduce their consequences have cognitive value. If, on the contrary, the initial ideas do not have cognitive value or, worse than that, are absurd, then the use of mathematical language as a tool of deduction causes harm. In this case, mathematical language turns from an instrument of cognition into an instrument of obfuscation. Deduction is neutral to the cognitive value of ideas: mathematization of nonsense is equally possible.

Successful application of mathematics in various sciences has caused an aura of prestige about scientific works that use mathematical symbolism. There is nothing wrong with that, since the right use of mathematics is really important in any science. A well-motivated use of mathematical formalism can enhance the value of a scientific paper or a book. In case of an abuse of mathematics, however, mathematical symbolism acquires a purely social function of creating an aura of prestige about works whose cognitive value is null or, at best, very low. In this case, the manipulation of mathematical symbolism, the play with symbols, belongs to phenomena of the same order as the ritual dances of an African tribe. The manipulation of mathematical symbolism becomes a sign of an affiliation with an exclusive social group. The magic of the play with symbols can have an effect comparable to the effect of drugs. The participants in the play get high and then fall into a trance that makes them feel they are in exclusive possession of God's truth.

## 8. The Notion of Semiotic Reality

As an alternative to the notion of psychological reality, which is, as was shown in section 1, irrelevant to linguistics, I propose the notion of *semiotic reality.*

I define semiotic reality as *the specific properties of sign systems and all necessary or possible consequences of these properties.*

The fundamental assumption is that natural language, like any kind of sign system, has a unique status: genetically it is the product of human consciousness, but ontologically it is independent of human consciousness. Language is a social phenomenon, and social phenomena should not be confused with psychological phenomena. Linguistics is not a branch of psychology. Linguistics is a branch of semiotics. The importance of semiotics for various branches of social science is comparable to the importance of physics for various branches of natural science.

Semiotic reality is a single empirical basis for testing linguistic theories. A cooperation of linguistics with psychology and other sciences can be fruitful only if linguistics is conscious of semiotic reality as its single empirical basis.

The founders of modern semiotics and linguistics Charles Sanders Peirce (Peirce, 1931–1935) and Ferdinand de Saussure (Saussure, 1959) clearly characterized the unique ontological status of language as a social phenomenon.

The basic fact about semiotic reality is that it is the domain of the coupling of thought and phonic substance. Saussure wrote:

> Language might be called the domain of articulations. . . . Each linguistic term is a member, an *articulus* in which an idea is fixed in a sound and a sound becomes the sign of an idea.

> Language can also be compared with a sheet of paper: thought is the front and the sound is the back; one cannot cut the front without cutting the back at the same time; likewise in language, one can neither divide sound from thought nor thought from sound; the division could be accomplished only abstractly, and the result would be either pure psychology or pure phonology.

> Linguistics then works in the borderland where the elements of sound and thought combine; *their combination produces a form, not a substance.* (Saussure, 1959: 112–13)

(Saussure uses the term *phonology* in the sense of what is called *phonetics* in contemporary linguistics.)

By claiming that language is form, not substance, Saussure meant that sound and meaning are linguistic facts only insofar as they are not separated from each other: sound separated from meaning is merely a phonic substance, not a linguistic fact; meaning separated from sound is merely a conceptual substance—a logical phenomenon rather than a linguistic fact. Stating the crucial significance of his claim that *language is a form, not a substance,* Saussure wrote:

> This truth cannot be overstressed, for all the mistakes in our terminology, all our incorrect ways of naming things that pertain to language, stem from the involuntary supposition that the linguistic phenomenon must have substance. (Saussure, 1959: 122)

Saussure's statement that language is form, not substance, is well known, but the meaning and implications of this statement are poorly understood.

Semiotic reality is determined by the Principle of Semiotic Relevance (which was formulated and explained in chapter 1, section 1): *Only those distinctions between meanings are relevant that correlate with distinctions between their signs, and, vice versa, only those distinctions between signs are relevant that correlate with the distinctions between their meanings.*

All other principles and laws that characterize semiotic reality are rooted in the Principle of Semiotic Relevance.

An important characteristic of natural language is its *hierarchical stratification into functional levels*, as was shown in chapter 1, section 1. The Principle of Semiotic Relevance and the Principle of Hierarchical Stratification constitute basic constraints on the degree of abstractness allowable in linguistics. Linguistic abstractions that conflict with these principles must be rejected, because they distort semiotic reality.

As constraints on the degree of abstractness, the Principle of Semiotic Relevance and the Principle of Hierarchical Stratification have two functions: 1) a preventive function and 2) a heuristic function. The preventive function of these principles is that they prevent linguistic abstractions that distort semiotic reality, such as deep structure or underlying phonemic representation in generative phonology. The heuristic function of these principles is that they lead to novel significant insights into the nature of semiotic reality.

The history of science and mathematics shows that significant progress has sometimes been achieved by imposing constraints on initial assumptions of a scientific or mathematical system. Thus, by eliminating Postulate V of Euclidean geometry, a new non-Euclidean geometry was created. Another example of a constraint is the hypothesis of the impossibility of measuring simultaneously the exact position and the exact momentum of a physical particle—Heisenberg's Indeterminacy Principle. Such constraints have played a very large part in the development of new fundamental theories in physics.

As was shown in the foregoing chapters, disregard of semiotic reality leads to disastrous consequences for linguistics, such as autonomous syntax, deep structure, generative phonology, a confusion of logical and linguistic analysis, a confusion of synchrony and diachrony, and so on. Here I will consider some more examples of this disaster.

In their book on the sound pattern of English, Chomsky and Halle suggest that alternations such as *resign : resignation* and *paradigm : paradigmatic* can be accounted for by providing a unique base for each morpheme (Chomsky, Halle, 1968: 234). Thus, Chomsky and Halle posit *rē=sign* as the systematic phonemic representation of *resign*. The equality sign = represents a special morpheme boundary, which is necessary in the following rule:

(1)     $s \rightarrow z$ in the context: *Vowel*=____*Vowel*

Chomsky and Halle posit *s* in the underlying form, because they claim that the same morpheme occurs in words such as *consign* where the same boundary = is recognized.

A question arises: Is *sign* in *resign* identical with *sign* in *consign?* Are they allomorphs of the same morpheme?

The answer is negative. If we analyze the meanings of *resign* and *consign*, we can easily see that from a synchronic point of view, *resign* cannot be divided into two morphs *re* and *sign*, nor can *consign* be divided into two morphs *con* and *sign*. From a synchronic point of view, *resign* and *consign* have nothing in common with each other except a partial similarity of their physical shapes: neither the word *resign* nor the word *consign* is related to the word *sign*.

Chomsky and Halle clearly disregard the function of words as signs. They ignore the problem of justifying synchronic identifications of morphemes. What basis could we provide for saying that *resign* is related to *sign*? If the only basis for saying so is the physical similarity of *sign* with *-sign* as a part of *resign*, we can use the same basis for saying that *mother* is related to *moth*, *liquor* to *lick*, *season* to *sea*, *butter* to *butt*, and *arsenal* to *arse*.

The identity of *sign* with *-sign* in *resign* and with *-sign* in *consign* claimed by Chomsky and Halle is a fiction that conflicts with the synchronic structure of English.

Since the phoneme *g* is present in *resignation* and absent in *resign*, Chomsky and Halle propose a rule that changes *g* into a fricative γ. This rule is stated as follows: *g* changes into γ when it occurs before a syllable-final *n*. Then the following rules are applied: 1) a rule changing the lax vowel *i* into the tense vowel *ī* when *i* occurs before γ; 2) a rule of γ-deletion when γ occurs before syllable-final *n*; 3) a rule of vowel shift; and 4) a rule of diphthongization. Chomsky and Halle represent *resign* phonetically as *riyzayn* and derive this phonetic form from the underlying phonemic representation *rē=sign* as follows:

(2)    *rē=sign*         Underlying phonemic representation
       *rē=zign*         Voicing of *s*
       *rē=ziγn*         Change of *g* into γ before syllable-final *n*
       *rē=zīγn*         Tensing of a vowel before γ
       *rē=zīn*          Drop of γ
       *rē=zǣn*          Vowel shift
       *riyzǣyn*         Diphthongization

The diphthong *ǣy* is modified to *ay* (= *aı*) by another rule.

The above derivation is characteristic of generative phonology. This derivation is a pure fiction that conflicts with the synchronic structure of contemporary English.

Since generative phonology disregards the semiotic properties of language as a sign system, it provides no constraints on abstractness. As a result, generative phonology abounds with fictions that, far from having any cognitive value, present a distorted picture of the phonological system of language. Some generativists, such as Lightner (1971), find it possible to take the underlying phonemic representation of English back to a Proto-Germanic stage. According to Lightner, contemporary English has the alternations *f* and *p*, ð and *t*, *h* and *k*, as in the following words:

(3)    *foot : pediatrician*
       *father : paternal*

*full : plenary*
*mother : maternal*
*brother : fraternal*
*heart : cardiac*
*horn : unicorn*
*hound : canine*

One may argue that Lightner goes too far, that Chomsky and Halle would not approve of Lightner's approach. If Halle and Chomsky did not approve of Lightner's approach, that would be sheer inconsistency on their part. Lightner is consistent; he reduces the principles of generative phonology to their absurd conclusions. And so do other pupils of Chomsky and Halle—S. Shane, J. Harris, C. Kisseberth, M. Kenstowicz, and W. A. Foley, to mention a few. No matter whether or not Chomsky and Halle approve of various absurdities in the works of their pupils, their own work is absurd enough in itself. All works in generative phonology—earlier works or the most recent ones—are based on the same principles, which are completely bankrupt.

Let us now turn to an example of fictions in syntax.

In discussing the theory of passivization in relational grammar (chap. 3, sec. 2.2), we came across sentences such as

(4)  a.  *Peter gave money to Nancy.*
     b.  *Peter gave Nancy money.*

Relational grammar claims that (4b) is the result of a relational change in (4a): *Nancy* is advanced from 3 to 2 and *money* is put en chômage. In other words, *Nancy*, which is the indirect object in (4a), becomes the direct object in (4b), while *money*, which is the direct object in (4a), becomes a chômeur in (4b).

I presented counterexamples that refute the claim of relational grammar that *money* is a chômeur in (4b). Thus, in some English dialects (4b) is passivized as

(5)  *Money was given Nancy.*

(5) shows that *money* is the direct object rather than a chômeur in (4b). Examples from other languages given above show that passivization of an indirect object has nothing to do with its alleged promotion to a direct object and the alleged demotion of the direct object to a chômeur. As a matter of fact, (4b) is a variant of (4a) rather than the result of the promotion of *Nancy* from the indirect object to the direct object.

The claim of relational grammar that *Nancy* is the direct object and *money* is a chômeur in (4b) is a fiction. Using the syntactic terminology of relational grammar, we can claim that actually *Peter* is the subject, *money* is the direct object, and *Nancy* is the indirect object in (4b), as well as in (4a).

The source of the above fiction of relational grammar is a disregard of the meaning of the sentences. Both (4a) and (4b) have the same meaning; they differ only with respect to the presence or absence of the preposition *to* and the different sequencing of terms. The change of (4a) into (4b) must be regarded as a syntagmatic process that does not affect either the meaning of the sentence or the relations between terms. Therefore, (4b) is nothing but a variant of (4a). In accordance with the Principle of Semiotic Relevance, only those syntagmatic processes must be considered relevant that are correlated with semantic processes. If given syntagmatic processes are not correlated with semantic processes, they must be considered irrelevant, and the syntactic structures resulting from them must be regarded as variants of the basic syntactic structures.

The foregoing shows the significance of semiotic reality as an empirical basis of a linguistic theory.

The failure of generative-transformational grammar, relational grammar, and Montague grammar is a natural and necessary consequence of their disregard of semiotic reality.

The strength of applicative grammar and the two-level phonological theory is that they are built upon the notion of semiotic reality as a single empirical basis of linguistics.

Applicative grammar was brought into existence by forces that determine the inner logic of the development of linguistics. These forces are semiotic problems. The results of the works of Peirce and Saussure led to the development of modern linguistics, to the creation of semiotic concepts, forming a new picture of language. Applicative grammar is a natural outcome of this development, but it is neither an ultimate truth nor the only possible linguistic theory based on semiotic concepts. One may accept or reject applicative grammar, but one must see clearly that any serious alternative to applicative grammar must be based on semiotic concepts.

# Notes

## 1. The Aim and Structure of the Semiotic Theory of Language

1. (p. 7) All the above estimates are reported in Miller, 1981.

2. (p. 9) A similar example is used in Reformatskij, 1960. The term *stratification* has been used in other senses by Lamb (1966a, 1966b, 1973a, 1973b, 1982) and Lockwood (1972) (also cf. Makkai, 1972 and Makkai and Lockwood, eds., 1973). Whereas applicative grammar is a self-contained system in its own right, it is ultimately not incompatible with Lambian cognitive stratificationalism. The reader should be most careful in drawing facile comparisons.

3. (p. 11) The Principle of Semiotic Relevance, which constitutes a basis for proper methods of abstraction in linguistics, can be traced back to the Principle of Abstract Relevance (*Prinzip der abstraktiven Relevanz*) proposed by Karl Bühler (1931: 22–53). Bühler's principle was meant only as a general point of view; it did not specify the correlation between sound differences and meaning differences as an essential condition for constraining linguistic abstractions.

4. (p. 16) A similar critique of the notion of homonymy is given by Zawadowski (1975: 117–26). Zawadowski correctly points out that different signs have the same form, and therefore homonymy is a theoretically invalid notion; he suggests replacing the notions of homonym and homonymy with the notions 'polysemous sign' and 'polysemy', which correspond to my notions of 'polyvalent sign' and 'polyvalence', based on the Principle of Semiotic Relevance and the Principle of Suspension. For lack of an explicit formulation of the Principle of Semiotic Relevance and the Principle of Suspension, Zawadowski does not explain why different signs cannot have the same form and why the same sign can have different meanings. I am at odds with his narrow conception of the sign as merely a sound sequence. Thus, for him, *bear* is the same sign in (5a), (5b), (5c), and (5d), while I distinguish three signs here: 1) *bear*; 2) *bear+place of a term*; 3) *bear+ place of a predicate*.

5. (p. 17) A detailed critique of Saussure's notion of the bilateral sign along similar lines is given by Zawadowski (1975: 120–26).

6. (p. 30) The latest version of generative grammar is presented in Chomsky's *Lectures on Government and Binding* (1981). Although the new version greatly differs from the first version presented in 1957, the basic principles of Chomsky's linguistic theory have not changed.

7. (p. 31) I must mention a few linguistic theories that view language in the spirit of modern semiotics. These are:

1) L. Hjelmslev's glossematics (Hjelmslev, 1961);
2) Sydney M. Lamb's stratificational linguistics (Lamb, 1966a, 1966b, 1973a, 1973b, 1982; Lockwood, 1972; Makkai, 1972);
3) Kenneth L. Pike's tagmemics (Pike, 1967, 1970, 1982; Pike and Pike, 1982, 1983);
4) M.A.K. Halliday's systemic grammar (Halliday, 1973, 1974, 1978);

5) I. A. Mel'čuk's 'meaning↔text' model (Mel'čuk, 1974).
Of course, these linguistic theories greatly differ both from each other and from my linguistic theory. Still, the semiotic view of language is their common ground.

## 2. Phonology

1. (p. 33) Speaking of Eastern Armenian, I mean literary Eastern Armenian as represented by educated Yerevan speech (Yerevan is the capital of Eastern Armenia). It should be noted that in some dialects of Eastern Armenian, $p^-$, $t^-$, and $k^-$ are pronounced with glottal closure which is released only after the release of the articulatory oral closure; they belong to a class of consonants called 'ejectives'. Ejectives occur also in Georgian and thirty-six other Caucasian languages and are found in many languages of the world (Catford, 1982: 70).

2. (p. 65) The reader will find a detailed description of distinctive features from an articulatory, acoustic, and perceptual point of view in Jakobson and Waugh, 1979.

3. (p. 70) As far as Russian language data are concerned, A. Martinet inaccurately points out that in Russian all components of a composite word, with the exception of one, lose their proper stress, because in Russian there also exist composite words every element of which preserves its proper stress, either as a primary or as a secondary stress, as, for instance, *kòneférma* 'horse farm', *pàrnokopýtnye* 'artiodactyla', *slàborázvityj* 'underdeveloped', and others (cf. *Russkoe literaturnoe proiznošenie i udarenie*, reference dictionary under the edition of R. I. Avanesov and S. I. Ožegov, Moscow, 1960). However, in spite of the inaccuracy, Martinet grasped the phonological essence of the phenomenon: since in Russian the components of composite words preserve their proper stress only in a few cases, the number of stresses in a sentence does not enable us to judge the number of lexemes within that sentence, and, therefore, from the phonological standpoint, in Russian the accentual unit is not the lexeme but the word.

4. (p. 70) A similar approach to phonological syntagmatic units is used in Prieto, 1975.

5. (p. 92) For morphophonology, or morphophonemics, see Jakobson, 1971; Hockett, 1958: chap. 16 and 32; Kuryłowicz, 1977; Lamb, 1978; Martinet, 1965; Matthews, 1974: chaps. 11–12; Stankiewicz, 1979.

## 3. Genotype Grammar

1. (p. 97) At this stage of the discussion, I do not question the conventional notions of subject and object. It will be shown below that these notions are inadequate for the purposes of linguistic theory.

2. (p. 103) The first to formulate the Applicative Principle was the Russian mathematician M. Schönfinkel, who formulated the bases of combinatory logic developed by the American mathematician H. B. Curry (Schönfinkel, 1924; Curry and Feys, 1958; Fitch, 1974).

3. (p. 106) On the notion of immediate constituents, see Wells, 1947 and Gazdar, 1981.

4. (p. 117) The notion 'functional transposition' and notions 'primary function' and 'secondary function' can be traced back to the works of Slotty (1932), Kuryłowicz (1936), and Bally (1944). The notion 'functional superposition' introduced in this book is new.

5. (p. 195) The terms *operationality* and *operationality primitive* correspond to Curry's terms *functionality* and *functionality primitive* (Curry and Feys, 1958: 262–66). Within the conceptual system based on the notion of the operator, I prefer the terms *operationality* and *operationality primitive*, since the operator is a function taken as a non-set-theoretical concept, and the term *functionality* involves associations with the function conceived of as a set-theoretical concept.

6. (p. 224) Section 3.13.7 of this chapter incorporates some material from the book *Theoretical Aspects of Passivization in the Framework of Applicative Grammar* by J.-P. Desclés, Z. Guentchéva, and S. Shaumyan (1985), to which I here apply some different theoretical viewpoints.

7. (p. 238) The characterization of reflexivization presented in section 13.8 of this chapter is a continuation of the research started in the paper "Reflexive Constructions: Towards a Universal Definition in the Framework of Applicative Grammar" by J.-P. Desclés, Z. Guentchéva, and S. Shaumyan (1986).

8. (p. 253) Zellig Harris has published books in which he used the concepts of operator and other related concepts (Harris, 1968, 1982). What is presented by Harris is not a linguistic theory proper but descriptive methods applied to a particular language—English. Harris operates with strings in the spirit of his previous works in descriptive linguistics. He is not interested in investigating language on the level of functional units. The level of abstraction is the same as in his previous works on transformations.

The basic notion of Harris's books is transformation. Harris understands transformations not as operations on trees, as does Chomsky, but as operations on strings. Transformations are systematic relations between sentences conceived of as strings of words. Technically, a transformation is an unordered pair of linguistic structures taken to be structurally equivalent in a certain sense. In order to obtain transformations, a set of constants called operators is applied to sentences. Analysis of transformations in terms of operators, in Harris's sense, is simply another way of describing the system of transformations presented in his previous works (Harris, 1957, 1965).

9. (p. 254) Among various works on analyses of natural languages from a logical point of view, one can mention, for example:

1) Carnap, R., "Meaning and Synonymy in Natural Languages" (in Carnap, 1956: 233–48);
2) Reichenbach, H., "Analysis of Conversational Language" (in Reichenbach, 1947: 251–354);
3) Quine, W. V., *Word and Object* (Quine, 1960).

10. (p. 269) It should be noted that a sharp critique of various orthodox versions of transformational grammar has been produced by some transformationalists who have departed far from its tenets in trying to mend its broken fences. Among them, James McCawley (1979, 1980, 1982) deserves mention in the first place.

11. (p. 283) In addition to works on the theory of combinators mentioned above, I would like to mention an excellent book for the general reader by Smullyan, 1985.

## 4. Phenotype Grammar

1. (p. 284) See the discussion of the notion of the word in Sapir, 1921; Bloomfield, 1933; Lyons, 1968; Matthews, 1974; Mel'čuk, 1976, 1982.

2. (p. 290) Since the main goal of this study is the clarification of the contemporary issues of grammar and phonology, I have been less interested in the otherwise fascinating and rather important area of lexicon and of one of the lexicon subsets, what is called *bound* or *phraseological expressions* (such as *to kick the bucket, red herring, ham and eggs*). In the framework of applicative grammar, rather extensive theoretical studies have been carried out of the organization of the lexicon with a special reference to Russian; see Shaumyan and Soboleva, 1968; Soboleva, 1972, 1973, 1978, 1981, 1983; Al'tman, 1981, 1983; Barčenkova, 1981; Ginzburg, 1973, 1981.

3. (page 297) There is no generally accepted notion of linguistic category. Some linguists define a linguistic category as a set of mutually exclusive meanings shared by a class of linguistic objects. Under this definition, the number in English is a linguistic category, but the singular number or the plural number is not; the grammatical case in

Latin is a linguistic category, but the nominative case, the genitive case, the dative case, etc. are not. Under my definition, both the number and the singular number or the plural number are linguistic categories; both the grammatical case and the nominative case, the genitive case, the dative case, etc. are grammatical categories.

## 5. Linguistic Methodology

1. (p. 307) For a detailed discussion of the concept of 'psychological reality', see Black and Chiat (1981). The authors argue correctly that the notion of psychological reality not only has been irrelevant to the practice of linguistics itself but also has had negative effects on the development of psycholinguistic theory. They conclude that the notion of psychological reality must be abandoned.

# References

Abelson, Harold, and Sussman, Gerald Jay, with Sussman, Julie. 1985. *Structure and Interpretation of Computer Programs*. Cambridge: MIT Press, McGraw-Hill Book Co.

Allen, W. S. 1965. "On One-Vowel Systems." *Lingua* 13:111–24.

Al'tman, I. V. 1981. "Otglagol'nye gnezda. Tipologija i semantika. I." In *Problemy strukturnoj lingvistiki. 1979*, ed. V. P. Grigor'ev. Moscow: Nauka.

———. 1983. "Otglagol'nye gnezda. Tipologija i semantika. III." In *Problemy strukturnoj lingvistiki. 1981*, ed. V. P. Grigor'ev. Moscow: Nauka.

Anderson, S. R. 1976. "On the Notion of Subject in Ergative Languages." In *Subject and Topic*, ed. C. N. Li. New York and London: Academic Press.

Aronoff, M. 1976. *Word Formation in Generative Grammar*. Cambridge: MIT Press.

Aronson, Howard I. 1977. "English as an Active Language." *Lingua* 41: 206–216.

Ashby, W. Ross. 1956. *An Introduction to Cybernetics*. London: Chapman and Hall.

Avanesov, R. I., and Ožegov, S. I. 1960. *Russkoje literaturnoe proiznošenie i udarenie*. Moscow: Prosveščenie.

Bach, E., and Harms, R., eds. 1968. *Universals of Linguistic Theory*. New York: Holt, Rinehart and Winston.

Backus, J. 1978. "Can Programming Be Liberated from the von Neuman Style? A Functional Style and its Algebra of Programs." CACM 21:613–41.

Bally, Charles. 1944. *Linguistique générale et linguistique française*. 2d ed. Berne: Editions Francke.

Barčenkova, M. D. 1981. "Granicy slovoobrazovatel'nogo gnezda." In *Problemy strukturnoj lingvistiki. 1979*, ed. V. P. Grigor'ev. Moscow: Nauka.

Bar-Hillel, Yehoshua (with C. Gaifman and E. Shamir). 1964. "On Categorial and Phrase Structure Grammars." In *Language and Information*. Jerusalem: Academic Press.

Beach, W. A.; Fox, S. E.; and Philosoph, S., eds. *Papers from the Thirteenth Annual Meeting of the Chicago Linguistic Society*, pp. 689–705. Chicago: University of Chicago, Department of Linguistics.

Becker Makkai, Valerie, ed. 1971. *Phonological Theory: Evolution and Current Practice*. New York: Holt, Rinehart and Winston. 2d ed. Lake Bluff, Ill.: Jupiter Press (1978).

Black, Maria, and Chiat, Shulamuth. 1981. "Psycholinguistics without Psychological Reality." *Linguistics* (1981): 37–61.

Blake, Berry J. 1977. *Case Markings in Australian Languages*. Linguistic Series, no. 23. Canberra: Australian Institute of Aboriginal Studies.

Bloomfield, L. 1933. *Language*. New York: Holt, Rinehart and Winston.

Boas, F., and Deloria, E. 1941. "Dakota Grammar." *Memoirs of the National Academy of Sciences*, vol. 23.

Bohr, Niels, 1948. "On the Notions of Causality and Complementarity." *Dialectica*, vol. 2. International Revue of Philosophy of Knowledge, Zurich, Switzerland.

———. 1958. *Atomic Physics and Human Knowledge.* New York: John Wiley and Sons.

Box, G. E. P. 1966. "Use and Abuse of Regression." *Technometrics* 8, no. 4.

Bresnan, Joan W. 1978. "A Realistic Transformational Grammar." In *Linguistic Theory and Psychological Reality*, ed. M. Halle, J. Bresnan, and G. A. Miller. Cambridge: MIT Press.

———. 1982. "The Passive in Lexical Theory." In *The Mental Representation of Grammatical Relations*, ed. Joan W. Bresnan. Cambridge: MIT Press.

Bresnan, Joan W., ed. 1982. *The Mental Representation of Grammatical Relations.* Cambridge: MIT Press.

Bresnan, Joan W., and Kaplan, R. M. 1982. "Lexical-Functional Grammar: A Formal System for Grammatical Representation." In *The Mental Representation of Grammatical Relations*, ed. Joan W. Bresnan. Cambridge: MIT Press.

Bühler, Karl. 1934. *Sprachtheorie.* Vienna: Verlag von Gustav Fischer.

Carnap, Rudolf. 1956. *Meaning and Necessity: A Study in Semantics and Modal Logic.* Chicago: University of Chicago Press.

———. 1962. *Logical Foundations of Probability.* 2d ed. Chicago: University of Chicago Press.

Catford, J. C. 1977. *Fundamental Problems of Phonetics.* Bloomington: Indiana University Press.

Chomsky, Noam. 1957. *Syntactic Structures.* The Hague: Mouton.

———. 1961. "On the Notion 'Rule of Grammar'." In *Proceedings of Symposium in Applied Mathematics*, vol. 12 (*Structure of Language and Its Mathematical Aspects*).

———. 1964. *Current Issues in Linguistics.* The Hague: Mouton.

———. 1965. *Aspects of the Theory of Syntax.* Cambridge: MIT Press.

———. 1978. "On the Biological Basis of Language Capacities." In *Psychology and Biology of Language and Thought*, ed. G. A. Miller and E. Lennberg. New York: Academic Press.

———. 1981. *Lectures on Government and Binding.* Dordrecht: Foris Publication.

———. 1982. *Some Concepts and Consequences of the Theory of Government and Binding.* Linguistic Inquiry Monograph, no. 6. Cambridge: MIT Press.

Chomsky, Noam, and Halle, Morris. 1968. *The Sound Pattern of English.* New York: Harper and Row.

Chung, S. 1976. "An Object-Creating Rule in Bahasa Indonesia." *Linguistic Inquiry* 7:41–87.

Churchward, C. M. 1953. *Tongan Grammar.* London: Oxford University Press.

Clements, G. N., and Keyser, S. J. 1983. *CV Phonology: A Generative Theory of the Syllable.* Cambridge: MIT Press.

Colarusso, J. 1975. "The Northwest Caucasian Languages: A Phonological Survey." Ph.D. dissertation, Harvard University.

Cole, Peter, and Sadock, Jerrold M., eds. 1977. *Grammatical Relations (Syntax and Semantics* 8). London and New York: Academic Press.

Comrie, Bernard. 1976. "The Syntax and Semantics in Causative Constructions: Cross-language Similarities and Divergences." In *The Grammar of Causative Constructions*, ed. M. Shibatani, pp. 261–312. New York and London: Academic Press.

———. 1977. "In Defense of Spontaneous Demotion: The Impersonal Passive." In *Grammatical Relations*, ed. Peter Cole and Jerrold M. Sadock. London and New York: Academic Press.

———. 1978. "Ergativity." In *Syntactic Typology*, ed. W. P. Lehman, pp. 329–94. Austin: University of Texas Press.

Copeland, James E., ed. 1984. *New Directions in Linguistics and Semiotics*. Houston: Rice University Studies.

Curry, Haskell B. 1961. *Some Logical Aspects of Grammatical Structure*. In *Structure of Language and Its Mathematical Aspects*, ed. Roman Jakobson.

————. 1963. *Foundations of Mathematical Logic*. New York: McGraw-Hill Book Co.

Curry, Haskell B., and Feys, Robert. 1958. *Combinatory Logic*, vol. 1. Amsterdam: North Holland Publishing Co.

Curry, Haskell B.; Hindley, J. R.; and Seldin, J. P. 1972. *Combinatory Logic*, vol. 2. Amsterdam: North Holland Publishing Co.

Desclés, Jean-Pierre. 1985. "Predication and Topicalization: A Formal Study in the Framework of Applicative Languages." *Second Conference of the European Chapter of the Association for Computational Linguistics*, Geneva, March 28 and 29.

Desclés, Jean-Pierre; Guentchéva, Zlatka; and Shaumyan, Sebastian. 1985. *Theoretical Aspects of Passivization in the Framework of Applicative Grammar*. Amsterdam/Philadelphia: John Benjamins Publishing Company.

————. 1986. "Reflexive Constructions: Towards a Universal Definition in the Framework of Applicative Grammar." *Linguistical Investigations*, 2.

Dik, Simon C. 1978. *Functional Grammar*. Amsterdam: North Holland Publishing Co.

Dixon, R. M. W. 1972. *The Dyirbal Language of North Queensland*. Cambridge: Cambridge University Press.

————. 1979. "Ergativity." *Language* 55:59–138.

Dowty, David R. 1982a. "Grammatical Relations and Montague Grammar." In *The Nature of Syntactic Representation*, ed. G. Pullum and R. Jakobson, pp. 79–130. Dordrecht: Reidel.

————. 1982b. "More on the Categorial Analysis of Grammatical Relations." Mimeographed. Columbus: Ohio State University Press.

Doyle, L. B. 1965. "Seven Ways to Inhibit Creative Research." *Datamation* 11:2.

Einstein, A., and Infeld, L. 1961. *The Evolution of Physics*. New York: Simon and Schuster.

Fant, G. 1960. *Acoustic Theory of Speech Production*. The Hague: Mouton.

Fillmore, Charles J. 1968. "The Case for Case." In *Universals of Linguistic Theory*, ed. E. Bach and R. Harms. New York: Holt, Rinehart and Winston.

————. 1977. "The Case for Case Reopened." In *Grammatical Relations*, ed. Peter Cole and Jerrold M. Sadock. London and New York: Academic Press.

Fischer-Jørgensen, Eli. 1975. *Trends in Phonological Theory: A Historical Introduction*. Copenhagen: Akademisk Forlag.

Fitch, F. B. 1952. *Symbolic Logic: An Introduction*. New York: Ronald Press Co.

————. 1974. *Elements of Combinatory Logic*. New Haven: Yale University Press.

Foley, William A., and Van Valin, Robert D. Jr. 1984. *Functional Syntax and Universal Grammar*. Cambridge: Cambridge University Press.

Frege, G. 1884. *Die Grundlagen der Arithmetik*. Breslau.

————. 1893. *Grundgesetze der Arithmetik*. Jena: H. Pohle.

Gamkrelidze, T. V. 1966. "A Typology of Common Kartvelian." *Language* 42:68–83.

Gamkrelidze, T. V., and Mačavariani, G. 1965. *Sonant'ta sist'ema da ablaut'i kartvelur enebji*. Tbilisi.

Gazdar, Gerald. 1982. "Phrase Structure Grammar." In *The Nature of Syntactic Representation*, ed. G. Pullum and R. Jakobson. Dordrecht: Reidel.

Genko, A. N. 1955. *Abazinskij jazyk*. Moscow: Nauka.

————. 1957. "Fonetičeskie vzaimootnošenija abxazskogo i abazinskogo jazykov." Sakartvelos SSR Mecnierebata Ak'ademiis Apxaretis Enis, Lit'erat'urisa da Ist'oriis Inst'it'ut'is Šromebi, vol. 28.

Gentzen, G. 1934. "Untersuchungen über das logische Schliessen." *Math. Z.*, 39:176–

210, 405–431. French translation: "Recherches sur la déduction logique" (translated, with supplementary notes by R. Feys and J. Ladriere, of [ULS], Paris, 1955).

Ginzburg, E. L. 1973. "Issledovanie struktury slovoobrazovatel'nyx gnezd." In *Problemy strukturnoj lingvistiki 1972*, ed. S. K. Shaumyan. Moscow: Nauka.

———. 1981. "Preobrazovanija slovoobrazovatel'nyx gnezd. I." In *Problemy strukturnoj lingvistiki 1979*, ed. V. P. Grigor'ev. Moscow: Nauka.

Givon, Talmy. 1979. *On Understanding Grammar*. New York: Academic Press.

Gleason, H. A. 1955. *An Introduction to Descriptive Linguistics*. New York: Holt, Rinehart and Winston.

Grigor'ev, V. P., ed. 1978. *Problemy strukturnoj lingvistiki. 1976*. Moscow: Nauka.

———. 1981. *Problemy strukturnoj lingvistiki. 1979*. Moscow: Nauka.

———. 1983. *Problemy strukturnoj lingvistiki. 1981*. Moscow: Nauka.

Gruber, Jeffrey. 1965. *"Studies in Lexical Relations."* Dissertation, MIT.

Guentchéva-Desclés, Zlatka. 1976. *Présentation critique de modèle applicationnel de S. K. Šaumjan*. Paris: Dunod.

Halle, Morris. 1959. *The Sound Pattern of Russian*. The Hague: Mouton.

———. 1970. "Is Kabardian a Vowel-less Language?" *Foundations of Language* 6: 95–103.

Halle, Morris; Bresnan, Joan; and Miller, George A., eds. 1978. *Linguistic Theory and Psychological Reality*. Cambridge: MIT Press.

Halle, M., and Vergnaud, J.-R. 1979. "Metrical Phonology (A Fragment of a Draft)." Unpublished manuscript.

Halliday, M. A. K. 1973. *Explorations in the Function of Language*. London: Edward Arnold.

———. 1974. *Learning How to Mean*. London: Edward Arnold.

———. 1978. *Language as a Social Semiotics: The Social Interpretation of Language and Meaning*. Baltimore: University Park Press.

Hamm, J., ed. 1967. *Phonologie der Gegenwart*. Graz-Vienna-Cologne: Hermann Bohlaus Nachf.

Harris, Zellig. 1951. *Structural Linguistics*. Chicago: University of Chicago Press.

———. 1965a. "Co-occurrence and Transformations in Linguistic Structure." *Language* 33: 283–340.

———. 1965b. "Transformational Theory." *Language* 41: 363–401.

———. 1968. *Mathematical Structure of Language*. New York: Wiley.

———. 1982. *A Grammar of English on Mathematical Principles*. New York: Wiley.

Hindley, J. R.; Lercher, B.; and Seldin, J. P. 1972. *Introduction to Combinatory Logic*. Cambridge: Cambridge University Press.

Hindley, J.R. and Seldin, J. P. 1986. *Introduction to Combinators and λ-Calculus*. Cambridge: Cambridge University Press.

Hjelmslev, L. 1961. *Prolegomena to a Theory of Language*. English translation by Francis J. Whitfield. 2d ed. Madison: University of Wisconsin Press.

Hockett, C. F. 1954. "Two Models of Grammatical Description." *Word* 10: 210–33.

———. 1958. *A Course in Modern Linguistics*. New York: Macmillan Co.

Hook, Peter Edwin. 1984. "The Anti-absolutive in Kashmiri and Sumerian." *Papers from the Twentieth Regional Meeting of the Chicago Linguistic Society* (CLS 20), pp. 181–91. Chicago, Illinois.

Hudson, Richard A. 1980. "Constituency and Dependency." *Linguistics* 18: 179–98.

Humboldt, Wilhelm von. 1836. *Über die Verschiedenheit des Menschlichen Schprachbaues und ihren Einfluss auf die geistige Entwickelung des Menschengeschlèchts*. Berlin: Gedruckt in der Druckerei der Koniglichen Akademie der Wissenschaften.

———. 1971. *Linguistic Variability and Intellectual Development*. Coral Gables, Fla.: University of Miami Press.

Infeld, L. 1950. *Albert Einstein: His Work and Its Influence on Our World.* New York: Simon and Schuster.

Jain, Jagdish. 1977. "The Hindi Passive in Universal Grammar." Unpublished paper, San Francisco State University.

Jakobson, Roman. 1962. *Selected Writings. Vol. 1: Phonological Studies.* The Hague: Mouton.

———. 1968. *Child Language, Aphasia, and Phonological Universals.* The Hague: Mouton.

———. 1971a. "The Phonemic and Grammatical Aspects of Language in Their Interrelations." In Roman Jakobson, *Selected Writings,* vol. 2. The Hague-Paris: Mouton.

———. 1971b. *Selected Writings. Vol. 2: Word and Language.* The Hague-Paris: Mouton.

Jakobson, Roman, ed. 1961. *Structure of Language and Its Mathematical Aspects.* Proceedings of Symposia in Applied Mathematics, vol. 12. American Mathematical Society.

Jakobson, Roman, and Waugh, Linda. 1979. *The Sound Shape of Language.* Bloomington and London: Indiana University Press.

Jaskowski, S. 1934. "On the Rules of Suppositions in Formal Logic." *Studia Logica,* no. 1:5–32.

Johnson, David E. 1976. "Ergativity in Universal Grammar." Mimeograph.

———. 1979. *Toward a Theory of Relationally Based Grammar.* New York: Garland Publishing Co.

Joos, Martin, ed. 1966. *Readings in Linguistics I.* Chicago and London: University of Chicago Press.

Kahn, D. 1976. *Syllable-Based Generalizations in English Phonology.* Ph.D. dissertation, MIT, 1976. Published by Garland Publishing Co., New York, 1980.

Kaplan, Abraham. 1964. *The Conduct of Inquiry.* San Francisco: Chandler Publishing Co.

Keenan, Edward L. 1972. "Relative Clause Formation in Malagasy." In *Chicago Witch Hunt,* ed. Paul M. Peranteau, Judith N. Levy, and Gloria C. Phares, pp. 169–89. Chicago: Chicago Linguistic Society.

———. 1975. "Some Universals of Passive in Relational Grammar." *Papers from the Eleventh Regional Meeting of the Chicago Linguistic Society.* Chicago, Illinois.

———. 1976. "Toward a Universal Definition of 'Subject'." In *Subject and Topic,* ed. C. N. Li. New York and London: Academic Press.

Keenan, Edward L., and Comrie, Bernard. 1977. "Noun Phrase Accessibility and Universal Grammar." *Linguistic Inquiry* 8:63–69.

Kibrik, A. E. 1979. "Canonical Ergativity and Daghestan Languages." In *Ergativity: Towards a Theory of Grammatical Relations,* ed. F. Planck. London and New York: Academic Press.

Kiefer F., ed. 1973. *Trends in Soviet Theoretical Linguistics.* Dordrecht: Reidel.

Klimov, G. A. 1972. "K xarakteristike jazykov aktivnogo stroja." *Voprosy jazykoznanija* 4:3–12.

———. 1973. *Očerk obščej teorii ergativnosti.* Moscow: Nauka.

———. 1974. "K proisxoždeniju ergativnoj konstrukcii predloženija." *Voprosy jazykoznanija* 1:3–13.

———. 1977. *Tipologija jazykov aktivnogo stroja.* Moscow: Nauka.

Kneale, W., and Kneale, M. 1962. *The Development of Logic.* Oxford: Clarendon Press.

Kohler, Klaus J. 1981. "Timing of Articulatory Control in the Production of Plosives." *Phonetica* 38:116–25.

Kortland, F. H. 1972. *Modelling the Phoneme: New Trends in East European Phonemic Theory.* The Hague: Mouton.

Kuhn, T. 1962. *The Structure of Scientific Revolutions.* Chicago: University of Chicago Press.

Kuipers, A. H. 1960. *Phoneme and Morpheme in Kabardian.* The Hague: Mouton.

Kumaxov, M. A. 1973. "Teorija monovokalizma i zapadno-kavkazskie jazyki." *Voprosy jazykoznanija* 7:54–67.

Kuryłowicz, Jerzy. 1936. "Dérivation lexicale et dérivation syntaxique. Contribution à la théorie des parties du discours." *B.S.L.* 37:74–92. Reprinted in Jerzy Kuryłowicz, *Esquises linguistiques I.* Munich: Wilhem Fink Verlag.

———. 1948. "Contribution à la théorie de la syllable." *Biuletyn polskiego towarzystwa jezykoznawczego* 8:80–114. Reprinted in Jerzy Kuryłowicz, *Esquises linguistiques I.* Munich: Wilhelm Fink Verlag.

———. 1973. *Esquises linguistiques I.* Munich: Wilhelm Fink Verlag.

———. 1977. *Problemes de linguistique indo-européenne.* Wroclaw: Wydawnictwo Polskiej Akademii Nauk.

Ladefoged, Peter. 1977. *Preliminaries to Linguistic Phonetics.* Chicago: University of Chicago Press.

Lafitte, Pierre. 1962. *Grammaire Basque: Navarro-labourdain littéraire.* Rev. ed. Bayonne: Editions des "Amis du Musée Basque" et "Ikas."

Lamb, Sydney M. 1966a. *Outline of Stratificational Grammar.* Rev. ed. Washington, D.C.: Georgetown University Press.

———. 1966b. "Prolegomena to a Theory of Phonology." *Language* 42:536–73. Reprinted in *Phonological Theory,* ed. Valerie Becker Makkai. New York: Holt, Rinehart and Winston.

———. 1973a. "Linguistics and Cognitive Networks." In *Readings in Stratificational Linguistics,* ed. Adam Makkai and David G. Lockwood. Alabama: University of Alabama Press.

———. 1973b. "The Sememic Approach to Structural Semantics." In *Readings in Stratificational Linguistics,* ed. Adam Makkai and David G. Lockwood. Alabama: University of Alabama Press.

———. 1978. "Some Type of Ordering." In *Phonological Theory,* ed. Valerie Becker Makkai. New York: Holt, Rinehart and Winston.

———. 1982. "On Determining the Number of Strata in Linguistic Structure." In *The Ninth LACUS FORUM.* Columbia, S.C.: Hornbeam Press.

Langacker, Ronald W. 1976. *Non-distinct Arguments in Uto-Aztecan.* Berkeley and Los Angeles: University of California Press.

Langacker, Ronald W., and Munro, Pamela. 1975. "Passives and Their Meaning." *Language* 51:789–830.

Larsen, T. W., and Norman, W. M. 1979. "Correlates of Ergativity in Mayan Grammar." In *Ergativity,* ed. F. Planck. London and New York: Academic Press.

Laudan, Larry. 1977. *Progress and Its Problems: Towards a Theory of Scientific Growth.* Berkeley and Los Angeles: University of California Press.

Lawler, John M. 1977. "A Agrees with B in Achenese: A Problem for Relational Grammar." In *Grammatical Relations,* ed. Peter Cole and Jerrold M. Sadock, pp. 219–48. London and New York: Academic Press.

Lehiste, Ilse. 1984. "The Many Linguistic Functions of Duration." In *New Directions in Linguistics and Semiotics,* ed. James E. Copeland. Houston: Rice University Studies.

Lehman, W. P., ed. 1978. *Syntactic Typology: Studies in the Phenomenology of Language.* Austin: University of Texas Press.

Leontiev, V. 1971. "Theoretical Assumptions and Non-observed Facts." *American Economic Review* 61, no. 1 : 1–7.

Li, C. N., ed. 1976. *Subject and Topic.* New York and London: Academic Press.

Lightner, Theodore M. 1971. "Generative Phonology." In *A Survey of Linguistic Science*, ed. William Orr Dingwall, pp. 489–574. Linguistic Program, University of Maryland.

Lockwood, David G. 1972. *Introduction to Stratificational Grammar.* New York: Harcourt Brace Jovanovich.

Lomtatidze, K. V. 1967. "Abazinskij jazyk." *Jazyki narodov SSSR* 4, Moscow, pp. 123–44.

Lyons, John. 1968. *Introduction to Theoretical Linguistics.* Cambridge: Cambridge University Press.

McCawley, James D. 1979. *Adverbs, Vowels, and Other Objects of Wonder.* Chicago: University of Chicago Press.

———. 1980. "An Un-syntax." In *Current Approaches to Syntax*, ed. Edith A. Moravcsik and Jessica R. Wirth. New York: Academic Press.

———. 1982. *Thirty Million Theories of Grammar.* Chicago: University of Chicago Press.

Makkai, Adam. 1972. *Idiom Structure of English.* Mouton, Series Maior 48.

———. 1973. "A Pragmo-ecological View of Linguistic Structure and Language Universals." *Language Sciences*, October 1973, pp. 9–22.

Makkai, Adam, and Lockwood, David G., eds. 1973. *Readings in Stratificational Linguistics.* Alabama: University of Alabama Press.

Marantz, Alec. 1984. *On the Nature of Grammatical Relations.* Cambridge: MIT Press.

Markov, A. A. 1954. *Teorija algorifmov.* Moscow-Leningrad: Akademija Nauk. Translated by J. Schorr-Kon and the staff of the Israel Program for Scientific Translations and published by the latter organization under the title *The Theory of Algorithms*, Jerusalem, 1961.

Martinet, André. 1949. *Phonology as Functional Phonetics.* London: University of Oxford Press.

———. 1960. *Elements of General Linguistics.* Translated by Elizabeth Palmer. London: Faber and Faber.

———. 1965a. "De la morphologie." *La linguistique* 1 : 15–30.

———. 1965b. *La linguistique synchronique.* Paris: Presses Universitaires de France.

———. 1975. *Studies in Functional Syntax.* Munich: Wilhelm Fink Verlag.

Marx, Karl. 1977. *Capital: A Critique of Political Economy.* Vol. 1. Translated by Ben Fowkes. New York: Vintage Books, A Division of Random House.

Matthews, P. H. 1974. *Morphology: An Introduction to the Theory of Word-Structure.* Cambridge: Cambridge University Press.

Mel'čuk, I. A. 1974. *Opyt teorii lingvističeskix modelej "Smysl↔Text."* Moscow: Nauka.

———. 1976. *Das Wort.* Munich: Wilhelm Fink Verlag.

———. 1982. *Towards a Language of Linguistics: A System of Formal Notions for Theoretical Morphology.* Munich: Wilhelm Fink Verlag.

———. 1983. "Grammatical Subject and the Problem of the Ergative Construction in Lezgian." In *Papers in Linguistics 2. Studies in the Languages of the USSR.* Edmonton: Linguistic Research.

Miller, George A. 1981. *Language and Speech.* San Francisco: W. H. Freeman and Co.

Miller, George A., and Lenneberg, E., eds. 1978. *Psychology and Biology of Language and Thought.* New York: Academic Press.

Montague, Richard. 1970a. "English as Formal Language." In *Linguaggi nella società e nella tecnica*, ed. B. Visentini et al. Milan: Edizioni di Communitá. (Chapter 6 in Richard Montague, *Formal Philosophy.* New Haven: Yale University Press.)

————. 1970b. "Universal Grammar." *Theoria* 36:373–98. (Chapter 7 in Richard Montague, *Formal Philosophy*. New Haven: Yale University Press.)

————. 1974. *Formal Philosophy: Selected Papers of Richard Montague*. Edited by R. Thomason. New Haven: Yale University Press.

Moravcsik, Edith A. 1978. "On the Distribution of Ergative and Accusative Patterns." *Lingua* 45:233–79.

Moravcsik, Edith A., and Wirth, Jessica R., eds. 1980. *Current Approaches to Syntax (Syntax and Semantics 13)*. New York: Academic Press.

Nalimov, V. V. 1981. *In the Labyrinths of Language: A Mathematician's Journey*. Philadelphia: ISI Press.

Partee, Barbara. 1975. "Montague Grammar and Transformational Grammar." *Linguistic Inquiry* 6:203–300.

Peirce, Charles Sanders. 1931–1935. *Collected Papers* in six volumes, vol. 2. Cambridge: Harvard University Press.

Peranteau, Paul M.; Levy, Judith N.; and Phares, Gloria C., eds. 1972. *Chicago Witch Hunt*. Chicago: Chicago Linguistic Society.

Perlmutter, David M. 1978. "Impersonal Passives and the Unaccusative Hypothesis." *Proceedings of the Fourth Annual Meeting of the Berkeley Linguistic Society*. Berkeley, California.

————. 1980. "Relational Grammar." In *Current Approaches to Syntax*, ed. Edith A. Moravcsik and Jessica R. Wirth. New York: Academic Press.

Perlmutter, David M., and Postal, Paul M. 1974. "Lectures on Relational Grammar at Summer Linguistic Institute of the Linguistic Society of America." Amherst, Massachusetts.

————. 1977. "Towards a Universal Characterization of Passivization." *Proceedings of the Third Annual Meeting of the Berkeley Linguistic Society*. Berkeley, California.

————. 1984a. "The 1-Advancement Exclusiveness Law." In *Studies in Relational Grammar 2*, ed. D. M. Perlmutter and Carol G. Rosen. Chicago and London: University of Chicago Press.

————. 1984b. "Impersonal Passives and Some Relational Laws." In *Studies in Relational Grammar 2*, ed. D. M. Perlmutter and Carol G. Rosen. Chicago and London: University of Chicago Press.

Perlmutter, David M., and Rosen, Carol G., eds. 1984. *Studies in Relational Grammar 2*. Chicago and London: University of Chicago Press.

Peškovskij, A. M. 1928. *Russkij sintaksis v naučnom osveščenii*. Moscow: Gosudarstvennoe pedagogičeskoe izdatel'stvo.

Petznik, G. W. 1970. *Combinatory Programming*. Ph.D. dissertation, University of Wisconsin. University Microfilm Publication 70-24812.

Pike, Kenneth L. 1967. *Language in Relation to a Unified Theory of the Structure of Human Behavior*. The Hague: Mouton.

————. 1970. *Tagmemic and Matrix Linguistics Applied to Selected African Languages*. Norman: Summer Institute of Linguistics of the University of Oklahoma.

————. 1982. *Linguistic Concepts: An Introduction to Tagmemics*. The Hague: Mouton.

Pike, Kenneth L., and Pike, Evelyn G. 1982. *Grammatical Analysis*. Arlington: Summer Institute of Linguistics and University of Texas.

————. 1983. *Text and Tagmeme*. Norwood, N.J.

Planck, Franz, ed. *Ergativity: Towards a Theory of Grammatical Relations*. London and New York: Academic Press.

Popper, K. 1959. *The Logic of Scientific Discovery*. London.

Postal, P. M. 1977. "Antipassive in French." *NELS* 7 : 273–313. (Also in *Linguisticae Investigationes* 1 [1977]: 333–374.)

Prieto, Luis J. 1975. *Études de linguistique et de sémiologie générale.* Geneva: Librairie Droz.

Pullum, G., and Jakobson, R., eds. 1982. *The Nature of Syntactic Representation.* Dordrecht: Reidel.

Quang, Phuc Dong. 1971. "English Sentences without Overt Grammatical Subject." In A. M. Zwicky et al., eds., *Studies Out in Left Field: Defamatory Essays Presented to James McCawley,* pp. 3–10. Edmonton: Linguistic Research.

Quine, W. V. 1960. *Word and Object.* Cambridge: MIT Press.

Quirk, Randolph; Greenbaum, Sidney; and Leech, Geoffrey. 1972. *A Grammar of Contemporary English.* London: Longman.

Reformatskij, A. A. 1960. *Vvedenie v jazykoznanie.* Moscow: Gosudarstvennoe učebno-pedagogičeskoe izdatel'stvo ministerstva prosveščenija RSFSR.

Regamay, C. 1954. "A propos de la 'construction ergative' en indo-aryen moderne Sprachgeschichte und Wortbededtung." *Festschrift Albert Debrunner,* pp. 363–84. Bern: Francke.

Reichenbach, H. 1947. *Elements of Symbolic Logic.* New York: Macmillan Co.

Rosser, John Berkeley. 1935. "A Mathematical Logic without Variables." *Annals of Mathematics* 36, 2d ser., pp. 127–50.

———. 1984. "Highlights of the History of the Lambda-Calculus." *Annals of the History of Computing* 6, no. 4 (October 1984): 337–49.

Sapir, Edward. 1917. "Review of 'Het passieve Karakter van het verbum actionis in talen van Noord-America'" by C. C. Uhlenbeck. *IJAL* 1 : 82–86.

———. 1921. *Language: An Introduction to the Study of Speech.* New York: Harcourt, Brace and Co.

Saussure, Ferdinand de. 1879. *Mémoire sur le système primitif des voyelles dans les langues indo-européennes.* Leipzig.

———. 1966. *Course in General Linguistics.* New York: Philosophical Library.

Ščerba, L. V. 1948. *Fonetika francuzckogo jazyka.* Moscow: Prosveščenie.

Schenker, Alexander M. 1986. "On the Reflexive Verbs in Russian." *International Journal of Slavic Languages and Poetics* 33.

———. 1985. "W sprawie się raz jeszcze." *Język Polski* 64, pp. 9–23.

Schmalstieg, William R. 1982. "The Shift of Intransitive to Transitive Passive in the Lithuanian and Indo-European Verb." *Baltistica* 18, no. 2 (1982).

Schönfinkel, M. 1924. "Über die Bausteine der mathematischen Logik." *Mathematischen Annalen* 92 : 305–316.

Schwartz, J. 1962. "The Pernicious Influence of Mathematics on Science." *Logic, Methodology, and Philosophy of Science, Proceedings of the 1960 International Congress.* Palo Alto, Calif.: Stanford University Press.

Sechehaye, A. 1926. *Essai sur la structure logique de la phrase.* Paris: Champion.

Shannon, C. 1956. "The Bandwagon." *IRE Trans. IT-2(1) : 3.*

Shaumyan, S. K. 1965. *Strukturnaja lingvistika.* Moscow: Nauka.

———. 1968. *Problems of Theoretical Phonology.* The Hague: Mouton.

———. 1971. *Principles of Structural Linguistics.* The Hague: Mouton.

———. 1974. *Applikativnaja grammatika kak semantičeskaja teorija estestvennyx jazykov.* Moscow: Nauka.

———. 1977. *Applicational Grammar as a Semantic Theory of Natural Language.* Chicago: University of Chicago Press.

———. 1980. "Semantics, the Philosophy of Science, and Mr. Sampson." *Forum Linguisticum* 1, no. 1.

Shaumyan, S. K., ed. 1972. *Problemy strukturnoj lingvistiki 1971*. Moscow: Nauka.
———. 1973. *Problemy strukturnoj lingvistiki 1972*. Moscow: Nauka.
Shaumyan, S. K., and Soboleva, P. A. 1958. *Osnovanija poroždajuščej grammatiki russkogo jazyka*. Moscow: Nauka.
———. 1963. *Applikativnaja poroždajuščaja model' i isčislenie transformacij v russkom jazyke*. Moscow: Nauka.
Shibatani, M., ed. 1976. *The Grammar of Causative Constructions (Syntax and Semantics 6)*. New York and London: Academic Press.
Slotty, F. 1932. "Problem der Wortarten." *Forschungen und Fortschritte 7* (1932).
Smullyan, Raymond. 1985. *To Mock a Mocking Bird: And Other Logic Puzzles Including an Amazing Adventure in Combinatory Logic*. New York: Alfred A. Knopf.
Soboleva, P. A. 1972. "Modelirovanie slovoobrazovanija." In *Problemy strukturnoi lingvistiki*, ed. S. K. Shaumyan. Moscow: Nauka.
———. 1973. "Derivational Structure of the Russian Lexicon." In *Trends in Soviet Theoretical Linguistics*, ed. F. Kiefer. Dordrecht: Reidel.
———. 1978. "Slovoobrazovatel'naja struktura slova i tipologija omonimov." In *Problemy strukturnoj lingvistiki*, ed. V. P. Grigor'ev. Moscow: Nauka.
———. 1981. "Asimmetrija slovoobrazovatel'nyx processov i slovoobrazovatel'nyx otnošenij." In *Problemy strukturnoi lingvistiki*, ed. V. P. Grigor'ev. Moscow: Nauka.
———. 1983. "Transformacionnye polja applikativnoj poroždajuščej grammatiki i modelirovanie složnyx slov." In *Problemy strukturnoi lingvistiki*, ed. V. P. Grigor'ev. Moscow: Nauka.
Stankiewicz, E. 1979. *Studies in Slavic Morphophonemics and Accentology*. Ann Arbor: Michigan Slavic Publications.
Stoy, J. E. 1977. *Denotational Semantics*. Cambridge: MIT Press.
Szemerényi, O. 1964. "Structuralism and Substratum: Indo-Europeans and Semites in the Ancient Near East." *Lingua* 13, pp. 1ff.
———. 1977. "Sprachtypologie, funktionelle Belastung und die Entwicklung in indogermanischer Lautsysteme." *Acta Iranica*, Leiden, pp. 339–93.
Tchekhoff, Claude. 1978. *Aux fondements de la syntaxe: l'ergatif*. Paris: Presses Universitaires de France.
Tesnière, L. 1934. "Comment construire une syntaxe." *Bulletin de la Faculté des Lettres*, Strasbourg, May–June.
———. 1966. *Éléments de syntaxe structurale*. 2d ed., rev. and corrected. Paris: Librairie C. Klincksieck.
Thomason, Richmond H. 1974. "Introduction." In Richard Montague, *Formal Philosophy*. New Haven: Yale University Press.
Trubetzkoy, N. 1969. *Principles of Phonology*. Translated by Christiane A. M. Baltaxe. Berkeley and Los Angeles: University of California Press.
Uspenskij, B. A. 1965. *Strukturnaja tipologija jazykov*. Moscow: Nauka.
Van Valin, R. D. 1977. "Ergativity and Universality of Subjects." In *Papers from the Thirteenth Annual Meeting of the Chicago Linguistic Society*, ed. W. A. Beach, S. E. Fox and S. Philosoph, pp. 689–705. Chicago: University of Chicago, Department of Linguistics.
Vennemann gennant Nierfeld, Theo. 1978. "Universal Syllabic Phonology." *Theoretical Linguistics* 5, no. 2/3 (1978).
Wardrip-Fruin, Carolin. 1982. "On the Status of Temporal Cues to Phonetic Categories: Preceding Vowel Duration as a Cue to Voicing in Final Stop Consonants." *Journal of the Acoustical Society of America* 71:187–95.

Wells, Rulon S. 1947. "Immediate Constituents." *Language* 23:81–117. Reprinted in *Readings in Linguistics I*, ed. M. Joos. Chicago and London: University of Chicago Press.

Wilensky, Robert. 1984. *LISPcraft*. New York-London: W. W. Norton and Co.

Winston, P. H., and Horn, B. K. P. 1984. *LISP*. 2d ed. Reading, Mass.: Addison Wesley.

Xolodovič, A. A. 1974. *Problemy grammatičeskoj teorii*. Leningrad: Nauka.

Zawadowski, Leon. 1975. *Inductive Semantics and Syntax*. The Hague: Mouton.

# Subject Index

Subject Index includes symbols of basic constants of applicative grammar and abbreviations of names of its formal concepts and rules. References are to pages where the symbols and abbreviations are defined or explained.

# Language Index

# Name Index

In the name index bold type figures indicate quotations from the author

351

## DATE DUE

| | | | |
|---|---|---|---|
| | | | |
| | | | |
| | | | |
| | | | |
| | | | |
| | | | |
| | | | |
| | | | |
| | | | |
| | | | |
| | | | |
| | | | |
| | | | |
| | | | |
| | | | |
| | | | |
| | | | |
| 261-2500 | | | Printed in USA |